SYSTEMS ANALYSIS & DESIGN FUNDAMENTALS

SYSTEMS ANALYSIS & DESIGN FUNDAMENTALS

A BUSINESS PROCESS REDESIGN APPROACH

NED KOCK

TEXAS A&M INTERNATIONAL UNIVERSITY

3/07

SAGE Publications
Thousand Oaks ▪ London ▪ New Delhi

For information:

 Sage Publications, Inc.
2455 Teller Road
Thousand Oaks, California 91320
E-mail: order@sagepub.com

Sage Publications Ltd.
1 Oliver's Yard
55 City Road
London EC1Y 1SP
United Kingdom

Sage Publications India Pvt. Ltd.
B-42, Panchsheel Enclave
Post Box 4109
New Delhi 110 017 India

Printed in the United States of America.

Library of Congress Cataloging-in-Publication Data

Kock, Ned F., 1964-
Systems analysis and design fundamentals: a business process redesign
approach / Ned Kock.
     p. cm.
Includes bibliographical references and index.
ISBN 1-4129-0585-0 (cloth)
   1. Information technology—Management. 2. Management information systems.
3. System analysis. 4. System design. I. Title.
HD30.213.K644 2007
658.4'038011—dc22

                        2006001785

This book is printed on acid-free paper.

06 07 08 09 10 10 9 8 7 6 5 4 3 2 1

Acquisitions Editor:	Al Bruckner
Editorial Assistant:	MaryAnn Vail
Project Editor:	Tracy Alpern
Copy Editor:	Jennifer Withers
Proofreader:	Andrea Martin
Typesetter:	C&M Digitals (P) Ltd.
Indexer:	Wendy Allex
Cover Designer:	Candice Harman

Contents

Preface   **vii**

Acknowledgments   **xiii**

    Chapter 1: Introduction   1

Part I: Emerging Trends in Business   **13**

    Part I Case: The FBI's Virtual Case File   13

    Chapter 2: Data, Information, and Knowledge

        Flow in Business Processes   16

    Chapter 3: Return on Investment in Technology   41

Part II: Understanding Business Processes   **59**

    Part II Case: DoD's Software Procurement From CSC   59

    Chapter 4: The Past, Present, and Future of

        Business Process Redesign   62

    Chapter 5: Business Process Modeling

        Approaches and Diagrams   79

Part III: Changing Business Processes   **107**

    Part III Case: IBM Global Financing's Credit Issuance Process   107

    Chapter 6: Selecting a Target for Successful

        Business Process Redesign   110

    Chapter 7: Representing Information and Knowledge

        in Business Processes   123

    Chapter 8: Redesigning Business Processes   136

Part IV: Technology-Based

Business Process Implementation   **153**

    Part IV Case: Investars, Inc.'s Outsourcing of

        Programming to Belarus   153

    Chapter 9: Using IT to Enable New Process Designs   156

    Chapter 10: Redesigning Little Italy Restaurants   176

Part V: Advanced Technology Issues   **195**

    Part V Case: Denver International Airport's
        Baggage Handling System   195
    Chapter 11: Database Design Concepts and Issues   198
    Chapter 12: Object-Oriented Design Concepts and Issues   215
    Chapter 13: Business Process Automation With ASP   229
    Chapter 14: Conclusion   251

Appendix A: Complete ASP Code Examples   **263**

Appendix B: Answers to Review Questions   **293**

Bibliography   **299**

Index   **313**

About the Author   **321**

Preface

The Goals of This Book

Textbooks are, more often than not, aimed at providing a comprehensible review of a particular topic, in many cases dedicating a great deal of text to the discussion of concepts related to the topic in question. This book tries to break away from that general mold. It does cover material that can be used to teach courses on a particular topic, namely the topic of systems analysis and design, but in a very applied manner. Moreover, it proposes a new approach to teaching systems analysis and design, centered on the notion of business process redesign. The writing of this book was motivated by three main goals.

The first goal was to provide a relatively succinct review of the most fundamental concepts, methods, and issues that are relevant to systems analysts today. The second goal was to integrate systems analysis and design with business process redesign, since the two usually go hand-in-hand in the real world of business. The third goal was to provide a book with a very practical, or applied, flavor.

The resulting book goes beyond what one would normally find in a systems analysis and design text in terms of business process redesign, as well as related emerging trends in business. As such, it attempts to break new ground in the teaching of systems analysis and design, by preparing students to operate in work environments where rarely straight automation of business process (i.e., without being preceded by business process redesign) leads to significant gains in quality or productivity.

The practical, or applied, flavor of this book comes from an attempt to illustrate all of the stages involved in improving a business process with the support of information technologies. These stages include business process modeling, redesign, and automation. The approach employed for business process modeling and redesign used in this book focuses on a communication flow view of business processes and related techniques, some of which were developed by the author based on his research. The automation stage is illustrated in this book through coding examples utilizing a widely used Web-based software development technology known as active server pages (ASP).

Organization and Contents of This Book

This book is made up of 14 chapters and two appendices. Most of the chapters are grouped into five main book parts. The content presented in the chapters flows in such a way to introduce the student to fundamental ideas; develop and support with evidence the new approach to systems analysis and design proposed through the book; and finally, offer advice to students on how to implement that approach. The appendices provide the computer programming code for the different modules of a Web-based system developed to illustrate key concepts and ideas, and answers to review questions available at the end of each of the chapters.

Part I comprises Chapters 2 and 3 and discusses various emerging trends in business that provide a motivation for the systems analysis and design views put forth in this book. Part II addresses business process redesign from a historical as well as methodological perspective. It consists of Chapters 4 and 5 and provides an understanding of how and why business processes should be modeled as a preparation for their redesign. Part III incorporates Chapters 6, 7, and 8. It focuses on how business processes can be redesigned before they (i.e., the new, redesigned, processes) are implemented with information technologies. Part IV, which includes Chapters 9 and 10, discusses issues in connection with information technology–based implementation of business processes. Finally, Part V of the book discusses advanced technology issues in Chapters 11, 12, and 13. It covers a range of advanced technology topics that are traditionally found in systems analysis and design courses, such as database and object-oriented design concepts and issues.

Each of the chapters is designed to add cumulatively to the main message of the book. As such, Chapter 1 sets the stage for the rest of the book. It looks back at systems analysis and design from a historical perspective, tying it to the evolution of computing. In doing so, this chapter introduces the main topics covered in more detail in later chapters, providing a basis on which the relevance of those topics for systems analysis and design can be understood.

Chapter 2 defines and discusses three central concepts of the book: data, information, and knowledge. The concepts are presented as related but fundamentally different from each other, which is important to emphasize for a couple of reasons. The first reason is that exchanging a lot of data does not mean the same as communicating a substantial amount of information; the second is that information cannot be effectively processed without knowledge. The discussion of these three concepts sets the stage for the methodological arguments made throughout the book.

Chapter 2 also introduces and discusses the concept of hypercommunication, characterized by the excessive exchange of data and information in business processes. It is argued that hypercommunication is one of the main problems facing businesses today. The chapter discusses the main underlying reasons for this excessive exchange of data and information in business processes, which are (a) a high data/information ratio in the exchanges, (b) a high fragmentation of knowledge among different organizational functions (e.g., manager, inventory supervisor, computer support specialist), and (c) an insufficient degree of knowledge sharing across different organizational functions.

The current state of knowledge in connection with returns on investment in technology is summarized in Chapter 3, which places emphasis on information technology–related returns. This chapter shows that, up until the early 1990s, information technology implementations in organizations had led to almost negligible returns in labor productivity—a finding that is often referred to as the *technology productivity paradox*. The chapter then shows that increasing (but still modest) returns started occurring in the 1990s, which coincides with the emergence of the business process redesign movement. One of the core messages of that movement is that information technology implementation projects should always be preceded by business process redesign. With this message, the chapter provides a strong motivation for the systems analysis and design orientation proposed in this book.

Historical reviews are particularly useful as motivators of new perspectives. Chapter 4 discusses the evolution of business process redesign methods, which coincided with the evolution of key schools of management thought, from scientific management to reengineering. It argues that the current focus of business process redesign approaches on activity flows, rather than information flows and knowledge distribution, has a historical basis and creates a number of problems. The chapter proposes some key ideas based on practical business examples, several of which refer to the relatively high importance of looking at and improving the web of communication interactions in business processes.

Chapter 5 discusses several business process modeling approaches as well as respective diagrams. For each approach, the chapter includes a discussion of its main focus, advantages, and limitations in comparison with the communication flow–oriented business redesign methodology proposed in the book. Main approaches covered here include activity flow–oriented approaches, the data flow diagramming approach that is often presented as part of the traditional systems analysis and design approach, the communication flow–oriented approach proposed in the book (whose several components are discussed in more detail in later chapters), object-oriented approaches, and holistic systems approaches.

Not all business processes can be successfully redesigned in a major way. Chapter 6 is founded on this reality. This chapter discusses techniques to select business processes for successful redesign. It discusses considerations such as cost-benefit analyses, support from management, and employee resistance, as well as factors that influence business process "rigidity," such as regulations (e.g., those found in government processes) and expensive workflow control applications previously implemented (which can be a major source of resistance due to the personal and financial investments attached to them).

Chapter 7 takes a few additional steps in clarifying certain issues in connection techniques for modeling and analyzing the flow of information and the distribution of knowledge (or expertise) in business processes. It proposes an approach to show how to differentiate between the flow of information and of knowledge in a business process, talks about the difference in media requirements for information and knowledge communication, discusses rules for coming up with the appropriate size of a communication flow diagram, and discusses how to break down large communication flow diagrams into smaller ones.

The important relationship between information and knowledge, discussed in previous chapters, is highlighted in Chapter 8. This chapter discusses new techniques for the redesign of business processes with a focus on the flow of information and the distribution of knowledge in them. It shows where to replace synchronous with asynchronous communication, how to reduce information duplication and overflow, and how to effectively reduce contact points in a business process. The chapter also shows why knowledge transfer should be minimized in the execution of business processes, particularly "operations" processes (also known as supply-chain processes), and maximized in specific types of business processes called "organizational learning" processes (e.g., training processes, socialization processes, R&D processes, strategy definition processes). Also provided here is a discussion on how to move "organizational learning" activities from operations processes to organizational learning processes.

Chapter 9 discusses ways to generate what are referred in this book as *rich pictorial representations* of redesigned business processes and how to move from these to practical information technology implementations. It discusses three main business process implementation strategies: business process outsourcing, commercial package customization, and in-house development. The chapter discusses the advantages and disadvantages of each implementation strategy, as well as situations in which one strategy is particularly better than the others.

Case studies have been successfully used in the business literature to illustrate key concepts and ideas. Chapter 10 embraces that tradition by employing a detailed case study to describe a practical business application of the ideas, methods, and techniques discussed in previous chapters. This is done here generally following the Harvard case study method, which usually involves an in-depth analysis of business context and a conceptual illustration that is not overly simplified. The goal is to show more or less how a real business process redesign project would be carried out, using the general redesign approach proposed in this book. The case study involves the redesign of the order fulfillment process of an Italian restaurant chain, referred to here as Little Italy Restaurants.

Chapter 11 covers a number of database design concepts and related techniques that are useful in the implementation of redesigned business processes, particularly those implementations that involve in-house software development projects. Key concepts and related techniques covered in this chapter are sequential and structured files, entity-relationship diagramming, database normalization, data warehousing, and data mining.

The object-oriented paradigm has become widely successful within the software development community. Chapter 12 focuses on object-oriented design concepts and issues. This chapter introduces the notion of a software object as an abstraction that allows computer programmers to "encapsulate," and thus protect from improper access, both data and data manipulation code. A brief discussion of object-oriented programming is then provided, followed by a discussion of object-oriented analysis and design. Two forms of object-oriented programming are subsequently discussed. The first involves the creation of software object classes, whereas the second involves the use of previously created software object classes.

Chapter 13 is dedicated to exploring how a specific technology, namely ASP, can be used to implement Web-based systems. This implementation is presented as the culmination of the several steps toward business process improvement discussed in previous chapters of the book. Chapter 13 shows that ASP-based prototype development can be implemented through a relatively "high-level" environment, which is usually made up of several software development products developed and commercialized by Microsoft Corporation, including Access (a database development environment), FrontPage (a Web pages and applications development environment), and Internet Information Services (a Web server software). ASP-based development is chosen as a focus of this chapter because it is one of the most widely used development approaches, from a commercial perspective.

A summary of the most important points discussed in the book is provided in Chapter 14. In addition, this chapter discusses future challenges facing managers and how they can be addressed through the methodology proposed in the book. The chapter argues that new activities should be added to the new business process and some fine-tuning should be conducted before the new business process is ready for final implementation with information technology. Among the activities that need to be added to the business process are those that enable future continuous improvement, such as quality metrics collection and related business process reviews. Also, the chapter argues that the impact of business process redesign changes on business process team members (i.e., employees) should be assessed and rewards (social and financial) should be created for those from whom extra time, effort, and dedication will be required to make the new business process work.

Appendix A includes ASP code examples for the Little Italy Restaurants Web System, which is discussed earlier in the book together with an introductory discussion of ASP as a basis for the implementation of redesigned business processes. The code is preceded by screen snapshots illustrating the features implemented through it. Necessary HTML elements (e.g., <form> . . . </form>) routinely used with ASP code are also included.

Appendix B includes answers to the review questions, which are provided at the end of each chapter. The review questions are designed to help students recapitulate the main concepts and ideas discussed in each chapter. While they appear to be fairly simple at first glance, those review questions are worded in such a way that they require some thinking to be answered correctly. For example, review questions worded in a positive and negative way are alternated, which requires focused attention to answer the questions correctly.

Supplemental CD Materials

A CD accompanies this book. The CD contains a variety of multimedia materials. Among those materials are PowerPoint slides covering key systems analysis and design concepts and techniques, various examples of diagrams and tables, and annotated templates for course project reports. These materials should be useful to both instructors and students in systems analysis and design courses employing traditional as well as online delivery methods.

Also included on the CD are multimedia materials that can be used by instructors and students in courses employing traditional methods but that will be particularly useful for online courses. These multimedia materials include a few introductory video clips highlighting key aspects of the book, audio clips associated with each of the PowerPoint slides provided, and full-motion screen-captured demonstrations of the use of some of the tools discussed in the book. All of these multimedia materials are provided in nonproprietary formats, which can be played from most freely available multimedia players (e.g., Windows Media Player and RealPlayer).

Acknowledgments

The author would like to acknowledge the invaluable cooperation of the many organizations that have been involved in research projects conducted by him in the past 15 years. Those projects served as a basis for research findings that underlie several of the ideas discussed in this book. Whenever specific projects that involved sensitive issues are discussed in the book, those projects are discussed in a somewhat disguised way, to protect the confidentiality of the organization, the organization's members, and other project stakeholders.

Among the many organizations whose projects served as the basis for this book are the following: Accenture, AmBev, American Customer Drying, Bigchalk.com, Bristol-Myers Squibb, Computer Sciences Corporation, Day and Zimmermann, Delaware Investments, Ford Motor Company, Holiday Boutique, HSBC Bamerindus Bank, Johnson & Johnson, Lockheed Martin, Marriott Hotels, Metro One Communications, New Zealand Ministry of Agriculture and Fisheries, PricewaterhouseCoopers, ProQuest, Rio de Janeiro State Construction Company, Temple University, True North, U.S. Department of Defense, Volkswagen, and Westaflex.

Parts of this book are based on some of the author's previous publications, whose text is used here in an adapted way and with permission from the publishers. Several sections of Chapter 2 have been based on the book titled *Business Process Improvement Through E-Collaboration: Knowledge Sharing Through the Use of Virtual Groups*, published by Idea Group Publishing. Several sections of Chapter 5 are based on the article titled "Communication-Focused Business Process Redesign: Assessing a Communication Flow Optimization Model Through an Action Research Study at a Defense Contractor," published in Volume 46, Issue 1 of the journal *IEEE Transactions on Professional Communication*.

Last but not least, the author would like to thank his family. This book is dedicated to them.

CHAPTER 1

Introduction

This chapter takes a look back at systems analysis and design as a discipline that emerged primarily from another related discipline, computer science. It is argued here that systems analysis and design's origins led to the current orientation in university circles toward in-house automation as an approach to organizational improvement using information systems. This, in turn, led to a corresponding neglect of business process redesign and other alternatives, such as customization of off-the-shelf packages and business process outsourcing. This chapter calls for a change in the practice and teaching of systems analysis and design—a call that this book aims at answering.

Computer Science as a New Discipline

Even though computers have been around since the 1940s, the birth of computer science as an independent discipline dates back only to the 1960s. The foundations of this new discipline came from the related fields of mathematics and electrical engineering. Mathematics was the source of one of the key ideas that led to the development of the computer, which is that data can be represented in a binary way by sequences of zeroes and ones (called bits). Electrical engineering provided the basic technologies necessary to support the development of electronic devices and circuits that would store and operate on bits.

In the years that followed its emergence as an independent discipline, computer science was primarily concerned with the development and teaching of ideas aimed at the solution of early problems associated with large computers, called mainframes. With the increasing use of mainframes in organizations, one of the key problems at the time was the reduction of the cost of using mainframes. One solution was to allow more than one user to exploit a mainframe's computing power and storage resources at the same time. Another was to make it easier for users to provide sequences of instructions to be executed by mainframes. This context provided the impetus for the development of a variety of operating systems and programming languages.

Many subdisciplines have sprung up from the computer science discipline. Those subdisciplines specialized in certain areas such as operating systems, computer programming, computer architectures, artificial intelligence, database design, computer networking, language processing, and data encryption—just to name a few, some with broader scopes than others. The many developments in connection with computer programming are particularly relevant for our understanding of the emergence and current state of the discipline of systems analysis and design.

In the absence of higher-level programming languages, early computer programmers had to write instructions for the execution of computer-based tasks using what is known as "machine language." This fundamentally numeric language can be understood and executed directly by a computer, without the need for any conversion or translation. However, machine language is difficult for humans to use. It consists of sequences of zeroes and ones representing operation codes and computer memory addresses.

Because of the difficulties associated with the use of machine language, assembly language was devised to provide computer programmers with slightly greater convenience. Assembly language enabled computer programmers to express machine language instructions in alphabetic symbols, also called mnemonic codes (e.g., AD, SUB, OR), instead of sequences of bits. Assembly language was easier to use than machine language but still far removed from the way humans normally communicate with each other.

Machine and assembly languages are often referred to, respectively, as first- and second-generation computer languages. The birth of third-generation computer languages begins with FORTRAN (a name that stands for Formula Translation), which many believe to have been invented in 1956. FORTRAN was developed mainly to be used by scientists and mathematicians, and its notation was similar to mathematical notations. This presented some difficulty for it to be used in commercial applications, which in turn led to the development a few years later (in about 1960) of another programming language, known as COBOL (an acronym that stands for Common Business-Oriented Language). Later, yet other programming languages were developed, some more user-friendly than others, including the widely popular BASIC (Beginner's All-Purpose Symbolic Instruction Code), as well as the also popular Pascal and C programming languages.

As the use of programming languages increased, so did the complexity of programming projects. This ushered a new discipline into existence, generally called software engineering. This new discipline was primarily concerned with tools and techniques aimed at improving productivity and quality in large computer programming projects. In the late 1970s, Tom DeMarco, one of the pioneers in the fields of software engineering and systems analysis and design, wrote a seminal book in which he argued in favor of structured methods for software development. The methods proposed by DeMarco included several ideas on how to effectively document the systems development process so that the correction of software errors (a.k.a. bugs) could be accomplished in a timely and cost-effective way.

DeMarco's ide͛   ͢g audience since it was clear then that most
computer systen   ͛ bugs when they were finally delivered to
the users. That   ͣputer systems. The correction of
those bugs w͛   ͛ maintenance costs of computer syster   ͛ sometimes as high
as 80% or

In the   ͛asks associated w͛   ͛nce costs by
reduc   ͛ally referred to
as C

ns Analysis and Design

J. Da͛   ͢t discussed the origins of
systems ana͛͟   ͣolution of Business System
Analysis Techniques   *Computing Surveys.* According
to Couger, the origins of s͛   ͢ date back to the 1900s, when
Frederick Taylor developed techn͛   ͛ process flow analysis. However,
Couger also recognized that Taylor's ͣ͟   ͛ placed emphasis on the flow of
materials through business process, a general trend that persisted until the 1950s,
when techniques aimed at the analysis of business processes and related design of
computer-based systems to automate those processes began to appear.

Other authors argue that the origins of systems analysis and design are more
recent, and rooted in the need to cope with computer system complexity. The argument goes more or less like this. As computer programs have become more complex, so has the realization that advanced specification, careful planning, and the
generation of related documentation were "necessary evils" to ensure the success of
complex computer systems development projects. And so systems analysis and
design was born, at least as we know it today. That is, systems analysis and design
emerged from the need to perform certain activities around, and particularly prior
to, the steps involved in developing a computer system using software engineering
tools and techniques.

Why refer to tasks such as advanced specification, careful planning, and the
generation of related documentation as "necessary evils"? The reason is how those
activities are likely to be perceived by people who write computer code for a
living—something that many of the early software engineers did, day in and day
out. From a computer programmer's point of view, those tasks are, well, fairly boring. Many of those who have been full-time computer programmers for a few years
view computer programming as a fun, albeit somewhat solitary, activity. It is safe to
say that most programmers prefer to start programming right away when a business process–related problem is posed to them. Specification, planning, and documentation are not nearly as fun as computer programming, at least not in the eyes
of the people who ultimately develop software.

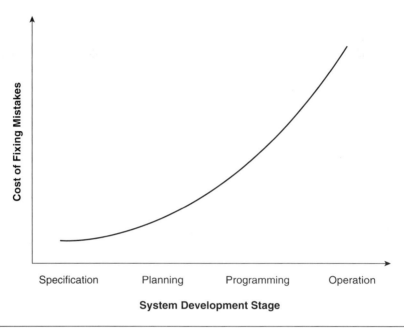

Figure 1.1   Costs of Fixing Bugs at Different System Development Stages

One of the key reasons why preparatory tasks such as specification, planning, and documentation became very important in complex software development projects was the recognition that the cost of fixing mistakes increases sharply as a project moves from preparatory tasks to system implementation and operation (or use). This is illustrated in Figure 1.1, where the relationship between the cost of fixing mistakes and the stage of a computer system development project is shown as being an exponential relationship. Most of the traditional literature on systems analysis and design is consistent with this depiction of the relationship.

Figure 1.1 also suggests that for the majority of systems development projects, particularly the ones where not a lot of emphasis is placed on pre-programming activities, most of the costs tend to be associated with fixing problems in the systems after they are being used. That is, most of the costs tend to be maintenance costs that are incurred after the system is under operation.

The above conclusion is consistent with a notion that has often been called by software developers the "software crisis," which many argue persists to this day. The idea behind the software crisis is that the quality of most of the computer systems developed is way below what it could be if proper precautions were taken. However, it has been difficult to identify exactly what can be done to provide a solution to the crisis. One of those who pointed out the existence of a software crisis in a high-profile manner was Roger Pressman, a software engineering and systems analysis and design pioneer and author of the seminal book *Software Engineering: A Practitioner's Approach.*

The software crisis is characterized by a few key statistics that stand out among others. Only about a third of all system development projects are considered successful by the users of the system. Only about half of all the system functions incorporated during development are utilized by the final users of the system; examples of system functions would be a file encryption option of an accounting system and a charting feature of a sales forecasting system. More than two thirds of all system development costs are maintenance costs; that is, those costs are associated with fixing problems in systems that are already under operation.

The Software Development Life Cycle Model

Early ideas in connection with systems analysis and design led to the development of the waterfall model of systems development, which is also known as the software development life cycle model. It is called the "waterfall" model because its graphical representation reminded its developers of a waterfall. Some may say that this is a little bit of a stretch, but with some effort, one can indeed see some similarity with a waterfall (see Figure 1.2). While sometimes depicted in different ways by different authors, it can be generally seen as comprising the following main steps: requirements definition; analysis; design; specification; database analysis; database design and specification; coding, testing, and implementation; and operation and maintenance. Table 1.1 shows a brief description of each of these steps.

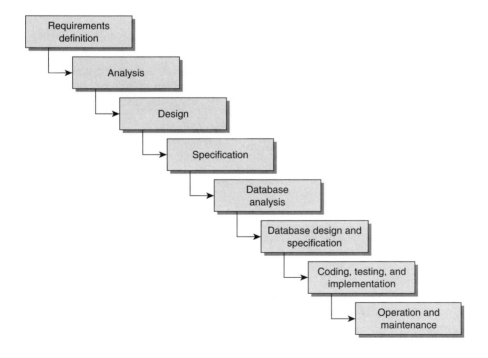

Figure 1.2   The Waterfall, or Software Development Life Cycle, Model

Table 1.1   Software Development Life Cycle Steps

Step	Brief Description
Requirements definition	Interviews are conducted, and a textual description of a business process and related problems are generated.
Analysis	The business process is graphically represented through data flow diagrams. Data flow diagrams are standardized representations of the flow of data in a business process.
Design	A computer program depiction called a structured chart is developed. Structured charts are standardized representations of the flow of data between computer program modules.
Specification	A high-level specification of the computer program modules, using structured English, is developed. Structured English is a midpoint representation that looks like a computer program, but without all the details that a computer program must have to be understood by a computer program compiler or interpreter (e.g., program lines do not have to end with a specific symbol such as the ";" used to signal the end of a line of code in the C programming language).
Database analysis	Entity-relationship diagrams are developed. Entity-relationship diagrams represent the different structured files in a database and their relationships with each other.
Database design and specification	Database files (also called tables) are designed and specified, which essentially means that the structure of the tables, the names of their fields, and the data types of those fields (e.g., numeric, date) are specified in detail. Also in this step, the data tables are normalized—a task whereby duplication of data in different files of the database is minimized.
Coding, testing, and implementation	The computer program is finally implemented, often using computer-aided software engineering tools and/or computer programming environments.
Operation and maintenance	The computer system is used, and errors in the system are corrected. Also in this step, new features are added to the computer system due to business process–related changes brought about by new market demands.

As it can be seen in Table 1.1, the software development life cycle model of systems analysis and design is aimed at automating business processes. So much so that it starts with the generation of a textual description of a business process and related problems. The automation through a computer program is aimed at solving the problems identified and associated with the business process in question. However, the software development life cycle model does not address the issue of business process redesign—an omission that has led to criticism from systems analysts and information technology managers. The problem with this lack of concern with business process redesign is that often computer systems end up being used to automate disorganized and inefficient business processes, something that could be reasonably avoided if a business process redesign step were incorporated into the software development life cycle. This theme will be picked up later in this chapter and also in other chapters of this book.

The software development life cycle description provided in Table 1.1 is somewhat database oriented. That is, it assumes that the computer program generated will be used primarily to maintain a database. This is why the steps that follow the "specification" step are called "database analysis" and "database design and specification." The reason for this focus on databases is that most commercial systems follow it. On the other hand, this does not mean that all projects conducted according to the software development life cycle will be database oriented. So, there may be variations in the software development life cycle from project to project.

Also, certain steps of the software development life cycle, as described in Table 1.1, are somewhat dated. Good examples are the "design" step, which has traditionally employed structured charts; and the "specification" step, which has traditionally made use of structured English. Structured charts usually show how computer program modules relate to each other. Structured English is a computer program specification that uses English, looks a lot like the Pascal programming language, and is produced as an intermediate step before software coding. Systems analysts have traditionally utilized the design and specification steps to communicate to computer programmers some of the details of a computer system, as far as its code is concerned, without the systems analysts having to actually write any computer code.

The design and specification steps of the software development life cycle lost much of their usefulness to systems analysts and computer programmers as a result of the development of computer-aided software engineering tools. Those tools generate computer programs automatically, and often transparently, based on higher-level representation of the computer system. That is, when using computer-aided software engineering tools, the computer programmer may never even see the underlying computer program, as he or she may design the system by manipulating only high-level elements such as icons and diagrams.

Computer-aided software engineering tools have been evolving over the years, leading to what some refer to as computer-aided *systems* engineering tools. Often, the same acronym, namely CASE, is used for both types of tools. This may lead to some confusion because computer-aided systems engineering tools tend to support substantially more systems analysis and design steps than computer-aided software engineering tools. For example, computer-aided systems engineering tools may incorporate project management features such as visualization and tracking of systems analysis and design tasks through Gantt charts. Such charts allow a project to be depicted as a series of interrelated tasks, which are usually shown on the chart as horizontal bars.

The waterfall, or software development life cycle, model was developed based on early and pioneering ideas in connection with systems analysis and design. Later, an alternative to the software development life cycle model was proposed. That alternative model became generally known as object-oriented analysis and design, which followed in the footsteps of the highly popular notion of object-oriented programming.

Object-oriented programming is a generic term used to refer to computer software development approaches in which computer program modules are developed as part of what are known as software objects. The central component of a software object is its data definition, which usually includes a set of variables. A distinctive characteristic of object-oriented programming is that only special program modules can modify the content of the variables that make up a software object. Those program modules share one special characteristic, which is that they are part of the software object whose variables they can modify. A widely popular object-oriented programming language is C++, which itself is an adaptation for the also popular structured programming language C.

Apparently due to the success of object-oriented programming, the 1990s saw the emergence of object-oriented analysis and design as a widely touted approach for business process analysis, as well as computer systems design and specification. Object-oriented analysis and design (discussed in more detail later in this book) has apparently been presented as an approach that allows computer systems developers to move swiftly from analysis and design to coding using object-oriented programming techniques. And it seems that object-oriented analysis and design has been reasonably triumphant in connection with that arguably narrow goal. However, unlike its object-oriented programming cousin, object-oriented analysis and design has been only modestly successful from a more general perspective.

The Industry–University Gap

Mathematicians, engineers, and computer scientists have been a key force behind the technological achievements from the development of the first modern computer to the emergence of the Internet. And those technological developments have deeply affected organizations, large and small, for profit and not. This has led to the view that organizations need mathematicians, engineers, and computer scientists to run their information technology operations. This view is also reflected in how universities have designed their information technology courses and academic program offerings over the years.

As discussed before in this chapter, systems analysis and design emerged within the context above as an attempt to bring organization and planning to the craft of computer systems development. As such, systems analysis and design has often been seen as a management-oriented discipline inserted into computer science programs. And, since computer science programs have tended to be more technology oriented than business oriented, it has been a natural consequence that the initial emphasis of systems analysis and design has been on the application of computing technologies to automate business processes.

Moreover, the association with computer science programs has led many systems analysis and design instructors, sometimes due to sheer pressure from technophile students interested in learning how to build computer applications, to place strong emphasis on the development of computer applications.

The above state of affairs has led to a number of problems, of which two are particularly relevant for the arguments presented in this book, to some extent because they have been exacerbated by universities and their difficulty adapting to change driven by industry needs.

Among the problems mentioned, the first that comes to mind is that current approaches to systems analysis and design, because of their inherited emphasis on the application of computing technologies to automate business processes, do not address the issue of business process redesign. The second problem is that the strong emphasis on the development of computer applications in current systems analysis and design has led many to be blindsided by what has become a reality in the 1990s and 2000s. That reality is that the vast majority of information technology–enabled projects are implemented through either customization of off-the-shelf computer packages or business process outsourcing.

A good example of customization of off-the-shelf packages (i.e., software packages that can be purchased in a box or as part of an Internet download package) has been the enterprise systems craze of the 1990s. Several Fortune 500 companies purchased and installed large systems (e.g., SAP/R3) to automate many of their activities in an integrated way. In many cases, the activities automated cut across the entire supply chain of the company, going from order taking to product delivery.

Many information technology executives firmly believe in the following motto: If you can buy a software solution, don't even think about building it yourself. There are exceptions to the rule of thumb implied by the motto, which will be discussed later in this book. Nevertheless, it is pretty clear that the proliferation of software development companies in the United States and around the world, particularly since the 1980s, almost guarantees that just about any software need has an off-the-shelf software package developed to address it.

A good example of business process outsourcing is the hiring, again by several Fortune 500 companies, of outside information technology service providers to run help desk operations (e.g., support to office computer applications) for those Fortune 500 companies. These providers of help desk support are sometimes located in different countries and accessible through a toll-free number. Their telephone support, in connection with generic applications such as word processing and spreadsheets, is sometimes better than the support previously provided internally by the companies that outsourced the support.

The advent of the Internet made it increasingly easier to implement business process outsourcing in connection with a variety of support areas. For example, many companies routinely outsource the hosting of their Web sites to other companies, usually known as Internet service providers (or ISPs). Another example of business process outsourcing enabled by the Internet is the farming out by several companies of the software asset management process to specialized service providers, which conduct regular software audits on the companies' application servers through the Internet. Software asset management is the business process whereby companies keep track of their installed software applications and respective licenses. This tracking is aimed at helping them avoid heavy fines in the event that any of their installed software is pirated.

The Need for a New Approach

Systems analysis and design is often seen as a course on how to design computing solutions to business problems. Whether the problems are fictitious or not, this emphasis on the development of computer applications is inconsistent with two key realities. The first is that business process redesign should precede computer-based automation; in fact, in some cases, only business process redesign, without any computer-based automation, leads to significant productivity gains for organizations. The second is that emphasizing computer application development, as possibly the main component of systems analysis and design, creates a narrow perception that is inconsistent with the reality that the vast majority of computer technology–enabled projects are implemented through either customization of off-the-shelf computer packages or business process outsourcing.

This book's solution to the notorious difficulty in teaching systems analysis and design is a simple one. It essentially entails teaching systems analysis and design with an emphasis on business process redesign and with an eye on industry trends and practical needs of organizations.

The above orientation is well aligned with the widespread adoption of enterprise systems since the 1990s. Those systems are often called "enterprise resource planning," or ERP, systems. The reason why the above orientation is well aligned with the widespread adoption of enterprise systems is that it in fact addresses a key problem almost always faced by organizations deploying those systems. Although enterprise systems can lead to major gains in productivity, by integrating information from different organization areas (e.g., sales, production, accounts receivable), they often require that key organizational processes be redesigned before they are deployed. Many examples exist in the business literature of organizations that have spent millions of dollars implementing enterprise systems, only to see those implementations fail due to incompatibilities between the organizational processes and the functionality provided by the enterprise systems.

The organizational revolution brought about by the advent of the Internet also supports the view that systems analysis and design should be taught and practiced with an emphasis on business process redesign. The Internet allows the streamlining of key business processes, such as order and production processes, so as to bring the customer much closer to the organization. It also enables the dramatic reduction of traditional supply-chain costs and order-to-delivery times, as exemplified by companies such as Dell and Amazon.com. However, those improvements can only be realized when traditional business processes are redesigned to take advantage of the new public information-sharing infrastructure provided by the Internet.

Summary and Concluding Remarks

This chapter looks at how systems analysis and design evolved as a discipline. Such evolution is complex and arguably closely intertwined with the evolution of computing. A key argument is put forth, namely that the evolution of systems analysis and design led the discipline to inherit a preference toward business process automation through in-house systems development as a way to improve organizations through the use of information technology. This has arguably led to a corresponding neglect of business process redesign and other alternatives, such as customization of off-the-shelf packages and business process outsourcing. The problem, as more and more organizations are finding out, is that those alternatives are often preferable to business process automation through in-house systems development.

This chapter resorts to some history to justify a key argument for a transformation of systems analysis and design, which is perhaps long overdue. Essentially, the argument is that modern systems analysis and design should be practiced and taught with an emphasis on business process redesign. This chapter calls for a related change in the practice and teaching of systems analysis and design, a change for which this book is presented as an initial answer, though a partial one that needs to be complemented by broader initiatives. Among those broader initiatives are accreditation standards for educational institutions, firms, and individuals selling systems analysis and design training and services—a theme that is picked up later in this book.

The aforementioned discussion is seen as important for the purposes of this book for two reasons. The first reason is that it gives the reader an overview of how systems analysis and design has evolved, which provides the basis on which the reader can understand how systems analysis and design is perceived by many today. The second reason is that the discussion provides the basis on which the reader can understand where the author is coming from, so to speak, which hopefully will clarify from the outset why the book covers the topics that it does, and why it covers those topics in the way that it does.

Review Questions

1. Computer science is not:
   (a) An independent discipline that dates back to the 1960s.
   (b) A discipline that emerged from the need to use assembly language.
   (c) A discipline that is taught in universities.
   (d) A discipline that encompasses several other important subdisciplines.

2. Systems analysis and design has:
   (a) Traditionally placed little emphasis on business process redesign.
   (b) Traditionally been hailed as the most exciting computer-related discipline by students.
   (c) Often been associated with the marketing discipline, particularly in schools of business.
   (d) Originated the discipline of object-oriented programming, through the language C++.

3. It is incorrect to say that the software development life cycle is:
    (a) An approach to systems analysis and design.
    (b) Seen as an abstraction resembling a waterfall-like structure.
    (c) An object-oriented methodology.
    (d) A byproduct of earlier ideas, including software engineering ideas.

4. Which of the following activities is not part of one of the steps in the traditional software development life cycle?
    (a) Generating textual description of a business process and related problems.
    (b) Graphically representing a business process through data flow diagrams.
    (c) Developing a high-level specification of the computer program modules, using structured English.
    (d) Developing a set of object-oriented representations of a business process.

5. It is incorrect to say that:
    (a) Systems analysis and design has traditionally been seen as a software development-oriented discipline.
    (b) Object-oriented programming has been very successful.
    (c) Systems analysis and design has traditionally placed little emphasis on business process redesign.
    (d) The software development life cycle disappeared in the 1990s.

Discussion Questions

1. Let's assume that medical doctors developed systems analysis and design primarily to address their professional needs. What would their version of systems analysis and design look like? Illustrate your answer through the development of a software development scenario where it is clear that the needs addressed are related to the medical profession.

2. As mentioned earlier in this chapter, the software development life cycle usually involves the design and specification of one or more databases. This implies that databases are a fundamental component of most (if not all) computer systems. Is this really the case today? Come up with a business software development scenario that illustrates a possible project in which database design and specification plays a minor role (if any). The scenario developed by you should be as realistic as possible.

PART I

Emerging Trends in Business

Part I Case:
The FBI's Virtual Case File

The Federal Bureau of Investigation (FBI) is the main investigative agency of the U.S. federal government. It dates back to 1908, when then U.S. Attorney General Charles J. Bonaparte established it under the name of "Bureau of Investigation" within the Department of Justice. The FBI was later reorganized under J. Edgar Hoover, who was appointed FBI Director in 1924 and successively reappointed until his death in 1972.

The FBI is responsible for investigating cases in which U.S. federal laws, as opposed to state and local laws, are suspected of being violated. The range of possible types of cases under the purview of the FBI is quite broad, involving computer crime, embezzlement, money laundering, organized crime, and terrorism. The passage of the Civil Rights Act in 1964 expanded the scope of crimes handled by the FBI, making it responsible for enforcing the prohibition of discrimination based on race, color, religion, or national origin. The FBI is also responsible for compiling a comprehensive summary of criminal activity in the United States and disseminating that to other federal agencies in the United States.

In 2001, the FBI hired the San Diego, California–based firm Science Applications International Corporation (SAIC) to build a case and evidence management software application called Virtual Case File (VCF) system. It hoped to replace a legacy case management system, called the Automated Case System, which no longer fit its needs. The obsolescence of the legacy system was chiefly due to changes in technology that affected the way other agencies stored and communicated data. Among the legacy system's problems was that it made it difficult for FBI agents to both import from and share data with external agencies' databases.

The terrorist attacks of September 11, 2001, led to new demands that would have to be met by the VCF system. For example, the legacy system that it was slated to replace did not have advanced data search capabilities, a limitation that became a serious point of concern during the congressional investigations following the terrorist attacks. According to one congressional testimony, field agents could not perform what are known as Boolean data searches through the Automated Case System. These are data searches in which combinations of qualifiers such as *and, or,* and *not* are used to narrow down data. An example of a Boolean search would be one that would allow FBI agents to identify individuals who were suspected members of terrorist associations and who had recently obtained flight training.

By early 2005, the FBI had spent about $170 million developing the VCF system, and a consensus started to emerge that the project had miserably failed to achieve its goals. While the VCF system was originally due in December 2003, only about 10 percent of the planned capability of the VCF system was available for use by FBI agents and other users in early 2005. At full capacity, the VCF system should have provided fully integrated criminal case and evidence data management, as well as varying levels of access and reporting to its data based on users' security clearances.

Within a few months into 2005, FBI Director Robert Mueller III indicated that the VCF system project was being abandoned. Mueller had previously admitted that the FBI had squandered $104 million on the development of VCF software that would unlikely be reused. The remainder of the total $170 million in funds had been spent on items that could be used for other purposes, such as generic computers and other general-purpose equipment items.

Procurement of a new system soon began, under a new name: the Sentinel Project. According to the FBI, the Sentinel Project would lead to the development of a system with case and evidence management tools, automated workflow control, and advanced search and reporting capabilities. This was essentially the same functionality set originally envisioned for the VCF system.

Several independent reports have been commissioned by the FBI and other agencies to investigate the VCF project and help understand what went wrong with it. Among those reports was one issued by the U.S. Department of Justice's Office of the Inspector General and another by the U.S. National Research Council (which is part of the U.S. National Academies, together with the National Academy of Sciences and the National Academy of Engineering).

One of the main conclusions of the above-mentioned reports was that the FBI had neglected to clearly understand how its internal organizational processes would have to be adapted to the new environment in which it operated and how those processes and related organizational regulations had to be modified to fully utilize the VCF system. Compounding those problems were technological changes that made much of the functionality in the VCF system unusable. For example, to be imported into the VCF system, external data had to be provided in certain formats. However, those who were in a position to provide that external data were also changing their technological infrastructure, creating a disconnect that often made data sharing impossible.

Moreover, the reports pointed out that the mission of the FBI had dramatically changed since the September 11 terrorist attacks, and, with that change, several of its organizational processes also had to change. However, the FBI seemed to have neglected to take those changes into account in the development of the VCF system. As a result, the functionality provided by the VCF system, as originally planned, would not meet the new intelligence gathering and counterterrorism mission of the FBI.

Sources

Dizzard, W. P. (2004, July 19). FBI to run old case system while it fields VCF. *Government Computer News.*

Dizzard, W. P. (2005, May 13). New system to replace FBI Virtual Case File. *Washington Technology.*

Frieden, T. (2005, February 3). Report: FBI wasted millions on "Virtual Case File." Retrieved from CNN.com

Kuchinskas, S. (2005, January 14). FBI's Virtual Case File flops. *Enterprise Magazine.*

The National Academies. (2004). *The FBI's trilogy information technology modernization program—Summary.* Washington, DC: Author.

Perera, D. (2005, January 14). Virtual case file a virtual bust. Retrieved from FCW.com

Schrage, M. (2005, April 15). Ignoring the obvious. *CIO Magazine.*

CHAPTER 2

Data, Information, and Knowledge Flow in Business Processes

This chapter operationally defines and discusses three central concepts of this book: data, information, and knowledge. These three concepts are so widely used today that defining them may sound a little too academic. Nevertheless, these concepts are too important for this book to be used in a loose way (which is what usually happens if they are not at least "operationally" defined). The operational definitions proposed here are not meant to be absolute or to invalidate definitions proposed by other authors. The goal here is to present definitions that will make sense in the context of this book and of the other concepts, methods, and techniques discussed in later chapters.

The concepts of data, information, and knowledge are presented as closely related yet fundamentally different from each other, which is important to emphasize for a couple of reasons. The first reason is that exchanging a lot of data does not mean the same as communicating, or transferring, a lot of information. That is, quite a lot of data can be transferred with little communication of information—as in a long e-mail that is not fully understood by its recipient. The second reason is that information cannot be effectively processed without knowledge, and knowledge varies from individual to individual. Individual knowledge variations depend on things such as an individual's cultural and educational background. The discussion presented here sets the stage for the methodological arguments made throughout the book.

Related but Different Concepts

We hear the words *data*, *information*, and *knowledge* quite often being used as if they were synonymous. However, there are subtle but very important differences among these concepts, and the nature of these differences is a relatively complex one. Moreover, from a business process design perspective, data, information, and knowledge serve purposes that are quite different from each other.

The contribution of information technology (IT) vendors has perhaps been unmatched in its potential to add to our confusion over the distinction between data and information. Examples can be found in almost any specialized IT vendor publication, in conversations with IT company sales representatives, and even in public speeches by IT "gurus" representing vendors. For example, at an international information systems conference the author attended, one of the senior vice presidents of a large software development company referred to the advantages of a well-known commercial group support system in the following terms:

> . . . information overflow can be considerably reduced . . . for example, a few weeks ago I prepared a 2 megabyte report and sent it via electronic mail to ten people. Each of these ten people forwarded a copy of the report to about ten other people . . . as a result, my report had generated a flow of 200 megabytes of information in the network, in less than four days. . . .

In the example above, the speaker was referring to data, which can be measured in megabytes, as synonymous with information. This can often be misleading, because large sets of data may have very low information content, depending on how well prepared the receiver of the data is to make sense of it. Mistakenly identifying data as information is as commonplace as confusing knowledge with information.

It is curious that the confusion over what information and knowledge are has been nurtured even by some of those who are widely recognized as among the forerunners of the study of information and knowledge and their impact on organizations and society. For example, not too long ago, Peter Drucker, a highly regarded management guru, stated that

> . . . the business, and increasingly the government agency as well, will be knowledge-based, composed largely of specialists who direct and discipline their own performance through organized feedback from colleagues and customers. It will be an information-based organization. . . . Today's typical organization, in which knowledge tends to be concentrated in service staffs perched rather insecurely between top management and the operating people, will likely be labeled a phase, an attempt to infuse knowledge from the top rather than obtain information from below.

Arguably, the eloquent and widely cited statement above was referring to information and knowledge as though they were synonymous. But, again, why should we worry about the different nature of data, information, and knowledge? One reason is that, by not distinguishing among these concepts, we may not be aware that an "ocean" of data may contain only a small amount of information that is of any value to us, and sifting through this ocean of data may be severely time-consuming. Another reason is that, without understanding the different nature of these concepts, we cannot fully appreciate how business process improvement can contribute to knowledge sharing, a theme that permeates several of the issues discussed in this book. But there are other reasons, and they relate to the nature of our understanding of the world, or the way we make sense of the world around us.

The world is not only what we perceive it to be through our senses. It is a combination of these perceptions and what is stored in our body, and mostly in our brain, in the form of neural networks. We can develop our neural networks by interacting with the environment surrounding us, which includes other human beings. However, to interact with other human beings, we need to externalize what is stored in our neural networks by means of a code. Other human beings should understand this code so communication of what is stored in our brain can actually take place.

One interesting thought experiment that illustrates the difference between data and information, discussed briefly next, points at the different information content that one e-mail message may have for different recipients. Let us suppose that an e-mail message written in Spanish (a specific code) is sent to two different recipients, one who can speak Spanish and one who cannot. In this example, let us also assume that the e-mail takes up the same disk space of about 3.6 kilobytes on the computers of each of the recipients, which is a measure of the amount of *data* related to the message.

In the aforementioned thought experiment, the *information* content of the e-mail is much higher for the recipient who can read Spanish than for the recipient who cannot. As mentioned, this provides a good illustration of the difference between data and information. If data and information were the same, they should not yield different "amounts" when measured for the same object (in this case, the e-mail message in Spanish).

The distinction between knowledge and information is a bit more abstract than that between information and data. To make this distinction as clear as possible, let us consider the following dialogue between a doctor and her patient:

Doctor: So, what brings you here today?

Patient: I don't know, doctor; I've been feeling a bit strange in the last couple of weeks.

Doctor: What do you mean by "strange"?

Patient: Burning eyes, stuffed nose . . . and these things come and go several times a day.

Doctor: Any headaches or fever?

Patient: A little bit of fever, but no headaches.

Doctor: Well, we'll run a checkup on you, but I think you probably have an allergy.

The patient was feeling the symptoms of what could be an allergy, and therefore he went to see his doctor—an expert who likely *knows* more about medicine than the patient himself. The patient described his symptoms, and the doctor made a tentative diagnosis: ". . . you probably have an allergy." Is what the patient told the doctor enough for anyone without any medical expertise to come up with the same tentative diagnosis? Maybe, but if this were always the case, very few people would agree to pay doctors for consultations. Doctors arguably possess more of something that patients do not have, something typically referred to as *knowledge*, in the specific field of medicine.

Is the nature of the expert knowledge possessed by the doctor, in this case, the same as that of the perception of symptoms experienced by the patient? No, for the simple reason that expert knowledge can be used to generate conclusions based on the description of symptoms—something that the descriptions alone cannot. Therefore, the natures of *descriptions* and *expert knowledge* are different, and it can be shown that neither of them is the same as the nature of data. This also suggests that the descriptions are instances of something unique, which is referred to here as *information.*

Data Are Used to Store and Convey Information and Knowledge

The usual sense of the term *data*, even if not explicitly stated, is that of carriers of information and knowledge. Data flow in organizational processes between the functions that carry out process activities. This flow takes place through various media, particularly paper, digital electrical impulses (e.g., electronic data interchange systems), analog electrical waves (e.g., analog telephone), electromagnetic waves (e.g., radio), and air vibrations (e.g., face-to-face conversation). Data can also be stored for later use in different storage media, such as magnetic media (e.g., hard and floppy disks), paper, and volatile digital memories (e.g., memory chips in personal computers).

Data are either transferred or stored through a process of "changing," or generating perturbations on, a given medium. A blank sheet of paper, for example, can be used for data storage (e.g., to write down an address of a colleague) or transfer (e.g., to write a memo to an employee) by applying ink on it. Or, from a more business-oriented perspective, if a machine operator wants to tell his supervisor about a problem with a metal-shaping machine, he can approach his supervisor and speak to her face-to-face. In doing so, he uses his vocal cords to generate vibrations in the air (volatile data) that will be received and decoded by the recipient through her hearing organs.

The main point here is that data will only become information or knowledge when they are interpreted by human beings, or, in some cases, artificial intelligent agents (the latter is a special case that is not addressed in depth in this book[1]). Data can be stored and transferred by organizational process functions (e.g., forklift operator, inventory manager) through changes in storage and communication media that will be interpreted by other organizational process functions.

The measurement of data depends on the medium used to store or transfer it, as well as on the code used. In most organizational processes, data can be measured in words or symbols, when the medium used is paper, and bits or bytes, when the medium used is a digital one.

In many ways, a bit can be considered the smallest and most fundamental unit of data. It can take only two values: 0 (or false) and 1 (or true). A group of 8 bits forms a byte. And, since the number of possible bytes is 2^8, or 256, there can be a direct correspondence between bytes and certain symbols (e.g., the letters of the English alphabet and other alphabets). One such set of symbols, largely used to convert alphanumeric characters into bytes and vice versa, is called the ASCII code (American Standard Code for Information Interchange). Most operating systems in personal computers use the ASCII code, or an extended version of it, to map symbols that have meaning to human beings (e.g., letters and numbers) into bytes stored in any of the computers' data storage devices (e.g., memory chips, hard disk).

Information Is Eminently Descriptive

From a business process–oriented view, information can be seen as carried by data and as being eminently *descriptive*. From a linguistic perspective, the typical instance of information is the utterance called *assertion*. One example of assertion is "Today is a sunny day." Independently of what this assertion means exactly (the word "sunny" can mean different things to different people, from sparsely clouded to clear-sky weather), it provides a *description* of the current state of the environment surrounding us. If the environment is seen as an object, the assertion can be seen as defining an attribute of the object, in this case the *weather*, as *sunny*.

Information can be qualified in different ways—it can be more or less complete or accurate, and it can refer to the past, present, and future. For example, the assertion "Today is hot!" conveys less accurate information than the assertion "Today's temperature is 85 degrees Fahrenheit and the humidity level is 90 percent." Both assertions describe the present, that is, today. The assertion "The temperature on this day during the past 3 years has averaged 87 degrees Fahrenheit" also provides information about the past. The assertion "Tomorrow, the top temperatures will be in the low 90s" provides a description of the future. Although similar to descriptions of the past and the present, descriptions of the future, by their own nature, *always* carry a certain degree of uncertainty.

Knowledge, which will be discussed in more detail in the next section, is often used to generate more information, based on information at hand. The information generated in that way (or *inferred*) is usually not obvious and therefore possesses some added value in relation to the primary information received as an input by the knowledge holder. One example is the generation of information about the future (e.g., the weather in New York tomorrow) based on information about the present and past (e.g., the weather patterns in New York during the past 2 years, up to now). This type of information about the future is produced by meteorologists, based on their knowledge about the science of weather forecasting. That information is then bought by news services, which in turn broadcast the information to their audiences and, in the process of doing so, manage to make some money out of it.

The Monetary Value of Information

One interesting aspect of information is that its value, that is, how much someone is willing to pay for it and can benefit from it, seems in general to directly correlate some of its attributes. Among those attributes are its *advanceness*, that is, how much time in advance it describes the future; its *accuracy*, that is, how accurate the description is; and its *completeness*, that is, how complete the description is.

Let us look at the different nature of the attributes above in a business context. The "corporate war" between Coca-Cola and Pepsi in the 1980s was largely one of product differentiation. Both Coca-Cola and Pepsi tried to increase their shares of the "cola" soft drink market by launching new differentiated (e.g., diet) products ahead of each other. Consider the similar situation of two companies, A and B, competing for 2 million customers in the same industry. Each customer consumes a product supplied by both companies. Analogously to the "cola" war, the product is essentially the same, the main difference being the brand. Each customer consumes 70 units of the product, which cost $3 each, every year, making it a $420 million per year market. Company A has 90 percent of the market, or $378 million, while Company B has the other 10 percent, or $42 million. Both companies sell with a pretax profit margin of 17 percent, which yields approximately $64 million for Company A and $7 million for Company B in absolute pretax profits.

Now suppose that Company B decides to launch into the market a new product whose development time is approximately 9 months. The product has the potential to bring Company B's market share up to 20 percent and send Company A's share down to 80 percent. This would raise Company B's pretax profits up to about $14 million and make Company A's profits plummet to nearly $57 million. From Company A's perspective (and the value of information always depends on its user and the context in which the user is), one piece of information—that Company B is going to launch a new product—can make a lot of difference. This piece of information can have a high advanceness if it is provided to Company A well in advance of the product launch, enabling it to take appropriate countermeasures. The same piece of information can have a high accuracy, providing accurate details about the product that is going to be launched (e.g., it might include the precise date of launch). The information can also have high completeness, providing a rich description of the new aspects of the product (e.g., the new flavor, the sweetener used).

If Company A has no access to information about the new product launch or, say, obtains some inaccurate information a few weeks before the new product is launched, it will have to endure a loss in pretax profits of $7 million—this is the worst-case scenario. However, if it gets its hands on accurate and complete information early enough, it can take preventive measures to at least reduce its losses. For example, if the information is obtained more than 9 months in advance (i.e., has high advanceness) but leaves uncertainty about the characteristics of the product (i.e., has low accuracy and completeness), then Company A might have to develop a range of new products to dampen Company B's new product's potential impact on market share. Its profits may still be reduced due to increased product

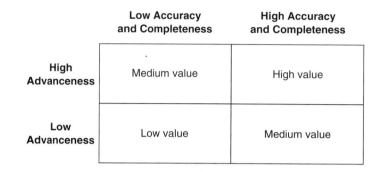

	Low Accuracy and Completeness	High Accuracy and Completeness
High Advanceness	Medium value	High value
Low Advanceness	Low value	Medium value

Figure 2.1   The Value of Information

development costs, but not to the same extent that they would if no information were available.

Having access to detailed information about Company B's new product (i.e., highly accurate and complete information) only 4 months before the launch (i.e., low advanceness information) may lead to a similar end result. That is, Company A may be able to develop an intermediary product that would reduce Company B's new launch's impact on market share.

The best scenario is perhaps that in which Company A has access to highly detailed information (i.e., highly accurate and complete information) about Company B's new launch early enough (i.e., the information has high advanceness) so it can develop a similar new product and get it out into the market before Company B does the same with its new product. According to our initial assumptions, this could potentially bring Company A's market share up to 95 percent and increase its profits by about $4 million.

In the example above, no information, or information with low accuracy, completeness, or advanceness, would be of low value to Company A. Information with high accuracy and completeness, but low advanceness (or vice versa), would have a medium value, as it could prevent a loss of $7 million in pretax profits a year. Finally, information with high accuracy, completeness, and advanceness would have a high value, enabling an increase in profits of $4 million a year. This relationship between information value and its attributes is illustrated in Figure 2.1.

Although the example above is concerned with a decision-making process at the strategic level, we can extrapolate the relationship between information value and the attributes advanceness and accuracy to most organizational processes. Simply put, business process–related information seems to be an important enabling factor for the members of a business process team (that is, those who perform business process activities) to do their job efficiently and effectively, whatever the business process is.

Knowledge Is Eminently Associative

While information is eminently descriptive, and can refer to the past, present, and future, knowledge is by its nature eminently *associative*. That is, it allows us to "associate" different world states and respective mental representations, which are typically linked to or described by means of pieces of information (i.e., knowledge allows us to link different pieces of information and make decisions based on that). The associative aspect of knowledge can be seen as being of two main types, namely *correlational* or *causal*.

Correlational knowledge usually connects two or more pieces of information that describe events or situations that have happened, are happening, or will happen at the *same* time. Causal knowledge connects pieces of information that describe the state of the world at *different* times. For example, consider the associative knowledge represented in the following decision rule: "If John has a high fever and is sneezing, then John has likely a cold." The knowledge embodied in this decision rule is of the correlational type, because it affirms that someone who has a high fever and is sneezing is in fact displaying typical cold symptoms—that is, "fever," "sneezing," and "cold" typically happen at the same time.

Another example, now of a different type of knowledge, is provided by the rule: "If John smokes a lot, then he will probably die of lung cancer." This decision rule expresses causal knowledge. As such, the rule connects two events that take place at different times: John smoking a lot, in the present, and John dying of lung cancer, in the future. This type of knowledge has been studied extensively by epistemologists (i.e., researchers and philosophers who study the nature of knowledge) and is what philosopher of science Daniel Dennett referred to when he stated the following in his seminal book *Consciousness Explained*:

> The brain's task is to guide the body it controls through a world of shifting conditions and sudden surprises, so it must gather information from that world and use *swiftly* to "produce future"—to extract anticipations in order to stay one step ahead of disaster [original emphasis].

Knowledge drives the flow of myriad decisions that have to be made even in the simplest organizational processes. Steel plants, for example, rely on process teams to load and operate smelters. Consider the causal knowledge expressed in the rule: "If the smelter is set at a temperature of 3,000 degrees Celsius, then a 1-ton load of steel will be smelted in 43 minutes." This is one of the pieces of knowledge that allow a smelter operator to predict that a batch of solid steel weighing about 1 ton will be in liquid form approximately 43 minutes after it is loaded into the smelter, if the smelter is set properly. This prediction allows the smelter operator to program a stop in the smelting process at the right time and let the liquid steel flow out of the smelter, which would save energy. Considering the high temperatures involved, the energy savings could be substantial.

For teamwork to yield effective and efficient outcomes, those who perform activities in a business process must share a certain amount of knowledge. In the example above, those who use the steel in liquid form for shaping steel parts should ideally hold at least part of the knowledge held by the smelter operator. If they know of the "43-minute rule," they can also predict that a batch of steel will be ready within 43 minutes from the time it is loaded in solid form. This will enable them to have their own equipment prepared at the right time to work on the liquid steel.

Knowledge has been distinguished from information and also linked with decision making in different fields of research and academic disciplines. In the field of artificial intelligence, for example, information has been typically represented through what has often been referred to (in a nontraditional dictionary sense) as "facts," which are similar to assertions. Knowledge, on the other hand, has been expressed by means of a number of different representations, such as semantic networks, frames, scripts, neural networks, and production rules. The most common form of knowledge representation in practical knowledge–based computer systems is through production rules. Production rules are conditional statements in *if-then* form, like the ones used to exemplify knowledge in this section.

In the fields of psychology and social cognition, knowledge has been expressed through "schemas" and "cognitive maps." These are, in turn, seen as mental structures that guide individual and group behavior and that use as their inputs environmental stimuli obtained through the senses. The concept of schema was developed as a reaction to studies of memory pioneered in the late 1800s by Ebbinghaus, which made use of arbitrary materials and sensorial stimuli to determine factors that influence the formation of memory and recall of information. The development of the concept of schema is credited to Frederick Bartlett, who used the American Indian folk tale "The War of the Ghosts" to show that existing mental structures strongly influenced memory formation and recall. Such existing mental structures, which were used by Bartlett's study subjects to process information coming from the tale, were called schemas. Essentially, Bartlett showed that individuals possessing different schemas would interpret the tale, which is filled with strange gaps and bizarre causal sequences, in substantially different ways. By doing this, Bartlett also showed that the different pieces of knowledge possessed by different individuals led them to interpret information in fundamentally different ways.

In biology in general, and, more particularly, in neurobiology and related fields, knowledge is typically seen as associated with long-term nerve-based memory structures whose main goal is information processing. Information, on the other hand, is seen as usually associated with short-term neural connections that appear to "vanish" from conscious memory after a while. For example, the knowledge of how to operate a telephone is stored in long-term memory structures, whereas the information represented by a telephone number is stored in short-term memory structures.

The Monetary Value of Knowledge

Knowledge is usually much more expensive than information to produce and transfer. For example, information in the form of mutual fund indicators (e.g., quarterly earnings, monthly price fluctuation) is produced by means of little more than simple calculations performed on data about share prices and their fluctuation over a time period. The knowledge of how mutual fund indicators fluctuate, however, requires years of analysis of relevant information to be built. This analysis of information leads to the development of knowledge that allows an expert investor to select the best mutual funds on which to invest her money given the configuration of the economy.

Comparative studies of experts and nonexperts suggest that knowledge is usually acquired through an inductive process in which generalizations are made based on the frequency with which a certain piece of information occurs. A different and less common method used to generate knowledge is deduction, whereby hidden knowledge is produced based on existing knowledge through a set of logical steps. This latter method has been used in the development of a large body of knowledge in the form of "theorems," particularly in the fields of mathematics and theoretical physics.

An example of knowledge building through induction is that conducted by novice investors in the stock market. The observation that shares of a small number of companies in high technology industries have risen 10 percentage points above the Standard & Poor's 500 average index during a period of 6 months may prompt a novice investor to put all of her money into these shares. A professional investor, however, knows, based on, say, 10 years of experience as a broker in the stock market, that a 6-month observation period is not long enough to support such a risky decision and opts for a more diversified portfolio. In cases such as these, the novice investor will eventually lose money, particularly because her decision to sell will probably follow the same pattern as her decision to buy. It will be based on inferences based on a time span that is too short, leading her to buy shares that are overvalued and sell these shares when they are undervalued. Most nonprofessional investors seem to follow this recipe, which in most cases leads to disastrous consequences.

The example above illustrates a key finding from research on cognitive psychology: People tend to infer knowledge based on the observation of a small number of events, that is, on limited information. Moreover, once mental knowledge structures are developed, changing those structures can become more difficult than developing them from scratch. A conversation that the author had a while ago with a university colleague illustrates these cognitive biases. The colleague in question had gone to two different agencies of the New Jersey Motor Vehicle Services (MVS) where he met employees who, in his view, lacked sympathy and friendliness. He also had gone to a similar agency in the state of Pennsylvania, whose employees he found to be very nice. Later, during a chat with friends, he said, "All MVS employees in New Jersey are very grumpy, difficult to deal with. . . . The state of Pennsylvania is much better in that respect." It was pointed out to him that he had just made a gross generalization, given the small sample of MVS agencies visited—only two in New Jersey and one in Pennsylvania. Although he agreed with that, he was nevertheless adamant that he would never go to a New Jersey MVS agency again, unless it was absolutely necessary. If this were the case, he said he would ask a less "touchy" person to go—his wife.

The development of theories of knowledge (or epistemologies) and scientific methods of inquiry has been motivated by a need to overcome cognitive biases such as those illustrated above. This has been one of the main common goals of such thinkers as Aristotle, René Descartes, Gottlob Frege, Bertrand Russell, Karl Popper, and Thomas Kuhn. Epistemologies and scientific methods have provided a basis for the conduct of research in general, and in consequence for technological advances that have shaped organizations and society. Every year, hundreds of billions of dollars are invested in research, with the ultimate goal of generating highly reliable and valid knowledge. And the market value of organizations is increasingly assessed based on the amount of knowledge that they possess, rather than on their material assets base.

Paul Strassmann, an information economics researcher and former information technology executive at companies such as Xerox, Kraft Foods, and the U.S. Department of Defense, suggests that variations in the perceptions of organizational knowledge account for the growing trend toward apparently incorrectly overvaluing or undervaluing stocks in the share market. According to Strassmann, the incorrect perception that a stock is overvalued or undervalued stems from the failure of current accounting systems to account for the knowledge assets of organizations. Undervaluing stocks was occurring less often when Strassmann conducted his seminal studies on the topic in the late 1990s. He presents an impressive array of data to support this idea. Abbott Laboratories is one of the companies he used to illustrate this point.

The market value of a publicly traded company is calculated based on the stock price and the number of existing shares of the company, through the multiplication of those two items. Over a period of 7 years from 1987 to 1994, the ratio between Abbott's market value and its equity had swung from five up to nearly eight and back down to about seven. However, the ratio between market value and "equity plus knowledge assets" remained almost constant over that period, smoothly gravitating around two. This supports Strassmann's position that the market perceives the accumulation of knowledge assets, which is reflected in the high correlation between share prices of organizations and their knowledge assets, even though the knowledge assets are not shown on a company's balance sheet. In his influential report titled *The Value of Computers, Information and Knowledge*, Strassmann stated,

> The sustained stability of the market-to-capital ratio which accounts for the steady rise in the knowledge capital of Abbott Laboratories confirms that the stock market will recognize the accumulation of knowledge as an asset even though the accountants do not. The stock market will also reward the accumulators of knowledge capital because investors recognize that the worth of a corporation is largely in its management, not its physical or financial assets.

When we move from a macroeconomic to a microeconomic perspective and look at the business processes of a firm, the trend toward valuing knowledge seems to be similar to the one just described. Knowledge allows for the prediction of business process–related outcomes, from the more general prediction of a group of customers' acceptance of a new product to much more specific predictions, such as slight manual corrections needed on a computer board surface after it goes through an automatic drill. Correlational knowledge enables chemical process–control workstation operators at a chemical plant to link a sudden rise of an acidity gauge to an incorrect setting of the amount of flow through a pipe valve. This enables the operators to take the appropriate measures to bring the acidity level down to normal.

The workers who hold bodies of expert knowledge are rewarded according to their ability to use them to perform process activities in an efficient and effective way. This is typically achieved through linking different types of information, which can be done through formal education or personal experience (i.e., the building of mental knowledge bases) and through inferring information about the future based on information about the past or present (i.e., predicting the future). Organizational wealth is closely linked to the ability to build and use technological artifacts to control future states of the environment in which organizations operate, whether those environments be economic, physical, cultural, or others. However, this control is impossible without the related ability to predict the future, which in turn relies heavily on causal knowledge.

Organizational knowledge is believed to be the single most important factor that ultimately defines the ability of a company to survive and thrive in a competitive environment. This knowledge is probably stored mostly in the brains of the workers of the company, although it may also be stored in computer systems, databases, and other archival records (e.g., printed reports). Whatever form it takes, knowledge is a commodity. And, as such, it can be bought and sold, which makes its value fluctuate more or less according to the laws that regulate supply and demand.

Abundant knowledge, which can be represented by a large number of available professionals with the same type of expertise, becomes cheap when supply surpasses demand, which is typically reflected in a decrease in the salaries of some groups of professionals. On the other hand, a situation in which some types of highly specialized knowledge are in short supply, while demand grows sharply in a short period of time, can lead the knowledge holders to be caught by surprise when faced with unusually high bids from employers (a pleasant surprise, at least while the situation persists).

For example, Web Java programmers were being offered salaries of up to $170,000 early in 1996, even though the demand for their new expertise was virtually nil until 1995. This was the year Java was first released by Sun Microsystems, 2 years after the University of Illinois began the distribution of its Web browser Mosaic. In 2002, in the aftermath of the infamous tech-stock bubble burst, many Web Java programmers were having difficulty finding a job, much less making anything near $80,000 a year.

The Relationship Connecting Data, Information, and Knowledge

Although they are different conceptual entities, data, information, and knowledge are inextricably connected. This may be one of the reasons why they are so often confused. As discussed before, data are perturbations on a communication or storage medium that are used to transfer or store information and knowledge. Therefore, knowledge and information can be neither communicated nor stored without data.

Information is used to describe the world and can provide a description of the past, present, and future. Information about the future always carries a certain degree of uncertainty. Correlational knowledge allows for the linking of different pieces of information about the present. In this case, usually some of the information pieces are known and used as a departure point, and the other pieces are hidden and allow for relevant decisions. Causal knowledge enables the production of information about the future, typically based on information about the past and the present. That is, information is generated based on both correlational and causal knowledge. However, the reverse relationship is also valid; that is, knowledge can be generated based on information.

In fact, the main process by which reliable knowledge is produced is the systematic analysis of information about the past. Such analysis typically leads to the observation of patterns that are combined into predictive and associative rules (i.e., knowledge). Consider, for example, the following case involving Hopper Specialty and NCR. In 1987, Hopper Specialty, a retail vendor of industrial hardware in Farmington, New Mexico, decided to purchase a computerized inventory management system from NCR, a large developer of computer hardware and software, headquartered in Dayton, Ohio. The system in question was called Warehouse Manager and was installed in 1988. Several problems surfaced immediately after the system had been installed.

According to Hopper Specialty's representatives, the system never worked as it was supposed to, displaying an assortment of problems such as extremely long response times, constant locking up of terminals, and corrupted data files. In 1993, more than 5 years after the system was installed, Hopper Specialty cancelled the contract with NCR and sued the company, claiming that it had suffered a loss of $4.2 million in profits due to problems caused by the installation and use of Warehouse Manager. NCR's lawyers immediately asked that the lawsuit be dismissed on the grounds that it was filed too late—New Mexico's statute of limitations for this type of lawsuit is only 4 years.

Ethical considerations aside, NCR's lawyers had access to information and knowledge that allowed them to safely move for a case dismissal. The valuable information here regards New Mexico's statute of limitations and can be expressed by the assertion: "In New Mexico, a lawsuit such as the one filed by Hopper Specialty should be filed within at least 4 years after the alleged breach of contract occurs." The knowledge possessed by NCR's lawyers allowed them to build a link between information about the law, in this case the statute of limitations, and the likely consequence (information about the future) of grounding their defense on New Mexico's statute of limitations. This knowledge can be summarily expressed by the rule: "*If* we move for a case dismissal based on New Mexico's statute of limitations, *then* it is likely that the case will be quickly dismissed by the judge presiding over the case."

Figure 2.2 depicts the relationship between data, information, and knowledge based on the case discussed above. The following printed or electronic documents store information that could be used by NCR's lawyers to defend their company in the lawsuit filed by Hopper: the lawsuit notification, the contract between NCR and

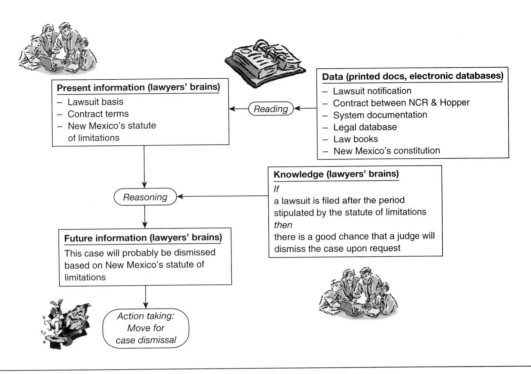

Figure 2.2   The Relationship Connecting Data, Information, and Knowledge

Hopper, Warehouse Manager's documentation, a legal database of previous legal cases, law books, and New Mexico's constitution.

The above items are physical or electronic records, that is, data, which had first to be read by NCR's lawyers so they (i.e., the lawyers) could extract some pieces of relevant present information (i.e., information about the present situation). Examples of such pieces of relevant information are the terms of the contract between NCR and Hopper, and New Mexico's statute of limitations.

Present information can then be combined with knowledge linking the main goal of a generic statute of limitations and the likely consequences of anyone not observing the lawsuit filing expiry period stipulated by it. This combination of knowledge and information allows for the prediction of the future with a certain degree of certainty, that is, the generation of information about the future. In the case of NCR versus Hopper, this future-related information was the prediction that the presiding judge would dismiss the case based on New Mexico's statute of limitations. NCR's lawyers therefore took the appropriate action of moving for a case dismissal.

As it can be seen from the discussion in this chapter, data, information, and knowledge are closely related but different concepts. Perhaps their discussion in this chapter has been a little too extensive for a book aimed at managers, professionals, and business students, but it is reasonable to assume that many readers will want to reread this chapter while digesting the ideas presented in future chapters. This chapter provides an important conceptual foundation for the understanding of many of the notions presented in future chapters.

The Hypercommunication Syndrome

Hypercommunication is a phenomenon characterized by people trying to communicate and absorb more information than they need or are able to handle in order to accomplish tasks and achieve goals in connection with tasks. Note that no reference to *knowledge* communication is made here, because it appears that this is really an *information*-related problem. This is as much a business or organizational phenomenon as it is a societal one.

We waste a lot of time and effort accumulating, ranking, and filing business forms, reports, memos, and e-mails that we never use in business activities, and we lead other people to make the same mistake by sending them forms, reports, memos, and e-mails as well—thereby implying that they should process all the information contained in those items.

Similarly, we also waste much time and effort reading in magazines and watching on TV things that we will never put to practical use in our personal lives, and we lead other people to fall into the same trap by telling them all about what we read or watched on TV, thus subconsciously making them feel guilty about not knowing those things already.

We would be better off saving some of that time and effort by redesigning business processes and rethinking personal habits with an eye on what we try to communicate to others and what we allow to be communicated to us.

Saying that too much communication is taking place in organizations means nothing unless we qualify what we are saying by defining communication's relationship with other concepts. Among those concepts, three of the most important are *task*, *goal*, and *process*. As a general rule, we achieve a goal in connection with a task through a process. For example, our goal may be to design a new car model that will sell 100,000 units in the United States, which is a goal in connection with the task of designing the new car model, which is accomplished through a process, namely the sequence of activities involved in designing the new car model.

Generally speaking, it is because we try to exchange too much information to accomplish organizational goals in connection with tasks and through processes that we create hypercommunicative environments. Thus, it should come as no surprise that a good way of preventing hypercommunication is to focus our attention primarily on the information that is needed to perform a process, which will allow us to accomplish a task and achieve a set goal in connection with the task.

Exchanging Much More Data Than Information

Processes are sequences of interrelated activities that are carried out by individuals. Usually the individuals involved in the execution of a process need to exchange information (and, to a much lesser extent, knowledge) among themselves to complete each of the iterations of the process (e.g., assembling one car in a car-assembly process). Information is always transferred through data, which in turn may take many shapes and flow through several different media. For example, transient data in the form of air vibrations may be used to convey information through the telephone, which is an electronic communication medium. More permanent data, in the form of printed forms, for instance, may be used to convey information through the internal mail system of a company.

Data, sometimes a lot of it, can be transferred without information being communicated. For example, let us suppose a situation in which an English-speaking information technology consultant called Karen sends an e-mail with 4 kilobytes of data, written in English, to two of her colleagues. One of her colleagues, John, speaks English. The other, Juan, speaks only Spanish—something that Karen was not aware of when she sent him the e-mail in English.

In the aforementioned situation, exactly the same amount of data, 4 kilobytes, has been transferred from Karen to John and Juan. However, the amount of information communicated by Karen to Juan has arguably been much smaller than that communicated to John—perhaps zero, if Juan knows absolutely no English.

As can be inferred from the example above, being unable to "decode" data can be one of the reasons why sometimes data is transferred but no information is communicated. Another reason is simply the exchange of data that is not relevant or that is too much to be handled effectively by the recipient of the data. For example, one of the main mechanisms for information communication in organizations is the business form, whether it is paper-based or electronic. A form is a collection of fields—for example, a Web-based book order form completed on Amazon.com's Web site. If a form is poorly designed and contains many more fields than necessary, as in many university registration and medical doctor offices, a great deal of the work involved in filling them out ends up being lost. They will become meaningless data that will also contribute to making the job of the user of the form (e.g., a university registrar or a medical office employee) harder, because he or she will have to filter out the relevant pieces of data from an unnecessarily complicated form and turn them into usable information.

The Irreversible Trend Toward Knowledge Fragmentation

Knowledge, whether stored in the brain or in computer databases, is necessary for the processing of information. Information processing, in turn, has been identified as the main reason why organizations exist. That is, purposeful organization of people, capital, and other resources is necessary so information processing can be done efficiently and effectively. Information processing, in turn, is seen as a fundamental step in the generation and delivery of products and services by organizations to their customers.

Knowledge exists in organizations in a dispersed way and is predominantly held by the individuals who perform process activities. The notion of group (or team) knowledge expands the locus of knowledge, from the individual toward the group. Group knowledge is the collective knowledge possessed by groups of individuals involved in the execution of organizational processes, regardless of process scope.

Such processes can be as diverse as the processes of "home loan approval" and "hamburger preparation."

Due to its associative nature, the continuous buildup and intensive use of knowledge is a necessity in a complex society that relies on complex organizations to produce and deliver the products and services it consumes. *Complexity* implies a large number of associations or interdependencies, whether we look at society from an environmental, artifact-oriented, sociological, psychological, or any other relevant perspective. Knowledge creation feeds complexity and vice versa, in what could be seen as an open-ended spiral.

For example, new discoveries about a terminal disease and its genetic roots can trigger the development of new technologies and drugs for treatment and prevention of the disease. This in turn can lead to the development of new equipment and new drug manufacturing companies. New governmental market regulations may follow. New militant groups fighting for their rights may emerge as those who have the genes that cause the disease organize themselves against possible discrimination by insurance companies. New research fields, theories, and academic disciplines may be spawned.

As knowledge becomes more voluminous and complex, so does the need for knowledge specialization by individuals. Through formal and informal education as well as practice, experts in fields as diverse as accounting and medicine absorb and use specialized knowledge that is not held by large sections of the population in general. The market rewards knowledge specialization and expertise through higher-paying jobs and social status.

Several difficult-to-overcome obstacles, particularly in the form of time constraints, prevent individuals from becoming experts in several different knowledge specialties at the same time. For example, studies by Herbert A. Simon and colleagues on expertise in connection with playing chess, which later were used as a basis to understand expertise and its impact in many other areas, suggest that a chess player cannot reach the grandmaster level in fewer than 9 or 10 years, regardless of how hard he or she tries and how intelligent he or she is. Analogously, a medical doctor specializing in brain surgery and a civil engineer specializing in the design of tall commercial buildings will need a certain number of years to acquire all the knowledge involved in doing what they do well, regardless of how hard they work and how intelligent they are. This will eventually ensure that no brain surgeon will know enough about building design to be able to design tall commercial buildings and vice versa; that is, they will be experts in only one main area or related areas, or they will not be good enough to be considered experts in any particular area.

A large and highly educated mass of people spanning many countries ensures that knowledge is created at a very fast rate so as to push individuals into focusing their learning efforts onto narrow fields of expertise. This leads to a growing knowledge fragmentation in organizations. A look at the shop floor of most automobile manufacturers provides what appears to be a good illustration of knowledge fragmentation. For example, an automaker's plant will often manufacture more than one car model (e.g., a plant by Volkswagen, General Motors, or Ford). Although an automaker usually designs each of the models assembled in its plants, most of the parts that go into the models come from third-party suppliers, which can easily amount to several hundreds for each automaker. Brakes, engine parts, or even something as simple as an exhaust pipe or a seat belt, are individually obtained from different suppliers and assembled into a car by the automakers. In fact, a common joke in the car parts industry is that automakers don't actually manufacture anything that goes into their cars.

Among the reasons why outsourcing the manufacturing of car parts is more economical for automakers than making those parts in-house is that the cost of keeping and managing the specialized knowledge that goes into economically and effectively building each car part is too high. Outsourcing pushes the responsibility of keeping and managing part-specific knowledge to the supplier.

The Lack of Knowledge Sharing in Organizational Processes

The example of automakers and their relationship with their suppliers of car parts is an interesting one; it illustrates not only knowledge fragmentation, but also the need for some degree of knowledge sharing. Although a supplier possesses the knowledge that goes into manufacturing each car part, an automaker's engineers still need to hold part of that knowledge in order to design their cars. For example, they need to know whether an air bag, which is manufactured elsewhere, will inflate properly if they reduce the size of the air bag's compartment. That is, sharing knowledge becomes a necessity if the automobile manufacturers and their suppliers are to build low-cost cars that meet car buyers' expectations. And such expectations are likely to be increasingly inflated in a highly competitive marketplace such as the one in which we live now.

At least one management movement has consistently argued for the development of knowledge creation and sharing capabilities within *and* between organizations as a fundamental step toward achieving heightened competitiveness. This management movement is known as the "learning organizations" movement and was pioneered by Chris Argyris in the 1970s and revived by Peter Senge and colleagues in the 1990s. To foster knowledge creation and sharing, it is argued that learning organizations should establish an organizational culture that is conducive to those activities. A climate of risk taking and experimentation has been found to be an important factor in establishing such organizational culture. Proponents of organizational learning argue that such a climate can be achieved through the adoption of new management practices and paradigms that stimulate creativity and proactive behavior, as well as social interaction.

In spite of attempts to create organizational cultures conducive to learning, the transferring of acquired knowledge from one part of an organization to another remains a complex and problematic undertaking. This is particularly unfortunate, as transfer of acquired knowledge across different organizational areas has been itself presented as one of the most important components of organizational competitiveness enhancement. As knowledge becomes more specialized, so does the need for information and knowledge sharing, which can be achieved through oral and written communication among those who possess different pieces of specialized knowledge. This need is motivated by the fact that even though knowledge has grown very specialized (or precisely because of it), most processes require the engagement of several individuals, each of them contributing their own expert knowledge. In organizations as well as in society in general, knowledge to carry out processes is rarely found in concentrated form.

Much research suggests that there is a positive correlation between the amount of knowledge shared by the members of a process team and the quality and productivity of the process. But there seems to be a threshold of knowledge sharing above which it becomes inefficient to share knowledge. That is, the members of a process team should share *some* of their knowledge but not all of it, simply because they cannot do so due to the cognitive and time limitations we discussed earlier.

The aforementioned discussion begs the question: How much knowledge needs to be shared? The answer to this question seems to be a relatively simple one. The members of a business process team should share enough process-related knowledge among themselves so that they can effectively participate in the improvement of the process. Note that reference is made here to *improvement* and not only execution, because to contribute to the execution of a process, not much knowledge about what other process members do may be needed, especially when standard procedures are followed. However, when decisions about nonstandard issues need to be made, quality and productivity may be strongly affected (e.g., when an airline crew member needs to make decisions regarding an emergency landing and he or she has no knowledge about what is involved in an emergency landing from the pilot's perspective).

In other words, as a general rule, if during a process redesign meeting some members of the process team do not understand the process well enough to propose changes in it or have a general understanding of the changes being proposed by other members, then the level of shared knowledge about the process needs to be raised. Ideally, the level of shared knowledge should be such that all process team members can propose changes to an existing process or have a good idea of the meaning of changes that are proposed by other process team members.

The Link Between Knowledge Fragmentation and Information Flow

If the fragmentation of knowledge in organizational processes is a driver of hypercommunication in processes in general, then one would expect to see a high correlation between the number of organizational functions involved in conducting processes (which imply areas of expertise, e.g., marketing consultant, mechanical engineer) and the number of information exchanges between those organizational functions in any sample of processes studied. This is exactly what was found in an organizational research and development project involving three diverse organizations: a car parts manufacturer in Brazil, a university in New

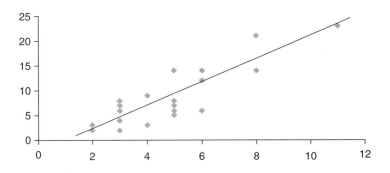

Figure 2.3   Link Between Process Functions (x-axis) and Information Exchanges (y-axis)

Zealand, and a semiautonomous branch of the New Zealand Ministry of Agriculture and Fisheries.

Figure 2.3 shows a scatterplot chart depicting the relationship of two numeric variables whose values were collected from 22 processes in the three organizations mentioned above. The two variables are process functions (e.g., mechanical engineer, quality inspector), plotted on the x-axis, and information exchanges in the process (e.g., mechanical part specifications form, quality inspection form), plotted on the y-axis.

As can be seen in Figure 2.3, the distribution of dots on the chart approximates a line, which suggests that the two variables are highly correlated, or, in other words, that the variables vary together. This was supported by the calculation of a widely used correlation measure, the Pearson correlation coefficient, between these two numeric variables. The coefficient was unusually high (0.86 out of 1) and suggested that the probability that these two numeric variables are highly correlated due to chance was lower than 1 percent.

The high correlation between process functions and information exchanges indicated by Figure 2.3 suggests the possibility of a certain degree of causality between knowledge fragmentation and information flow. That is, increased knowledge fragmentation may cause increased information flow. Or, in other words, whenever a lot of fragmented knowledge needs to be used in the execution of a process (i.e., people with different types of expertise need to collaborate), there will be a need for a lot of information flowing among the people who hold the different pieces of fragmented knowledge. This will, in the absence of knowledge sharing, invariably lead to hypercommunication.

As was seen earlier in this chapter, hypercommunication is a big problem for modern organizations, particularly hypercommunication of information. Hypercommunication seems to be associated with three main contemporary organizational phenomena: (a) We seem to exchange much more data than information in organizations; (b) the number of different areas of expertise (and, thus, experts) needed in most business processes is growing; and (c) there is not enough knowledge sharing among individuals involved in the execution of the same business process, which pushes them into exchanging much more information than they would otherwise need.

And, since hypercommunication is probably, at a deep level, motivated by communication instincts and cognitive limitations that we are unlikely to be able to "shake off" in the near future (unless we quickly find a way to reengineer the genetic makeup of our species), we have little choice but to find smart ways of dealing with hypercommunication in organizations, regardless of the communication instincts and cognitive limitations that are hardwired in our biological communication apparatus. A great deal of what several of the remaining chapters of this book attempt to do is to discuss and propose ways to make organizational processes more efficient and effective by attacking the hypercommunication problem.

Summary and Concluding Remarks

This chapter has dedicated a great amount of text to operationally defining, discussing, and illustrating three key business concepts: data, information, and knowledge. One could reasonably conclude that operationally defining concepts such as these, which are expressed through words that are part of our everyday life, is a bit too academic. Nevertheless, these concepts are too vital to the discussion of other topics covered by this book not to be at least operationally defined. Of course, the definitions provided here are meant to clarify the use of these concepts throughout the book, not to propose new definitions of these concepts that should be accepted by everyone and every possible academic and applied discipline. The definition of knowledge used here is arguably too simplistic to be used, say, as a basis for epistemological discussions—which are very important in the field of philosophy, particularly the philosophy of science. That is, the definitions proposed here are not one-size-fits-all definitions. The main objective here is to provide definitions that allow future chapters to discuss other business phenomena in a relatively precise and rigorous way.

In summary, data are carriers of information and knowledge. Data flow in organizational processes between the functions that carry out process activities through various communication and storage media, particularly paper, digital electrical impulses (e.g., electronic data interchange systems), analog electrical waves (e.g., analog telephone), electromagnetic waves (e.g., radio), and air vibrations (e.g., face-to-face conversation). Information can be seen as being eminently *descriptive*. For example, the assertion "Today is a sunny day" represents information, since it provides a limited *description* of the current state of the environment surrounding us. Knowledge is by its own nature eminently *associative*; that is, it allows us to "associate" different world states and respective mental representations. For instance, the decision rule "If John has high fever and is sneezing, then John has likely a cold" represents knowledge, because it affirms that someone who has a fever and is sneezing (descriptive terms that are associated with health conditions) is in fact displaying the typical symptoms of a cold (another health condition).

One of the key problems facing organizations today is that of hypercommunication, a phenomenon characterized by the excessive exchange of data and information in business processes. This chapter discusses three key underlying reasons for the hypercommunication phenomenon, namely (a) a high data/information ratio in the communication exchanges, (b) a high fragmentation of knowledge among different organizational functions (e.g., manager, inventory supervisor, computer support specialist), and (c) an insufficient degree of knowledge sharing across different organizational functions.

One could argue that to a large extent the hypercommunication problem is due to our human nature. We tend to embrace changes that look like progress, such as increasingly more sophisticated products. But there is a catch. That increasing sophistication is correlated with increasing complexity, which we have to do our best to handle, using computers and other tools to make up for the limitations of what is essentially a Stone Age brain. Most evolutionary psychologists assume that our brain hasn't changed much in the past 100,000 years, and life was much simpler then than it is now.

It is not the goal of this chapter to address solutions to the hypercommunication problem. This is done later in this book. This chapter brings the hypercommunication problem to the fore, explicitly recognizing its existence and some of the deep reasons for that existence. This sets the stage for the discussion of a number of techniques later in this book, many of which are aimed squarely at reducing hypercommunication in organizational processes.

Review Questions

1. Data are:
   (a) Stored only on electronic media and through magnetization.
   (b) Carriers of information, but not knowledge.
   (c) Carriers of knowledge.
   (d) Mental structures that are coded and decoded through communication.

2. Consider the following quote: "I prepared a 2 megabyte report and sent it via electronic mail to ten people. Each of these ten people forwarded a copy of the report to about ten other people . . . as a result, my report had generated a flow of 200 megabytes of information. . . ." In the preceding quote:
   (a) Information is confused with data.
   (b) Information is appropriately measured in bytes.
   (c) Information is appropriately measured in megabytes, since too much information flows in organizations nowadays.
   (d) Knowledge is confused with information.

3. Let us suppose that an e-mail message written in Spanish is sent to two different recipients. One of those recipients, Carlos, can read Spanish; the other, Angus, cannot. Which of the following statements is incorrect?
   (a) The amount of data transferred is about the same for both recipients.
   (b) Much more information is being transferred to Carlos than to Angus.
   (c) Knowledge may or may not have been transferred to Carlos.
   (d) Significantly more information is being transferred to Angus than to Carlos.

4. Consider the following conversation between a doctor and her patient:

   Doctor: So, what brings you here today?

   Patient: I don't know doctor; I've been feeling a bit odd recently.

Doctor: What do you mean?

Patient: I've been having burning eyes, stuffed nose . . . and these things come and go several times a day.

Doctor: Any headaches or fever?

Patient: No fever or headaches.

Doctor: We'll run a checkup on you. As you know, it's allergy season, and I think you probably have an allergy.

In the preceding conversation:
   (a) About 500 megabytes of information was exchanged.
   (b) The patient is obviously very angry with the doctor.
   (c) The patient conveys only information to the doctor.
   (d) The patient conveys a great deal of knowledge to the doctor.

5. Which of the following statements is correct?
   (a) The statement "Today is a sunny day" conveys knowledge.
   (b) A question can never convey information.
   (c) Face-to-face conversations don't rely on data.
   (d) The statement "This answer is the correct one" conveys information.

6. Regarding the monetary value of information, it is incorrect to say that:
   (a) Information is always more valuable than knowledge.
   (b) It may depend on an attribute called *advanceness*, which is essentially how much time in advance a piece of information describes the future.
   (c) It may depend on the accuracy of the piece of information in question.
   (d) Information has been valuable to Bill Gates in the past, when he built Microsoft from scratch into a large company.

7. Knowledge can never:
   (a) Be harder to acquire than information.
   (b) Be more difficult to produce than information.
   (c) Connect pieces of information that describe the state of the world at different times.
   (d) Be conveyed without the use of data.

8. Correlational knowledge:
   (a) Usually connects two pieces of data that are transferred at the same time.
   (b) Usually allows for the mental creation of connections between different pieces of data transferred asynchronously—that is, in a time-disconnected fashion, such as through e-mail.
   (c) Usually connects pieces of information describing events or situations that happen at the same time.
   (d) Usually connects knowledge about correlations between one piece of data and one piece of information—the latter often being larger than the former.

9. Consider the following rule: "If John smokes a lot, then he will probably die of lung cancer." The preceding rule:
   (a) Surely expresses information about John's state of mind.

    (b) Connects an event with another—both of which may or may not happen.

    (c) Describes John's current health condition.

    (d) Connects data about John's health state with knowledge about cancer.

10. The value of a particular professional knowledge or skill doesn't usually depend on:

    (a) The supply of that particular professional knowledge or skill in the market.

    (b) The amount of data used, at a particular point in time, to store that particular professional knowledge or skill.

    (c) The barriers that exist for someone to acquire that particular professional knowledge or skill.

    (d) The demand for that particular professional knowledge or skill in the market.

11. Hypercommunication is:

    (a) Primarily a knowledge-related problem that is unrelated to information communication.

    (b) Clearly not a big problem at all for organizations in general.

    (c) Primarily an information-related problem, and not as much a knowledge-related problem.

    (d) Primarily a computer software–related problem that is unrelated to information communication.

12. Hypercommunication is not characterized by:

    (a) People having to process substantially less information than they can.

    (b) People lacking the cognitive resources to process all the information that is "thrown" at them.

    (c) People lacking the time necessary to process all the information that is given to them.

    (d) People having to process substantially more information than they can.

13. Regarding the exchange of data and information, it is correct to say that:

    (a) We usually exchange 10 times more of the latter than of the former.

    (b) These two abstract entities are completely unrelated.

    (c) We usually exchange more of the former than we need to perform tasks.

    (d) We never exchange any of the former to communicate some of the latter.

14. Assuming a data exchange situation, it is incorrect to say that:

    (a) It may lead to no transfer of information.

    (b) It may take place without the use of any data transfer or storage medium.

    (c) It may lead to some transfer of information.

    (d) It may occur through the combined use of data transfer and storage media.

15. Which of the following is not a good example of knowledge fragmentation?

    (a) New discoveries about a terminal disease and its genetic roots trigger the development of new methods that require the revision of medical studies curricula to add new specialty tracks.

    (b) New discoveries about a terminal disease and its genetic roots trigger the elimination of several current medical specialties.

(c) New discoveries about a terminal disease and its genetic roots trigger the development of new types of equipment and, in consequence, new job specialties.

(d) New discoveries about a terminal disease and its genetic roots push hospitals into hiring new employees with specific types of expertise.

Discussion Questions

1. Consider the following scenario. Inflation in Argentina is now at 25 percent, and the Argentine government sticks to its U.S. dollar parity program, which means that the Argentine peso is pegged one-for-one to the U.S. dollar. Also, the typical Argentine bank pays the inflation plus 1 percent in interest to account deposits above 1,000 pesos. What can one do, from an investment perspective, to take advantage of this scenario? How can you express the knowledge necessary to answer the preceding question in the form of one or more *if-then* rules?

2. Come up with three examples of professional relationships between two individuals (e.g., a computer consultant and a lawyer) in which there is a great deal of knowledge that one individual needs but that only the other individual possesses. Does the difficulty in acquiring the bodies of unshared knowledge in question reflect well the market values (exhibited by the salaries likely paid to the different individuals) of those bodies of knowledge?

3. Which is the most important in defining the market value of a professional body of knowledge (e.g., the body of knowledge necessary to provide corporate tax law advice to a large company): (a) How difficult it is for individuals to acquire the professional body of knowledge in question, or (b) how much supply exists of individuals who possess that professional body of knowledge? Illustrate your answer through the development of a detailed business scenario.

4. Develop a business scenario where two different companies compete for a given market (e.g., the cola market in the example discussed in this chapter). The scenario developed by you should be as realistic as possible. Illustrate, through this scenario, how the value of information is likely to correlate the three attributes discussed in this chapter—that is, advanceness, accuracy, and completeness.

5. Are there other information attributes that correlate the value of information beyond the three discussed in this chapter—that is, advanceness, accuracy, and completeness? If yes, which are they? Develop a business scenario to illustrate your answer.

Note

1. The following book, although a bit old, provides a very good introductory discussion of key issues related to artificial intelligence: Russel, S., & Norvig, P. (1995). *Artificial intelligence: A modern approach.* Upper Saddle River, NJ: Prentice Hall.

CHAPTER 3

Return on Investment in Technology

This chapter summarizes the current state of knowledge in connection with returns on investment in technology, particularly information technology. Based on evidence from several seminal studies, it is pointed out here that, up until the early 1990s, information systems and related technology projects had led to almost negligible returns in terms of labor productivity. This finding can be seen as the dirty little secret of the information technology field, since computer hardware and software vendors rarely discuss it. In fact, many vendors who exhibit their products in computer conferences and user-oriented workshops do not seem to be aware of this finding. In academic circles, the finding is often referred to as the *technology productivity paradox.*

It is important to point out that the picture just painted is based on the quantitative summarization of aggregate evidence and thus should be taken with a grain of salt. After all, statistics is the discipline in which one person eats a whole chicken per week over a period of 1 year, another person eats nothing over the same period, and the final conclusion is that each person ate half a chicken per week during that year—a conclusion that, when looked at in isolation, would be incompatible with the latter person dying of hunger.

So, results of statistical analyses of data should be carefully scrutinized and, if possible, triangulated with other types of evidence. There are no doubt exceptions to the productivity paradox. Some individual companies have in the past achieved major productivity increases as a result of investment in information systems and related technologies. Also, from a sectorwide perspective, the manufacturing sector has historically reaped substantially more benefits from technology investments than the service sector.

Moreover, while investment in information technology has not led to significant increases in productivity during most of the 1990s, it is reasonable to argue that such investment has not been completely wasted. That investment has arguably led to other types of benefits in terms of increases in sales, improved customer satisfaction, and competitive advantages. One does not have to look further than the case of the Semi-Automatic Business Research Environment (SABRE) airline seat reservation system, developed jointly by IBM and American Airlines in the 1960s, which contributed to American Airlines becoming one of the dominant forces in the airline industry.

It is also argued here that increasing (but still modest) productivity returns on investment in information technologies started occurring in the 1990s, particularly the second half of the 1990s, which coincides with the emergence of the business process redesign movement. One of the core messages of that movement is that information technology implementation projects should always be preceded by business process redesign. Consistently with that message, this chapter adds to the arguments presented in previous chapters and provides yet another strong motivation for the adoption of the systems analysis and design orientation proposed in this book.

What Is Productivity?

Robert Solow, the recipient of the Nobel Memorial Prize in Economics in 1987, once remarked that, "We see computers everywhere except in the productivity statistics." Solow's remark is a reminder that the early promise of information technology to completely revolutionize business by making labor productivity skyrocket may not have turned out exactly as expected. However, before one can reach any further conclusions, it is important to understand what the abstract concepts of productivity and quality really mean and how they relate to the concept of competitive advantage.

Productivity in a business process is usually measured as the ratio between outputs and inputs. This measurement approach may lead to problems, as will be explained below. To illustrate this measurement approach, let's consider the following example. A car assembly process may produce 10 cars per day, with about 10 people working in the assembly line. Thus, the daily productivity of the car assembly process is 1 car per person. If the car assembly process is, say, automated in a particular smart way, it may as a result produce twice as many cars (i.e., 20 cars per day) using only five people as labor. Its daily productivity then would jump to 4 cars per person—a 400 percent increase in productivity.

It should be clear that this approach to productivity measurement is at best myopic. One reason is that it completely disregards the extra costs associated with automation, such as those related to equipment, software, and support personnel. Another reason is that it mistakenly uses actual production numbers to estimate productivity, rather than production capacity numbers, since actual production numbers may be affected by demand patterns that have nothing to do with productivity. If there is no demand for cars, production will go down regardless of how many car units an assembly line can produce.

A better way of measuring productivity in connection with a business process is, arguably, the ratio of production capacity and production costs. Production capacity is, roughly speaking, how many production units a business process is *capable* of producing, which means that this measure often has to be estimated based on actual output measures. Or, in other words, production capacity is the number of production units being generated by a business process under full demand conditions. The other component of the productivity measurement scheme proposed here, production cost, is the total cost associated with the production capacity of a business process, which would include direct as well as indirect costs.

A production unit of a business process is essentially what the process generates as its output to both internal and external customers, usually measured in a standardized way. For example, in a contract preparation process of a large law firm, the production unit could be one contract, if most contracts had a standard structure and size. In a car assembly process, the production unit would be one car, if the assembly line were dedicated to only one car model.

In idiosyncratic business processes, such as a flexible assembly line that produces a variety of car models, some kind of standardized production unit would have to be used so that productivity could be properly measured—for example, a standard car equivalent unit. Such standardized production units are analogous to the widely used full-time equivalent student (FTES) employed by universities to prepare their budgets; standardization here is necessary because not all university students are actually full-time students. For instance, a student whose paid coursework-related tuition is one third that of a full-time student would contribute approximately 0.33 FTES units to the university in terms of revenues.

Production costs may vary in a business process, without any variation in the number of inputs used in the process. For example, one can reduce the costs associated with a car assembly process by outsourcing the manufacturing of car parts to more efficient suppliers and thus reduce the cost of the parts that go into the final product, the car. Still, the same number of parts may be used. Also, using production costs rather than number of inputs in the calculation of business process productivity allows for the inclusion of support costs into the picture. For example, car assembly automation may reduce assembly labor costs but at the same time add equipment, software, and support labor costs to the process—someone will have to operate and maintain the car assembly automation system. In some cases, production costs are increased to a degree that productivity ends up going down, even though the management's impression is that it is going up, if the proper measures are not in place.

It is hoped that this discussion has been able to make a strong case for measuring productivity through the ratio (production capacity)/(production costs). For the sake of illustration, let us again consider the car assembly process example used earlier in this section. If a car assembly process can generate 10 cars of a particular model per day at a total cost of $100,000, including direct labor costs as well as parts and support costs, then the productivity of that process is 0.1 cars per thousand dollars. If through automation the process can now generate 20 cars per day at a total cost of $150,000, then the productivity is now approximately 0.13 cars per thousand dollars—a 30 percent increase in productivity.

What About Quality?

From a business process perspective, quality is essentially a measure of customer satisfaction with the outcomes of a business process. As such, quality assessment is much more subjective than the assessment of productivity. For example, in a car assembly process, productivity can be estimated directly based on business process attributes such as maximum output, costs of materials and labor, cycle time, and so forth. Quality measurement, on the other hand, often relies on customer perceptions about the car itself. And, if the customers do not like a particular car, they will not buy it, which means that any productivity gains that an automaker may have been able to achieve in connection with its assembly will never be realized. That is, quality and productivity are interrelated, and their relationship is a complex one (see Figure 3.1).

In Figure 3.1, the relationship between productivity and quality is illustrated based on the context created by a help desk operation. Help desk operations usually provide help and support to internal users of information technology in the organizations of which they are a part. In the example, a productivity improvement, that is, a decrease in the number of handoffs in a help desk process, leads to user problems being solved faster and is presented as improving the users' perceptions about the quality of the help desk process. Conversely, an improvement in the quality of the information used by those who solve technology problems sent to the help desk, that is, better categorization and definition of problems by a help desk

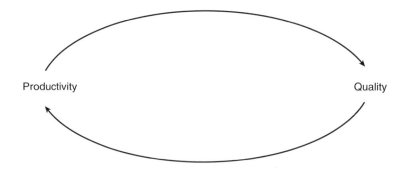

Lower process time/cycle time (for the whole process) will
invariably lead to increased customer satisfaction
(e.g., a decrease in the number of handoffs in a help desk
process leads to user problems being solved faster)

Productivity   Quality

Better-quality information will invariably lead to decreased need
for checks and controls
(e.g., better categorization and definition of problems by a help
desk operator leads to more efficient routing and escalation)

Figure 3.1   The Relationship Between Productivity and Quality

operator, leads to a more efficient routing and escalation of those problems, which is arguably a productivity-related improvement.

Figure 3.1 illustrates the relationship between productivity and quality in a way that also conveys an important idea, namely that quality and productivity matter to both external and internal customers. This is a point that was made quite strongly in the past by William E. Deming, the father of what became known as the total quality management movement. A classic book in which Deming makes this point, as well as other very important ones, is the book titled *Out of the Crisis*, published in 1986 by the Center for Advanced Engineering Study at the Massachusetts Institute of Technology.

While the external customers are the ones who usually pay the company for making and delivering its products (e.g., goods, services, information), the internal customers are usually employees and managers who use the output of certain business processes to produce other outputs. The sequence of business processes that connect several internal customers leading to the delivery of products to external customers is often referred to as the organizational supply chain, when taken as a whole integrated sequence of business processes.

Often, quality is assessed through rather crude percentage-based measures such as the number of defects per N units produced, where N may be a big number (e.g., 1,000). Those measures, whatever they are, ultimately try to assess customer satisfaction in a rather indirect way. Since customers do not like defective products, it is reasonable to assume that there is a correlation between percentage of defects and customer satisfaction. And, quite often, correlation is all that is needed to justify using one measurement in place of another. Sometimes that backfires, though, such as when one single defect leads to catastrophic consequences by causing a death-related accident. An ensuing lawsuit may lead the manufacturer to spend millions of dollars compensating a plaintiff (or class of plaintiffs) and spending even more recalling thousands of defective units already in the hands of other users.

Another, perhaps more sophisticated, way of measuring quality is to calculate the frequency distribution of answers to several question–statements, such as the question–statement "I'm satisfied with the service received from the help desk," using what is normally referred to as a multi-point Likert-type scale for each question–statement. One example of such type of scale would be a 7-point scale with the following answers: disagree very strongly, disagree strongly, disagree somewhat, neither disagree nor agree, agree somewhat, agree strongly, and agree very strongly (each of which would be coded as 1, 2, 3, 4, 5, 6, and 7, respectively). With such a multi-point scale, one could more finely gauge the general perceptions of business process customers regarding quality attributes of a product, be it a good, service, or something else (e.g., a computer program, a news article).

As previously mentioned here, whatever measurement approaches an organization takes, quality will often be more difficult to measure than productivity, and quality's measurement will usually be more subjective as well. In the approach above, the challenge is not only coming up with the right questions, but also convincing customers to answer them, as many hotel managers have found out the hard way. Who wants to fill out questionnaires when they are checking out of a room?

Of course, other approaches for measuring quality exist, such as paying a relatively small group of people to test and provide detailed comments on a product (this is often referred to as a focus group approach), or simply finding ways of closing the gap between the members of an organization and the organization's customers, which is highly advisable anyway. F. Gouillart authored an article published in 1994 by *Harvard Business Review* that became a classic on closing the gap between an organization's members and its customers. The title of the article is "Spend a Day in the Life of Your Customers."

Productivity Goes Down, and We Are Happy!

One of the key topics of this chapter is the apparently meager productivity gains traditionally associated with investment in information technologies. While those meager gains are generally presented as bad news, it must be noted that they are not always the result of mistaken decisions by senior information technology managers and other company executives. Sometimes, senior management intentionally agrees to put up with losses in relative productivity, because those losses are not that bad for their companies when looked at more carefully.

The above may sound a bit strange, so it would be useful to explain it with an example. Let us assume that a life insurance company has $1 billion in revenues, with a net profit margin of 20 percent, or $200 million. It would be reasonable for a company of this size to have an information technology division with a budget of at least $30 million, or 3 percent of its revenues. Now, let us also assume that the company is considering an information technology–related decision in connection with the deployment of a new computer program to its main outside partners, the insurance brokers. The deployment will cost the company $2 million.

The aforementioned deployment is likely to double the company's revenues, but the downside is that it will probably have a negative impact on productivity, which in turn is expected to reduce the company's net profit margin to 15 percent. The resulting picture will be a company making $2 billion in revenues, with a net profit margin of 15 percent, or $300 million; this reduction also takes into account the $2 million cost of the computer program deployment. Will the life insurance company's senior management agree to the deployment of the new computer program to its insurance brokers? Yes, it will, because having $300 million in cash is better than having $200 million. The conclusion is that the relative productivity of the company will go down, and this reduction will be a direct result of an investment in information technology.

This scenario is obviously a fairly simplified version of what would likely happen in reality, where many other factors would be at play, including political infighting, economic forecast uncertainties, and potential threats by competitors, just to name a few. Nevertheless, it illustrates an organizational reality that often biases results in connection with productivity gains resulting from information technology investments. Companies will often reduce their own productivity and profit margins to increase their revenues, as long as their cash flow situation improves, even if in the long run.

The above is accomplished sometimes by the company's increasing the size of the market as a whole and sometimes by the company's getting a greater market share without affecting the size of a stable market. An extreme example (usually of the latter) is the competitive strategy called "dumping," where a company will offer a product at a very low cost (sometimes for free) to become the dominant player in a certain market. It seems that this is what one of the most visible and valuable companies in the world, Microsoft, did in the 1990s when it gave away its Internet Explorer product to dominate the Web browser market, whose leader then was a company that had helped usher in the Internet revolution, Netscape.

The scenario that was laid out above is not aimed at setting the stage for the argument that there is no point in worrying about productivity gains resulting from information technology investments. We should indeed worry about those productivity gains and certainly try to increase them if we can. Nevertheless, the scenario laid out above sets the stage for the argument, which the author would like not only to make but also to stress here, that conclusions derived from the analysis of aggregate evidence regarding organizations' productivity measures and investments on information technology should be made very carefully. Simply put, sometimes the aggregate evidence does not tell us the whole story.

The Technology Productivity Paradox

The technology productivity paradox (a.k.a. the information technology productivity paradox) is a term apparently coined by Steven Roach sometime between the late 1980s and early 1990s; it is a term that has gained a lot of attention and been repeated many times since. Roach was then Morgan Stanley's chief economist and author of a widely cited study on service sector productivity and its relationship with investment in information technology. The term refers to the poor gains in productivity in the service sector in spite of heavy information technology investments by service companies such as banks, insurers, airlines, retailers, and telecommunications providers.

A senior manager at the consulting firm Booz, Allen and Hamilton discussed the technology productivity paradox regarding particular industries in the service sector in an article published in 1990 in the journal *Sloan Management Review*. The author, Gregory Hackett, aptly titled the article "Investment in Technology: The Service Sector Sinkhole?" He presented evidence suggesting that banks and insurance companies, in particular, have been ineffective at reaping productivity gains from information technology investment.

This scenario, interestingly, does not extend to manufacturing companies in general, which have generally been more effective than service companies in turning technology investments into productivity gains. This is illustrated in Figure 3.2, which provides a general and schematic view of productivity increases in the period that goes from the 1950s to the 1990s. Figure 3.2 provides a general idea of how productivity varied over time in the manufacturing and service sectors, as well as in the banking and insurance areas; the latter are a part of the service sector.

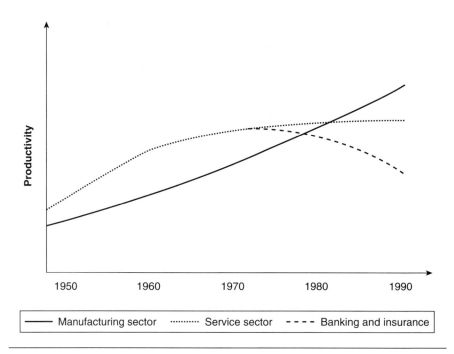

Figure 3.2   Productivity Growth From the 1950s to the 1990s

At this point, the reader may be thinking: "Well, the situation is not so bad. At least the manufacturing sector is doing well." The bad news, of course, is that the lion's share of the economic output of most developed and developing countries comes from the service sector, which usually accounts for 60 percent or more of those countries' employed workforce and gross national products. This means that, in the United States, for example, for every $10 spent, at least $6 goes to pay for service-related activities.

The period that goes from the 1950s until the 1990s saw a truly massive investment in information technology, a type of investment that has also steadily grown over the years, in spite of the fact that computer processing and memory capacity have been steadily growing over the years without a corresponding increase in the cost of computing technology. Given the high stakes of the technology spending game, the technology paradox attracted a tremendous amount of interest from the information systems research community and also much speculation about its reasons.

In a seminal article titled "Beyond the Productivity Paradox," published in the journal *Communications of the ACM*, MIT professor Erik Brynjolfsson and University of Pennsylvania's Wharton School professor Lorin Hitt argue that computer-based automation does not increase productivity per se. Computer-based automation provides, according to Brynjolfsson and Hitt, a basic ingredient that enables changes in organizational practices. Those changes in organizational practices do, in turn, have an effect on productivity. Because of this indirect relationship between investments in computing technologies and productivity gains, it seems that the time lag between investments and observable gains in productivity is longer than initially predicted, often exceeding 2 years, after which productivity gains are reaped for several additional years.

The argument that computer automation provides a basic ingredient that enables changes in organizational practices is similar to another idea proposed in the early 1990s by information technology and management consultant Michael Hammer and others, called business process reengineering. The original business process reengineering idea was simple and direct enough to capture vast interest in the business community, which led to what many would call a management revolution. While the original premises of business process reengineering lost some of their appeal, particularly due to some highly publicized failures, the notion that organizations should redesign their business processes before automating them has slowly taken hold in the business community. This is a topic that will be picked up later in this book, since it is at the core of the message that this book tries to convey.

Why Technology Investment Kept Going Up and Up

Given the poor returns in terms of productivity gains from technology investment, should not managers have pulled the plug on information technology spending early on? Why have they done the opposite and in fact increased spending in information technology during the period that goes from the 1950s to the early 1990s? The answers to these questions can be summarized in one simple statement: Productivity is not everything.

In other words, while productivity is very important in the long run, other factors, such as the need for and opportunity to achieve cash flow improvement, production flexibility, on-the-fly product customization, quick identification of new production trends, market share increases, and other related needs, also play an important role in information technology spending decisions. The common thread among those factors is that they all have the potential to affect the competitive advantage of an organization, some more than others, depending on the economic context in which the organization finds itself.

As we have seen earlier in this chapter, it may make sense for a company to put up with a reduction in productivity, as well as relative profits, as long as its cash flow situation improves from an absolute perspective. For instance, a 15 percent profit margin on $2 billion in revenues may be preferable to a 20 percent profit margin on $1 billion in revenues, if we assume that information technology spending can have that kind of positive effect on revenues. Why? Simply because $300 million in absolute profits (15 percent of $2 billion) is generally preferable to $200 million (20 percent of $1 billion). Many companies prefer to operate on a lower profit margin as long as they can dominate a market. Some retail chains are particularly good at alternating between periods of very low profit margins on certain retail items, undergone as a way of attracting new customers to their stores, and periods of above-average profit margins, implemented as a way of reaping the benefits of the previously gained extra market share.

There has been a great deal of research on the relationship between information technology spending and revenues and competitive advantage. In an article titled "Technology Investment and Business Performance," published in the journal *Communications of the ACM*, Georgia State University professor Arun Rai and colleagues show that technology spending quite often affects revenues in a positive way. At the same time, Rai and colleagues warned readers about the need for business process redesign, as illustrated by the following quote from their article.

> IT investments for improving the effectiveness of an organization's management require a simplification and redesign of management processes. In the absence of such redesign, IT investments may increase management expenses without concomitant increases in management productivity.

Being an early adopter of a technology has been presented by many as a risky thing to do and likely to have a negative impact on productivity, since the costs associated with being an early adopter are generally higher than those for late adopters—which is probably correct, for most organizations. This is a point made by a controversial article authored by Nicholas Carr titled "IT Doesn't Matter," published in *Harvard Business Review*. Carr has been one of the many technology pundits who have strongly criticized overspending in information technology by U.S. organizations. In his *Harvard Business Review* article, Carr also argued that it is unadvisable for companies to be early technology adopters.

Prior research, however, contradicts Carr's latter argument. One of the first studies addressing the business advantages of being a "first mover," or leader, in the adoption of a particular technology was conducted by Brian Dos Santos and Ken Peffers and published under the title "Rewards to Investors in Innovative Information Technology Applications: First Movers and Early Followers in ATMs" in the journal *Organization Science*. Their study spanned the period from 1971 to 1983 and included 2,534 banks from across the United States. The results of the study strongly suggested that the earliest adopters of automatic teller machine (ATM) technologies, the banks that adopted the technology between 1971 and 1973, gained market share and sustained those gains for a long time. On the other hand, the study shows that late adopters of the technology, banks that adopted ATMs between 1974 and 1979, generally did not gain any market share as a result of adopting the technology. These findings provide support for the notion that early adoption of new technologies has the potential to lead to long-term competitive advantages for the early adopters, even though the costs associated with being an early adopter may lead to short-term losses in productivity.

There are many other examples of companies that derived significant benefits from being early technology adopters. And, as mentioned before in this chapter, being an early technology adopter does not necessarily lead to gains in productivity, since leading the way in the adoption of a technology is usually more costly than adopting the technology after it has been tested by others. Classic examples of companies that gained significant competitive advantages from the early adoption of key information technologies are that of United Parcel Service and American Airlines.

United Parcel Service, a high-profile parcel delivery company, invested heavily in information technology during the early 1990s. Among other technology innovations, United Parcel Service led the way in its industry with the implementation of a parcel delivery-tracking system called TotalTrack, which is constantly updated with information about deliveries by truck drivers using a piece of equipment called the Delivery Information Acquisition Device (DIAD). By the late 1990s, United Parcel Service was by far the leader in its industry, a position that has been maintained over the years. United Parcel Service's leadership position has been often challenged by its main competitor, which coincidentally is also a leading new technology adopter, Federal Express.

American Airlines, an airline carrier, invested heavily in information technology in the 1960s and 1970s, particularly in connection with its airplane seat reservation system, called SABRE, one of the first air travel reservation systems to be widely used by travel agents in the world. SABRE is widely credited to contributing to American Airlines' dominance in the airline carrier industry in the 1970s and 1980s, together with United Airlines (which also developed its own reservation system, called APOLLO).

So, as can be inferred from the discussion above, there are many factors, other than productivity improvement, that may lead organizations to invest in information technologies. Among these are potential increases in revenues and improved competitive positioning, which may be achieved at the expense of productivity decreases, at least at first. But don't get the wrong idea; productivity does matter! The argument that is being put forth here is that technology investments do not necessarily go down because they do not lead to productivity gains, since those investments often lead to other benefits that may easily be seen as offsetting the lack of returns in terms of either production capacity increases or cost decreases.

Productivity Gains in the 1990s

The technology productivity paradox led many management and technology consultants and researchers to call for alternative approaches that would increase the chances that technology investment would lead to productivity gains. Particularly noticeable were the calls for organizational change approaches associated with the adoption of information technologies, which have apparently built on the general notion that the business processes that make up organizations should be redesigned with an eye on productivity and quality improvement *before* information technologies are used to automate them.

Perhaps because of the organizational responses to these calls for business process redesign, the productivity gains associated with information technology investments seem to have shown some improvement in the late 1990s, when compared with the previous 25 years. For example, a study conducted by the Center for Research on Information Technology and Organizations (CRITO) at the University of California at Irvine shows that, in the 1995–1999 period, annual labor productivity growth has been 4.3 percent in the manufacturing sector, which is higher than the labor productivity growth in several industries in the service sector for the same period. The same study shows, also for the 1995–1999 period, annual labor productivity growth rates of 1.7 percent for transportation services and 2.7 percent for finance, insurance, and real estate services.

While these numbers show a trend similar to that observed in the technology productivity paradox period, notably of better returns in the manufacturing than the service sector, the picture looks a little better for the service sector. Moreover, and perhaps more telling, the same study by CRITO shows that annual labor productivity growth during the 1995–1999 period has been 4.2 percent for industries where information technology was intensely used (most of which were from the service sector), as opposed to 1 percent for industries where information technology was not used very intensely.

These results suggest that productivity gains due to investment in information technologies have been improving since the mid-1990s, particularly in the service sector, since it is into that sector that historically most of the technology investments have been poured. It would of course have been interesting to analyze data in the early 2000s to see if that trend continued, but a major technology-related economic phenomenon happened, which is most likely to pose serious challenges for the interpretation of technology investment data collected in the early 2000s. The phenomenon was called the great technology bubble burst.

The Technology Bubble Burst

The technology bubble burst phenomenon was characterized by an unusual euphoria about technology companies, particularly companies whose products or services had anything to do with the Internet. Those technology companies that were publicly traded, with shares made available to the public in stock markets, saw their share prices (and thus market values) skyrocket. Many privately owned technology companies, trying to cash in, quickly became publicly traded through initial public offerings (a.k.a. IPOs) that often turned not very wealthy company founders into instant millionaires.

The technology bubble burst period occurred between approximately 1999 and 2001 and is illustrated by the variation in stock prices of publicly traded companies during that period (see Figure 3.3). During that period, technology companies attracted vast amounts of capital investment and also sold many products and services to technology users, which included other companies. As can be seen in Figure 3.3, investments in technology company stocks made around 1999 yielded huge returns by around 2000. However, those returns fell precipitously (to 1999 levels) around 2001. Unfortunately, a lot of individual investors purchased stocks when their prices were going up and then lost almost all of what they had invested about a year after.

The technology bubble burst poses a big hurdle to those interested in assessing returns on investment in technology in the 2000s. The reason is that a disproportioned amount of investment in technology was made during that period, and much of that investment was, in a sense, lost. That is most likely to have created a

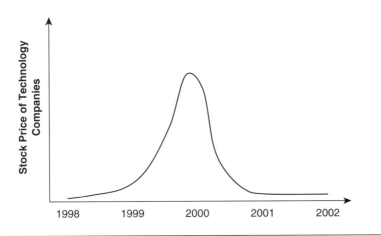

Figure 3.3   Stock Prices of Technology Companies During the Technology Bubble Burst

great deal of unused technology resources in organizations, which may or may not have contributed to increases in productivity, depending on how those organizations faced the situation.

Complicating this picture further is the fact that a great deal of investment in and before the year 2000 was aimed at addressing the so-called millennium bug problem. That is, many computer programs and databases stored dates with only two digits. This was seen as likely to lead to potentially catastrophic consequences if those programs and databases were not modified and replaced before the turn of the year. For example, a computer program that used the current date to make sales projections would be reset to the year "00" and would possibly make useless projections. Other computer programs were seen as more critical, such as those controlling crucial operations such as nuclear reactor plants and airline flight paths, since their malfunction could lead to serious accidents and much death and destruction.

Some have argued that the massive technology investments in the early 2000s have led to the creation of something called organization "slack" throughout the economy, or the ability to use idle resources to restructure one's operations. Since the early 2000s has been a period of economic recession, organizations have been pushed into resorting to worker layoffs and business process redesign to control costs. Given the aforementioned slack, the resulting picture may have been one of increased productivity, at least from a statistical standpoint. Some results suggest that this is the case, but the jury is still out as to the nature of productivity gains in connection with technology investment in the 2000s. One of the big problems with productivity gains obtained in periods of massive layoffs is that those gains may be short-lived, because massive layoffs are bound to eventually lead to a tightening of consumer demand (employees are consumers too), and thus losses of revenues. Without revenues, productivity gains simply cannot be realized.

Summary and Concluding Remarks

Many studies suggest that productivity gains associated with information technology investments have been okay in the period going from the 1950s to the 1960s and somewhat dismal in the period going from the 1970s to the 1990s. The irony here is that information technology investments have gone up substantially in the latter period, a situation that has been labeled the technology productivity paradox and that begs the question: Why do organizations keep investing in information technology?

The answer provided in this chapter is that information technology investments are made not only so that productivity gains can be achieved. Those investments may have other goals, such as increased customer satisfaction, increased production flexibility (which allows organizations to respond quickly to changes in market demand), and better competitive positioning. In some cases, productivity losses will be taken in return for increases in revenues—a situation that will often lead to a reduction in relative profits (e.g., 30 percent to 20 percent) but sometimes an increase in absolute profits (e.g., $100 million to $150 million).

Moreover, products, whether they are tangible (e.g., cars) or intangible (e.g., software), have become increasingly more complex over the years. That increase in complexity was not accompanied by an increase in the cognitive capacity of human beings. Our cognitive capacity today is functionally identical to the cognitive capacity possessed by our early *Homo sapiens* ancestors who emerged in Africa over 100,000 years ago. Therefore, we have had to rely increasingly on information technologies over the years to cope with complexity. Without technology investment, or rather, without *massive* technology investment, we would not have many of the goods and services we take for granted today.

But still, we have to face the challenge of increasing productivity gains resulting from information technology investment. As has been shown in this chapter, a great deal of the literature on the technology productivity paradox converges on one generic recommendation to address the poor investment returns underlying the paradox. The recommendation is that information technology should not be used simply to automate organizations, but instead should be used as an enabler of innovations implemented through organizational change. This book is closely aligned with that generic recommendation and is aimed at providing people with the concepts and methodological tools to implement that recommendation.

Review Questions

1. Measuring productivity as the ratio between outputs and inputs:
   (a) Is one of the best measurement approaches around.
   (b) Isn't actually used by anyone.
   (c) Is not a very good approach, except for factories, where it leads to excellent results.
   (d) Often disregards some legitimate productivity gains.

2. Which of the following statements is incorrect?
   (a) Productivity can be measured through the ratio of production capacity and production costs.
   (b) Productivity can never be objectively measured.
   (c) Productivity is one of the attributes of a business process.
   (d) Productivity may affect quality.

3. Which of the following statements in connection with quality is correct?
   (a) Quality assessment is much more subjective than the assessment of productivity.
   (b) Quality and productivity are completely unrelated.
   (c) Quality refers only to perceptions by external customers.
   (d) A seminal work on quality is *Out of the Crisis*, by Michael Hammer.

4. Which of the following statements is incorrect?
   (a) Investments in IT may lead to labor productivity improvements.
   (b) In some cases, it may make sense to invest in IT when profitability is expected to go down.
   (c) Technology investment may lead to increases in a company's revenues.
   (d) Investments in IT have historically led to significant increases in productivity.

5. It is correct to say, in connection with the technology productivity paradox, that:
   (a) It refers to poor gains in productivity in spite of heavy investments in IT, particularly in the service sector.
   (b) William Deming was the first to propose it as a theoretical idea.
   (c) The Internet bubble caused it.
   (d) The manufacturing sector has been the most affected by it.

6. The technology productivity paradox is:
   (a) A problem that affects only the manufacturing sector.
   (b) Probably bad for the U.S. economy.
   (c) A new management idea created by IBM.
   (d) A direct result of computer technology's reliance on electricity.

7. It is correct to say that:
   (a) Banking and insurance industries are particularly good examples of industries affected by the technology productivity paradox in the 1980s.
   (b) Banks and insurance companies did not benefit at all from IT investment in the 1980s.
   (c) If there were no IT investment in the banking and insurance industries during the 1980s, certainly the services delivered by them to customers would be much better now.
   (d) Banking and insurance industries are bad examples of industries affected by the technology productivity paradox in the 1980s, since their investments in IT usually led to formidable productivity gains.

8. Technology investment kept growing in the 1980s because:
   (a) It consistently led to gains in productivity, as well as in areas not necessarily related to productivity, such as revenues and competitive advantage.
   (b) It always increased the competitive advantage of any company that made a technology investment, especially in non–cutting-edge information technologies.
   (c) It led to gains in areas not necessarily related to productivity, such as revenues and competitive advantage.
   (d) All senior managers at the time were uneducated, had a poor understanding of their businesses, and knew very little about likely IT effects on organizations.

9. It is correct to say that:
   (a) The productivity gains associated with information technology investments seem to have shown some improvement in the 1980s, when compared with the previous 30 years.
   (b) The productivity gains associated with information technology investments have been quite spectacular in the 1990s, when they have grown more than 10 times higher than those of the previous 40 years.
   (c) The productivity gains associated with information technology investments have been horrible in the 1990s and much worse than in any of the previous 40 years.
   (d) The productivity gains associated with information technology investments seem to have shown some improvement in the late 1990s, when compared with the previous 10 years.

10. Which of the statements below, in connection with the technology bubble burst, is wrong?
   (a) It was caused by an unusual euphoria about technology company stocks.
   (b) It was largely a stock market–driven phenomenon.
   (c) It was based on speculation and probably on wrong ideas about the likely future demand for information technology products.
   (d) The explosion of what was then referred to as a virtual electronic bubble caused it.

Discussion Questions

1. What would have happened if there had been no investments in information technology in the banking industry in the 1970s and 1980s? Illustrate your answer through the development of a business scenario involving two fictitious banks, one that invested in technology and another that did not. The scenario developed by you should be as realistic as possible.

2. Try to reconcile your answer to Discussion Question 1, as well as the related scenario you created and conclusions you reached, with the technology productivity paradox notion. Are they compatible? Explain your answer.

3. Let's assume that you have just been asked to develop a forecast of productivity gains in connection with a large information technology project. Develop a business scenario of such a project in an organization in the service sector. The business scenario should illustrate how you would demonstrate, through some careful number crunching, that the information technology project would or would not lead to productivity gains. The scenario developed by you should be as realistic as possible.

4. Develop a well-crafted business scenario involving an information technology project, in an organization in the service sector, which clearly illustrates the relationship between quality and productivity. The scenario developed by you should be as realistic as possible.

5. Develop a well-crafted business scenario involving an information technology project at an organization that clearly illustrates that, in some situations, even though productivity and profitability may go down as a result of investment in technology, senior management may still end up happy with the overall results of the technology investment for the organization. The scenario developed by you should be as realistic as possible.

PART II

Understanding Business Processes

Part II Case:
DoD's Software Procurement From CSC

C omputer Sciences Corporation (CSC) is a large consulting and computer systems integration firm. CSC is also one of the largest providers of computer services to the U.S. Department of Defense (DoD). In 2000, CSC decided to redesign its outbound software development procurement process, whereby the DoD purchased software from CSC (from CSC's perspective, this is a sales process, as opposed to a purchasing process). An analysis of the DoD-CSC software development procurement process led to the identification of several problems, including the following.

One of the problems was that the work plan in the software development proposal developed for the DoD often did not include all the departments that participated in the actual work, which created internal budgeting difficulties. Another problem was that the justification of the items in the Basis of Estimates document, which forms the basis on which the budget is generated, often did not meet the needs of the DoD.

In addition to these problems, participating departments at CSC often were not informed on time about how much project funding was allocated to them, which often forced them to transfer initial overhead costs to other projects. Also, there were no process metrics in place, which made it difficult for the contracts manager at CSC to manage the quality and productivity of her process. Finally, there had been incidents in which proposal data was lost, leading to many hours of work being wasted. There was no disaster recovery procedure in place.

The business process redesign team had nine members, six from CSC and three from Lockheed Martin, another large company that was a subcontractor for CSC in many software development projects (Lockheed Martin also regularly subcontracted CSC in other projects). DoD members also participated in the project as information providers, but not as members of the business process redesign team.

The business process redesign team employed activity flow as well as communication flow representations to understand the process to be analyzed. The activity flow representation placed emphasis on the chronological flow of activities within the process and did not show how information exchanges took place in the DoD-CSC software development procurement process. The communication flow representation placed emphasis on the flow of information within the process—for example, the flow of forms and memos in the process.

The redesign team independently proposed nine major business process changes. Eight of those changes focused only on the communication flow of the target business process and led to changes in request for proposals (RFP) receipt and announcement, Alpha Negotiations (i.e., negotiations regarding project scope between the software development team and the DoD), and receipt and announcement of project awards. Only one focused on both the activity and the communication flow of the target business process and led to the inclusion of activities related to the compilation and regular review of process metrics.

The team then developed a "generic" information technology "solution" (i.e., a product-independent computer-based infrastructure and system specification) to implement the new business process. The solution was illustrated through a rich pictorial representation with icons representing computers, databases, and organizational functions. The redesign team members saw this pictorial representation as an important aid for them to explain the new process to CSC employees and DoD representatives. The pictorial representation was generated entirely based on the communication flow representation of the new process.

A focus group discussion was conducted with the members of the business process redesign team immediately after the above tasks had been completed. In this discussion, the members unanimously indicated that, based on their experience in the project, a focus on the communication flow of a business process was more likely to lead to successful redesign outcomes than a focus on the activity flow of the business process. However, there was no consensus on the reason for this. Some suggested that communication flow representations were easier to generate than activity flow representations of business processes. Others disagreed, arguing that while communication flow representations were more difficult to generate, they made it easier to spot business process improvement opportunities.

All of the process changes proposed by the redesign team were approved and subsequently implemented. The implementation of the process changes was accomplished through modifications in the computer system used by the DoD for procurement, known as Joint Computer-aided Acquisition and Logistics Support (JCALS), which had originally been developed by CSC. A business process performance review conducted approximately 6 months after the implementation of the changes indicated that the business process redesign had led to observable productivity and quality gains, and mitigation or elimination of several of the problems previously identified with the DoD-CSC software development procurement process.

Sources

CSC Web site: http://www.csc.com/

Kock, N. (2001). Changing the focus of business process redesign from activity flows to information flows: A defense acquisition application. *Acquisition Review Quarterly*, *8*(2), 93–110.

Kock, N., & Murphy, F. (2001). *Redesigning acquisition processes: A new methodology based on the flow of knowledge and information.* Fort Belvoir, VA: Defense Acquisition University Press.

CHAPTER 4

The Past, Present, and Future of Business Process Redesign

This chapter discusses the evolution of business process redesign methods. The discussion covers topics from as far back as Taylor's scientific management movement, passing through Deming's total quality management and Hammer's business process reengineering, and culminating with the current state-of-the-art of business process redesign. From this discussion, it will be clear to the reader that business process redesign is less of a business "fad" than some management pundits try to argue it is. The notion of business process redesign has a long history and permeates many more schools of management thought than it is usually given credit for.

It is also argued here that the current focus of business process redesign approaches on activity flows, rather than information flows and knowledge distribution, has a historical basis and creates a number of problems. This provides the basis on which key ideas are offered based on results of applied projects, several of which refer to the relatively high importance of looking at and improving the web of communication interactions in business processes. Those ideas are put to the test in the context of business process redesign projects conducted in four organizations. The results of those projects strongly support the ideas proposed.

Taylor's Principles of Scientific Management

Organizational development approaches centered on the idea of business process redesign became quite popular as we approached the new millennium, particularly due to the emergence of business process reengineering in the late 1980s and early 1990s. In spite of this recent popularity, an argument can be made that business process redesign is a much older approach than reengineering, one that has probably influenced management thinking since management's emergence as a separate field of study and practice.

According to this view, business process redesign can be seen as dating back to the early 1900s, when Frederick Taylor published one of the most important books in the history of management, *The Principles of Scientific Management*, launching the scientific management movement. The movement strongly influenced organizational development ideas and approaches throughout the second industrial revolution (1850–1950). During this period, business process redesign was primarily concerned with productivity (i.e., efficiency) improvement in manufacturing plants and was centered on the optimization of "times and motions" in situations of high work specialization and division of labor.

Taylor was faced with the challenge of increasing productivity in manufacturing plants employing a workforce that was largely uneducated and unskilled. His solution involved an emphasis on the use of standard work methods and strict division of labor. In Taylor's time, unlike today, manufacturing was the main wealth creator. As previously discussed in this book, today the service sector is the main contributor to the labor employment and (to a lesser extent) the gross national product of most developed and developing countries.

Accordingly, Taylor's approach involved breaking business processes down into simple activities that usually involved sequences of physical motions, which were then designed to be carried out in the minimum amount of time and with the minimum amount of effort by specialized manual workers.

The value of Taylor's approach in rationalizing production is indisputable, and its impact on the development of mass-production techniques has been widely recognized. However, it provoked resentment and opposition from labor and union representatives when carried to extremes, which seems to have happened often. This might have been at least partially motivated by Taylor's depiction of workers in general as mindless executors of activities designed by management, to whom (i.e., the workers, as opposed to management) he sometimes referred as being as "stupid" and destined to backbreaking manual work "as an ox."

The Humanists and Their Reaction to Taylor's Ideas

Even though it often raised factory workers' salaries, by tying individual financial compensation to increased productivity, Taylor's scientific management led to what many believe to have been a dehumanization of the workplace. This set the stage for more "humane" schools of management to emerge and flourish. The work of Elton Mayo in the early and mid-1900s and that of others such as McGregor, Maslow, and Herzberg represented the emergence of the "humanist" school of management, which tried to shift the focus of organizational development from "business processes" to "people."

The significance of Mayo's contributions to organizational development lies in his ideas about the importance of noneconomic rewards and personal satisfaction to employee productivity. His criticism of the model proposed by Taylor was rooted in the fact that it devised optimal work procedures and somewhat imposed them on the workers, through a system of simple financial incentives, without giving workers the opportunity to provide their own input. That is, Taylor's "sin," according to Mayo, was not to allow those who would have to put in practice key organizational changes to participate in the decision-making process that led to the changes.

Mayo provided scientific evidence that taking workers' attitudes and personal motivations into consideration when designing work paid off in economic terms. He investigated the relationships between people working together and, unlike Taylor, paid relatively little attention to such things as procedural routines, times, and motions. What both Taylor and Mayo shared, however, was their main goal, which was the improvement of organizations.

Mayo's most important research project was labeled "The Hawthorne Investigations." It was a 10-year project conducted at Western Electric Company's Hawthorne Works in Chicago. The project began in 1927 and involved around 20,000 subjects and 100 investigators. Its main focus was on the behavior of small groups under different physical working configurations and social stimuli. Among its main findings was the notion that, for the average worker, the desire to stand well with one's fellows and managers easily outweighs the influence of financial rewards and physical working conditions. This notion became known as the "Hawthorne effect."

The management thinkers associated with the humanist school of management were very successful during the mid-1900s. They are widely seen as having proposed ideas that minimized the importance of business processes as competitiveness drivers in organizations. The focus of their predictions was on people and how they react to work structures and incentives. But business process redesign was far from dead.

Total Quality Management

The work of the humanists set the stage for the emergence of what many saw as a more humane business process redesign school of thought, generally known as total quality management. This new school of thought not only succeeded scientific management as a business process–based method for organizational development, but also represented a shift in focus from productivity to quality in the improvement of business processes. While heavily based on statistical methods in its inception, this approach soon acquired a broader orientation.

Total quality management began in Japan after World War II, largely due to the work of William Edwards Deming and Joseph Juran, and is widely credited as having propelled Japan to economic superpower status. All the more impressive is that this happened within 35 years of the conclusion of a war that left Japan with a dilapidated industrial infrastructure and at the brink of a national disaster. In the 1980s, total quality management became widely practiced in the United States and other Western capitalist countries. Similar to scientific management, its primary focus was the improvement of manufacturing operations.

One of the fundamental ideas of total quality management is that work-related problems are largely caused by badly designed business processes and have little to do with workers' negligence or unwillingness to do a good job. In this sense, total quality management created an environment of increased accountability for those responsible for the design of business processes, who were usually managers. It made it difficult for those in positions of authority to blame their employees for low quality goods or services. The employees, in turn, were seen as inherently willing to do their best for the organization. This is a message that resonated with many of the ideas proposed by the humanists.

Business Process Reengineering

Business process reengineering replaced total quality management as the predominant school of thought in connection with business process redesign in the early 1990s. Michael Hammer (together with James Champy) and Thomas Davenport independently developed business process reengineering as, respectively, a better alternative (Hammer's version) and a complement (Davenport's version) to total quality management. Their work was based on the premise that the incremental gains in productivity obtained through the implementation of total quality management methods alone were insufficient for organizations to cope with the accelerated rate of change of the 1990s, brought about by new information technologies. Different from scientific management and total quality management, business process reengineering was presented as a method for the improvement of service as well as manufacturing operations.

In spite of being initially touted as a new idea, it became apparent that business process reengineering had built on ideas and methods that were similar to those proposed by Taylor's scientific management. This is particularly true of operational versions of business process reengineering, which, unlike more strategic ones, look into the inner workings of individual business processes to improve them. In fact, throughout the history of business process redesign, operational-level approaches to business process redesign consistently maintained a focus on activity flows (also known as "workflows"), or chronological flows of activities in business processes. One of the key arguments put forth in this book is that while this orientation makes some sense in materials-transformation business processes, whose final product usually is a tangible manufactured item (e.g., a car engine), this orientation is fundamentally inconsistent with the communication-intensive nature of the vast majority of business processes found in organizations today, where arguably much more information (an intangible item) is handled than materials (or tangible items).

Is Reengineering a Modernized Version of Taylor's Ideas?

Much research on business process redesign has been conducted since the 1990s, addressing important questions raised by reengineering. One area that has received relatively little attention, however, is that of business process representation frameworks and their impact on business process redesign. This is an important area of research because it addresses the way business process redesign practitioners look at business processes. That is, business process representation frameworks are essentially the representational "lenses" through which redesign practitioners "see" a business process.

The ways through which a business process is looked at are arguably likely to have a strong influence on how business processes are redesigned. For example, a focus on the flow of activities (or workflow) in a business process is likely to lead to changes in how *activities* flow in the business process, whereas a focus on the flow of information in a business process is likely to lead to changes in how *information* flows in the business process.

An analysis of business process redesign practices throughout the 100-year period from the development of scientific management to the emergence of business process reengineering suggests an interesting, perhaps cyclic, pattern. Even though business processes changed significantly since Frederick Taylor's times, the business process redesign practices employed then seem very similar to those of the 1990s and beyond. This seems to be particularly true in terms of the focus of business process redesign, which has consistently been the sequence of activities, or workflow, of a business process.

The scientific management method proposed by Frederick Taylor consisted in breaking down a business process into component activities, for which a pictorial as well as a quantitative model was generated. The pictorial model depicted the flow of execution of the activities and the associated motions, whereas the quantitative model included information about physical distances associated with motions and the times needed to perform each of the activities. Taylor showed that managers and consultants could empirically devise optimal or quasi-optimal business process configurations that could then be standardized through financial incentives to workers.

Many have argued that business process reengineering is a kind of modernized version of scientific management. Reengineering's popularity reached its peak by the mid-1990s and has slumped since due to a number of reported failures. James Champy, one of reengineering's pioneers, argued that 70 percent of all reengineering projects failed to achieve their goals. In spite of this, reengineering created renewed interest in business process redesign, making it (i.e., business process redesign) one of the most widely practiced modern forms of organizational development. However, unlike during the heyday of scientific management, when business process improvement meant materials flow improvement, today most of what flows in business processes is information. As pointed out by Peter Drucker in the early 1990s, "In 1880, about nine out of 10 workers made and moved things; today, that is down to one out of five. The other four out of five are knowledge people or service workers." This notion finds support from a 1996 study published in the journal *Business Process Re-engineering & Management* under the title "Product Flow, Breadth and Complexity of Business Processes: An Empirical Study of Fifteen Business Processes in Three Organizations." The study shows that, even in manufacturing organizations, approximately 80 percent of what flows in business processes is data (carrying mostly information), while the other 20 percent is made up of materials. In service organizations, those proportions are usually very close to 100 and 0 percent, respectively. These figures seem to confirm the claims, once thought to be visionary, that "we are living in an information society" and that "organizations have become information organizations" by social and organizational evolution pundits such as Alvin Toffler and Peter Drucker (the latter is considered to be the father of modern management theory). The high proportion of information flow is also consistent with the widespread use of information technologies in organizations and the increasing importance of information technologies in the improvement of business processes.

What About Communication Optimization?

In spite of the facts above, most business process redesign practices today mirror Taylor's approaches of the early 1900s in one key respect. They appear to be tailored to the optimization of the flow of materials, which involves sequences of interrelated physical actions and not the flow of information, which involves communication. This conclusion is reached based on the observation that most of today's business process redesign practices focus on the analysis of business processes as sets of interrelated activities and pay relatively little attention to the analysis of the communication flow in business processes. Systems analysis and design methods, on the other hand, do address communication in business processes. However, as previously mentioned in this book, systems analysis and design methods have traditionally been relegated to business process *automation* and have seldom been applied to business process *redesign*.

More recently, object-oriented analysis and design methods have contributed a more communication-oriented view of business processes. This is particularly true for those methods in connection with the unified modeling language (a.k.a. UML). But such methods have also been faulted by what some see as an excessive activity orientation. T. Chuang and S. Yadav coauthored an article published in the journal *Database for Advances in Information Systems* in which they made a similar argument and used that argument to explain the relative lack of success of object-oriented analysis and design methods in comparison with object-oriented programming methods.

A focus on the flow of activities makes particularly good sense in manufacturing processes, for example, assembly-line business processes, because those business processes usually involve sequential steps that add complexity and value to tangible items. Since manufacturing processes embody "action" in the physical sense, they can generally be easily represented as chronological sets of activities that bring tangible items together. Examples of such tangible items are car parts or chemical components, used to produce other complex and value-added tangible items, such as a car engine or a complex chemical product. That is, it is natural to think of manufacturing processes as sequences of activities. However, this is not the case with nonmanufacturing processes in general. In nonmanufacturing processes, the output is typically a service, which is usually consumed while it is produced, or an information product, such as a report or a computer program. It has been argued that in nonmanufacturing business processes in general, activity flow–based modeling attempts usually lead to overly complex and somewhat misleading representations, which are not useful for business process redesign.

Perhaps due to the fact that, until recently, manufacturing business processes played a key role in wealth creation, the most widely adopted normative approaches for business process redesign embody general guidelines that place no special emphasis on the redesign of communication activities, thus arguably disregarding the information-intensive nature of business processes. This is true for many large organizations, including the U.S. Department of Defense and its contractors, arguably the single largest group of employers in the United States. In the U.S. Department of Defense, the IDEF0 approach for business process redesign, an activity flow–based approach, has been chosen as the official business process redesign approach and is by far the most widely used. One widely used activity flow–oriented approach was proposed by J. H. Harrington in his classic book *Business Process Improvement*, where he goes as far as stating that "As a rule [information flow diagrams] are of more interest to computer programmers and automated systems analysts than to managers and employees charting business activities." This opinion was maintained in a highly influential follow-up book authored by J. H. Harrington and colleagues, titled *Business Process Improvement Workbook: Documentation, Analysis, Design, and Management of Business Process Improvement*. That opinion is obviously at odds with the notion that information processing is the main goal of business processes, which has been advocated by many, including renegade economist John Kenneth Galbraith (a former Harvard and Princeton professor, and key adviser to President John F. Kennedy). Nevertheless, that opinion is in line with reengineering's original claims and most of the current business process redesign practice.

Some Key Ideas Based on Practical Experiences

Members of the E-Collaboration Research Center at Temple University facilitated a series of business process redesign projects in organizations located primarily in and around the Philadelphia Metropolitan Area (which includes several townships in southern New Jersey). Evidence from those projects suggested that the flow of information could generally be seen as analogous to the flow of materials in business processes and that the former (i.e., the flow of information) could be subsumed by what is referred to here as the "communication flow," or the web of communication interactions of a business process.

One of the key findings of the aforementioned projects was that the communication flow structure of business processes was a particularly strong determinant of most of the quality and productivity problems associated with business processes, more so than either the activity flow or the material flow structure of the business processes. In other words, business processes that seemed optimized in terms of their communication flow appeared to present high levels of quality and productivity. Activity flow optimization did not seem to matter that much.

Figure 4.1 depicts a partial process including the ordering and production of auto parts. It highlights the differences between communication flow and activity flow representations of processes. Figure 4.1(a) focuses on the flow of communication in the process. Figure 4.1(b) focuses on the flow of activities. The communication flow representation is an adaptation of data flow diagrams and was generated following the modified format proposed in a 1999 book titled *Process Improvement and Organizational Learning*. That modified format is discussed in more detail later in this book. The activity flow representation follows the general format proposed by Harrington and colleagues for functional timeline flowcharts in their *Business Process Improvement Workbook*.

In Figure 4.1(a), plain rectangles represent organizational functions—that is, individuals, areas comprising groups of individuals, or organizations external to the process under consideration. Rectangles with rounded edges represent activities. Each activity is represented by the name of the activity, followed by the organizational function(s) that execute(s) the activity within parentheses. Drumlike symbols represent information repositories, and arrows represent the flow of information in the process. No knowledge is represented in this type of diagram (knowledge representation is something that will be discussed later in this book).

In Figure 4.1(b), organizational functions are shown at the top of each column, which contains (at lower parts, in the "body" of the column) the activities executed by each organizational function. Plain rectangles represent activities, and the text inside has the same meaning as in Figure 4.1(a). The arrows represent the flow of execution of the activities.

The evidence from the business process redesign projects facilitated by the E-Collaboration Research Center also suggested that, unlike in traditional systems analysis and design projects, business process redesign groups rarely favored communication flow representations of business processes over activity flow representations early on in their projects, apparently because the former were seen as more difficult to generate, or "less natural" than the latter.

That is, communication flow representations of business processes seemed to be perceived as more difficult to be generated than activity flow representations, apparently because the latter are better aligned with the way humans are cognitively programmed to envision "action" in the physical sense. That is, business processes, which essentially represent action, are more naturally seen as sequences of interconnected activities than communication interactions.

It appears from the aforementioned projects that a focus on the flow of communication within a business process usually leads to better business process redesign results than a focus on other elements, including activities, materials, or both. That is, even though some may perceive communication flow representations as more difficult to generate than activity flow representations, a focus on the former seems more advisable in business process redesign projects than a focus on the latter.

This assumption does not dismiss the usefulness of business process redesign techniques based on operations research, linear programming, and other traditional assembly-line and factory design techniques, whose focus on times and motions often leads to quantum-leap productivity gains. Rather, what is being

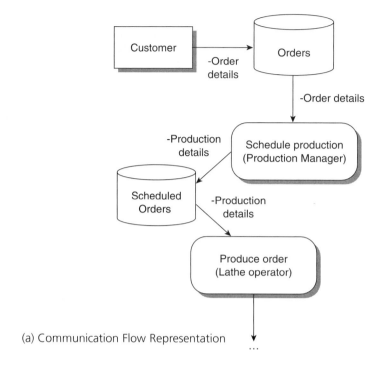

(a) Communication Flow Representation

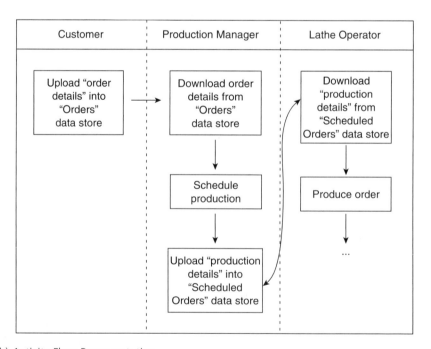

(b) Activity Flow Representation

Figure 4.1   Process Representations Used

argued here is that at the individual business process level, where usually redesign is done by looking at how elements (e.g., activities, materials, data) flow within the business process, a focus on communication interactions is likely to yield results that are, on average, better than if other elements were targeted. The key reason for this appears to be the higher frequency in organizations today of communication-intensive business processes, whose quality and productivity are more strongly determined by their flow of communication, than of non–communication-intensive business processes.

Redesigning Business Processes at Four Organizations

Let us look at evidence from some of the business process redesign projects run by the E-Collaboration Research Center, as a way of verifying the ideas outlined previously. Especially relevant is the verification of the idea that business process redesign yields better outcomes if it places more emphasis on communication flow redesign than on activity flow redesign. It is important to assess the validity of this idea because of the apparent past and current focus of business process redesign on activity flows.

The projects we are going to be looking at here involved four different organizations, with one business process redesign group conducted at each organization. Two of those organizations were manufacturing companies: American Customer Drying and Holiday Boutique. The other two were service organizations: Bigchalk.com, an online education services provider, and Temple University's help desk department.

Members of the E-Collaboration Research Center provided business process redesign training and facilitation to the members of business process redesign groups. Those groups involved external consultants, as well as employees and management of the organizations from which business processes were selected for redesign. The business processes that were redesigned as a result of the projects were quite important for the organizations involved.

The projects involved hands-on training in a variety of business process redesign methodologies, including activity flow– and communication flow–oriented methodologies. Following the initial training, business process redesign groups were formed by individuals to address key problems in connection with business processes involving their departments. Members of the E-Collaboration Research Center facilitated the work of those groups by meeting with them on a weekly basis during a period of approximately 4 months each. Each business process redesign group developed both communication flow and activity flow representations of their target processes. Those representations were similar to the representations shown in Figure 4.1.

While both types of representations contained different types of information, they generally embodied the same amount of information; that is, neither was substantially more information-rich than the other. This may sound a bit confusing, since communication flow diagrams are by definition more information oriented than activity flow diagrams. What is being pointed out here is that both types of representations provided comparable amounts of information *about the business processes* modeled through them.

After developing the communication flow and activity flow representations of their target business processes, each group independently proposed several major business process changes. Communication flow and activity flow representations of the new processes, with major changes incorporated into them, were then generated. Following this, each business process redesign group developed a generic information technology solution to implement the new process. These generic information technology solutions were essentially product-independent computer-based infrastructure and system specifications; that is, no infrastructure or software product names were mentioned (e.g., Cisco Router, Microsoft SQL Server). The generic information technology solutions were illustrated through rich pictorial representations with generic icons representing computers, databases, and organizational functions. These were followed by the actual implementation of the recommended business process changes, which typically lasted from 3 to 6 months, for each project.

After their business process redesign efforts were completed, the members of the business process groups were asked to answer questions aimed at comparing their perceptions regarding the use of communication flow and activity flow representations in their projects, along several variables. Figure 4.2 summarizes answers provided by business process group members to question–statements referring to

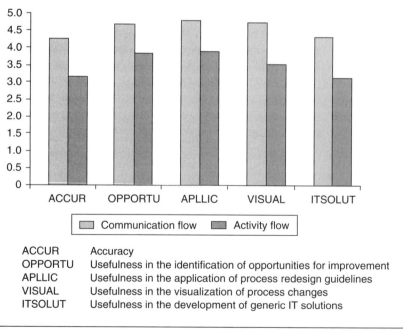

ACCUR	Accuracy
OPPORTU	Usefulness in the identification of opportunities for improvement
APLLIC	Usefulness in the application of process redesign guidelines
VISUAL	Usefulness in the visualization of process changes
ITSOLUT	Usefulness in the development of generic IT solutions

Figure 4.2   Perceptions Regarding Communication and Activity Flow
Representations

Table 4.1   Question–Statements Used for Each Variable

Variable	Question–Statements
ACCUR	• Activity flow representations are accurate representations of processes. • Communication flow representations are accurate representations of processes.
OPPORTU	• Activity flow representations are useful in the identification of opportunities for improvement. • Communication flow representations are useful in the identification of opportunities for improvement.
APPLIC	• Activity flow representations are useful in the application of process redesign guidelines. • Communication flow representations are useful in the application of process redesign guidelines.
VISUAL	• Activity flow representations are useful in the visualization of process changes. • Communication flow representations are useful in the visualization of process changes.
ITSOLUT	• Activity flow representations are useful in the development of generic IT solutions. • Communication flow representations are useful in the development of generic IT solutions.

the following variables: "accuracy," "usefulness in the identification of opportunities for improvement," "usefulness in the application of process redesign guidelines," "usefulness in the visualization of process changes," and "usefulness in the development of generic IT solutions." The question–statements used are shown in Table 4.1. The answers to those question–statements were provided on a Likert-type scale ranging from 1 (strongly disagree) to 5 (strongly agree). The heights of the bars in Figure 4.2 are the averages of the answers provided for each variable in connection with each of the two business process representation approaches, the communication flow and activity flow representation approaches.

As can be seen from Figure 4.2, the average scores for all the variables were higher for the communication flow than for the activity flow representation approach. Statistical tests indicate that those differences are statistically significant and not due to chance. According to those scores, perceived accuracy is approximately 34 percent higher in communication flow representations of business processes, when compared with activity flow representations. The scores also suggest that perceived usefulness in the identification of opportunities for improvement is about 22 percent higher in communication flow representations; perceived usefulness in the application of process redesign guidelines is about 23 percent higher; perceived usefulness in the visualization of process changes is about 34 percent higher; and perceived usefulness in the development of generic information technology solutions is about 38 percent higher in communication flow representations, when compared with activity flow representations.

Moreover, of all the 37 business process redesign decisions made by the four groups as a whole, 23 decisions (62.16 percent) were entirely based on communication flow representations of their target business processes. The other 14 process redesign decisions were distributed as follows: 4 (10.81 percent) were entirely based on activity flow representations of their target processes, and 10 (27.03 percent) were based on both types of representations. These trends toward employing communication flow representations were also tested for statistical significance. The results of those tests suggest a statistically significant preference for the use of communication flow representations when applying business process redesign guidelines—a preference whose likelihood of being due to chance is lower than one tenth of a percent.

It is reasonable to conclude, based on these results, that a focus on communication flow structures in business processes is indeed advisable as an alternative to the currently more widespread focus on activity flows. This is especially true when time constraints force practitioners to use one single business process redesign approach. With the fast pace of change in the business world, a pace that seems to be constantly increasing, this is likely to become more and more common. Systems analysts, who are more and more becoming business process designers as well, need to prepare themselves to deliver effect improvement solutions in a matter of months, rather than years. It is hoped that the orientation proposed by this book, and particularly the ideas and methods discussed in further chapters, will help systems analysts meet that challenge.

Summary and Concluding Remarks

Business process redesign approaches have become very popular in organizational circles, particularly since the emergence of the business process reengineering movement in the early 1990s. The key assumption underlying the development and use of business process redesign approaches is that processes can be understood and modified in such a way as to increase both their efficiency and the quality of their outcomes. In such approaches, business processes are seen as the basic units of value-added work in organizations.

In spite of being touted as a new and revolutionary idea, it can be argued that business process redesign has a long history, dating back to Frederick Taylor's scientific management movement. The scientific management method was concerned primarily with the improvement of manufacturing processes. It provided an approach through which managers could redesign processes to minimize times and motions in them and subsequently encourage workers to follow the new process designs by means of financial incentives. The approach has worked particularly well in processes that involved the handling of heavy materials and whose executors were largely uneducated and unskilled workers. In that context, the value of Taylor's scientific management method is undeniable, making it one of the most enduring and successful organizational development methods ever devised.

The time gap between the emergence of the scientific management method and the emergence of the business process reengineering movement amounts to almost a century. Many new organizational development approaches have been proposed in between. Notably, there was the humanist movement, which shifted the focus of organizational development from "processes" to "people," pioneered by Elton Mayo in the early and mid-1900s and extended by others such as McGregor, Maslow, and Herzberg. There was also the total quality management movement, which reverted to a focus on processes but with an emphasis on process quality rather than productivity. Deming and Juran pioneered the total quality management movement.

In spite of the time gap mentioned, many have argued that reengineering is in fact a modernized version of the scientific management method. When one looks at the original reengineering ideas and the process redesign approaches that followed, it seems that this argument is generally correct. The similarity between today's business process redesign practices and those propounded by the scientific management method has extended to one aspect that has negative implications for the contemporary practice of business process redesign. That aspect is the focus of much of today's business process redesign approaches on times-and-motions elements associated with activity flows (or workflows), which is reflected in an emphasis on modeling and understanding business processes primarily as chronological sequences of interrelated activities.

This chapter discusses the comparison of a communication flow–oriented approach to business process redesign, which is arguably well aligned with the information-intensive nature of most modern processes, with an activity flow–oriented approach, which reflects much of the current practice in connection with business process redesign. The comparison builds on projects that involved four different organizations, with one business process redesign group conducted at each organization. Two of those organizations were manufacturing companies. The other two were service organizations.

Evidence from those projects suggests that business process redesign group members perceived communication flow representations as better than activity flow representations across a number of attributes (accuracy, usefulness in the identification of opportunities for improvement, and others). The evidence also suggests that business process redesign group members employed communication flow representations of business processes more extensively than activity flow representations when making decisions in connection with business process redesign itself and information technology solutions to implement the redesigned business processes. This emphasis apparently had no negative impact on group success—in fact, the evidence suggests a positive impact. Moreover, it is fair to assume that business process redesign group members made a rational and relatively well-informed choice, particularly given that they were involved in "real" business process redesign projects, with all the personal risks associated with not doing a good job.

Review Questions

1. Business process redesign's origins:
   (a) Can be traced back to Taylor's scientific management movement.
   (b) Are based on Taylor's work conducted in collaboration with labor unions.

(c) Can be traced back to Taylor's development of the first mainframe computer.

(d) Cannot be traced back to Taylor's scientific management movement.

2. The total quality management movement did not:
   (a) Represent a shift in focus from productivity to quality in processes improvement.
   (b) Receive credit for having propelled Japan to economic superpower status.
   (c) Precede Taylor's scientific management movement.
   (d) Succeed Taylor's scientific management movement.

3. Which of the following statements is correct?
   (a) Business process reengineering was a completely new idea.
   (b) Business process reengineering was initially touted as a new idea.
   (c) Reengineering was a school of management thought pioneered by William G. Deming.
   (d) Strategic approaches to reengineering, as opposed to more operational approaches, look into the inner workings of individual business processes to improve them.

4. It is wrong to say that:
   (a) Research on business process representation frameworks has the potential to improve our understanding about some of the factors influencing business process quality.
   (b) The research area of business process representation frameworks and their impact on business process redesign has received relatively little attention up until the 1990s.
   (c) Research findings regarding business process representation frameworks can help us improve the way in which we improve business process productivity.
   (d) One research area that has received a lot of attention in the 1980s is that of business process representation frameworks and their impact on business process redesign.

5. Traditional systems analysis and design methods:
   (a) Address the flow of communication in business processes.
   (b) Do not address the flow of communication in business processes.
   (c) Address only the sequential flow of activities in business processes.
   (d) Fully address business process redesign issues, but unfortunately do not address business process automation issues.

6. Based on the business process redesign projects that were mentioned in this chapter, it is incorrect to say that:
   (a) The flow of information in a business process can be subsumed by the web of communication interactions of the business process.
   (b) The flow of information in business processes was studied more closely than the flow of knowledge in the processes.

(c) The flow of materials in business processes could be subsumed by the web of communication interactions of a business process.

(d) The flow of materials in business processes was seen as relevant for business process redesign in manufacturing processes.

7. One of the key differences between the communication flow and activity flow representations discussed in this chapter is that:

(a) The former type of representation shows the flow of information between organization functions, something that is not done by the latter.

(b) The former type of representation is significantly richer in terms of details than the latter.

(c) The latter type of representation shows the flow of information between organization functions, while the former doesn't show that flow.

(d) The latter type of representation is significantly richer in terms of details than the former.

8. Which of the following statements in connection with the project involving the four organizations mentioned before in this chapter is incorrect?

(a) Generally, the group members perceived communication flow representations as less accurate than activity flow representations.

(b) Generally, the group members perceived communication flow representations as more useful in the identification of opportunities for improvement than activity flow representations.

(c) Generally, the group members perceived activity flow representations as less useful in the application of process redesign guidelines than communication flow representations.

(d) Generally, the group members perceived activity flow representations as less useful in the visualization of process changes than communication flow representations.

9. When we look at the results of the project involving the four organizations mentioned before in this chapter, we can unequivocally conclude that:

(a) Perceived accuracy is higher in activity flow representations of business processes, when compared with communication flow representations.

(b) Communication flow representations are perceived as significantly more difficult to be generated than activity flow representations.

(c) Perceived accuracy seems to be higher in connection with communication flow representations of business processes than with activity flow representations.

(d) Activity flow representations are perceived as radically more difficult to be generated than communication flow representations.

10. Based on what was discussed in this chapter, which of the following statements is false?

(a) It is safe to say that business process redesign has a long history, perhaps dating back to Frederick Taylor's ideas.

(b) Taylor's management ideas have worked particularly well in processes that involved the handling of heavy materials.

(c) Many have argued, probably correctly, that reengineering is in fact a modernized version of the scientific management method.

(d) The popularity of business process redesign approaches in organizational circles has steadily decreased in the 1990s.

Discussion Questions

1. This chapter argued that, in today's organizations, there is a high proportion of communication-intensive business processes. It was also argued that those business processes' quality and productivity are more strongly determined by their flow of communication than non–communication-intensive business processes. Develop a business scenario that illustrates an exception to these "rules," for example, an organization where communication-intensive business processes are not that common. Why is this type of scenario not more common today? The scenario developed by you should be as realistic as possible.

2. Does the idea that human beings in general perceive communication flow representations as more difficult to be generated than activity flow representations make sense to you? Explain your answer, which may be "yes" or "no" (since it is based on your personal perception), based on the development of a business scenario illustrating your answer. The scenario developed by you should be as realistic as possible.

3. Develop a realistic business scenario that will serve as the backdrop for the development of two business process representations, one focused on the flow of communication and the other on the flow of activities of a key business process. The business process in question should be critical to a specific organization, which should be part of your business scenario.

4. Pair up with a colleague, and carefully redesign the business process generated in Discussion Question 3 with the goal of improving its quality and productivity. Do not worry about following specific business process redesign guidelines in this exercise; just use your common sense. Each of you should use one business process representation approach as the basis for your redesign. Once you are done, compare your redesigned process with that generated by your colleague. Are they different? If yes, try to explain why they are different based on what was discussed earlier in this chapter.

5. After you complete Discussion Question 4, answer each of the question–statements previously discussed in this chapter in connection with the second applied research project (the one involving four organizations). Compare your answers with the answers provided by business process group members previously discussed in this chapter. Are there any differences? If yes, try to explain why.

Business Process Modeling Approaches and Diagrams

Many issues in connection with business process redesign have been addressed since the 1990s, in large part in response to important questions raised by business process reengineering. Success factors and preconditions for effective business process redesign have been identified, new methods and techniques for managing change in connection with business process redesign projects have been proposed, potentially damaging "myths" have been identified, the role of information technology in business process redesign efforts has been clarified, and new insights on the implementation of new business process designs have been gained. Several of these issues are addressed in this book, many in later chapters.

One area that has received relatively little attention, however, is that of business process modeling approaches and their impact on business process redesign. This is an area where important questions remain to be answered. Business process modeling approaches influence the way in which business process redesign practitioners look at processes. That is, those approaches define the representational "lenses" through which people see business processes, which arguably are likely to have a strong influence on how business processes are redesigned. For example, as previously discussed in this book, a focus on the flow of activities in a business process (or "workflow") is likely to lead to changes in how *activities* flow in the process, whereas a focus on the flow of information in a business process is likely to lead to changes in how *information* flows in the process.

In this chapter, several business process modeling approaches are discussed, as well as respective representative diagrams. For each approach, a discussion of its main focus is provided, as well as a comparative discussion within the context of the communication flow–oriented business redesign methodology proposed in this book. Main approaches covered here include activity flow–oriented approaches, the data flow diagramming approach used in traditional systems analysis and design, the communication flow–oriented approach (which can be seen as a modified version of the data flow diagramming approach discussed before it), object-oriented approaches, and holistic systems approaches.

Why Model Business Processes?

As a concept becomes more abstract, so does generally the discrepancy in the ways different people may construe the concept. A concept that refers to a tangible object, like that of a wooden four-legged chair, for example, is likely to be understood more or less in the same way by two people. There will be visualization differences between the two people, which may be reconciled by further description (e.g., exact color of the chair, whether it is new or old), but those differences will not be as big as differences in connection with a concept that refers to an intangible item.

An intangible item is generally seen as an abstraction, something that exists in our minds and nowhere else. There are different levels or degrees of abstraction, with some abstract concepts being more abstract than others. For example, while a person is a tangible item, since he or she can be touched and exists in reality, a team of people is not. One does not bump into a team of people; he or she bumps into a person, who is a member of the team. In this instance, the team is an abstraction. But, since the abstract concept of a team of people is made up of tangible items, namely the team members, its level of abstraction is lower than that of the concept of team spirit, for example. The latter is not an abstract collection of tangible items. It is a somewhat ethereal quality that the team is supposed to have.

Business processes are abstract concepts that are in between the team and team spirit concepts discussed above in terms of degree of abstraction. With abstract concepts such as that of a business process, shared mental visualizations are much less likely to be achieved without substantial effort and clarification. One of the reasons for this difficulty is that abstractions are not perceived by our five senses as real objects like a chair is (e.g., we can see and touch a chair) and therefore must be understood based on abstract models. If these models do not exist or are too rough and incomplete, then a sense of perplexity ensues.

Business processes, as most abstract entities, need to be modeled in some way to be understood by different people. And, more importantly, two or more people must understand a business process in roughly the same way if they intend to be successful at redesigning it. Models, however, irrespective of how complex they are, are in most cases limited representations of whatever they are supposed to depict, whether those are real objects or abstract entities. In the same way that an airplane model (used for simulations) does not incorporate all of the elements of a real airplane (only the elements that are the most relevant for a particular simulation exercise), a business process model will not incorporate all of the elements of the process it is representing.

Several main types of business process modeling approaches, or views, are discussed in this chapter. Those views lead, as discussed previously, to incomplete representations of business processes and therefore should be understood in terms of their pros and cons in today's information- and knowledge-intensive organizational environments. From the perspective taken in this book, perhaps the most important criterion with which one could assess the practical value of a particular model is the likelihood that the model will serve as a solid basis for a successful business process redesign project.

A Business Process Example: Predictive Car Maintenance

Before we go any further into the discussion of business process modeling approaches, let us set the stage for that discussion with a business process example. The example refers to the predictive car maintenance process of a rental company. It involves obtaining and properly using information from customers of the car rental company about problems with the cars. The problems that are relevant are those that can be prevented in the future through predictive maintenance of cars, that is, through maintaining the cars (e.g., replacing certain parts) before the problems occur in the future. The example will be referred to in the discussion of each business process modeling approach.

The business process example starts with a customer filing a complaint online regarding problems with a car that the customer supposedly rented in the past. The details of the complaint filed by the customer are stored in an online file of car rental complaints. The assistant manager of the rental company then downloads the information about the complaint using a Web-based computer system called RentalWizard, which automatically generates a complaint form to be used for internal processing of the complaint. The assistant manager then places that complaint form in a box for later processing, together with other complaint forms.

Once every week, the assistant manager of the rental company reviews each complaint form, using a manual containing several rules for reviewing complaints. Those rules had been devised so that certain complaints could be filtered out (e.g., complaints not related to car maintenance problems) before they progressed any further in the business process. Once the assistant manager is finished reviewing each complaint form, he hand delivers a reviewed complaint form to the rental company's manager, briefly explaining why the complaint should proceed in the process.

The rental manager then hand delivers the reviewed complaint form to the assistant maintenance manager, again briefly explaining why the complaint should be processed. The assistant maintenance manager is the main point of contact for the rental company's manager in the company's maintenance department, which is the organizational unit that processes reviewed customer complaints.

The assistant maintenance manager then, upon receipt of a reviewed complaint form, places the form in a box for processing by the quality control specialist. The quality control specialist is an employee who formerly worked for a software development company that owns and commercializes a computer system called SmartFleet. The computer system cost the rental company approximately $800,000. It incorporates artificial intelligence algorithms that operate on predictive maintenance rules, which are both used and updated by SmartFleet based on each new complaint processed through the system and on details about previous maintenance activities. The algorithms allow the SmartFleet system to create a schedule of predictive maintenance activities (called "jobs") that reduces maintenance costs to a minimum while also reducing the likelihood of future car problems occurring while the cars are with the customers of the car rental company.

The schedule of predictive maintenance jobs generated by SmartFleet is a printed set of pages (one page per job), organized according to the order of execution prescribed by the computer system. The quality control specialist then places those pages in a box with other predictive maintenance jobs. The box is located at the entrance of the workshop used by the maintenance department. A team of mechanics from the maintenance department then processes each predictive maintenance job. Upon completion of each job, the team enters the details about each completed job into a fleet maintenance details file, using a data entry screen of the SmartFleet computer system.

Activity Flow–Oriented Approaches

Activity flow–oriented approaches are the most commonly used in business process redesign. Activity flow–oriented representations are also frequently referred to as "workflow" representations of business processes. Business process redesign approaches that build on activity flow representations are often referred to as workflow-oriented approaches to business process redesign.

Because of their popularity, many different activity flow–oriented business process representation conventions exist, each with its own set of standard symbols. A particularly popular set of business process representation conventions is that discussed by J. Harrington in his book *Business Process Improvement*. There, several different activity flow diagrams are discussed, among which is one of the most characteristic of the activity flow orientation in business process modeling: the functional flowchart.

Activity flow diagrams are aimed at clearly showing the chronological and sequential order of execution of the activities that make up a business process. Human beings tend to perceive business processes as representations of "action" in a physical sense. Therefore, activity flow diagrams are often perceived as being among the easiest to generate and understand, and certainly easier to generate and understand than diagrams placing emphasis on communication flow elements. A recent doctoral dissertation by Azim Danesh drives this point home, providing some empirical evidence in support of this perception. The dissertation is titled *IT-Enabled Process Redesign: Using Communication Flow Optimization Theory in an Information Intensive Environment* and was completed at Temple University.

This perception is not really caused by a higher complexity, in terms of number of symbols used in the diagram, of activity flow diagrams. The most likely reason for the perception is that activity flow diagrams are better aligned with the way human beings envision "action," particularly in the physical sense. The problem with this perception is that most business processes operate on intangible elements, particularly information, and also have intangible elements as their outputs.

Among activity flow–oriented business process representations, one of the most popular is the functional flowchart. Representing business processes through functional flowcharts generally involves using the set of symbols shown in Figure 5.1 to show how activities are carried out chronologically. The serial sequence of activities is highlighted in the representation, and so is parallelism among activities, when sets of serially linked activities are carried out at the same time and more or less independently.

In Figure 5.1, a rectangular shape represents an activity. Arrows indicate the flow of execution of activities. As mentioned before, when seen as a group, several arrows connecting a set of activities also serve to indicate the chronological order of execution of the set of activities. This is a distinguishing characteristic of activity flow–oriented business process representations that serves to differentiate them from other types of representations of business processes (e.g., data flow diagrams, discussed later in this chapter).

In Figure 5.1, the organizational function that executes an activity or set of activities is described at the top of a column containing the activity or activities. In addition to organizational functions (e.g., warehouse manager, quality control inspector), activities may also be executed by groups of organizational functions (e.g., warehousing department, quality control committee) or organizations external to the organization that houses the business process (e.g., a supplier or customer organization).

The aforementioned symbols are used in Figure 5.2 to represent the business process whose example was discussed earlier, which refers to a car rental company's predictive maintenance process. It is important to stress a point that will become clear as we progress through this chapter: While the diagram in Figure 5.2 may be seen as a good representation of how communication takes place in the predictive maintenance process, arguably that is not the case.

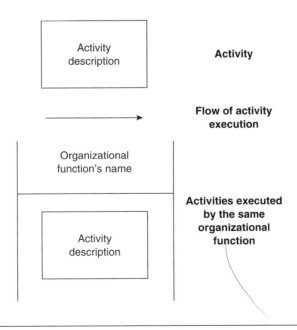

Figure 5.1   Activity Flow Representation Symbols

84

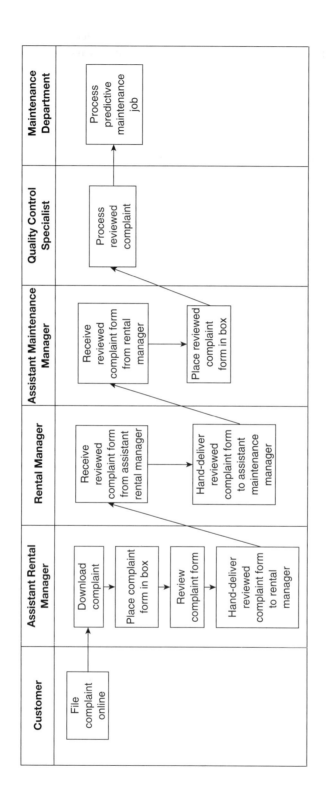

Figure 5.2   Activity Flow Representation Example

In fact, one of the key omissions of activity flow diagrams is that they do not provide much detail about business process data, neither in terms of flow nor in terms of storage. This makes an activity flow diagram a somewhat incomplete representation of the car rental company's predictive maintenance process, especially when compared with the communication flow–oriented representation approaches discussed later in this chapter. Nevertheless, many would probably view the activity flow representation shown in Figure 5.2 as a fairly clear and intuitively appealing representation of the car rental company's predictive maintenance process.

Activity flow–oriented representations of business processes, such as the one shown in Figure 5.2, are among the most popular in business process redesign circles, even though their use poses some serious obstacles to business process redesign practitioners. For example, they show practically no detail in connection with the web of communication interactions that make up most business processes today. And, as previously demonstrated in this book, most business process problems seem to stem from communication configurations that are suboptimal.

In the past, some adaptations of activity flow–oriented representations have been proposed with the goal of allowing for the representation of communication flow–related elements, such as data flows. However, because of the different nature of activity flow representations, those adaptations can sometimes be a little confusing from a business process representation standpoint. For example, one could try to represent the flow of data by associating it with the arrows shown in an activity flow representation (e.g., the one in Figure 5.2). However, strictly speaking, data do not flow from one activity to another. They flow from one data source to a data destination, for example, from one organizational function to another. Because of that, representing data as flowing between activities may be somewhat misleading when the time comes for business process redesign.

There are a number of variations of activity flow representations similar to the one shown in Figure 5.2. The workflow in Figure 5.2 is itself based on an adaptation of the American National Standards Institute's (ANSI) standard flowchart and has been extensively used in projects involving business process redesign groups. Flowchart variations are the block diagram, functional timeline flowchart, and geographic flowchart; see, for example, Harrington's book *Business Process Improvement* and the follow-up book *Business Process Improvement Workbook,* by Harrington and colleagues, for a more detailed discussion of those flowchart variations.

It has been argued that the use of activity flow representations of business processes is generally less advisable than the use of communication flow representations, particularly when the goal is business process redesign. However, there is at least one notable exception to this rule. Activity flow representations are probably better than communication flow representations when the business processes being modeled are manufacturing processes. This is particularly true for business processes that involve the assembly of a complex product (e.g., a car engine) based on a number of parts that are sequentially added to the unfinished product in an assembly line (until it becomes a finished product, of course). In the vast majority of other types of business processes, however, it is reasonable to argue that communication flow representations provide a better and more complete view of the elements that should be considered in a business process when the process is being redesigned.

The Data Flow Diagramming Approach

The traditional systems analysis and design approach, also known as the structured systems analysis and design approach, has served as the basis for hundreds of thousands of software development projects. This approach's main business process modeling diagram is the data flow diagram (or DFD).

Different sets of symbols and notations have been proposed in the past for data flow diagramming. Among the most important ones are those proposed by DeMarco and Yourdon and by Gane and Sarson, with the latter being used more extensively. Figure 5.3 shows the symbol set proposed by Gane and Sarson.

In Figure 5.3, a rectangular shape represents a data source or destination. A data source or destination represented through a rectangular shape may be an organizational function (e.g., warehouse manager, quality control inspector), a group of organizational functions (e.g., warehousing department, quality control committee), or an organization external to the organization that houses the business process (e.g., a supplier or customer organization).

As indicated in Figure 5.3, arrows indicate the flow of data, which are described by freestanding text located beside or near the arrows. Open rectangle shapes represent data repositories. Rectangular shapes with round edges represent activities,

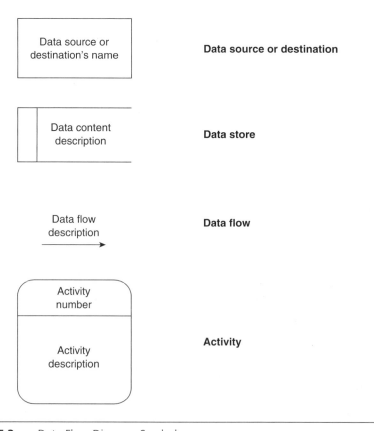

Figure 5.3   Data Flow Diagram Symbols

with the number of the activity being shown at the top of the shape. That number serves as a unique identifier for the activity and also indicates the approximate order of execution of the activity in relation to the other activities in the same business process representation.

Similar to the activity flow approach discussed in the previous section, activities are often referred to as business processes, or subprocesses, because they themselves can often be broken down into component activities. In this sense, the inner details of one activity in a business process can be represented as a separate business process diagram. The new diagram is at a different conceptual level of representation than the original diagram, where the business process was represented as a single activity. This is an issue that is discussed in more detail in this chapter, as well as later in the book.

In Figure 5.4, the aforementioned symbols are used to represent the business process example discussed earlier, which refers to a car rental company's predictive maintenance process. Certain types of relationships cannot be represented through data flow diagrams without the violation of widely accepted standardized diagramming rules and thus are not shown in Figure 5.4. This makes it a somewhat incomplete representation of the car rental company's predictive maintenance process.

Among the elements that are not shown in the data flow diagram in Figure 5.4 are the following: a customer providing information about car rental complaints, the knowledge repositories containing complaint review rules and predictive maintenance rules, the communication interaction between the rental manager and the

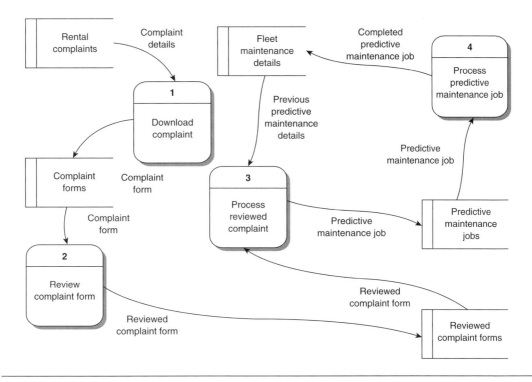

Figure 5.4   Data Flow Diagram Example

assistant maintenance manager, the indication in the activity symbols of which organizational function carries out each activity, and the indication in the activity symbols of which nontrivial tool or tools are used by an organizational function to carry out each activity.

The symbols showing a customer providing information about car rental complaints are not in Figure 5.4 because it would be a violation of standard data flow diagramming rules to represent a flow of data between a data source or destination and a data store. The same is true for the communication interaction between the rental manager and the assistant maintenance manager, since it would be a violation of data flow diagramming rules to represent a data exchange between two data sources or destinations. The knowledge repositories containing complaint review rules and predictive maintenance rules are not shown in Figure 5.4 because there are no data flow diagramming symbols that can be used to represent knowledge.

Arguably, the data flow diagram shown in Figure 5.4 also leaves out some details that are very important from a business process redesign perspective. For example, it will be seen later in this book that synchronous information communication interactions between two organizational functions (which involve a same-time interaction and do not usually rely on information repositories) are not very efficient ways of communication business process–relevant information. One example of synchronous information communication interaction is the one between the rental manager and the assistant maintenance manager. These types of interactions should usually be replaced with asynchronous communication interactions, where one employs an information repository for time-disconnected communication (e.g., an e-mail box, a voice messaging system). This would arguably streamline the business process and thus make it more efficient.

Generally speaking, business process problems such as the one just mentioned cannot usually be identified without the development of business process representations that make those process problems explicit. This is one of the main reasons why one would want to develop a slightly modified communication flow representation that incorporates many of the aspects of data flow diagrams but also eliminates some of its shortcomings (one such representation is discussed in the next section).

Often it becomes apparent that traditional data flow diagrams are difficult to be successfully used for representing problematic business processes, that is, business processes that badly need redesign, when modelers try to use computer-aided software engineering (or CASE) tools. The reason is that many of those tools attempt to enforce rather strictly standard data flow diagramming rules, which prevents business process modelers from representing processes as they really are.

The Communication Flow–Oriented Approach Proposed Here

This section discusses a modified communication flow–oriented representation, which to a large extent is based on data flow diagramming ideas. One of the key differences between the communication flow–oriented approach proposed in this section and standard data flow diagrams is that the communication flow representation approach discussed here attempts to overcome some of the limitations just discussed in connection with the traditional data flow diagrams. It does so employing a more relaxed set of diagramming rules. This added flexibility enables business process modelers to explicitly show more process inefficiencies that need to be addressed prior to automation through redesign.

Several different symbols are used to represent business processes through the communication flow–oriented approach proposed here (see Figure 5.5). A rectangular shape represents a data source or destination, where the data may carry information, knowledge, or both. A data source or destination represented through

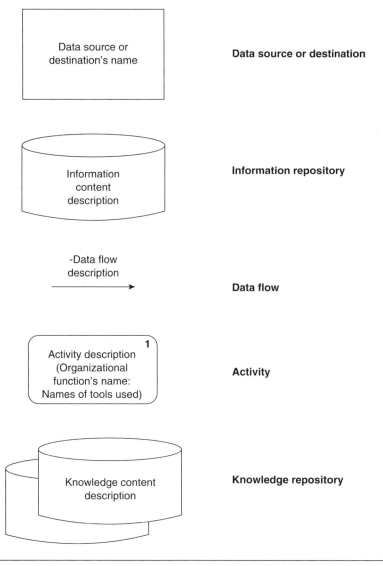

Figure 5.5   Communication Flow Representation Symbols

a rectangular shape may be an organizational function (e.g., warehouse manager, quality control inspector) or a group of organizational functions (e.g., warehousing department, quality control committee).

A data source or destination represented through a rectangular shape may also be an organization external to the organization that houses the business process. For example, it may be a supplier of car parts, where the business process under consideration is the car assembly line process in an automaker that outsources car parts manufacturing to several suppliers.

As noted in Figure 5.5, arrows indicate the flow of data, which is described by freestanding text located beside or near the arrows. When two arrows are near each other, an appropriate arrangement of the text is necessary to avoid confusion as to which arrow each piece of text description refers. Rectangular shapes with round edges represent activities. A number on the upper right corner indicates the approximate order of execution of the activity in relation to the other activities in the same business process representation. As with other types of business process representations, these activities are often referred to as business processes, or sub-processes, because they themselves can often be broken down into component activities. Drum shapes represent information repositories. Double drum shapes represent knowledge repositories.

The set of symbols shown in Figure 5.5 expands on the symbol set used earlier in this book in connection with standard data flow diagrams. That symbol set is expanded even further later in this book, with the goal of providing a richer and differentiated representation of information and knowledge flows and repositories in business processes. The reasons for expanding further the set of symbols used will be clearer then. For now, the comparison of different business process modeling approaches is primarily based on the symbol set shown in Figure 5.5.

In Figure 5.6, the aforementioned symbols are used to represent the business process example discussed earlier in this chapter, which refers to a car rental company's predictive maintenance process. In the business process representation shown in Figure 5.6, RentalWizard is the Web-based computer system that the assistant manager of the rental company uses to download information about user complaints. SmartFleet is the artificial intelligence–based computer system that creates a schedule of predictive maintenance activities on cars based on each new complaint processed through the system and on details about previous maintenance activities.

Note that, in Figure 5.6, the order of execution of activities is fairly clearly indicated through the numbers at the upper right corner of the activity symbols, which go from 1 to 4. This is not always the case with communication flow representations, because this type of representation is aimed primarily at making explicit the web of communication interactions that takes place in a business process. Some information- or knowledge-processing activities may take place recurrently, sometimes before *and* after other activities, which makes it difficult to figure out how to number them. In these cases, the decision on how to number them is a subjective one, which is left to the business process modeler or modeling team.

Also, the activity representations in Figure 5.6 have inside them the description of each activity. That description is followed, within parentheses, by the organizational function that carries out the activity and, in the case of activity numbers 2, 3,

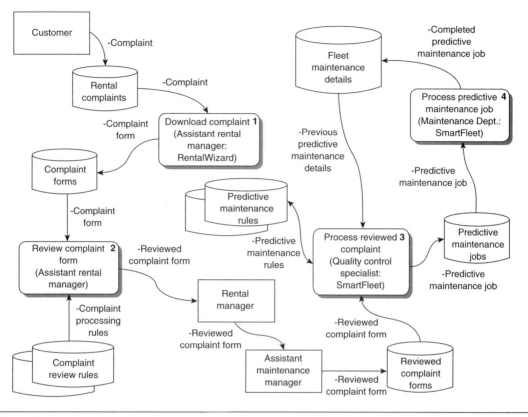

Figure 5.6   Communication Flow Representation Example

and 4, the main tool used by the organizational function to carry out the activity. Here, only specific and nontrivial tools are mentioned, such as specific computer systems, as opposed to nonspecific and somewhat trivial tools such as pen and paper. This is why no tool is mentioned in connection with activity number 1. The description of the activity is presented as a verb in the infinitive form followed by the object of the verb. For example, in activity number 1, the verb is *review* and the verb's object is *complaint form*.

Previously, this book discussed business process–oriented approaches to organizational improvement from a historic perspective. That discussion revealed several historic facets of business process redesign, including a preference toward activity flow–oriented approaches. The book then discussed some tests of the notion that a shift in focus from an activity flow to a communication flow orientation would lead to better results in terms of business process redesign.

In the aforementioned tests, communication flow representations that incorporated fewer of the elements shown in Figure 5.6 were used (e.g., activities were not numbered, and knowledge repositories were not represented). Nevertheless, those tests provided support for the notion that a shift toward a communication flow orientation would lead to improvements in business process redesign performance. This leads to the conclusion that the type of representation discussed above is likely to lead to comparable, if not better, results in similar tests. Among other reasons is that the new elements provide a richer view of business processes, while at the same time they appear to add little in terms of extra effort (although it seems that some extra effort is required) from the business process modelers to be used in the generation of the diagrams.

Object-Oriented Approaches

Ivar Jacobson has been one of the main proponents of the object-oriented view of business processes. He developed a methodology to model business processes as data objects, where the word "object" has a very specific and somewhat technical meaning. Jacobson's methodology, which is discussed in detail in the book *The Object Advantage* (by Jacobson and colleagues), is based on the concept of a software object (often referred to as simply "object"). A software object is essentially a data repository with several operations, or programming functions, associated with it. They are defined in such a way that any changes in the data repository's contents can only be carried out through those operations. The operations are also referred to as "methods" in the technical jargon of object-oriented programming. A software object typically stores data in its attributes, which are analogous to the attributes of real objects, like a chair. For example, the attributes of the object "chair" could be its "color," "weight," and "number of legs."

Object-oriented business process modeling has evolved as a component of object-oriented analysis and design, which in turn owes much of its existence to the success of object-oriented programming. One of the main goals of object-oriented analysis and design, as discussed earlier in this book, is to provide computer systems developers with methods and tools that allow them to move more quickly from analysis and design to coding using object-oriented programming techniques.

Different flavors of object-oriented analysis and design methodologies have emerged over time. Those methodologies were often differentiated from each other based on the standard notations for diagramming that each of them proposed for modeling business processes and other computer systems components, such as software objects. The different standard notations have been incorporated into several diagram types. Soon, a new set of standard notations for object-oriented analysis and design was developed, with the goal of unifying three existing methodologies. The three methodologies were the ones developed by Ivar Jacobson, Grady Booch, and James Rumbaugh. The new set of standard notations became known as the unified modeling language, or UML.

The unified modeling language consists of 12 types of diagrams and respective diagramming rules. The 12 diagram types are organized into three major categories: structural diagrams, behavior diagrams, and model management diagrams. Structural diagrams represent the structure and static relationship of software objects, such as the data and operation modules that are shared by software objects. Behavior diagrams represent the operation of a computer system in terms of its objects, such as the interaction of software objects with each other when the computer system is being executed. Model management diagrams represent the organization of computer system modules around software objects.

The cornerstone of object-oriented systems analysis and design employing the unified modeling language is the use-case diagram. The set of symbols shown in Figure 5.7 is the one commonly used to generate use-case diagrams. A humanlike stick figure represents an organizational function, called an "actor" in the technical lingo of use-case diagramming. A line, called an association, links an organizational function with one or more use-case symbols. An oval represents a use-case, which is similar to an activity in communication flow diagrams (the meaning is essentially the same as in the other diagrams discussed in this chapter as well). A rectangle is used to encase the set of symbols that are supposed to be part of, or associated with, the same computer system. Normally, this is done whether a computer system exists or not at the time of business process modeling, an approach similar to that followed in the traditional systems analysis and design approach.

Figure 5.8 employs the symbols discussed above to represent the business process example discussed earlier related to a car rental company's predictive maintenance process. As can probably be seen from Figure 5.8, the use-case diagram is, among the diagrams already discussed in this chapter, one of the most heavily oriented toward computer systems implementation. Rather than showing details that can be used for business process redesign, such as the communication interactions

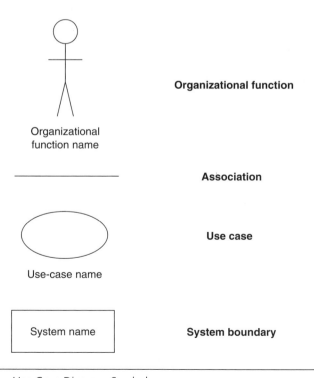

Figure 5.7   Use-Case Diagram Symbols

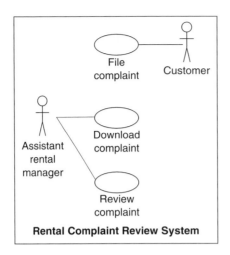 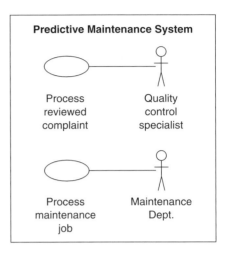

Figure 5.8   Use-Case Diagram Example

between different organizational functions, the use-case diagram organizes different activities and related elements into "systems." The separate sets of activities and related elements are encased in rectangles to signal that they are part of the same system. In this sense, use-case diagrams are a step forward in terms of pre-implementation analysis when compared with data flow diagrams, used in the traditional systems analysis and design approach. However, from a business process redesign perspective, use-case diagrams may be seen as a backward step, because they push systems analysts into thinking in terms of how to automate a business process before the business process is redesigned.

The object-oriented view of business processes can in fact be seen as an extension of the view provided by the traditional systems analysis and design approach. In this extended view, data repositories, often represented in data flow diagrams by open-ended rectangles, are subsumed by the activities that change the contents of those repositories. The data repositories and activities that change them become part of the same structure, which is then subsequently automated as a software object.

From a technology automation–focused perspective, especially where automation is conducted through in-house software development, there is a clear advantage in adopting object-oriented approaches to business process analysis and design. Many believe that object-oriented programming is increasingly becoming the dominant software development paradigm, particularly given that it has been adopted by most of the major players in the software development industry since the 1990s. And, as mentioned before, the object-oriented view of business processes allows for a relatively inexpensive transition between (a) business process analysis and redesign and (b) the development of new computer systems, using object-oriented programming techniques, to support the implementation of the new business processes.

However, business process redesign may end up suffering, or not being done at all, when one's focus is to move quickly from business process analysis to computer automation. In addition to this problem, there is an associated concern in connection with the somewhat technical, software programming orientation of object-oriented approaches. That orientation is highlighted by the fact that object-oriented approaches have been criticized by what some see as their excessively technical complexity. That complexity is often perceived as preventing users who are unfamiliar with object-oriented concepts and related technical jargon from effectively understanding those approaches and adopting them in business process redesign projects. Business process representation approaches based on the object-oriented paradigm, such as the unified modeling language, are often seen as too complex to be widely accepted and used in organizations, in spite of the fact that the unified modeling language has been endorsed by heavyweights of the computer community.

Holistic Systems Approaches

What is called here the "holistic systems" view of business processes is based on the traditional concept of system, that is, that of an assembly of interdependent parts that cannot be understood very well as only a function of its components. In this light, a system can be characterized by its emergent properties, which are system properties and therefore meaningless in terms of the individual parts or elements that make up the system. Peter Checkland and Jim Scholes illustrate the system concept in their very important book *Soft Systems Methodology in Action*: "The vehicular potential of a bicycle is an emergent property of the combined parts of a bicycle when they are assembled in a particular way to make the structured whole."

According to a strict interpretation of the holistic systems view and its application to business process analysis, one could operationally define business processes as abstract entities that represent the transformation of inputs into outputs. A business process's suppliers provide inputs. The business process's customers consume the outputs generated through the process, which have a value-added component to them, when compared with the inputs. That is, transformation of inputs into outputs is aimed at adding value to the customers of the business process. According to this interpretation of the holistic systems view, a business process representation would look somewhat like Figure 5.9 for the business process example discussed earlier related to a car rental company's predictive maintenance process.

As is probably obvious from Figure 5.9, the main problem with using only the holistic systems approach to business process modeling is that it provides little in terms of details about the inner workings of a business process. Nevertheless, the holistic systems approach is often successfully used as a precursor to a more operational approach, such as the data flow diagramming and communication flow–oriented approaches discussed earlier in this chapter. In fact, a specific class of data flow diagrams that are similar to the holistic system diagram shown in Figure 5.9 are part of well-established data flow diagramming standards, such as the one proposed by Gane and Sarson and discussed earlier in this chapter. They are often referred to as "Level 0" data flow diagrams, or "context diagrams." Their development regularly precedes the development of data flow diagrams that show in more detail the inner workings of business processes.

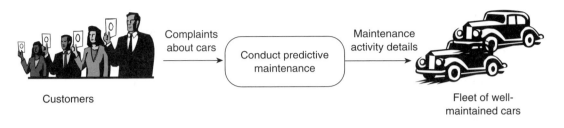

Figure 5.9   Holistic System Diagram Example

It is reasonable to argue that the holistic systems approach, when used in isolation, may be of little use to those whose job is to try to change a business process. In the holistic systems view, business processes are defined by means of sets of key emergent properties that characterize them, with the relationship between their inside activities and related components being of relatively small importance.

Nevertheless, the holistic systems view has proved to be quite useful in the analysis of very complex and messy business processes, even when used alone and separately from other business process views. One type of business process that is often complex and messy is that related to strategic decision making, where senior managers make decisions based on incomplete information about their organizations' operations and past performance. Strategic decision-making business processes are not usually amenable to modeling using communication flow–oriented or other operational approaches, such as the ones discussed earlier in this chapter, because the number of activities and related symbols required to fully represent them is often too large to allow for effective modeling.

For example, in a consulting project, a systems analyst tried to model one such process in an advertising company and ended up with a very complicated diagram made up of more than 150 activities and related symbols. One could reasonably argue that, in this case, taking a holistic systems approach would have led to a better understanding of the business process in question. However, given several constraints on time and financial resources, which often go unmentioned in popular business books, the management of the advertising company and the system analyst simply decided to move on to other more analyzable business processes and leave the complex and messy strategic management process alone.

What does the holistic system diagram in Figure 5.9 tell us about the car rental company's predictive maintenance process? One could argue that it tells us almost nothing, simply because it (the diagram) is too simplified a representation of the real process. Nevertheless, simplified representations may sometimes free our minds from unnecessary details that could prevent us from coming up with a creative solution to a serious problem. To illustrate this, let us look at the surprising ending of the car rental company's case—the case was introduced earlier in this chapter. This surprising ending is based on a case of a real car rental company.

In spite of the SmartFleet computer system, which cost the rental company approximately $800,000 and which incorporated artificial intelligence algorithms, the car rental company was still lagging behind the competition. Among other things, the company's operating costs were higher, and customer satisfaction with the cars was lower than the competition's!

Then, someone looking at a diagram similar to (but with a few more inputs and outputs than) the holistic diagram example shown in Figure 5.9 concluded that the car rental company was paying a whole lot of attention to the maintenance of their fleet. Car maintenance, the person argued, should not be one of the core competencies of any car rental company. In other words, that person argued that car maintenance was better left to the service departments of car dealerships, and that the car rental company should focus on the intricacies of the car rental service—which is not as easy a service to deliver with quality as it may look like at first glance.

To make a long story short, the car rental company decided to essentially throw away their SmartFleet computer system (which may sound somewhat unbelievable to some readers) and radically change their approach to dealing with customer complaints. They simply did what many of the large car rental companies do, which arguably is one of the best ways of running a car rental business. They started buying brand-new cars and selling them right before the manufacturer's warranty expired. This allowed the car rental company to virtually close down its car maintenance division and replace it with a car sales division. Brand-new cars were then purchased through bulk deals with manufacturers, and all the maintenance was subsequently run by dealerships associated with each particular car brand; for example, a local Ford dealership for the Ford car models purchased by the car rental company.

In the end, the car rental company realized that the costs of maintaining their fleet of cars were actually higher than the depreciation costs they had to incur by buying new cars and selling the cars right before the warranties expired. Moreover, having a fleet of newer cars increased customer satisfaction, not only because new cars do not usually present many problems, but also because customers usually prefer to drive new cars—the newer the car, the better, in the eyes of most customers. This is probably the type of conclusion that would not have been achieved without a holistic systems approach to business process redesign, where the business process ended up comprising activities cutting across the entire car rental company.

Types of Business Process Diagramming Tools

There are a number of commercial software tools that support the development of business process representations, and that number seems to be increasing by the day. Generally, those tools can be seen as belonging to one or both of two broad types. The first type is that of what is referred to here as "lean" diagramming tools, which are independent of specific CASE tools. As mentioned before in this chapter, CASE stands for computer-aided software engineering. CASE tools often allow one to move from business process representation to software development with mining coding. The second type of commercial software tools that support the development of business process representations is that of diagramming tools that are part of CASE tools.

Examples of the first type of business process diagramming tools mentioned above are Chartist, SmartDraw, DiagramStudio, is/Modeler, and Visio. Also in this category are diagramming tools that have other functions, such as PowerPoint, which was originally developed to be used as a professional slide creation and presentation tool.

Examples of the second type of business process diagramming tools mentioned above are System Architect and Silverrun. The main difference between the first and second types of diagramming tools is that tools in the latter type provide the functionality to generate software automatically based on business process diagrams, while the former usually does not. CASE tool–dependent diagramming tools are usually data oriented, supporting data flow diagrams as well as other types of diagrams that go beyond business process representations (e.g., entity-relationship diagrams, which are discussed later in this book).

One of the problems with using diagramming tools of the second type is that they usually enforce diagramming rules, such as the ones previously discussed in this chapter in connection with data flow diagrams. This can make it difficult to use Type 2 diagramming tools to represent all of the inefficiencies present in business processes that are being targeted for redesign. On the other hand, Type 2 diagramming tools may be quite useful to represent business processes that have undergone changes and that are ready for implementation through computer software automation.

CASE-independent business process diagramming tools may be quite complex and feature-rich, such as Chartist, from Novagraph, Inc., which allows for the development of just about any type of diagram (including the ones discussed in this chapter). Another example is Visio, from Microsoft Corporation, which began as a robust Type 1 diagramming tool. Over time, it has steadily moved toward becoming a full-fledged Type 2 diagramming tool, through the increasing incorporation of functionality to generate software automatically. These developments refer particularly to the generation of software for technologies that are part of the Microsoft Office Suite (e.g., Access).

Business process redesign, as well as other components of systems analysis and design, often involve individuals who are not geographically colocated and who need to communicate efficiently and effectively with each other. This makes it important that those individuals be able to easily share business process representations among themselves. In this sense, the use of diagramming tools that employ proprietary methods can be a problem, especially when the business process being targeted for redesign cuts across two or more organizations. In this case, different organizations would have to agree on which diagramming tool to use, as well as to purchase and train their employees on the use of the agreed upon diagramming tool. This can be a problem with many diagramming tools, whether they are of Type 1 or 2.

Building Business Process Diagrams Using PowerPoint

Two possible solutions to the aforementioned problem are (a) to employ diagramming tools that generate diagram files in standard public formats, which can be viewed and edited using a variety of different diagramming tools, or (b) to employ proprietary diagramming tools that are widely available. Since standard public formats for diagram files are still emerging, Solution (b) seems more feasible. And, one obvious way to implement Solution (b) is to use a ubiquitous diagramming (and presentation) tool such as PowerPoint. The problem then turns to whether PowerPoint can be used effectively as a diagramming tool, since it does not incorporate several of the features of more sophisticated Type 1 diagramming tools.

The next several paragraphs address this issue and assume some basic knowledge of PowerPoint. The basic knowledge includes the ability to create simple diagrams, store them in different PowerPoint slides, and save them in different PowerPoint files. The features discussed here are available in most versions of PowerPoint. They are illustrated through screen snapshots generated based on the version of PowerPoint that comes as part of the Microsoft Office 2000 Suite, generally known as PowerPoint 2000.

Most novice PowerPoint users face two nagging problems when using it to build diagrams—problems that often turn them away from using PowerPoint and toward more sophisticated Type 1 diagramming tools (often with steep learning curves). The first is the limited set of symbols available from PowerPoint. While nonexisting (and usually more complex) symbols can be built by combining existing (and usually simpler) ones available from PowerPoint's predefined symbols library, the problem then becomes how to make those combinations into one single complex symbol that can be easily resized and moved around the diagram.

Using the "grouping" feature of PowerPoint, which is available in most versions of the software tool, can solve this problem. This feature allows a user to combine any number of basic PowerPoint symbols into new complex symbols, which can then be moved around the diagram and even resized, as though they were basic PowerPoint symbols. Moreover, a new symbol created through the grouping feature of PowerPoint can be copied and pasted into separate diagrams, saved in separate slides.

Figure 5.10 illustrates how two "drum" symbols and a borderless text box (with the text "Predictive maintenance rules" in it) can be combined to create a knowledge repository symbol, which can be used as part of a communication flow representation of a business process. The slide containing those symbols is a blank PowerPoint slide, without any background images or colors, which is provided as a default slide type in most versions of PowerPoint.

The knowledge repository symbol shown at the bottom-right corner of Figure 5.10, which combines three others symbols, can be treated as one single symbol. For example, one click of the mouse on any part of the knowledge repository symbol is enough to select the entire symbol, which can then be moved around the diagram and linked (see discussion below) with other symbols.

The second main nagging problem faced by novice PowerPoint users when using it to build diagrams refers to the use of arrows to connect symbols. Arrows are used in most types of diagrams, including three of the four main diagrams discussed in this chapter. Often, arrows do not "follow" the symbols they are connecting, making it a very laborious process to move symbols around the diagram. When arrows do not "follow" the symbols that they connect, every time one of the symbols is moved to a different position in the diagram, the arrow associated with it has to be moved separately (and often resized so that it can "reach" both symbols).

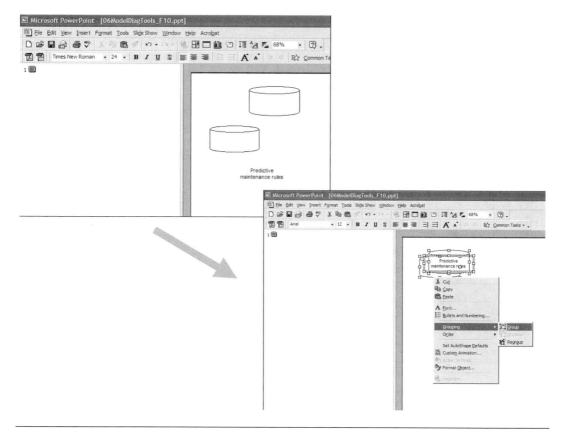

Figure 5.10   Grouping Disconnected Symbols

This problem can be solved by the use of connectors, which are offered in PowerPoint as an alternative to lines or arrows. Once two symbols are linked through a connector, the user does not have to worry about the connection when the symbols are moved around the diagram. The connector follows the symbols around the diagram, moving with them, and resizing itself as needed. Moreover, connectors can be defined as curved, which enables the user to have them go around other symbols in complex diagrams.

Figure 5.11 illustrates the use of connectors. At the top-left corner of Figure 5.11, two separate symbols are shown. They are part of the communication flow representation of the predictive car maintenance process discussed earlier in this chapter. One is a data source or destination symbol that represents a customer. The other is an information repository symbol that represents an online file of car rental complaints. On the right side and at the bottom left of Figure 5.11, we see the two symbols being connected by means of a curved connector.

Using the grouping and connector features, PowerPoint can be used to build relatively complex diagrams. If a business process representation is too large and needs to be broken down into two or more diagrams, those diagrams can be easily combined as part of one PowerPoint slide set and kept in the same file (usually with the .ppt extension).

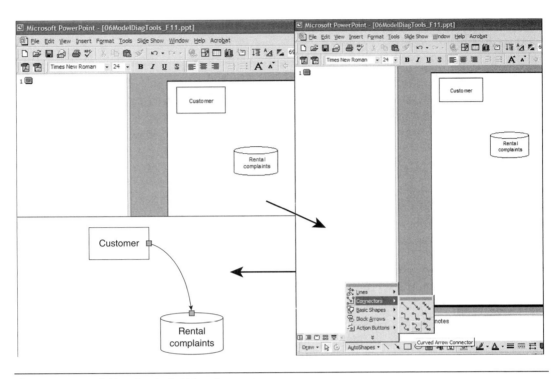

Figure 5.11   Linking Symbols Using Connectors

The same is true for complex business process representations that need to be "exploded" into other representations at different levels (this is an issue that is discussed in more detail later in the book). For example, a communication flow representation of a business process that cuts across an entire organization may not show enough details about certain activities that are carried out by specific divisions or departments of the organization. So it may be necessary to build business process representations of those activities. This is generally called "exploding" an activity into a diagram, by representing the inner details of the activity as a full-fledged business process. The resulting diagrams will be at different organizational representation levels, with the original diagram being what is often referred to as a Level 1 diagram and the resulting "exploded" diagrams being Level 2 diagrams. Diagrams at different levels can be grouped as sets of slides into different PowerPoint files for organization purposes.

PowerPoint is certainly not as powerful as other, more sophisticated, diagramming tools. Its diagramming functionality is more limited than that of Visio, for example. Nevertheless, it has the advantage of being quite widely used, which makes it easier to use for sharing business process representations electronically than other, less frequently used diagramming tools. Moreover, PowerPoint's limited functionality as a diagramming tool may make it easier to be learned, since the number of features that a user will have to learn will be smaller than if a more powerful diagramming tool were used.

Summary and Concluding Remarks

One area that has received relatively little attention within the business process redesign realm is that related to business process modeling approaches and respective diagrams, which in turn are likely to affect, perhaps strongly, how business process redesign is conducted. For example, a focus on the flow of activities in a business process is likely to lead to changes in how *activities* flow in the process, whereas a focus on the web of communication interactions of a business process is likely to lead to changes in how *communication* takes place in the process.

Why should one worry about modeling a business process? One of the main reasons is that, with abstract concepts such as that of a business process, shared mental visualizations are much less likely to be achieved without substantially more mental effort and clarification than with nonabstract concepts. Business processes, as most abstract entities, need to be modeled in some way to be understood by different people. And, more importantly, two or more people involved in the redesign of a business process must understand the process in roughly the same way if they expect to be successful.

Business process models are by and large incomplete representations of the abstract entities they are supposed to depict. This is generally true regardless of their type. In fact, this general rule of thumb applies to just about any type of model of virtually anything. That is, one characteristic that is shared by the vast majority of models is that they are incomplete and somewhat "rough" representations of reality. Each provides a specific "lens" through which we can see reality, which frequently filters out details that are often emphasized by other models.

This chapter discussed several approaches to business process modeling and respective diagramming techniques. The approaches discussed were activity flow–oriented approaches, the data flow diagramming approach used in traditional systems analysis and design, the communication flow–oriented approach proposed in this book (whose several components are discussed in more detail in later chapters), object-oriented approaches, and holistic systems approaches.

In light of this chapter's discussion of different business process modeling approaches and diagrams, one could be tempted to ask the question: Why not use several different approaches in combination as a basis for business process redesign and subsequent computer automation projects? After all, some approaches seem to be better at highlighting certain aspects of a business process than others. This is indeed advisable in some cases, since the likely outcome is a very complete and multifaceted view of the business process in question. However, it may be problematic in some situations.

The problem with using different approaches in combination is that business process redesign and automation projects usually are not very successful if it takes too long for the project team to complete their work. And, taking too long to generate a model, the business process being targeted for redesign is likely to extend the duration of a business process redesign project beyond what is acceptable.

A recent study of several business process redesign projects conducted by *CIO Magazine*, a leading publication among information technology executives, suggests that the optimal duration of business process redesign projects is somewhere around 3 months, not considering the time to implement the business process changes.

If time were not a constraint and plenty of it were available, it would probably be okay to look at a business process from several different angles. This would be enabled by the use of several different business process modeling approaches and diagrams. However, the reality of business projects in most organizations is often different.

Most business processes cut across two or more departments, which essentially means that a cross-departmental team will often have to be put together for just about any business process redesign project. The cross-departmental team will have to identify problems associated with the business process, as well as clearly delineate the process's boundaries; otherwise, the team may embark in an open-ended project that will never be completed. Then, the team will have to understand the business process in some detail, propose changes in it, and investigate ways in which those changes could be implemented using information technologies.

Arguably, it is very difficult to accomplish all of the above in approximately 3 months if several different business process modeling approaches and diagrams are used. An alternative, which is probably advisable in most business process redesign projects, is for business process redesign teams to choose one or two approaches at most and stick with them for the duration of their project. Based on the above discussion, it would be reasonable to argue that the communication flow–oriented approach should be chosen, in combination with the holistic approach—the former providing a view of the "trees," so to speak, while the other provides a view of the "forest as a whole."

Review Questions

1. Why do business processes need to be modeled?
   (a) Because they are tangible entities that need to be understood in the same way by several people to be successfully improved.
   (b) Because they are abstract entities that need to be understood in the same way by several people to be successfully improved.
   (c) Because they are abstract entities that do not need to be understood in the same way by several people to be successfully improved.
   (d) Because they are abstract entities that do not need to be understood more or less in the same way by several people to be successfully improved.

2. Which of the following statements does not refer to a difference between the business process and chair concepts?
   (a) The former is a concept that refers to an abstract entity.
   (b) The latter is a concept that refers to a tangible entity.
   (c) Both are concepts that refer to abstract entities.
   (d) One of them is a concept that refers to an abstract entity; the other is not.

3. In the communication flow–oriented approach proposed here:
   (a) A rectangular shape represents an entity that may send or receive information, knowledge, or both.
   (b) A rectangular shape represents an activity that may carry information, knowledge, or both.
   (c) A rectangular shape represents an activity that may lead to the exchange of information, knowledge, or both.
   (d) A rectangular shape represents a repository of information, knowledge, or both.

4. In the communication flow–oriented approach proposed here, a number on the upper right corner of a rectangular shape does not represent:
   (a) The approximate order of execution of an activity in relation to the other activities in the same business process representation.
   (b) The most likely order of execution of an activity in relation to the other activities in the same business process representation.
   (c) The approximate order of execution of an activity, from an activity flow perspective, in relation to the other activities in the same business process representation.
   (d) The approximate order of storage of information in an activity in relation to the other activities in the same business process representation.

5. Data flow diagrams have been developed primarily to:
   (a) Represent business process activities as they would most likely be after computer automation.
   (b) Represent business processes as they would most likely be with computer automation.
   (c) Represent data tables and relationships as they would most likely be after computer automation.
   (d) Represent business processes in such a way that makes it very easy to identify all possible opportunities for redesign.

6. Which of the statements below describes a relationship that cannot be represented through data flow diagrams without breaking widely accepted diagramming rules?
   (a) An assistant manager downloading a complaint from the Web.
   (b) A manager processing a complaint downloaded from the Web.
   (c) A knowledge repository containing complaint review rules.
   (d) A manager processing a complaint received in paper form.

7. Activity flow–oriented approaches:
   (a) Are the most commonly used in business process redesign.
   (b) Are the least commonly used in business process redesign.
   (c) Are not discussed by J. Harrington in his book *Business Process Improvement*.
   (d) Are often perceived as being among the hardest to generate, and certainly harder to generate than communication flow diagrams.

8. Which of the following symbols is not used in business process representations generated through functional flowcharting?
   (a) A rectangular shape.
   (b) An arrow.
   (c) A column containing one or more activities.
   (d) A drumlike shape.

9. The unified modeling language (UML):
   (a) Is a set of standard notations for object-oriented analysis and design that was developed with the goal of unifying the methodologies developed by Ivar Jacobson, Grady Booch, and Al Gore.
   (b) Is a set of standard notations for object-oriented analysis and design that was developed with the goal of unifying three existing methodologies.
   (c) Is a set of standard notations for object-oriented analysis and design that was developed with the goal of unifying data flow diagram notations developed by DeMarco and Yourdon.
   (d) Is a set of standard notations for systems analysis and design that was developed with the goal of unifying the diagramming techniques developed by Gane and Sarson.

10. Which of the following statements is not consistent with the interpretation of the holistic systems view discussed in this chapter?
   (a) It provides little in terms of details about the inner workings of a business process.
   (b) It contributes to one's understanding of business processes in terms of broad elements that characterize them.
   (c) It provides more in terms of details about the inner workings of a business process than most activity flow–oriented views.
   (d) It can be used in the redesign of business processes.

Discussion Questions

1. Develop a textual description of a business process like the one in the section describing the predictive car maintenance process of a rental company in this chapter. The business process example you will develop should be of a company outside the car rental industry and should be as realistic as possible.

2. Develop a communication flow–oriented representation of the business process example you developed in response to Discussion Question 1, using the related diagram symbols previously discussed in this chapter. Also, develop a data flow diagram of the business process example you developed in Discussion Question 1, using the data flow diagram symbols previously discussed in this chapter in connection with the traditional systems analysis and design approach to business process modeling. What are the differences between the two representations? How could those differences affect the outcomes of a business process redesign project targeting the business process example you developed?

3. Develop an activity flow–oriented representation of the business process example you developed in response to discussion Question 1, using the related diagram symbols previously discussed in this chapter. Compare it with the communication flow–oriented representation you developed in Discussion Question 2. What are the differences between the two representations? How could those differences affect the outcomes of a business process redesign project targeting the business process example you developed?

4. Develop an object-oriented representation of the business process example you developed in response to Discussion Question 1, using the use-case diagram symbols previously discussed in this chapter in connection with object-oriented approaches. Compare that representation with the communication flow–oriented representation you developed in Discussion Question 2. What are the differences between the two representations? How could those differences affect the outcomes of a business process redesign project targeting the business process example you developed?

5. Develop another textual description of a business process example like the one you generated in response to Discussion Question 1, but based on a different business process of your choice. Generate a representation of the new business process example using the object-oriented approach discussed in this chapter. Redesign the business process developed here and the one developed in response to Discussion Question 1. For the latter, use the communication flow–oriented representation. The goal of the redesign should be to reduce process costs. You don't have to use specific redesign guidelines—just use your common sense. Generate business process representations of the redesigned processes. In your opinion, did the difference in modeling approaches used affect the effectiveness of the business process redesign outcomes? Explain your answer.

PART III

Changing Business Processes

Part III Case:
IBM Global Financing's
Credit Issuance Process

BM Global Financing (IBM-GF) is a fully owned subsidiary of International Business Machines Corporation (IBM). IBM is an Armonk, New York–based global information technology company. IBM-GF provides lease and loan financing to external and internal IBM customers, usually through contracts involving repayment in 2 to 5 years. It was previously called IBM Credit Corporation.

In its early years, IBM-GF provided financing services through a business process that was rather cumbersome. The process started when an IBM sales representative was near closing a deal for the sale of an IBM product or service. IBM sold computers, software, and many information technology–related services (e.g., integration of different software applications, technology consulting, and outsourcing). Much like a car salesperson, the IBM sales representative would call in with a request for financing from IBM-GF on behalf of the customer. The person taking in the call would then write down the details of the request and send that to the Credit Department.

Upon receipt of a financing request, a credit specialist in the Credit Department would enter the request's details into a computer system. The credit history of the requestor would then be checked, as well as the potential customer's ability to repay the borrowed amount. Some calculations based on the basic information provided by the potential customer would be used for the latter. For example, in the case of a privately held company interested in buying IBM products or services on credit, useful information would be the company's revenues, cash flow, and profitability.

Once the credit specialist was done with the credit checks, he or she would write the results down on a piece of paper and send it to IBM-GF's Business Practices Department, which would in turn prepare a "loan covenant." A loan covenant is an agreement between the borrower and the lender where the borrower agrees to fulfill certain responsibilities and refrain from certain acts (e.g., incurring further debts beyond a certain level). The loan covenant would be prepared based on a standard template, and using a specialized computer system.

Once the request had been processed by the Business Practices Department, it would go to a pricing specialist, who would enter the request details into a spreadsheet. The output would be the recommended interest rate to be charged from the customer, which the pricing specialist would then write down on a piece of paper and send to an administrative assistant. The administrative assistant would then prepare a quote letter that would be delivered to the sales representative via Federal Express.

The entire business process took on average 6 days to be completed. Sometimes it would take as long as 2 weeks. Many sales representations were unhappy with the length of time that the process took to be completed. It essentially gave the potential customer on average 6 full days to think through the deal, possibly finding another lender (e.g., a bank), or call the whole deal off due to "buyer's remorse." Compounding the long wait time was the fact that whenever the sales representative called in to ask about the status of the financing request, rarely could anyone give a quick answer. The request was usually buried somewhere within the process awaiting action.

It became clear that something had to be done to improve the process. Initially, one solution was to create a control desk function that would track the request through the process and inform sales representatives about each request's status. While that solved the problem of the sales representative not knowing the status of his or her request, it added more time to the processing of requests, since the several members of the process team (credit specialist, pricing specialist, etc.) would have to inform the control desk whenever a request reached them. Now the processing time was increased to 7 days on average.

Eventually, senior managers at IBM-GF did a full analysis of the credit issuance process. They found out that, when they factored out the amount of time the financing request was sitting on the different specialists' desks awaiting processing, the total time needed to fully process a financing request was only 90 minutes. Moreover, their analysis strongly suggested that all activities in the process could be almost completely automated and carried out by a generalist, since they involved very standardized procedures. Only in a few cases was a specialist's intervention actually needed.

The process was redesigned so as to completely eliminate handoffs. Now, only one person, a generalist, would take the financing request through all the steps of the credit issuance process. The generalist would do that using a computer system that incorporated the functionality of the previously separate computer systems used by the several specialists involved in the process. In the special cases in which the generalist did not have the knowledge to proceed with the processing of a financing request, he or she would consult with a specialist.

This redesign led to an extraordinary improvement in the overall performance of the process. The previous 7-day turnaround time was reduced to only 4 hours. Because specialists would not now be involved in processing all financing requests, fewer specialists were needed. That is, there was a reduction in head count and thus in overall process costs. Finally, the number of financing requests that the new process would be able to handle increased 100 times, and the level of satisfaction experienced by customers and sales representatives was substantially increased.

Sources

Hammer, M. (1990). Reengineering work: Don't automate, obliterate. *Harvard Business Review,* *68*(4), 104–114.

Hammer, M., & Champy, J. (1993). *Reengineering the corporation.* New York: Harper Business.

IBM Global Financing Web site: http://www-1.ibm.com/financing/us/

CHAPTER 6

Selecting a Target for Successful Business Process Redesign

Selecting business processes that are amenable to successful redesign at a given point in time is not a trivial task. Local business processes, that is, processes whose activities are contained in one single department or area and which are being considered for small changes, are less of a problem than cross-departmental processes being targeted for radical redesign. The argument can be made that local business processes can be improved in an incremental way and that doing so is a relatively low-risk endeavor.

In fact, conducting continuous and incremental business process redesign is always a good idea. Not only does this hold the promise of bringing about improvements in the quality and productivity of the processes targeted, but it also promotes knowledge sharing among business process team members. Knowledge sharing among those who carry out a business process, in turn, tends to improve business process efficiency by reducing the need to exchange knowledge at process execution time. As previously discussed and further emphasized later in this book, exchanging knowledge is generally more difficult and time-consuming than exchanging information.

The picture may not be so rosy for all types of business process redesign projects, though. The higher the degree of change sought, the greater are usually the risks involved in not being successful. More radical business process redesign projects, such as those normally referred to as business process reengineering projects, usually involve broader processes that cut across more business areas. Consequently, those projects affect more people and have a higher number of stakeholders. Moreover, those projects typically involve higher implementation costs as well, often in the form of more expensive resource reallocation, technology implementation, and training initiatives.

Not all business processes can be successfully redesigned in a major way. This chapter discusses techniques to select business processes. The techniques are particularly useful in major redesign projects, which are normally those redesign efforts that target broad cross-departmental business processes. This chapter also discusses key business process selection considerations such as cost-benefit analyses results, level of support from management, and degree of employee resistance, as well as factors that influence process "rigidity." Among those rigidity factors are regulations (e.g., those found in government processes) and expensive workflow automation technologies previously implemented (which can be a major source of resistance due to the personal and financial investments attached to them).

Identifying Problems First

Whether a business process redesign project is of the incremental or the radical type, it is hard to convince anyone of the importance of the project without first identifying problems with the business process. Most people will resist attempts to change a business process that is apparently working well. Thus, it is important to identify organizational problems first, and then select a business process for redesign based on the problems. The problems may refer to productivity or quality issues.

In the identification of organizational problems, the business process redesign practitioner is likely to find another obstacle when asking people about productivity and quality-related problems. Many organizational members are unlikely to admit to problems in their areas. And, if they do, their managers may deny the existence of problems. One reasonably effective way of overcoming this initial barrier is to refer to problems not as "problems" but as "opportunities for improvement." This is a softer, more benign term, which will usually elicit the same types of responses as the "P word," without the same level of resistance.

Let us illustrate the problem identification step through an example involving the facilitation of the work of a redesign group targeting a high-enrollment computing course at a university in New Zealand. The university had recently set up a successful advanced computer literacy course. The course covered a number of software applications, including e-mail, group decision support systems, Internet Web browsers, word processors, spreadsheets, and database management systems.

While successful, with about 100 enrollments per semester, the course had recently been the focus of an avalanche of student complaints, which were perceived by management as negatively affecting the university's image. Most of the complaints were linked to the frequent computer problems that were being experienced by students when trying to run their practical course assignments in the computer laboratory.

The person most directly involved with the practical component of the course was the course tutor, who was responsible for practical demonstrations in a computer laboratory during the time slots assigned for the course. Both students and management had urged the course tutor to come up with innovative solutions to reduce or eliminate the computer problems experienced by students. His first step was to bring together members of the two departments directly involved in the practical component of the course, a computer support department and an academic department.

Those members were initially reluctant to meet and discuss the problems because of previous conflicts between the two departments, who blamed each other for the problems in the course. However, they eventually agreed to participate in the business process redesign group led by the course tutor when they knew that the discussion would take place through an e-mail–based electronic collaboration system. The electronic mediation was perceived by most of those prospective members as likely to lead to a less formal and less confrontational discussion, different from what would in their view likely happen in face-to-face meetings.

The group leader posted a message to the group containing a list with eight problems and three business processes, suggested as the main causes of the problems and thus as the target for redesign. This posting was followed by four replies with comments on the leader's message, whose content led to the selection of two business processes for redesign. Those business processes comprised course preparation and delivery activities. The group then went on to discuss and agree on several changes on both business processes.

All changes were implemented either before or during the course semester, and their impact was assessed through a survey of student perceptions about the course. The survey covered most of the points targeted by the business process improvement group, and its results indicated a remarkable improvement in the quality of the course, when compared with the results of a survey performed in the previous semester.

The success of this project was in large part due to the proper identification of problems in the first place. It of course helped that the problems were clearly identifiable (sometimes this is not the case), that they were obviously associated with quality and potentially productivity concerns, and that those problems were seen as needing urgent attention by the university's management because they created an "image issue" for the university as a whole. That is, in the views of several members of the university's management, the course problems were negatively affecting the image of the university as a whole, even though they were restricted to a single course.

Basic Cost-Benefit Analyses

While some business process redesign projects can be started right after the identification of problems and related business processes, others cannot. The redesign projects that can be started right away are typically those aiming at relatively low-cost and incremental changes in small-scope business processes, which is arguably the case of the course redesign project example discussed in the previous section.

The business process redesign projects that cannot usually be started right after the identification of problems are typically those targeting broad processes for major redesign, chiefly because of the magnitude, risks, and possible costs involved in those projects. In those cases, analyses of costs and benefits of the redesign effort are necessary to build the required management and employee support for the business process redesign project. More often than not, the benefits must significantly outweigh the costs, even if in a subjective way, for the business process redesign project to get the "go-ahead." Tables 6.1 and 6.2 show simple estimates of costs and benefits for a business process redesign project involving the warehousing of products of an online electronics store.

The costs estimate in Table 6.1 assumes that the business process redesign group will have five members. Four of those members will be internal to the organization, namely the project manager, warehouse manager, warehouse assistant manager, and inventory coordinator. The other member, the project facilitator, will be a consultant hired from outside the organization. The costs estimate in Table 6.1 also assumes that the business process redesign group will come up with a redesign proposal report in 12 weeks, for which it will have six face-to-face meetings (and thus travel and accommodation expenses) and six teleconferencing meetings (and thus specific communication costs). The travel and teleconferencing expenses are related to the participation of the project facilitator. The other members work in different offices of the same building, which makes it easy for them to get together face-to-face. It is also assumed that e-mail and the Web will be used for communication between meetings and document sharing, respectively. With the exception of the organization's teleconferencing room, which is budgeted for separately, the use of the organization's technology infrastructure (e.g., telephones, e-mail, local and wide area networks, Web servers) and clerical resources (e.g., secretaries, webmaster) is

Table 6.1   Costs Estimate for a Business Process Redesign Project

AA	Personnel wages	
AA1	Project manager (12 wk × 10 hr × $100)	$12,000.00
AA2	Warehouse manager (12 wk × 4 hr × $50)	$2,400.00
AA3	Warehouse assistant manager (12 wk × 4 hr × $25)	$1,200.00
AA4	Inventory coordinator (12 wk × 20 hr × $20)	$960.00
AB	Total personnel wages (total for AA)	$16,560.00
AC	Fringe benefits (25% of AB)	$4,140.00
AD	Total personnel	$20,700.00
AE	Consultant services	
AE1	Project facilitator (12 wk × 10 hr × $250)	$30,000.00
AF	Total consultant services (total for AE)	$30,000.00
B	Equipment/software (dedicated laptop)	$2,500.00
C	Materials and supplies (disks, books)	$500.00
E	Travel and accommodation (6 mtgs × [$150 hotel + $500 fare])	$3,900.00
F	Communication costs (6 teleconf × $300)	$1,800.00
O	Total direct project costs (AD + AF + B + C + E + F)	$59,400.00
P	Overhead (25% of O)	$14,850.00
Total project costs		*$74,250.00*

Table 6.2   Benefits Estimate for a Business Process Redesign Project

AA	**Productivity gains**	
AA1	Warehouse space reduction and related savings (per year)	$50,000.00
AA2	Improved cash flow and related gains (1% of revenues per year)	$1,000,000.00
AB	**Total productivity gains**	**$1,050,000.00**
BB	**Quality gains**	
BB1	Shorter order-to-delivery time	N/A
BB	**Total quality gains**	**N/A**
	Total project gains (productivity and quality)	***$1,050,000.00***

covered by the overhead of 25 percent applied to the total of the direct costs involved in the project. This is a typical and reasonable overhead percentage for most projects, with higher numbers being used in certain types of projects—for example, universities often charge 50 percent in overhead for research projects, particularly projects financed by research organizations such as the U.S. National Science Foundation.

The internal personnel listed in Table 6.1 are salaried employees. Many organizations will not explicitly consider salaried employees when developing the cost items of a business process redesign project, sort of pretending that salaried employees are paid whether they work on the project or not. The assumption is that assigning them to a business process redesign project will lead to no extra costs for the organization. This of course overlooks the fact that, if the organization makes good use of its human resources, reassigning a salaried employee from a revenue-producing activity (e.g., order delivery) to a support activity in a business process redesign project will have some negative impact on the organization's revenues. This type of oversight can easily happen, which is why it is important to be as thorough as possible when estimating the costs of a business process redesign project.

In the estimates of benefits shown in Table 6.2, there are two items that account for productivity gains. One of those items refers to $50,000 per year in savings from the reduction of warehouse space needed, and related cost reductions. Examples of those cost reductions are lower rent, if the warehouse is rented, and lower utility bills, due to the need to maintain appropriate temperatures in a smaller area. The other item related to productivity gains is a $1 million increase in gains from an improved cash flow, which assumes that the new redesigned warehousing process will increase inventory turnaround in approximately 50 percent. That means that the organization's cash flow situation will improve substantially, since the time between the electronic item getting to the warehouse and being sent to customers will decrease, and so will the amount of the organization's cash "parked" at the warehouse—in the form of inventory. This better cash flow situation can be taken advantage of by the organization in a number of ways, one of which is a better cash investment strategy. Since the organization in our example has $100 million in yearly revenues, it is estimated that the improved cash flow situation will lead to gains of about 1 percent of total yearly revenues, or $1 million.

Of course, some benefits may not be as easily quantifiable as some costs, as indicated by the "N/A" (not available) estimates for quality gains in Table 6.2. Nevertheless, those benefits should also be mentioned, even if they cannot be quantified. It is important to stress that, in most projects, it is a good idea for the project manager (who is usually responsible for cost-benefit analyses) to be very honest about all the costs and benefits up front. Hidden costs can be a major problem in a project, and eventually, those costs may lead a project to be dropped, with the foreseeable negative career consequences for those in charge of the project.

Early on in business process redesign projects, some of the costs may not be that clear, either. However, one thing to bear in mind at this stage of a business process redesign project is that it is usually a good idea to separate costs associated with the business process redesign task from costs associated with the full implementation of the redesign. This was done above. No new information technology implementation costs were mentioned, and those would obviously kick in when the new redesign changes were to be implemented. This should, of course, be mentioned to whoever is reviewing the cost-benefit analysis. It is very hard to estimate implementation costs before the business process redesign is complete. As mentioned before in this book, business process redesign projects may lead to radical changes in how the organization operates, which may even include the outsourcing of an entire division of a company, and the creation of new divisions. Therefore, implementation of business process changes can vary widely in terms of approach used, and thus, implementation costs are very difficult to estimate in advance.

Costs associated with the business process redesign task involve primarily the costs associated with analyzing and redesigning a business process from a conceptual perspective. The costs associated with the full implementation of the redesign may involve substantially higher expenses, which could comprise hardware, software, consulting, and training expenses associated with automating activities in the new, redesigned business process.

So, from a cost-benefit analysis perspective, a much more attractive picture can be put forth for consideration by management (the group of people that typically approve spending) for business process redesign, looked at from a conceptual standpoint, than for the actual implementation of business process redesign decisions and recommendations. But that picture should be tempered with warnings that the implementation costs are yet to come. In the aforementioned example, if the new process implementation costs were to amount to $500,000 and if the forecasted gains were to be fully realized, the total cost-benefit picture after implementation would still be very attractive. The project would pay for itself and generate about a half-million-dollar gain on top of that in the first year after the implementation of the business process redesign changes.

Support From Management

As previously discussed in this book, the business process reengineering approach was first proposed around the early 1990s, in two main "flavors," or versions. One of the initial versions of reengineering was more radical, was proposed as a replacement for total quality management, and was less information technology oriented.

Michael Hammer and colleagues proposed that more radical version. The other version of reengineering was less radical, was proposed as a complement to total quality management, and relied more heavily on the use of information technology. This version's main proponents were Thomas Davenport and colleagues.

The business process reengineering idea spread like fire in the 1990s, perhaps more than any other business idea before it. However, by the end of the 1990s, the word "reengineering" became synonymous with failure, with other more benign views of it gravitating around that of an ineffective business fad. Two of the key reasons for that were the number of reported cases of failed reengineering projects in the business and academic literature and a widely cited study by James Champy, one of the original developers of the reengineering idea. Champy's study pointed at a 70 percent failure rate for business process reengineering projects.

There have been many studies of successful and failed reengineering projects conducted with the goal of identifying success and failure factors. One of the key reasons for failure, according to many of those studies, is lack of management support. Much of the business process redesign facilitation practice strongly supports that finding. Without strong management support, it is very difficult to impart change to an organization. There are many reasons for this, with one of the most important being that most people's initial reaction to change suggestions is a somewhat blind resistance to the changes.

Now, assume that a business process redesign group has selected a business process that they want to target for redesign. What level and degree of management support do they need? The answer to that question is that, more often than not, they need very strong support from who is often referred to as the business process "owner" and from the level of management immediately above him or her (i.e., above the business process owner). The business process owner is the individual responsible for the outcomes of the business process. Take, for example, the food preparation process of a restaurant. The owner of that process is the restaurant's chef, who coordinates the work of his or her team of cooks.

A few years ago, a consultant facilitated the redesign of a computer help desk process at a relatively large company—$3 billion–plus in yearly revenues. The business process owner was the help desk manager, who was willing to redesign the computer help desk process because of the many systemic problems with the process. For example, computer problems requiring a high level of expertise in certain areas, such as computer networking, were routinely assigned to the wrong people, causing serious delays in their effective solution. The computer help desk process involved, directly and indirectly, about 20 individuals. A business process redesign group was put together. However, the support of the help desk manager was not enough to get the business process redesign project off the ground, primarily because several of the computer experts who helped solve computer problems reported to the help desk manager only on a part-time basis. There was a need to obtain strong support from the next level of authority, namely the chief information officer of the company. Once that support was gained, all of the employees involved in the computer help desk process bought into the redesign idea, and the business process redesign project was completed successfully.

There seem to be two main reasons why strong management support is needed for business process redesign success. One is the sense of importance that management support gives to a project, in the eyes of the employees who will participate in and/or be affected by the outcomes of the business process redesign project. The other reason is the apparent assurance that comes from management support that the resources necessary to carry out the business process redesign and implement the new process will be made available. After all, no one wants to propose redesign changes that will eventually be ignored.

Employee Resistance

While management support may go a long way in reducing employee resistance to a business process redesign initiative, unfortunately that is not always the case. And, if there is strong employee resistance to a redesign project, that project will most likely fail—for the simple reason that those who would supposedly execute the activities of the new process will simply refuse to do so. This is particularly true in organizations where employees are unionized and in organizations where employees participate in organizational governance committees. Organizations as varied as large automakers and agricultural cooperatives have governance committees. Some organizational governance committees have enough power to be able to oust a chief executive officer or a chairman of the board.

For example, in a large business process redesign project, the target for redesign was one of the core processes of a civil construction company—the process whereby civil construction projects were planned and managed. That redesign project touched virtually all areas of the construction company, which happened to have a strong labor union. And the labor union was deeply opposed to the redesign project.

This complex and problematic situation was solved like many similar situations are. First, the business process redesign group obtained strong management support, which was in large part there already, since it had been the construction company's chief executive officer who championed the business process redesign project in the first place. The next challenge was to make the business process redesign project attractive to the employees as a whole, and particularly to key employees who were very influential within the union. That was achieved by setting aside a budget to provide training, financial rewards, flexible time, and a variety of other benefits to the employees. All of those benefits were, in one way or another, tied to the employees' participation in the business process redesign project.

Employee resistance to changes brought about by business process redesign is often motivated by those employees' lack of involvement in the change decisions. This is particularly true in organizations where employees are expected to have a say in major organizational change decisions. Examples of those organizations are universities, where administrators (e.g., the president, provost, and deans) are expected to share the university governance with certain elected employee groups (e.g., the faculty senate). In these types of situations, the involvement of employees in business process redesign decisions is very important for the successful implementation of those decisions.

While not as common as employee resistance, major business process redesign projects may face resistance from outside groups. One example of such outside groups is that of shareholders. In fact, shareholder activism seems to have increased since the 1990s, which has created some difficulties for senior executives to implement much needed organization changes in several companies. The senior management teams of companies like Hewlett-Packard, Computer Associates, Disney, and even Microsoft have had to face serious scrutiny from shareholder groups before having major organizational changes approved and implemented. Typically, shareholder concerns can be addressed only by carefully developed and convincingly positive cost-benefit analyses.

Business Process Rigidity

Let us assume that a business process redesign group appropriately identifies organizational problems and business process boundaries, develops a carefully prepared and convincing cost-benefit analysis, gains support from management, and successfully eliminates all sources of employee resistance. Even then, there is still something that can prevent successful business process redesign, something that is referred to here as business process "rigidity."

Business process rigidity is essentially a systemic resistance to change, which is inherent to a business process and often unrelated to what management and employees think about the idea of redesigning the business process in question. There are many factors that may influence the degree of rigidity of a business process. One of the factors is the amount of previous investment in information technology used to automate the business process. The higher that investment, the less likely it is that business process redesign will be considered, because of the possibility that redesign changes will require new information technologies to be implemented and thus prevent the previous information technology investment from yielding the expected return. For example, if a company invests $1 million in a computer system to automate a business process, it is unlikely that it will consider that business process a good target for radical redesign—unless the redesign changes can be implemented with the same system, which unfortunately is not very often what happens in real business process projects.

In a 1998 article titled "Government Transformation and Structural Rigidity: Redesigning a Service Acquisition Process" published in the journal *Acquisition Review Quarterly,* two other factors are identified as very strong determinants of business process rigidity. The article is based on a study of business process redesign practices, particularly in highly regulated organizations. The two rigidity factors are presented as interacting with each other, and the article shows evidence that it is their combination that arguably leads to the highest levels of business process rigidity. One of those factors is the degree of legal regulation in connection with a business process. The other is the degree of functional heterogeneity in connection with a business process.

The degree of legal regulation affecting a business process is directly related to the degree of government regulation regarding the business process; that is, the more the government is involved, the more laws exist regulating a particular type of organizational endeavor. For example, the new drug development process carried out by large pharmaceutical companies in the United States is a highly regulated process, with many of the regulations enforced by government agencies such as the U.S. Food and Drug Administration.

A consultant once facilitated a business process redesign group at a large pharmaceutical company in New Jersey that tried to radically redesign a new drug development process. The final result was that the group was able to make very small changes in the process, because most redesign ideas that they came up with clashed with government regulations. Those ideas could not be implemented without legal violations that would most certainly subject the company to heavy fines and sanctions. Some of the regulations that affected the new drug development process made a lot of sense and were in place to protect consumers. Other regulations were simply unnecessary and out of sync with the times—for example, regulations regarding certain types of paperwork that prevented computer-based routing of documents and use of electronic signatures.

Another pattern that is suggested by several consultants' past experience conducting and facilitating business process redesign projects is that the level of business process rigidity increases when a high degree of regulation affects a business process that also has a high degree of functional heterogeneity. The degree of functional heterogeneity of a business process can be measured by counting the number of different organizational functions or teams involved in the execution of the process (e.g., help desk manager, chief information officer, networking team). Functional heterogeneity in organizational processes has been found to be highly correlated with the number of knowledge specialization areas involved in business processes, that is, the number of different types of expertise required to perform the business process. For example, a business process aimed at developing a new car model likely has a higher degree of functional heterogeneity (i.e., more people with different kinds of expertise involved in the process) than a business process aimed at preparing a hamburger at a fast food restaurant.

Demands for high functional heterogeneity lead to a high number of functional roles in business processes, which then often become the focal point around which legal regulation is created and passed. A good example here is the legal prescription that budgets of large civil construction projects be prepared by a group of "recognized experts," and the related criteria prescribed by law to identify and hire those experts. Legal regulation solidifies the procedures involving each one of the organizational functions performing business process activities, turning each organizational function into a potential focus of resistance against process change, especially change of a radical nature.

Summary and Concluding Remarks

This chapter identified several elements that can be used to select business processes for redesign so that the probability of success of the redesign project is maximized. One of those elements is a set of problems that are caused by a business process and whose level of annoyance is high enough to motivate employees and managers to spend the time and effort necessary to redesign the business process that is at the source of the problems. The more urgent the problems that are seen by managers and employees, the higher is the priority that will be given to a business process redesign effort.

Other important elements used to select business processes for redesign are the cost-benefit comparison and management support associated with the redesign project. If costs significantly outweigh benefits, then it is probably a good idea to forget about redesigning the business process in question and to move on to a different business process. Similarly, if there is not enough management support for a business process redesign project, then it is better to move on to another business process project with greater management appeal.

Another important element that can be used to select business processes for successful redesign is the level of employee resistance to change associated with a business process. Employee resistance can be reduced or eliminated by making the business process redesign project attractive to employees through various kinds of social and work-related rewards. However, sometimes that is not possible because the management is not willing to commit the necessary resources or make the required concessions—for example, management is not willing to set aside a budget to provide training, financial rewards, and other benefits to the employees. In those cases, it is probably a good idea to move on to a business process where employee resistance is very low or nonexistent.

Business process rigidity is also an element that plays a key role in the selection of business processes for successful redesign. Business process rigidity is essentially a systemic resistance to change that is associated with a number of factors. Among those factors, the most important are the amount of previous investment in information technology used to automate the business process, the degree of legal regulation in connection with the business process, and the degree of functional heterogeneity in connection with the business process. Particularly resistant to change are business processes where a high degree of legal regulation is combined with a high degree of functional heterogeneity. Those business processes will not change unless changes in legal regulations occur first. The latter are notoriously difficult to accomplish, usually requiring strong political connections, deep pockets, and years of lobbying.

Review Questions

1. Why is it difficult to obtain appropriate answers when asking people about productivity and quality-related problems involving their departments or areas?

   (a) Many organizational members are unlikely to admit to problems in sales departments.

   (b) Many organizational members are unlikely to admit to problems regarding issues outside their main topics of expertise.

   (c) Many organizational members are unlikely to admit to problems in other people's areas.

   (d) Many organizational members are unlikely to admit to problems in their areas.

2. What costs are not usually included in initial cost-benefit analyses of business process redesign projects?
   (a) The costs associated with any information technologies used in the business process redesign effort.
   (b) The costs associated with conducting business process redesign meetings.
   (c) The costs associated with implementing the redesigned business process.
   (d) The costs associated with overhead expenses, such as clerical support.

3. What immediate levels of management support does a business process redesign group need to be successful?
   (a) The group needs support from the business process "owner" and the level of management immediately above that of the process "owner."
   (b) The group needs decisive and unequivocal support from the chief executive officer and the chief information officer.
   (c) The group absolutely needs strong support from the chief executive officer, the chief information officer, and, most importantly, the chief business process redesign officer.
   (d) The group needs decisive and unequivocal support from the chief shareholder lobbyist, particularly in privately owned companies, and the chief information officer.

4. Which among the options below is not a good way of reducing employee resistance to business process redesign?
   (a) Carefully preparing cost-benefit analyses that convincingly show a positive return from business process redesign–related market share expansion.
   (b) Carefully preparing cost-benefit analyses that convincingly show a likely positive return from business process redesign–related layoffs and organizational downsizing.
   (c) Carefully preparing cost-benefit analyses that convincingly show a positive return from business process redesign in terms of revenue expansion and increased worker flexibility brought about by telecommuting opportunities.
   (d) Carefully preparing cost-benefit analyses that convincingly show a positive return from business process redesign associated with a variety of employee rewards and new personnel benefits.

5. Business process rigidity is positively correlated with:
   (a) The degree of legal regulation affecting a business process.
   (b) The lack of functional heterogeneity of a business process.
   (c) The combination of process-embedded information technology resources and the lack of government regulation affecting a business process.
   (d) The ratio between the degree of legal regulation affecting a business process and the degree of functional heterogeneity of the business process.

Discussion Questions

1. Develop a detailed scenario that involves a business process in a nonprofit organization (e.g., a university, a social services–related government agency, a faith-based organization) and a series of problems associated with the business process. Develop a basic cost-benefit analysis for a project aimed at redesigning the business process.

2. Expand the scenario in Discussion Question 1 (without completely modifying it) to include elements that would suggest a lack of management support and unionized employee resistance. Develop a set of integrated solutions to address the problems associated with the lack of management support and unionized employee resistance.

3. Expand the scenario resulting from Discussion Question 2 (without completely modifying it) to include elements that would add so much rigidity to the business process that it would be impossible to successfully redesign it. Suggest what you think would be needed to bring about changes in the business process by using your creativity and trying to think in broad terms (including nationwide changes in the law, if necessary).

CHAPTER 7

Representing Information and Knowledge in Business Processes

Previously in this book, we operationally defined the concepts of data, information, and knowledge. That was done because those concepts are widely used in the business literature with myriad meanings and also because those concepts are too important for this book to be used in a loose way, which is more often than not what happens when they are not at least operationally defined. According to the operational definitions presented earlier, data are used to store and convey information and knowledge, information is eminently descriptive, and knowledge is eminently associative.

Previous chapters also discussed the apparently irreversible trend toward knowledge fragmentation. It was pointed out in those chapters that knowledge exists in organizations in a dispersed way and that knowledge is predominantly held by the individuals who perform business process activities. Over time, business process–related knowledge seems to be increasingly becoming more voluminous and complex, as competition drives products (e.g., car engines, health insurance services) into becoming more elaborate and complex. As knowledge becomes more voluminous and complex, so does the need for knowledge specialization by individuals.

Earlier chapters also put forth the notion that communication flow models of business processes are particularly useful tools for business process redesign and discussed how those models could be generated. A set of symbols was proposed that can be used to represent data sources and destinations, information repositories, knowledge repositories, data flows, and activities.

This chapter takes a few additional steps in clarifying certain issues in connection with techniques for modeling and analyzing the flow of information and the distribution of knowledge (or expertise) in business processes. The chapter proposes an approach to differentiate between the flows of information and of knowledge in a business process, addresses the difference in communication media requirements for information and knowledge communication, presents rules for coming up with the appropriate size of a communication flow diagram, and discusses how to break down large business process representations into smaller ones.

Representing the Flow of Knowledge in a Business Process

Previously in this book, the example of a predictive car maintenance process at a rental company was used to illustrate different business process modeling approaches and related diagrams. One of those approaches was the communication flow–oriented approach, proposed in this book as the one likely to lead to the best business process redesign results in most circumstances.

The diagramming technique discussed in connection with the communication flow–oriented approach earlier in this book did not incorporate all of the necessary elements for the representation of knowledge flow. The necessary elements for the representation of knowledge repositories were discussed there, but not those for the representation of knowledge flow. Figure 7.1 shows an example of the communication

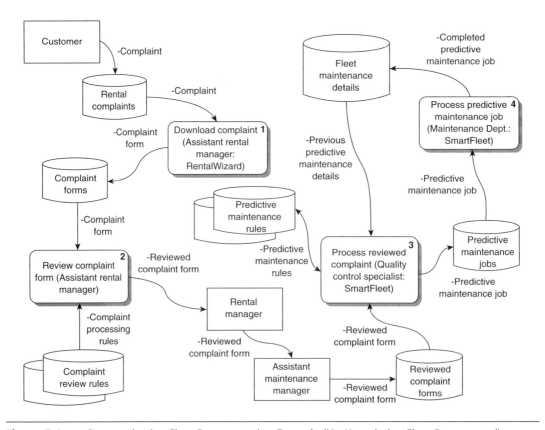

Figure 7.1   Communication Flow Representation Example (No Knowledge Flow Represented)

flow–oriented diagramming technique discussed earlier in this book (copied from a previous chapter).

Let us briefly review the business process represented through Figure 7.1. It involves obtaining and properly using information from customers of a car rental company about problems with the cars that the rental company rents to its customers. The car problems that are relevant are those that can be prevented in the future through predictive car maintenance, whereby the cars are essentially fixed before the problems actually occur.

The business process starts with a customer entering a complaint online regarding problems with a car. The details of the complaint are stored in an online file of car rental–related complaints. The assistant manager of the rental company then downloads the complaint details using RentalWizard, a Web-based computer system that automatically generates a complaint form to be used for internal processing of the complaint. The assistant manager then places the complaint form in a box for later processing.

The rental company's assistant manager reviews each complaint form using a manual containing several rules for reviewing complaints. Those rules, which incorporate knowledge, were devised so that certain complaints, such as complaints not related to car maintenance problems, could be removed from the process before they progressed any further—since they would not likely be solved through that particular process. Upon completion of the review of each complaint form, the assistant manager hand delivers each reviewed complaint form to the rental company's manager. The rental company's manager, in turn, hand delivers the reviewed complaint form to the assistant maintenance manager, who is the main point of contact for the rental company's manager in the company's maintenance department.

Upon receipt of a reviewed complaint form, the assistant maintenance manager places the form in a box for processing by the quality control specialist, who operates SmartFleet. This is an expensive and elaborate computer system that incorporates artificial intelligence algorithms, which also incorporate knowledge. The algorithms are used to create a schedule of predictive maintenance activities with the goal of reducing maintenance costs to a minimum while also reducing the likelihood of future car problems occurring while the cars are with the customers who rented them.

The quality control specialist then places each printed schedule of predictive maintenance activities in a box with other predictive maintenance jobs. The box is located at the entrance of the workshop used by the maintenance department and is used by a team of mechanics from the maintenance department to process each predictive maintenance job. Whenever a job is completed, the team uses a data entry screen of the SmartFleet computer system to enter the details about the completed job into a fleet maintenance details file.

A simple solution to the problem of representing knowledge flow in a business process such as the one described above is indicated in Figure 7.2. The solution is an adaptation of a solution that was proposed in a 2001 report titled *Redesigning Acquisition Processes: A New Methodology Based on the Flow of Knowledge and Information*, published by the Defense Acquisition University Press, and was subsequently used by branches of the U.S. Department of Defense and several of its contractors. The solution essentially entails explicitly indicating by means of a

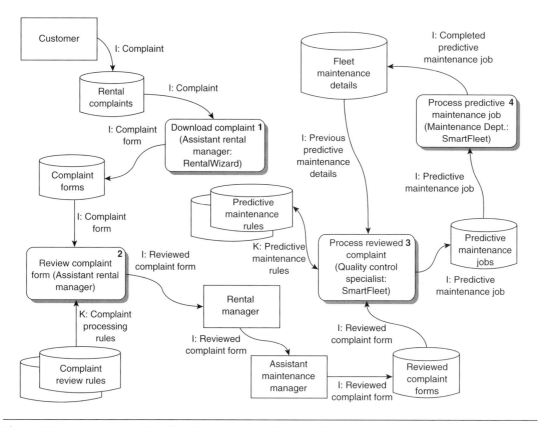

Figure 7.2   Communication Flow Representation Example (Knowledge Flow Represented)

letter (either *I* or *K*) whether a data flow is primarily a flow of information (*I*) or knowledge (*K*).

This solution is fairly simple and complements the differentiation of repositories of information and knowledge through the use of drum shapes, for information repositories, and double drum shapes, for knowledge repositories. The obvious question at this point is, Why is it important to represent knowledge flow in a business process? The reason is the problematic situation created by the flow of knowledge at business process execution time in certain types of business processes, which is discussed in the following section.

Knowledge Communication and Business Process Execution

In many situations, trying to communicate knowledge at business process execution time leads to productivity and quality-related losses. To establish which situations lead to such losses, we first have to distinguish between two generic types of business processes: operational business processes and organizational learning processes.

Operational business processes are those that refer to the operations of an organization and that directly contribute to the creation of goods or services that are responsible for the revenues received by the organization. Operational business processes are usually designed once and then repeated many times to generate wealth by adding value to products that flow through them. For example, a car part assembly-line process is initially put together and then repeated many times, each time producing a car part in a predictable manner. Operational business processes are also frequently redesigned after their initial design to adapt to changes in the economic environment, new technologies, pressures from competitors, and other factors.

Obviously, the frequency of redesign of operational business processes must be much lower than their frequency of execution. For example, for a car assembly-line process that is executed 10 times a day, thus producing 10 cars daily, it is reasonable to assume that the process can be redesigned once or at most twice a year. Redesigning the car assembly-line process five times per year may be too much and may lead to a number of productivity and quality problems, since each new redesign may require halting production temporarily, rewriting manuals, installing new equipment, training workers on the new redesigned procedures, and other related accommodations.

A different type of business process is what is often referred to as a support business process, which essentially is a set of interrelated activities that are aimed at supporting operational business processes. For example, the business process responsible for the maintenance of car part production equipment is a business process that supports the car part assembly-line process, which in turn is an operational business process.

Organizational learning processes are a subtype of the support business process type. Organizational learning processes are usually aimed at knowledge acquisition and sharing. The goal of that knowledge acquisition and sharing is essentially to improve the productivity and outcome quality of operational business processes, although the target of improvement may also be a support business process, including an organizational learning process as well (why simplify something when it can be complicated, right?).

Let us now go back to the original question, which is, Why is it important to represent knowledge flow in business processes? The key reason is that knowledge flow at business process execution time should be minimized in operational business processes, which cannot be achieved if we don't know that it is flowing—hence the need for some form of representation. This assumption is based on past research and experience redesigning business processes. The underlying idea here can be clarified through a basketball game analogy.

The college basketball team run by the University of Connecticut, the Huskies, was arguably a very successful team in 2004, when it won the coveted National Collegiate Athletic Association championship. The Huskies achieved such an honor by carrying out what could be seen as an operational process, the process of playing basketball games against other competing teams, over and over again. Each time the Huskies carried out that game process, they used a number of techniques and strategies, which could be quite complex depending on the opponent and other factors—for example, altitude and thus air pressure in the city they were playing, which could prompt a sequence of substitutions during the game so that certain players would not feel too tired to play at their full potential. Those techniques and strategies most likely involved a great deal of knowledge about what would work under a variety of circumstances.

Saying that knowledge flow should be minimized during the execution of operational businesses processes carried out in a car part factory is analogous to saying that the time to devise basketball game techniques and strategies and train the Huskies' players on them is not when a game is being played, but before that. Even though some learning will take place during a game, the best approach is to impart most of the knowledge in connection with basketball game techniques and strategies on the Huskies' players before the game. This, in turn, is analogous to saying that knowledge flow should take place primarily in organizational learning processes involving the employees of a factory (e.g., equipment operation and car part manufacturing training).

Media Naturalness and Knowledge Communication

Notwithstanding the above discussion, sometimes at least some knowledge must flow during the execution of a business process, and there is no way around that. Therefore, it is important to think of ways in which that flow can be improved as much as possible so that all the knowledge needed at a certain point in a business process flows quickly and smoothly from its source to its destination. While the knowledge source may or may not be an individual (e.g., it may be a printed manual or a computer system), the knowledge destination more often than not will be an individual.

One of the most important considerations in situations when knowledge must flow during the execution of a business process is that regarding the communication medium through which the knowledge will flow. Here, the concept of media naturalness comes into play. Media naturalness refers to the degree of similarity between a given communication medium and the face-to-face communication medium. The more similar the communication medium is to the face-to-face medium, the higher the naturalness of the communication medium in question is.

There are several main elements that define the naturalness of a communication medium, namely the ability of the communication medium to support a sense of colocation; the degree of synchronicity supported by the medium; and the ability of the medium to support communication employing speech, facial expressions, and body language. For example, a shared Web-based virtual work space, with online discussion boards and virtual file cabinets, is more natural than e-mail, because the former provides a higher sense of colocation than the latter. Similarly, a desktop video-conferencing communication system provides a more natural communication medium than a desktop audio-conferencing system, because the former supports communication employing facial expressions, which the latter does not. An instant messaging system is more natural than e-mail, because the instant messaging system supports a higher degree of synchronicity (i.e., same-time interaction) than e-mail.

Recent studies have shown that knowledge communication is better accomplished through media of high naturalness. Let us take, for example, the situation in which an electrical engineer needs to convey complex knowledge about the operation of a robotics device to another peer engineer. Much research suggests that, if effectively conveying that complex knowledge face-to-face took about 30 minutes, it would probably take 5 to 10 times longer, or about 2.5 to 5 hours, to effectively convey the same body of knowledge over e-mail. That additional time and effort would typically be spent in the preparation of e-mail messages, several of which would be clarifications on previous messages, since e-mail communication is usually more ambiguous than face-to-face communication. Finally, the person conveying the knowledge, as opposed to the receiver, would more often than not be the one having to spend most of the additional time and effort involved in effectively communicating the body of knowledge in question.

A low degree of naturalness does not have a significant effect on the quality of the communication when what is being communicated is primarily information. For example, sending someone the location of a particular car part in a warehouse can be done just as effectively via e-mail as it would face-to-face, as long as there is no need to explain or support learning about anything. It seems that the problem is really when we try to explain things over a low naturalness medium.

One may argue that this idea is incompatible with the notion that most of what we learn comes from books like the one you are reading right now. Well, there is no doubt that a great deal of the knowledge we acquire on a daily basis is obtained through books, but that does not mean that we would not acquire the same knowledge just as effectively if we were seated in front of the author and having a face-to-face conversation. Obviously, the costs of interacting face-to-face with each reader would be prohibitive to the book's author, which is why a mass communication medium is used.

Having said the above, let us also look at the following example, involving a computerized individual tax return preparation system called TurboTax (which is used extensively by individuals living in the United States). This system allows individuals to file their tax returns electronically, over the Internet, taking them through the several steps involved in doing so (e.g., entering their wages for the previous year, devising deduction options, entering deductions, calculating credits and refunds). TurboTax incorporates many of the elements of a step-by-step manual on how to prepare a tax return.

A while ago, TurboTax's developer decided to incorporate video clips where experts explained some of the most complex issues involving personal income taxation law, which users particularly liked because that made it much easier for them to understand the complexities associated with certain aspects of personal income taxation law. In doing that, TurboTax's developer in fact increased the naturalness of the medium used to convey complex knowledge, in a way that supports the ideas proposed in this chapter. The ability to see and hear someone, even without the ability to interact in real time with the person, does seem to make it easier for us to understand what the person is trying to explain.

So, if there is no way around having at least some knowledge flowing during the execution of a business process, then it is a good idea to support that flow with communication media incorporating a high degree of naturalness. When designing and implementing communication tools, the information technology manager should bear in mind not only that the degree of naturalness should be as high as possible, but also that other factors must be taken into consideration, such as some of the advantages provided by certain media elements that make them less natural. For example, for people working in different time zones, a low level of synchronicity is very useful, since those people cannot easily interact at the same time, even though it decreases naturalness and thus makes communication of complex knowledge more difficult.

Breaking Down Large Diagrams Into Smaller Ones

What is a large business process diagram? This is an important question, because a business process diagram that is too large will also appear to be very complex to those looking at it, which in turn will lead to a certain level of perplexity by those who are in charge of redesigning the business process. That perplexity will more often than not prevent a business process redesign group from optimally redesigning the business process, since different group members have different kinds of expertise that they bring to bear when suggesting changes in a business process. Without fully understanding how a business process works, at least some of the business process group members will be unable to contribute valuable business process redesign suggestions.

One broad rule regarding the cognitive capacity of human beings in general and that can be used to answer the above question is George Miller's "magical number 7 rule," discussed in detail in his article titled "The Magical Number Seven, Plus or Minus Two: Some Limits on Our Capacity for Processing Information," published in 1956 by the journal *The Psychological Review*. Generally speaking, the magical number 7 rule states that human beings cannot remember more than seven (plus or minus two) different types of sensorial stimuli, when those stimuli are provided within a short time interval. The rule refers primarily to our short-term memory limitations and not to limitations in our long-term memory. For example, while a new telephone number is stored in our short-term memory, the process of using the telephone device is stored in our long-term memory. Incidentally, short-term memories are often associated with what was defined earlier in this book as information, whereas long-term memories are chiefly associated with what was defined earlier as knowledge.

To illustrate Miller's rule, let us assume that 60 symbols, like δ, θ, α, Ω, Φ . . . , were shown to several individuals during a 1-minute slide session; that is, each symbol would have been displayed on a screen for about 1 second, and would have been followed by the next symbol, and so on. The magical number 7 rule predicts that when we averaged the number of symbols that were remembered correctly by the several individuals, that number would be very close to 7. And the magical number 7 rule does not apply only to visual stimuli. It also predicts that the number of remembered stimuli would be on average seven, whether those stimuli were tactile, auditory, or gustative, for example.

Of course, if the following series of 26 symbols were shown at once to several individuals, those individuals would probably be able to remember all of them correctly: a, b, c . . . x, y, z. The reason is because the individuals would be able to group the symbols together and see them as one main entity (the alphabet), which would essentially mean the same as being shown only one single symbol. This grouping of symbols phenomenon has been referred to in the past more generally as "cognitive chunking." Similar phenomena have led to the development of a new theory, often called the cognitive chunking theory. The theory has a variety of practical applications, from diagramming to Web site development.

From a business process diagramming perspective, we can assume that the central elements of a diagram are the activity symbols, since most of the other symbols gravitate around activities. That is, we can assume that the viewers of a business process diagram will tend to look at activities as the principal elements of the diagram and mentally attach other symbols to the activity symbols associated with those other symbols. For example, an information repository that is used by an activity would be seen as attached to that activity.

The above is true even though the most important element from a business process redesign perspective is the web of communication interactions in the business process. The reason is that communication interactions revolve around activities, because without activities, there would be no reason for business process–related communication. As pointed out by Winograd and Flores in their seminal book *Understanding Computers and Cognition,* communication both enables and underlies action in business processes.

Thus, it is reasonable to assume that a business process diagram that has more than seven activity symbols in it would be considered somewhat large and likely to cause some confusion to individuals trying to understand it. Just for the sake of illustration, it is useful to point out that the diagrams shown previously in Figures 7.1 and 7.2 in this chapter are well below that limit, since they both have four activity symbols in them.

So, what if a business process is complex enough to require, say, 20 activity symbols to be properly represented? In this case, taking the following two diagramming steps would be recommended: (a) grouping activities so that no more than seven are shown in each business process diagram and (b) breaking down diagrams into several levels, with the lowest level being labeled "Level 1" and the higher levels being business process representations of lower-level activities (where those activities are seen as business processes themselves). See Figure 7.3 for an illustration of this approach.

As can be seen in Figure 7.3, lower-level activities are "exploded" into higher-level business process diagrams; that is, the new higher-level diagrams are essentially detailed representations of the inner workings of activities in the previous lower-level diagrammatic business process representation. The higher-level business process diagrams use the same symbols as the lower-level diagrams. At this point, it is reasonable to ask, How many levels of business process diagrams should one have?

The answer to the above question is simple, if somewhat subjective. The number of levels of diagrammatic representations of business processes depends on how much detail is necessary for effective business process redesign. Generally speaking, in communication flow representations of business processes, the explosion of an

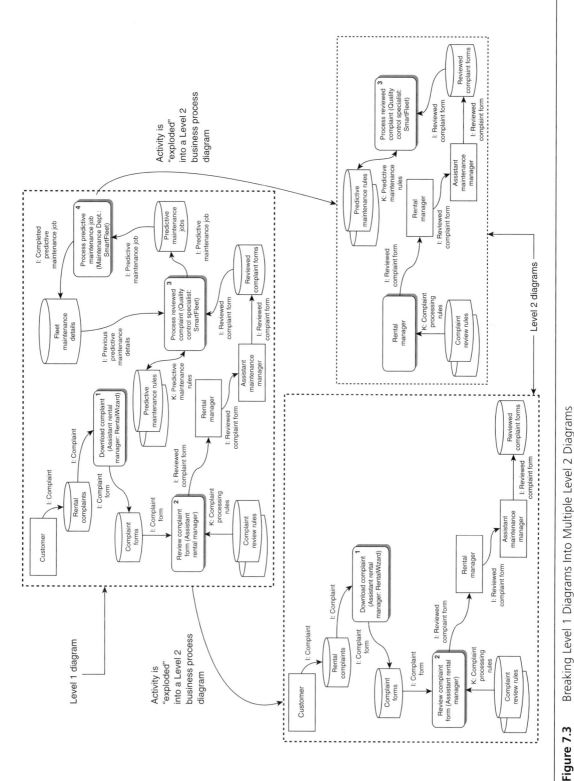

Figure 7.3 Breaking Level 1 Diagrams Into Multiple Level 2 Diagrams

activity into a higher-level business process diagram stops when only one person carries out the activity in question. That is, if an activity in a business process does not involve several people in its execution, there is no good way of improving by looking at how communication takes place in the activity, primarily because there is no interpersonal communication going on. Like many other rules of thumb provided in this book, there are exceptions to this rule—for example, very complex activities that are carried out by only one person, but in multiple steps over a period of time. From a practical perspective, much of the industry-oriented research so far, as well as the experience of business process redesign practitioners, suggests that it is not usually a good idea to go beyond Level 3 representations in one single business process redesign project.

Summary and Concluding Remarks

This chapter has expanded on the discussion of topics addressed in earlier chapters, such as business process modeling and the different nature of information and knowledge. In particular, the chapter has offered a simplified approach to differentiate between the flows of information and of knowledge in a business process representation. The approach essentially entails explicitly indicating by means of a letter (either I or K) whether a data flow is primarily a flow of information (I) or knowledge (K).

The chapter has also discussed the differences in media requirements for information and knowledge communication, arguing that more natural, or face-to-face–like, communication media are particularly useful when the amount of complex knowledge being communicated increases. In many situations, trying to communicate knowledge at business process execution time leads to productivity and quality-related losses. The general rule that natural media should be used to support complex knowledge communication applies to situations where at least some knowledge must flow during the execution of a business process.

Finally, this chapter has discussed some basic rules for coming up with the appropriate size of a communication flow diagram, and a relatively straightforward approach to break down large business process representations into smaller ones. Generally speaking, the activities in a business process should be grouped so that no more than seven activities are shown in a single diagram. When that threshold is surpassed, it is recommended that diagrams be broken down into several levels, with the lowest level being labeled "Level 1" and the higher levels being business process representations of lower-level activities.

Review Questions

1. Why is it important to represent knowledge flow in a business process?
   (a) Because it is useful to identify and eliminate instances in which data flows at business process execution time in certain types of business processes.

(b) Because it is useful to identify and eliminate instances in which knowledge flows at business process execution time in certain types of business processes.

(c) Because it is useful to identify and eliminate instances in which information flows at business process execution time in certain types of business processes.

(d) Because it is useful to identify and eliminate instances in which knowledge flows in most types of business processes, especially organizational learning processes.

2. Which of the following is not an example of an attempt to communicate knowledge at business process execution time?

   (a) A car factory employee uses what he learned at General Motors University to become a very productive engine assembler.

   (b) A car factory employee learns a great deal from the assembly-line manager on how to assemble engines while that employee assembles the engine of a new Chevrolet Blazer.

   (c) A car factory employee learns from the quality control manager techniques on how to look for statistical engine nonconformities while that employee assembles a set of engines for several Chevrolet Avalanche 1500s.

   (d) The assembly-line manager at a car factory explains to an employee how to assemble engines while that employee assembles the engine of a new Subaru Forester.

3. What defines the degree of naturalness of a communication medium?

   (a) The level of asynchronicity of the communication medium.

   (b) Whether the communication medium employs mainframe-based video-conferencing features or not.

   (c) The degree of similarity of the communication medium to AOL's instant messaging system.

   (d) The degree to which the communication medium incorporates all of the elements found in face-to-face communication.

4. Which of the following situations is incompatible with Miller's magical number 7 rule?

   (a) A person who is shown 100 unrelated symbols every 15 minutes during 30 days remembers all of them.

   (b) A very controlling manager at a health insurance company, who likes to centralize work-related decisions, is able to keep track of the activities performed by no more than five subordinates who report directly to her.

   (c) A person who is shown 100 unrelated symbols during a 1-minute session remembers all of them.

   (d) A controlling and autocratic manager at a car rental company is able to keep track of the status of work performed by no more than seven subordinates who report directly to him.

5. Communication flow diagrams with more than seven symbols should:
   (a) Be broken down into higher-level diagrams.
   (b) Be broken down into higher-level diagrams as soon as the number of activities reaches 14, which is 7 times 2, according to Miller's "magical number 7 times 2" rule.
   (c) Be ignored as long as the number of functions in the diagram is negatively correlated with the complexity of the business process.
   (d) Be used only in activity-oriented business process redesign projects.

Discussion Questions

1. Develop a detailed scenario involving a knowledge-intensive business process in a service sector organization (e.g., a university, a consulting services firm). The business process in question should incorporate at least three knowledge repositories and three interactions comprising flow of knowledge. Develop a communication flow representation of the business process in question.

2. Develop a detailed scenario involving an online customer service process provided by a service sector organization (e.g., an online stockbroker, an Internet-based networking equipment store). The business process in question should incorporate several types of communication interactions (e.g., providing support to customers who forgot their passwords, listing stocks in order of transaction volume during the day) involving the exchange of information or knowledge, but not both at the same time. Develop a practical list of recommended computer-based communication tools (e.g., e-mail, instant messaging, desktop video conferencing) for each of the communication interactions, and provide an explanation of why each recommendation has been made.

3. Develop a detailed scenario involving a complex business process in a manufacturing sector organization (e.g., a car factory, a hardware developer). The business process in question should be complex enough so that a Level 1 communication flow representation of it would require more than 20 activity symbols. Develop a set of communication flow representations of the business process in question, where the representations are at diagrammatic Levels 1 and 2.

CHAPTER 8

Redesigning Business Processes

This chapter discusses several new techniques for the redesign of business processes. Those techniques focus on the flow of information and the distribution of knowledge in business processes. They focus on where to replace synchronous with asynchronous communication in business processes, how to reduce information duplication and overflow, and how to effectively reduce contact points in business processes. The ultimate goal of these techniques is to improve business process quality and productivity.

This chapter also shows why two key goals in connection with knowledge transfer should be achieved through business process redesign. One of those goals is that knowledge transfer should be minimized in the execution of business processes, which may seem a bit paradoxical, particularly in "operational" processes, also known as supply-chain processes. The second goal is that knowledge transfer should be maximized in specific types of business processes called here "organizational learning" processes. Examples of those processes are training processes, socialization processes, R&D processes, and strategy definition processes. Finally, this discussion is complemented by a discussion on how to move organizational learning activities from operational business processes to organizational learning processes.

Encouraging Asynchronous Communication of Information

When people exchange information as part of a business process, they can do that synchronously or asynchronously. Synchronous exchanges of information involve people interacting at the same time, while asynchronous exchanges involve people interacting at different times. One example of synchronous communication is a telephone conversation, because both people involved in a telephone conversation have

**Karen needs to tell John about a new consulting contract she
secured, which he should follow up ASAP.**

Karen tries to call John
several times, but he's out
talking to a customer.
The calls disrupt her activities.
She spends 35 minutes in total
trying to talk to John before
she gives up.

Karen e-mails John about
the new contract, using a
specific e-mail account
that John created only for
this purpose, which takes
her only 7 minutes.

Synchronous

Asynchronous

Figure 8.1   Encouraging Asynchronous Information of Communication

to participate in the conversation at the same time. If the conversation takes place via
e-mail, it then becomes an example of asynchronous communication, because it is
no longer necessary for the two individuals interacting via e-mail to do so at the
same time (e.g., an e-mail message may be prepared and electronically mailed in the
morning by its sender, and read and replied to in the evening by its recipient).

It has been observed, especially in formal business interaction, that, almost
always, asynchronous communication of information is more efficient than synchronous communication (see Figure 8.1). As far as the quality of the communication is concerned, that is, whether communication attempts really lead to
information being transferred effectively, past research has found little difference
between synchronous and asynchronous communication of information. In summary, more often than not, asynchronous communication of information is less
costly and faster than synchronous communication of information, with no real
impact on the quality of the communication. So, we should encourage asynchronous communication of information in business processes as much as possible.

The above remarks may sound a little bit counterintuitive to many people, who
would probably argue that in most business situations it is important to meet face-
to-face (and thus synchronously) to clarify business issues. This is probably true
regarding communication aimed at clarification of issues, but it should also be
noted that issue clarification more often than not involves the exchange of *knowledge*, not only information. That is, what is being argued here in connection with
asynchronous communication applies chiefly to information, not knowledge. If one
needs to exchange knowledge with someone else, to explain why an activity in a
business process needs to be conducted in a particular way, for example, then by all
means, walk over to that person and talk face-to-face or pick up the telephone and
chat with her synchronously. It can be rather annoying and inefficient to have to
explain something to somebody (e.g., why we ask customers to sign the same insurance policy twice) via e-mail. And previous research has shown that, when complex
issues are being discussed, it can be as much as 10 times more time-consuming to

discuss them electronically (often because we have to be so careful in our writing to avoid misunderstandings).

So, if Mary needs to explain to John why the temperature of a chemical process should be kept at a particular level, then Mary will be better off setting up a meeting with John and explaining that to him face-to-face than e-mailing him. But if Mary needs only to tell John what the temperature level in question is, because John already possesses the necessary knowledge about the process to use that piece of information effectively, then Mary will be better off e-mailing John than meeting with him face-to-face.

There are two other situations in which synchronous communication is more desirable than its asynchronous counterpart (all business process redesign guidelines have their exceptions and should never be used blindly). The first is when personal information needs to be provided to someone, particularly information that carries a high emotional content. Sending that type of information asynchronously, which typically involves the use of electronic communication media, often gives the recipient the impression that we don't care much about him or her. The second is when the information is of an ethically or legally sensitive nature, which generally means that it can be used in a lawsuit (or as a basis for filing criminal charges) against the person providing it. Here, asynchronous methods of communication are undesirable because, by definition, asynchronous communication requires the use of some kind of data repository (e.g., an e-mail box), which means that a record of the communication is generated. And it is not absurd to imagine that prosecutors and attorneys may use records in legal proceedings, sometimes in a twisted way, to make a legal point against those who generated the records. For example, in 1998, the U.S. Department of Justice, together with 19 states, filed an antitrust legal action against Microsoft Corporation, alleging that Microsoft engaged in anticompetitive practices over a period of time against developers of competing Internet browsers, most notably Netscape Communications. In that legal action, some of the key evidence used against Microsoft came in the form of e-mails exchanged among its executive officers (including Microsoft's top executive at the time, founder Bill Gates).

Nevertheless, when *information* is what is being exchanged and it is not of a personal or ethically/legally sensitive nature, asynchronous communication is generally a better choice. There are many losses associated with synchronous communication, which make asynchronous communication a desirable alternative. For example, synchronous communication over the phone often leads to time being wasted in communication interaction setup activities (i.e., activities involved in getting the two people on the phone at the same time), since the individual starting the communication interaction has to wait for the other person to be found. Synchronous phone communication can also lead to other time losses, like those associated with having to play telephone tag (as colleagues make themselves unavailable for telephone calls to avoid being disrupted all the time). Also, communication tends to be less objective when it takes place face-to-face or over the phone, as the immediate social presence of another real human being will prompt many people to discuss other issues (e.g., gossip) that are unrelated to the specific information that needs to be conveyed.

**For asynchronous communication to occur between
Karen and John, there needs to be an information repository
linking them – e.g., John's e-mail box.**

Karen e-mails
John about the
new contract.

Sales rep.
Karen

-New
contract

John's e-mail box

-New
contract

Senior
consultant
John

Figure 8.2   Information Repositories as Enablers of Asynchronous
Communication

Asynchronous communication can be implemented with simple artifacts such as
in- and out-boxes, fax trays, billboards, and e-mail boxes (see Figure 8.2). These artifacts work as dynamic, as opposed to static, information repositories—the difference
here is that dynamic repositories (e.g., a student information entry form) store
information on a much less permanent basis than static repositories (e.g., a student
information file). An example of dynamic information repository is an e-mail box
used by a college professor to store exam answers sent to him by students who took
an exam online (and didn't cheat, of course). Another would be a wooden tray where
waiters and waitresses leave for kitchen employees those little forms with information about what customers ordered for dinner, so that those employees can prepare
the dishes exactly like the customers ordered them (and never send out medium-
cooked steak, for example, when customers ask for it to be well-done).

Reducing Information Duplication
in Static Repositories

As mentioned, static repositories, as opposed to dynamic repositories, hold information on a more permanent basis. A student file maintained by a primary school,
for example, is a static repository of information. Conversely, the data entry form
used to temporarily store information about a student that will be entered into the
student file is not a static repository. The latter is a dynamic information repository.

Duplication of information in different static repositories often creates incon-
sistency problems, which may have a negative impact on productivity and quality.
Among the most common and damning of these problems is that of identical

business process activities being carried out inconsistently because those who carry out those activities make use of one of the static data repositories but not the other. And, while some of those activities may appear simple and inconsequential, their execution in a context of static information repository duplication may have significant negative business consequences down the road.

An interesting and illustrative situation is that of a large automaker's purchasing division. The division frequently interacted with hundreds of suppliers of car parts, such as suppliers of brakes, windshield wipers, and exhaust pipes. In fact, the automaker did not seem to manufacture many of the parts that went into the cars it sold through dealers; just about everything was outsourced to suppliers who worked in close partnership with the automaker. This was an interesting arrangement for the automaker, especially because the automaker's purchases accounted for most of the revenues of each of its individual suppliers, which in turn made the suppliers particularly dependent on the automaker's business.

The automaker had recently implemented a computerized supplier management system to streamline and improve the quality of its relationship with its suppliers. The system was also aimed at improving the efficiency of the parts purchasing process, by reducing the time between the identification of a need for parts by the automaker (e.g., a need for a batch of windshield wipers for a particular car model) and the actual delivery of those parts.

However, there were some problems with the computerized supplier management system. The computer database had presented some problems, which seemed to be related to the large and expensive hard disk being used, and therefore was deemed unreliable. As a reaction to those problems, the automaker's purchasing division tried to keep its old manual and paper-based process running in parallel with the computerized system (just to be on the safe side). The result was that two large static data repositories were being duplicated.

The duplication was causing a considerable number of purchasing problems, and also a substantial amount of money to be lost by both the automaker and the suppliers. For example, since both the computerized and manual systems were in place, some purchasing division employees felt that they could use either system. That led to inconsistencies in the computerized and manual data repositories, which in turn caused orders for parts to sometimes be placed twice, once using the computerized system and then again using the manual system. Since the automaker's factory had been designed based on lean manufacturing principles, it had limited warehousing space. Thus, the duplicated orders often led to the additional unused parts being stored in inappropriate places, and, in consequence, becoming defective prior to going into the assembly line. Sometimes the automaker put up with the costs of those defects, while other times the suppliers were made to pay for them; even though it was not their fault, the suppliers would not risk losing their business with the automaker over a dispute in connection with defective parts.

This situation persisted for a while, until the automaker's purchasing division was convinced by a group of consultants that they should have had only one supplier management system in place: the computerized one. What about the problems with the computerized system? Well, it turned out that those problems were relatively easy and inexpensive to solve. The solution essentially involved creating storage redundancy by employing a technical solution that later became widely known as disk mirroring using a redundant array of independent disks (RAID-1). Through this technical solution, information is stored concurrently into more than one hard disk at a time. This means that, in the case of two disks being used in a RAID-1 configuration, both would have to fail at the same time for information to be lost, which is statistically improbable. When one looks at the technical literature, it seems that most problems that can lead to duplication of information in different static repositories are easily resolved with technical solutions.

It is important to stress that what is called here information duplication in static repositories actually refers to operational duplication, where the same type of information is entered by people and retrieved separately to and from different static repositories. Those repositories may be computer based or not—it doesn't matter. The notion of operational duplication does not apply to two types of database technologies that may appear to involve duplication, namely backup and synchronization.

When a computer-based information repository is backed up, a copy of it, often compressed, is created on a data storage medium. That copy, or backup, is not used for information entry and retrieval in connection with any business process, with the exception of a data recovery process. Or, in other words, the backup data is only used in special circumstances, such as when the original data are accidentally lost.

While the notion of data synchronization is similar to that of data backup, synchronization usually serves different purposes. One type of common synchronization is that carried out regularly by owners of personal digital assistants (PDAs), which usually involves synchronizing a set of PDA files (e.g., calendar, address book) with their mirror files sitting on the hard disk of a personal computer. Another type of synchronization, sometimes called remote synchronization (see Figure 8.3), involves replicating changes made to a computer-based database to another, remotely located database. For example, let us assume that the sales department of an industrial scale manufacturer is located in Portland, Oregon, and that its engineering department is located in Philadelphia, Pennsylvania. Both departments enter information into, as well as retrieve information from, a product database, which stores details about the company's many products, including their technical specifications and prices. As soon as new information is entered into the database in one location (e.g., Portland), a synchronization software application updates the database in the other location (e.g., Philadelphia), and vice versa.

In both types of synchronization discussed, a synchronization software application works in the background to ensure that only one logical data repository is maintained, even though physically different copies of the data repository exist in different locations. That is, from the users' perspective, only one version of the data repository is maintained, and thus there is essentially no duplication of information in different static repositories. The same is true for backups. In fact, synchronization and backup technologies often solve many of the problems that could lead to information duplication in different static repositories.

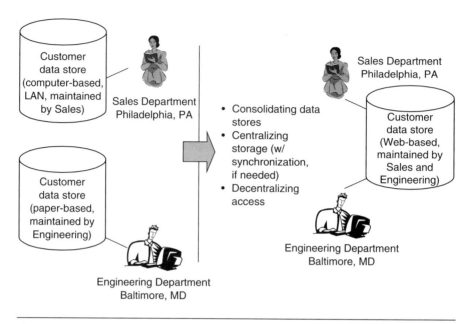

Figure 8.3   Reducing Information Duplication in Static Repositories

Eliminating Unnecessary Information Flow

Excessive information flow is often caused by an excessive preoccupation with control, sometimes caused by previous problems in connection with a business process—for example, an order taken by a sales representative that went wrong, which prompts the sales representative to keep track of everything that happens with future orders. In this sense, excessive information flow is often caused by a lack of focus on the information that really matters.

Consider the following example. Digital scales sales representative John wants to please his customers by keeping track of everything that occurs, from production to delivery, related to his orders. He fails, because he ends up spending too much time processing information, which prevents him from spending valuable time with current and prospective customers. Moreover, most of the information he collects, processes, and stores is not the type of information that he will use in his interactions with his current and prospective customers. Conversely, sales representative Karen wants to please her customers by learning from past experience what may go wrong with her orders and selectively keeping track of certain stages in production and delivery. She succeeds.

On top of often leading to excessive and unnecessary information flow, control activities do not usually add value to customers. They are often designed to prevent problems from happening as a result of human mistakes. In several cases, however, control itself fosters neglect, with a negative impact on productivity, because controls often *encourage* human mistakes. For many readers, this may sound rather strange, but consider the following line of reasoning. An engine assembly-line worker may not be careful enough when performing an engine assembly activity if he knows that there will be some kind of control down the assembly line to catch his mistakes.

Additionally, some types of control, such as those aimed at preventing fraud and targeting groups from which fraud is not very likely, may prove to be more costly than no control at all in connection with the groups targeted. Some car insurance companies, for example, have found out that the cost of accident claim inspections, for a sizeable percentage of their customers, is much more expensive than the average cost of frauds that that group may commit.

Let us consider, for example, a car insurance company that has a client base of 3 million people, and that about 500,000 (or about 17 percent) of those people are part of a group for which the likelihood of fraud is 5 percent or less, and that, when that fraud occurs, it involves inflating the amount of the claims by an average of 50 percent. That is, there is a 5 percent or less likelihood that those customers will do things like getting into an accident that damages their front fender and ending up having that fixed as well as their windows tinted on the insurance company (which, of course, the insurance company would not like, had they known about it). Let us also assume that the car insurance company gets claims from about 10 percent of those 500,000 customers every year, and that the average amount claimed is $500. Finally, let us assume that the cost of inspecting each car whenever a claim is filed is $50; remember that these inspections are aimed at preventing fraud. The bottom line is that the total amount spent in inspections, in this example, is $2.5 million per year, whereas the total amount lost due to fraud, if there were no inspections, would be about $1.9 million. That is, not only is the company wasting about $625,000 a year, it is also annoying those customers who are unlikely to cheat (the vast majority, or 95 percent) with unnecessary inspections. Or, in other words, if the company performed no inspections for those customers, they would be more satisfied, and the cost for the company would in the end be lower.

But let's go back to the issue of unnecessary information flow and its elimination. Excessive information flow is often caused by information being perceived as an important component of processes, which it indeed is. The problem is that this perception drives some people to an unhealthy information hunger. This causes information overload and the creation of unnecessary information processing functions within organizations, such as middle managers, whose main responsibility is to relay information from the top of the organization to the bottom and vice versa, without adding anything to it. Some of these folks even think that what they do gives them some measure of job security, because, they think, information is power. The problem with that line of thinking is that what those middle managers do is relatively easy to automate, which is why they are often the first to lose their jobs as a result of business process reengineering.

Information overload leads to stress and, often, the creation of information filtering roles, in addition to the information buffer roles mentioned. These roles are normally those of aides or, again, middle managers, who are responsible for filtering in the important bit from the information coming from the bottom of and from outside the organization. Conversely, excessive information flowing top-down forces those middle managers to become filter-messengers, to the damage of more important roles—such as making good hiring decisions and motivating their employees.

A former colleague is a good illustration of that (let us call him Mario, which is not his real name). Mario was the lead consultant in an information technology–enabled restructuring project that involved an entire organization. Mario's main job seemed to be to talk with the company's chief executive officer and inform his team about the chief executive officer's most relevant decisions. That was done in such a way that was clearly a big waste of time, especially because Mario always kept the consulting team somewhat in the dark. He would usually come to the team, often late in the afternoon, make the team members stop what they were doing, and tell them something like this: "I talked with the chief executive officer today again. I can't tell you everything about what we discussed, but I can say this. . . ." What usually followed was some piecemeal information on the status of our project, whether there would be a follow-up project (many consulting firms try to secure follow-up projects as a way of increasing their revenues), and so on. Some months later, the team members found out that Mario had been fired. Apparently, the consulting firm's brass did not see Mario's information-filtering role as a value-adding one and decided to replace him with someone who could actually do something other than what they perceived as simply schmoozing with the chief executive officer.

Selecting the information flows that appear to be important in business processes and eliminating the rest can be a simple yet effective approach to reduce information flow. Since much information flows through organizational forms, whether those forms are paper based or electronic, reducing information flows often becomes an exercise of streamlining and, in many cases, downright elimination of forms. Sometimes, reducing the number of contact points in a business process (a guideline that is discussed in the next section) also will go a long way in terms of eliminating unnecessary information flow in the process.

As for the roles played by information buffers and filters (see Figure 8.4), those can more often than not be easily eliminated by effectively employing commercially available systems, such as electronic collaboration and decision support systems. For example, information that is supposed to flow top-down in a life insurance company, from the executive officers to all of the employees, no longer has to be passed down by middle management employees through each of the successive hierarchical levels of the company. It can simply be broadcast by the executive officers to the entire company via e-mail. Conversely, information about operations (e.g., number of phone calls taken in different geographic areas, percentage of phone calls that led to a signed policy) can be automatically and directly summarized to senior managers by decision support systems (sometimes referred to as online analytical processing systems) running on those managers' personal computers, building on data stored in operations data management systems.

Mark, Sophia, and Anthony work at a car dealership.

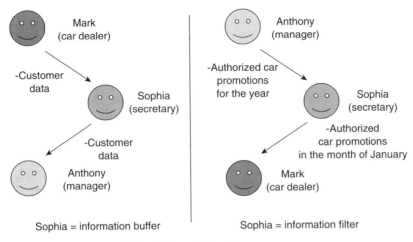

Two situations are illustrated: left = buffer; right = filter.

Figure 8.4   Information Buffers and Filters

Reducing Contact Points in a Process

Contact points are interactions between two or more people, both within the process and outside. This includes contacts between organizational functions involved in the execution of business processes, as well as contacts between business process team members and their external customers. For example, the organizational functions inventory control assistant and productions manager in a shoe manufacturing company may discuss daily the status of the inventory in connection with several shoe models. Those discussions are contact points. Contact points may also refer to interactions between organizational functions and customers. For example, in an airplane run by American Airlines (or any other airline carrier), each interaction between a steward and a passenger is a contact point.

Usually, in business processes that do not involve interaction with customers, unnecessary contact points are often the cause of bottlenecks and related delays, which increase the cycle time of the entire business processes unnecessarily. A bottleneck is an activity of a business process in which inputs accumulate before they can be processed to generate outputs. For example, let us imagine a credit institution where lending contract proposals have to be approved by a lending manager. Let us then assume that the lending manager also needs to interact with two very busy people, namely the chief financial officer of the credit institution and its general counsel, before she approves any lending contract proposal. The fact that those two contact points (between the lending manager and the chief financial officer as well as the general counsel) exist in the lending contract approval process turns the approval activity handled by the lending manager into a bottleneck. Without those contact points in the business process, the lending manager would have to be allowed to grant or deny approval to lending contract proposals without consulting with those two other people, which could substantially reduce the business process cycle time.

One could think that slashing contact points involving business process team members is okay but that those contact points between business process team members and external customers are untouchable. After all, in many cases, it is during contact points with business process team members that customer perceptions about quality are formed. Those contact points are what the former chief executive officer of Scandinavian Airlines, Jan Carlzon, famously referred to as "moments of truth."

However, having too many of Carlzon's "moments of truth" in a business process can be a problem, since inconsistent experiences in those contact points may lead to customer perplexity and dissatisfaction. The bottom line is that there is always a probability that a contact point between a business process team member and a customer can go wrong and leave the customer with a bad impression about the organization. In fact, one interesting phenomenon regarding contact points with customers is that people in general tend to form perceptions about the entire organization (e.g., an airline carrier) based on a few interactions with its representatives (e.g., a check-in counter employee, a baggage handler). Thus, as counterintuitive as this may sound, reducing contact points, even those with customers, is generally an advisable business process redesign strategy. With few contact points, quality may be monitored and improved in a much more effective manner. That is, it is much easier to monitor customer perceptions in situations where there are a small number of contact points. This makes it easier to improve business process quality.

Also, in many situations, a reduction in the number of contact points may streamline a business process and, at the same time, improve customers' quality perceptions about the business process. For example, in certain self-service restaurants (e.g., a seafood buffet restaurant in Las Vegas) and furniture warehouses (e.g., Ikea), the points of contact have been successfully reduced to a minimum (see Figure 8.5). In a self-service buffet restaurant, for example, the customers come in,

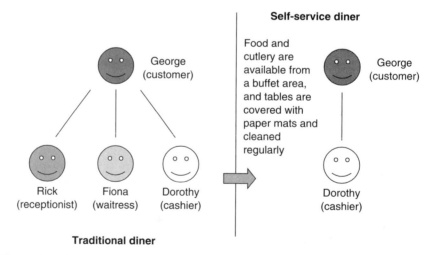

The number of contact points is 3 times higher in the situation depicted on the left.

Figure 8.5   Reducing the Number of Contact Points in a Process

eat whatever they want, and then pay a set amount at the cashier when they leave. However, as with all of the business process guidelines discussed in this book, one cannot slash contact points blindly. Still using the restaurant industry as an example, turning a service-oriented French restaurant in New York, where customers go specifically for the elaborate service (e.g., to impress their guests), into a self-service buffet is likely going to push it into bankruptcy.

Minimizing Knowledge Transfer in Operational Processes

As previously mentioned in this book, operational business processes are those that refer to the operations of an organization. They are, in essence, business processes that directly contribute to the creation of goods or services that are responsible for the revenues received by the organization. As a basis for comparison, a different type of business process refers to those sets of interrelated activities that are aimed at supporting operational business processes and that do not directly contribute to an organization's revenues. For example, in a university, teaching is a type of operational business process, whereas instructional support (e.g., providing projectors to be used by instructors in classrooms) is a type of support business process. The type of business process referred to in the next section as organizational learning, which is essentially an organizational development process (i.e., a business process aimed at improving other business processes), is a support process.

Much research done in connection with business process management in the past has suggested one interesting idea in connection with operational business processes: Process team members should strive to exchange enough information to carry out activities in those processes (bearing in mind the previously discussed business process redesign guidelines), but not knowledge, at process execution time. For example, if an employee responsible for an activity of a chemical mixing process (this is what pharmacists usually do when they prepare prescription medication orders) needs to *learn* how to conduct that activity while executing it, more time would be spent communicating about the activity than if only discrete pieces of information were being exchanged. In other words, there would be losses in efficiency due to communication patterns in the business process.

So, how can we minimize knowledge transfer in operational business processes? One could argue that such minimization will occur naturally over time, because, after a few learning-while-doing interactions, the amount of knowledge that will need to be transferred among process team members (particularly from the veterans to the rookies) will slowly decrease, eventually reaching a point close to zero (a point in time where virtually only information will have to be transferred). This will likely happen in organizations where business processes do not change often and where there is no turnover—organizations that are unfortunately very rare today, if they exist at all. Most, if not all, organizations will change due to pressures associated with competition, changing customer demands, and new technologies. Also, most, if not all, organizations will have a certain level of turnover, with people leaving the organization and being replaced by others who may bring in fresh new views yet still have to learn a great deal about the organization and its business processes.

The solution, then, is to foster knowledge sharing in nonoperational processes, such as organizational learning processes. That will hopefully create the proper contexts in which process team members will all hold the knowledge necessary to optimally (or at least quasi-optimally) execute operational processes. It is important to stress that, for this to be achieved, that knowledge needs to be acquired *before* the time of execution of those processes. We can use a sports analogy to emphasize this point. The right time for the members of a soccer team to learn about a particular game strategy to be used against a tough opponent is before, not during, the championship final.

Maximizing Knowledge Transfer in Organizational Learning Processes

Knowledge transfer among business process team members should be maximized through organizational learning processes, which in turn should take place *before* the routine execution of the operational processes, where the transferred knowledge is supposed to be used. This may sound a little bit esoteric at first hearing, but it is a guideline that many organizations follow, whether they know what business process redesign is or not. For example, new employees often receive orientations in their first days after joining an organization. The main goal of those orientations, which are usually coordinated by human resource departments, is to impart to those new employees the knowledge necessary to enable them to go about doing their work without getting lost and asking too many questions—that is, to enable those new employees to hit the ground running, so to speak.

This business process redesign guideline is based on a simple assumption, which can be illustrated through the following example. If each member of a team of six employees responsible for the execution of a telephone line repair process has a good deal of knowledge about what the others do, even if what they do requires a great degree of specialized knowledge (e.g., internal and external telephone line repair), then the communication among those employees will become more efficient and the productivity of the process as whole will be increased. The external telephone line repair guy will tell the internal line guy that the external multiplexing device is properly grounded and will not have to explain what "multiplexing" and "grounded" mean to his colleague. This, in turn, will enable them to finish their work faster, and more effectively.

The question then becomes, How do we foster knowledge sharing? For those who read the previous chapter, the answer to this question will have a familiar ring to it. While pure training activities (as in the new employee orientation mentioned before) are the usual alternative employed here, there is another, perhaps more desirable option. That option was suggested by a 2003 study report titled "Can Lean Media Support Knowledge Sharing? Investigating a Hidden Advantage of Process Improvement." The option is *business process redesign*.

This study looked at business process exchanges in operational as well as business process redesign processes. This may sound a bit confusing, but business process redesign is also conducted through a set of interrelated activities and thus can be seen as a business process as well—some might prefer the term *meta-process* to refer to the process carried out by a business process redesign group. One interesting aspect of the study, for the purposes of this book, is that it involved a knowledge content analysis of communication exchanges in two different types of processes whose definitions have already been discussed here: operational and business process redesign.

The analysis suggested strongly that individuals participating in groups conducting business process redesign efforts tend to engage in more than twice as many knowledge-bearing exchanges as individuals conducting activities in operational processes, which is a big difference from a statistical analysis standpoint. That is, the study suggested that participating in business process redesign initiatives is a catalyst for knowledge sharing in groups.

This discussion indicates that a relatively new and unorthodox approach to promote inter-functional knowledge sharing is to have workers participate in business process redesign groups. But one might ask, Why use business process redesign as a mechanism to encourage knowledge transfer, when there are other more traditionally used and targeted mechanisms, such as training sessions and committee meetings?

One answer to this question is that business process design, unlike more traditional knowledge transfer activities such as training sessions and committee meetings, has other numerous side effects that are obviously beneficial, perhaps the most important among them being business process improvement itself. Another answer is that business process redesign discussions can be more engaging than training sessions and committee meetings, given the importance of their outcomes for those involved. After all, it is likely that most of the members of a business process redesign group will have to live with (and will be affected by) the business process changes they propose and agree upon.

Summary and Concluding Remarks

This chapter discusses several new techniques for business process redesign, all of which focused on the flow of information and the distribution of knowledge in business processes. Those techniques addressed the need to replace synchronous instances of communication of information with asynchronous ones, reduce information duplication in static repositories, eliminate unnecessary information flow, reduce the number of contact points in a process, minimize knowledge transfer in operational processes, and maximize knowledge transfer in organizational learning processes. The chapter also shows that one key type of organizational learning process is the business process redesign process (or meta-process) itself.

The techniques discussed in this chapter are only a subset of all the techniques that could be discussed based on the communication flow optimization paradigm adopted by this book. Nevertheless, it is reasonable to believe that such a subset of techniques can lead to significant levels of quality and productivity improvement in most business processes, even those that do not seem to be terribly communication intensive at first glance. Obviously, it is important to note that, since the techniques discussed in this book are aimed at improving the flow of information and storage of knowledge in business processes, those processes that involve no flow of information and storage of knowledge cannot benefit from them, and those processes that involve little of those elements cannot greatly benefit from the techniques. This caveat, however, likely applies to a very small number of business processes. Rarely does one come across processes that cannot be substantially improved from an information and/or knowledge perspective.

Review Questions

1. Asynchronous communication is:
   (a) Preferable when what is being communicated is mostly knowledge.
   (b) Not indicated when communicating primarily information.
   (c) Usually more efficient than synchronous communication for business interactions in general.
   (d) Illustrated by a telephone conversation.

2. To implement asynchronous communication of information, we need:
   (a) To always spend a great deal of effort.
   (b) To convince people to talk over the phone more often.
   (c) To develop, as professionally as possible, at least three normalized databases.
   (d) To create information repositories, if they don't yet exist.

3. Static information repositories do not differ from dynamic information repositories in that:
   (a) Both store information.
   (b) They store information over different lengths of time.
   (c) They are usually implemented in different ways.
   (d) Dynamic repositories often store information in a temporary way.

4. Which of the following describes a problem that has been created chiefly by the duplication of information in static repositories?
   (a) Two sales teams at Alpha Corp. engage in predatory competition against each other, which negatively affects both of their sales performances.
   (b) Carl misplaces chemical materials, which have a short lifetime, in the storage warehouse of his factory, which leads to the loss of those items.
   (c) John and Mary order the same batch of parts twice, because John uses a computerized inventory control system and Mary uses a paper-based one.
   (d) Mark forgets that he invoices one of his customers, and then invoices that customer again, which leads to several complaints and, ultimately, the loss of the customer to a competitor.

5. Which of the following describes what clearly seems to be a negative business consequence of excessive information flow?
    (a) Half of the middle managers at a large insurance company spend most of their time summarizing operations information to support senior management decision making.
    (b) Too many parts are used in a new car model, making it overpriced in comparison with competing models.
    (c) When forecasting sales for the coming year, a sales department manager uses information that has been produced by a decision support system.
    (d) The chief information officer of a company is fired after refusing to abandon a project that is obviously going to fail.

6. It is correct to say that a contact point is always:
    (a) A point at which food changes hands in a restaurant.
    (b) A communication interaction between a waiter and one of his customers.
    (c) An e-mail interaction between any two individuals.
    (d) A point where there is interaction between two or more people.

7. Contact points have not:
    (a) Been called "moments of truth" by a former chief executive officer.
    (b) Been hailed as the solution to all business problems.
    (c) Been reduced in buffet restaurants, when compared with traditional restaurants.
    (d) Led to increased customer satisfaction with service speed in certain industries.

8. Regarding knowledge transfer in business processes, we can safely say that:
    (a) It should be minimized during the execution of operational business processes.
    (b) It should be maximized during the execution of operational business processes.
    (c) It leads to decreased outcome quality in business processes in general.
    (d) It always increases the need for information transfer in organizational learning processes.

9. Which of the following statements is not true?
    (a) Management should foster knowledge sharing in nonoperational processes, such as organizational learning processes.
    (b) Organizational learning processes can improve business productivity by fostering knowledge transfer among business process team members.
    (c) New employee orientations are not the absolutely best alternative to encourage knowledge transfer among members of a business process team.
    (d) New employee orientations are not at all conducive to knowledge transfer.

10. It is correct to say that:
    (a) Knowledge transfer should take place always after the routine execution of operational processes.

(b) Since business process redesign is also conducted through a set of interrelated activities, it can thus be seen as a business process as well.

(c) Prior research has shown that individuals participating in groups carrying out operational processes tend to engage in more than twice as many knowledge-bearing exchanges as individuals conducting activities in business process redesign efforts.

(d) Minimization of knowledge transfer in operational processes never occurs naturally over time as a result of learning-while-doing interactions.

Discussion Questions

1. Consider the following scenario. You have just been hired as general manager of a home improvement store that sells a variety of tools and parts. Let's call this store United Hardware. This is a store like Home Depot and Lowe's, but, unlike those, it is not part of a chain of stores. The store makes a lot of money selling big items such as lawnmowers, scales, and electronic home security equipment, which are items that have a large profit margin. However, there is one big problem: The store is losing money on the sale of small items such as nuts, nails, and screws. How would you deal with this problem? How does your solution relate to the issues discussed in this chapter?

2. What other techniques could be used to redesign business processes, beyond the ones discussed in this chapter? Illustrate your answer through the development of a detailed business scenario.

3. Develop a business scenario where a number of problems exist that can be addressed through business process redesign. The scenario developed by you should be as realistic as possible. Develop a business process representation associated with the scenario you created. Then carry out the two following steps: (a) Apply the business process redesign techniques discussed in this chapter, and develop a representation of the new redesigned business process; and (b) then apply the new techniques you developed in response to the previous discussion question, and develop a representation of the resulting business process. Is there a big change between the representations generated in Steps (a) and (b)? Why?

4. Can the techniques discussed in this chapter be used in both continuous (e.g., total quality management–like) and radical (reengineering-like) business process improvement projects? Illustrate your answer through the development of two business scenarios, one for each type of business process improvement project (i.e., continuous and radical).

5. Among the techniques discussed in this chapter, are there a few that would be particularly useful for organizations where the main service provided to external customers is knowledge transfer (e.g., universities)? Why?

PART IV

Technology-Based Business Process Implementation

Part IV Case:
Investars, Inc.'s Outsourcing
of Programming to Belarus

Investars, Inc. was founded in 1999 in Hoboken, New Jersey. At the time, it was called Netologic, Inc. It provided financial analysts and their customers with analyses of stocks ratings, statistical comparisons, and other quantitative data related to financial instruments. Over time, Investars moved into other, more sophisticated financial services areas. Among other things, it questioned the value of the advice provided by many of the top brokerage firms and developed a method of measuring the value of that advice. At the time of this writing, Investars had grown in size and importance and had established its main office in New York City.

Investars' approach to promoting its services was an aggressive one. It pulled no punches when referring to the performance of brokerage firms. For example, it once stated that in a period of 5 years in which it had analyzed the stocks ratings issued by brokerage firms and the actual returns of those stocks, only four of the top brokerage firms had a positive overall return on the ratings they published on stocks. Investars strongly criticized top stock analysts for often not telling the entire truth about a stock's actual performance, due to fear of losing customers. An instance of this would be analysts' rating a stock that they do not consider worth buying as a "market performer" or "weak buy."

One might think that Investars' aggressive approach to marketing its services could have led to strong attacks by powerful brokerage firms (e.g., Merrill Lynch, Credit Suisse First Boston) and possibly hurt the company's prospects. But what almost killed Investars while it was still in its infancy (and while it was still called Netologic) was its inability to find computer programmers. In the few years following its initial establishment in 1999, Investars' main quantitative analysis tool was still under development. But, at that time, computer programmers were in high demand and very expensive. Simply put, Investars had a very hard time finding computer programmers, and, when it could find them, they were out of its price range.

Computer programmers were in high demand around 1999 for two main reasons. One was the infamous "Year 2000 problem," which pushed many organizations into revamping the software code of their many systems to make sure that no dates were stored using only two digits. Dates stored using only two digits would make those systems see the turn to a new millennium as the return to the year "00." The second reason why computer programmers were in such high demand around 1999 was the also infamous "technology bubble" seen in that period. One of the characteristics of the technology bubble, which "burst" soon after the year 2000, was a large amount of venture capital being poured into start-up technology companies. This was especially true for start-ups that were based on Internet products or services; those startups often received generous funding to implement silly ideas.

Investars' senior management team was becoming desperate, even resorting to trying to learn programming themselves through "for dummies" books series. Their funding was not enough to maintain them for much longer; they needed a final product and paying customers really soon. Also, the amount of funding available did not allow them to afford computer programmers at the salary levels then prevalent in New York, New Jersey, and other areas with a large concentration of computer programming labor.

Then, Investars' senior management found out about Elance Online, an online outsourcing service provided by Mountain View, California–based Elance, Inc. Through Elance Online, companies such as Investars could advertise a variety of projects (including software development projects) and receive competitive bids from all over the world.

Through Elance Online, Investars hired a group of computer programmers from Belarus to complete a few well-defined projects. That relationship with the Belarusian programmers soon blossomed into a more formal agreement and eventually led the American company to establish a permanent operation in the Belarusian city of Mogilev. At the time, the company employed several Belarusian computer programmers at a cost of approximately $12 per hour each (including benefits). That was about a third of what it would have to pay for computer programmers with equivalent knowledge and skills in New York City.

As a result of having outsourcing computer programming to Belarus, by 2004 Investars was able to expand its revenues by more than $1 million and become profitable. Also, the expansion of its revenues and market base had led Investars to create new jobs in New York City as well, in areas where outsourcing would not be an option. Usually, activities that involve close interaction with customers and knowledge of a company's product (such as Investars' quantitative analysis product) cannot easily be outsourced.

Sources

The Bank of New York. (2002, July 8). BNY Jaywalk, Inc. implements Investars performance measurement to meet new guidelines for research disclosure. The Bank of New York Press Release.

Investars, Inc. Web site: http://www.investars.com

McGeehan, P. (2001, May 29). Market place: Study questions advice from brokerage firms. *New York Times.*

Shira, B. (2004, June 21). Small business stays alive by outsourcing. *Crain's New York Business.*

CHAPTER 9

Using IT to Enable
New Process Designs

Many methodologies aimed at developing computer systems to support work practices in organizations have been proposed in the past. As previously discussed in this book, the vast majority of them have been targeted at the automation of business processes, without much concern for pre-automation changes in the business processes. But there are exceptions to this rule. One such exception is the visionary work conducted by Peter Checkland in the early 1980s on soft systems methodology. Soft systems methodology was proposed well before the business process reengineering movement burst into the corporate management scene and the consequent worldwide interest in business processes and their redesign as a way to achieving bottom-line organizational improvements and productivity, quality, and competitiveness. The core ideas of Checkland's soft systems methodology are discussed in his many publications, including his seminal book titled *Systems Thinking, Systems Practice*.

Checkland's soft systems methodology addressed one key problem found in many contemporary business process redesign projects—namely, how does one go from a relatively abstract business process representation, such as a communication flow diagram, to a clear pre-implementation understanding of how technologies will be used to enable a new business process? To solve a similar problem, this chapter proposes something called *rich pictorial representations* of the new business process, which are inspired by a similar concept proposed by Checkland as part of the soft systems methodology. Given the multitude of commercially available charting tools today, with a large variety of free iconic pictorial representations of technology components (e.g., servers, routers), this chapter's suggestion of rich pictorial representations goes a bit beyond what was proposed in the soft systems methodology in terms of depiction of actual technology configurations. The goal here is to help a business process redesign team move somewhat smoothly from representation to practical information technology implementation.

However, once a clear view of how technology can be used to implement a new business process is achieved, important decisions still have to be made as to what strategy will be used in that implementation. For example, long gone are the days in which the only computer software implementation option available was to develop a computer system in-house, by using employees as computer programmers or hiring programmers from outside to code the system. In fact, today, with the proliferation of packaged software to automate a large variety of business processes that are common to many organizations (e.g., customer relationship management, data mining, inventory control, cash flow control), in-house development is likely to be the most costly and less advisable option.

So, what other options are available? This chapter discusses three main business process implementation strategies, which underlie three different options. One is the aforementioned *in-house development* option, which essentially consists in "creating" a technology solution in-house, that is, inside the organization that houses the business process being implemented. Another strategy discussed is *commercial package customization*, which entails buying a packaged technology solution to implement the new business process and using it with some modifications aimed to accommodate (if necessary) business process idiosyncrasies. Finally, a third strategy discussed is *business process outsourcing*, which essentially entails farming out the execution of the business process to an outside organization.

Rich Pictorial Representations of New Business Processes

There is a joke in automobile manufacturing circles that carmakers do not make the cars they sell. There is some truth to that joke, in that, indeed, the vast majority of the parts that go into a car are bought by automobile manufacturers from car parts suppliers and then assembled in a car manufacturing plant. This is the case with most, if not all, large automobile manufacturers—DaimlerChrysler, Ford, General Motors, Subaru, Toyota, Volkswagen, and so on. The reason for this is that outsourcing the manufacturing of a large number of car parts to suppliers is, from an automobile manufacturer's perspective, a better economic alternative than manufacturing all of those parts in-house.

While this solves certain problems and increases car manufacturing's overall efficiency, it does create some challenges in areas such as supply chain and inventory management. Managing car part inventories is usually a headache for automobile manufacturers. Not surprisingly, a lot of research has been conducted in connection with the improvement of car part inventory management processes. As a result, some automobile manufacturers devised somewhat unorthodox and innovative inventory management practices, among which is that of shifting, in a well-structured and coordinated way, the responsibility of keeping track and maintaining optimal car part inventory levels to the suppliers themselves.

Figure 9.1 shows a simplified communication flow representation, without any depiction of knowledge repositories or knowledge flow, of a supplier-driven car

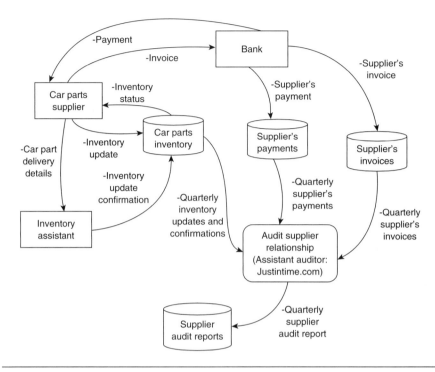

Figure 9.1   Simplified Communication Flow Representation Example

part inventory management process. In that business process, each of the suppliers of car parts (e.g., brakes, windshields, transmissions) monitors and controls the inventory of its parts that is kept in an automobile manufacturer's plant. The business process is depicted from the perspective of the automobile manufacturer, which is why certain entities like the cart parts supplier and the bank that pays the supplier are represented in a summarized way, without details about their inner business processes.

In the representation in Figure 9.1, the car part supplier monitors the inventory levels of its car parts that are sent to and used by the automobile manufacturer. When those levels fall below a certain threshold, the car parts supplier immediately sends a new batch of car parts to the automobile manufacturer, without the automobile manufacturer having to ask for those parts. This saves time and money on the automobile manufacturer's end and enables better planning on the car parts supplier's end.

Since the diagram shows only communication flows, the key indication in it that a new batch of parts is being sent is the data flow related to car part delivery details. A few days after the car parts are scheduled to be delivered to the automobile manufacturer, the car parts supplier sends an invoice to a bank that handles the supplier's payment according to a previous agreement established among the bank, the automobile manufacturer, and the supplier.

The bank makes this payment automatically upon receipt of an invoice from the supplier, which is one of the characteristics that make this type of supplier-driven inventory management process a rather unorthodox one. In most cases, one would expect the payment to be made only after receipt of the car parts by the automobile manufacturer. One reason for this is the issue of what happens if the supplier engages in some kind of fraud. For example, what if the supplier charges the automobile manufacturer for car parts that are not delivered?

The above problem, as well as other related problems, is addressed by a quarterly audit conducted by an assistant auditor using a Web-based application hosted by an outside company called Justintime.com (a fictitious name), which specializes in helping put into operation the type of supplier-driven inventory management approach discussed here. If an audit points at irregularities, the automobile manufacturer replaces the offending supplier with a competitor. This leads to certain costs for the automobile manufacturer, but the supplier is the one that suffers the most because, in most practical cases, car parts suppliers are highly dependent on the automobile manufacturers they sell to. In some cases, as much as 80% of a car parts supplier's business comes from a single automobile manufacturer. The possibility of losing such a high proportion of business is likely to be a strong deterrent to fraud.

Now, notice that we are already touching upon some technology implementation details mentioned in the discussion of the business process (e.g., the use of Justintime.com's Web-based application). However, it is hard to have a clear idea of how the business process is actually implemented, with the support of technology, based only on the diagrammatic representation used in Figure 9.1 and the related textual description that accompanies that diagrammatic representation. The kind of representation used, a communication flow representation, provides reasonably good support for communication flow–oriented business process redesign discussions and related decisions. Nevertheless, unfortunately that type of representation is too abstract to provide an effective view of how the business process will be automated, which is the next major step following business process redesign. This is addressed through intermediate representations, called here rich pictorial representations, such as the one shown in Figure 9.2.

Notice that the rich pictorial representation shown in Figure 9.2 makes explicit how information technology will be used to implement the business process previously shown in Figure 9.1. However, it does not go into so much detail as to make it impossible to have the complete representation in one single diagram. For example, the names of the computer systems used are largely omitted, and so are the specifications of the hardware used. Nevertheless, some of the elements in Figure 9.2 add substantial insight into how databases will be implemented with the use of Web servers and accessed remotely through Web browsers. As such, the diagram in Figure 9.2 provides an effective complement to the more abstract diagram shown in Figure 9.1.

The symbols used in rich pictorial representations are not standardized. Also, there are no rules as to what should be represented and what should not. Nevertheless, common sense suggests that widely used technologies, such as Web browsers and servers, be represented in one way or another. Also, it is usually a good idea to make use of graphical representations that resemble the actual elements they are aimed at representing. For instance, a humanlike figure should be used to represent a particular organization function, a computerlike icon should be used to represent a Web server, and so on.

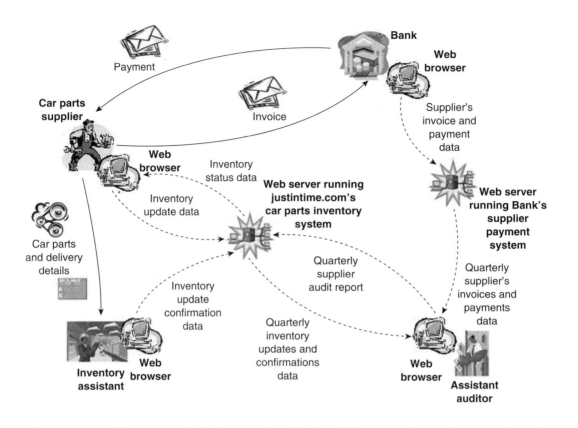

Figure 9.2   Rich Pictorial Representation Example

Users of rich pictorial representations are also free to use any method or tool to generate the representations. Some may prefer to hand draw rich pictorial representations. Others may prefer to hand draw the figures they will use, scan them, and then bring them into a charting tool and edit them as needed. Yet others, less inclined to put to use the artistic abilities that nature endowed them with, may prefer to use charting tools with predefined icons, figures, and symbols. There are many such tools in the market, some more expensive than others.

The advantage of using commercial charting tools is sometimes eclipsed by the fact that their files are saved in proprietary formats, which makes it difficult to share them electronically with a large number of users. And not being able to share diagrams electronically with a large number of users is likely to be a major obstacle in many business process redesign efforts. So, sometimes it is a good idea to compromise a bit, by using relatively standard software in a creative way. For example, one may use a component of Microsoft's ubiquitous Office suite, such as PowerPoint, for charting, taking advantage of the software's own charting tools and predefined clip-art elements. The diagram in Figure 9.2 was generated using Microsoft's PowerPoint and a set of icons and symbols available free from the developer to licensed users.

Business Process Implementation Strategies

Rich pictorial representations are aimed at providing a relatively clear view of how technology can be used to implement a new business process, without too many details about that technology-based implementation. There is a reason for this paucity in terms of details. The reason is that today there are many approaches for implementation, and often the least advisable is what is called here *in-house development*—that is, building a technology solution to implement a new business process essentially from scratch.

Up until the 1980s, it was relatively common to think of the task of automating business processes as one of primarily computer programming. That is, one would choose a computer programming language and development suite that he or she was familiar with and then code away for months (in some cases, years) until a computer system was ready for use. For instance, one would choose the programming language Pascal, a structured programming language that was seen as a major step up from unstructured computer programming languages such as BASIC. Then, the person would choose, say, Turbo Pascal as a programming suite and code away—usually in partial seclusion, and with minimal contact with the future users of the computer system being developed.

As discussed in previous chapters of this book, the above approach has probably contributed to the dismal results seen in terms of productivity returns up to the 1980s, and it is not surprising why, when we take a look back from today's perspective. Long gone are the days in which the only technology implementation option available to companies was to develop solutions in-house, often by using employees as computer programmers. Today's proliferation of packaged software to automate a large variety of business processes that are common to many organizations is one of the main phenomena that rendered in-house development unproductive.

Another element has been added to the mix with the emergence of business process outsourcing, or the farming out of entire business processes to outside organizations. With business process outsourcing, a company with hundreds of employees would not simply outsource the development of a computer-based payroll solution to be operated in-house. Rather, the company would hire an outside firm to run the entire payroll process for it. Business process outsourcing has been around for many years, but it has been receiving particular attention since the early 2000s as a worthwhile alternative for many organizations. This has been particularly true of very labor-intensive business processes that organizations in free market–oriented developed countries with high labor costs, such as the United States, can outsource to organizations in other countries where the cost of labor is much lower. One example is the business process associated with providing low-level help desk support for office applications; another is the business process associated with telemarketing.

In the next few sections, three key alternatives are discussed, some of which have been briefly reviewed above, for the implementation of redesigned business processes. The alternatives are discussed in the following order. *Business process outsourcing* is discussed first, followed by *commercial package customization*, and then *in-house development.* Arguably, this order reflects the general order in which those alternatives should be considered in practical situations, primarily because the suggested order also reflects the contemporary business practice of most organizations. Currently, about 80 percent of all technology implementation projects aimed at automating business processes rely on business process outsourcing and commercial package customization. Only about 20 percent of those projects rely on in-house development.

Business Process Outsourcing

The chief information officer of a health services organization in Philadelphia with $1.5 billion in annual revenues provided an interesting case of an outsourcing project. He was talking about a business process outsourcing project he had just successfully seen to completion and about the financial outcomes of the project. In a nutshell, what he and his senior information technology management did was outsource all of the information technology support processes, whose services were formerly provided by the unit he led to the internal users of his health services organization.

However, the aforementioned business process outsourcing arrangement was a rather unorthodox one. No one was fired. A contract was signed between the health services organization and the outsourcing services provider to ensure that there would be no layoffs for at least 3 years. Moreover, all of the information technology employees continued occupying the same desks, using the same equipment, and coming to work as usual. The biggest difference for those employees was that they now received their paychecks (or direct bank deposits) from an organization different from the one that they worked at, namely the outsourcing services provider. The health services organization became their customer.

Nevertheless, the chief information officer reported information technology savings in the neighborhood of 20 percent for the health services organization, as a result of the outsourcing. Was it a cut in employee benefits that led to the savings? The answer is "no," which is a bit perplexing. How did those savings come about, then? The explanation was a rather simple one. The company to which the information technology support processes were outsourced had other large customers, which meant that their information technology budget was a sizeable one. If they had, say, 10 outsourcing customers, where each had an individual information technology budget of $40 million, then the total information technology budget of the outsourcing organization would have been $400 million. A sizeable budget in turn allowed the organization providing outsourcing services to negotiate much better deals with hardware manufacturers and, most importantly, better licensing deals with software developers.

Understandably, having a budget of $400 million for software license purchases gives a company a much higher bargaining power than having a budget of $40 million. That increase in bargaining power easily translates into software licensing savings, which may be very substantial. For example, a 10 percent savings in a $400 million budget is $40 million, which was close to the entire budget of the health services organization that outsourced its business process. And a 10 percent savings in connection with licensing fees translates into a modest reduction in vendors' profits, especially given that large software developers like Microsoft and IBM often have juicy gross profit margins, in some cases as much as 70 percent or more on some of their software products.

This example illustrates an advantage of business process outsourcing that is not always self-evident to those who consider it as an alternative to implement new business processes using information technologies. Business process outsourcing also brings other advantages, such as that of allowing an organization to focus on its core competencies and farm out those business processes that can be categorized as support processes. One example of support process is the payroll management process—what kind of organization can argue that payroll management is one of its core competencies, with the exception of a payroll management services organization?

Another advantage of business process outsourcing, particularly in the case of business processes that are peripheral to the core competencies of an organization, is often an increase in the quality and productivity of the business process outcomes. The reason for this is that employees of an organization who are not involved in performing tasks related to one of the core competencies of the organization are often treated as "second-class citizens" within the organization, which decreases their morale and negatively affects their performance. That is a situation that may change substantially with business process outsourcing.

Let us look at an example that illustrates this notion. Let us imagine an information technology support unit of a large bank. Among the bank's main lines of business is that of lending money to individuals and organizations in exchange for interest payments (and the return of the principal after some time, of course). Arguably, providing information technology support is not one of the core competencies of the bank. Therefore, an employee who specializes in the intricacies of the lending process could be seen as a more "mainstream" employee within the bank than another employee specializing in information technology support. Among other differences, the former (mainstream employee) may reasonably expect to become the chief executive officer of the bank one day, whereas for the latter, this expectation would be much less reasonable. In other words, it is much harder to "climb up the corporate ladder" if one is not involved with one of the core processes of the corporation, which naturally limits the career options of employees in support areas.

Now, this situation would change substantially if the bank outsourced its information technology support processes to an outside organization—an information technology services organization. The employees of this information technology services organization would all be involved in the core processes of their organization, even though they would be carrying out business processes that are similar to those performed by employees of an information technology support unit of the bank, if there were one. The career progress prospects for the employees of the outsourcing services provider would be, at least in perception, much more promising than for the employees of an information technology support unit of the bank, which could make the former more productive and more motivated to please their external customers.

Notwithstanding the benefits associated with business process outsourcing, there are also some potential problems. Every form of outsourcing involves a certain degree of dependence on the outside organization to which one or more business processes are being outsourced. Conducting business process outsourcing with an outside company that is about to go bankrupt, for example, may lead to disastrous consequences. There have been cases in the past in which that was exactly what happened. For example, in a Society for Information Management workshop, a large chemical company representative reported on an outsourcing contract that went bad. The chemical company hired, through an outsourcing contract, a help desk services firm to provide internal help desk support to all of the chemical company's employees. Apparently, the help desk services provider, in an effort to underbid its rivals, underestimated its own expenses in connection with the provision of help desk support. To make a long story short, after many problems with the quality of the support provided, the large chemical company ended its contract with the outsourcer, which was then close to bankruptcy.

Also, outsourcing usually involves contracts between organizations, and if those contracts are not carefully prepared, they may lead to major problems for the parties in the contract. While firing an employee in breach of contract may lead to some legal liability and related expenses, breaching a multimillion-dollar contract with an outsourcing services provider may lead to legal problems of much greater magnitude. One of the key issues in connection with outsourcing contracts is that of defining appropriate service quality metrics, that is, measurements that can be used to assess whether contractual obligations are being met. For example, let us assume that a multinational engineering company hires an Internet service provider in the United States to (a) provide the engineering company's employees in the United States with access to the Internet and (b) host and provide Web access to a large customer relationship application that sales representatives of the engineering company can utilize from anywhere in the world.

Now let us also assume that the outsourcing contract, while specifying that access will be provided on a 24/7 basis, does not make any statements in connection with the latency (or delay) of the data provision. In that case, if it takes 30 minutes for a sales representative to obtain the full address of a customer, most of the sales representatives will not use the Web-based customer relationship application. However, from a contractual perspective, the engineering company will have little recourse.

Business process outsourcing may take a variety of forms and cover numerous types of business processes. For instance, many organizations today outsource their hardware and software management processes, whereby they keep track of their equipment and software, and make sure that they comply with the licensing agreements they signed. This makes particular sense if the organization purchases most of its hardware or software from one main vendor and that vendor also offers hardware or software management services through outsourcing arrangements. Let us take General Motors, for example. If General Motors were a Microsoft "shop," that is, if most of its software were purchased from Microsoft, it would make sense for General Motors to farm out the process of software asset management to Microsoft. By doing so, General Motors would shift the responsibility to Microsoft to ensure that General Motors' software licensing agreements with Microsoft were being followed—at a cost, of course, namely the cost of the business process outsourcing contract.

Commercial Package Customization

Commercial package customization is perhaps the most widely used alternative for the implementation of business processes, with business process outsourcing inching forward and soon likely to become a close second. Commercial package customization refers primarily to software. The reason why it is presented here after business process outsourcing is that it is usually a good idea to look at it after a review of available outsourcing options. For most business processes, there will be commercial packages available, which may not be the case with outsourcing. Moreover, a review of outsourcing options may suggest some interesting metrics that the organization can use to review commercial package customization solutions.

In essence, commercial package customization entails purchasing a commercial software package "off the shelf," so to speak, to automate a given business process. The software package is usually installed in one or more of the organization's computers, be they servers, client desktops, or both (in the case of client-server computer software). For standardized business processes that are very similar across a large number of organizations, commercial package customization is usually a good solution, if business process outsourcing either is not an option or is too expensive an option.

While to many people commercial package customization may bring to mind the idea of installing a few hundred dollars' worth of office software applications on a desktop and configuring them for personal use, there are substantially more expensive and broader examples of commercial package customization. One rather extreme example, from an organizational perspective, is that of enterprise systems—also known as enterprise resource planning, or ERP, systems. Enterprise systems are large and expensive software applications that automate, usually in a tightly integrated way, several business processes of an organization. The business processes automated sometimes comprise most of an organization's processes, ranging from order taking to production and delivery processes.

Before the advent of enterprise systems, which occurred mostly in the 1990s, it was difficult for organizations to automate several of their business processes in an integrated way. What is meant here by integrated automation is essentially a type of automation in which business processes share data with one another. What usually happened before enterprise systems became commonly used in organizations was the automation of business processes in a localized manner, which often led to organizations' having many different computer systems working in isolation.

This situation can be illustrated through an example. Consider a sales division of a large company that automates its new product marketing process using a marketing management computer system, while the engineering division of the same company automates its new product development process using a new product development computer system. The problem is that both systems would have to store some of the same information. For instance, while contact information about the company's customers is obviously needed for the marketing management system, it is also needed for the new product development system, since key customers have to be contacted frequently and asked to provide their input regarding the desirability of the features of the new products being developed. Since the two computer systems work in isolation, one of the inevitable outcomes is information duplication and inconsistencies—for example, differences in the contact information kept by the two systems about a customer.

The name of the business process implementation alternative discussed in this section is commercial package *customization*, where the term *customization* means alteration of the computer application purchased through configuration or programming. Many commercial software packages allow users to add or modify features through programming using a software package–specific language or programming environment. A good example is one of the best-selling enterprise systems, SAP/R3, which is commercialized by the large German software development company SAP AG. Not only can SAP/R3 be configured in many different ways, it also can have its functionality modified and extended through a programming language called ABAP (known in some circles as "German COBOL").

Even small and relatively inexpensive computer applications allow for major customization through myriad configuration options and programming. For example, some of the main components of the Microsoft Office suite, namely Word, Excel, and Access, can have their functionality substantially expanded through macros (i.e., program modules that automate manual operations). Those macros are coded in a programming language called Visual Basic for Applications (VBA), which is "native" to the Microsoft Office suite and is common to most of the suite's components.

Upon purchasing a commercial package, an organization has the option of not customizing it or customizing it minimally. Of course, this saves time and labor resources, but it also prevents the organization from implementing business process features that are unique and that could give the organization an edge over its competitors. Since commercial packages are usually developed to support business processes that are somewhat standard (e.g., cash flow control, ISO 9000 compliance reporting), the commercial package customization options are usually there to allow just that, that is, the implementation of business processes with unique features.

The issue of whether one should customize or not customize commercial software packages is one that has attracted a substantial amount of attention, particularly from information technology managers, since it involves a key decision that all those who purchase commercial software packages have to make, usually right after they buy the packages. Many information technology managers know from experience that while customization can lead to differentiation, it can also lead to poor returns in terms of productivity gains associated with investment in software.

To address this issue, members of the MIS and Decision Sciences Department at Texas A&M International University have conducted an analysis on data collected from 116 information technology executives in charge of enterprise systems contracting. The analysis built on the information technology paradox phenomenon discussed earlier in this book. Briefly recapping what was discussed before, the phenomenon is primarily characterized by organizations in the service sector having historically dismal productivity returns on information technology investment, especially when compared with manufacturing sector organizations.

Given that, the analysis was aimed partly at finding out whether service sector organizations generally displayed a preference toward customization of software packages, while manufacturing sector organizations displayed the opposite preference, which combined would help explain the information technology productivity paradox. That is, if the information technology productivity paradox is correct, it is reasonable to expect that service sector organizations will generally present lower levels of return on information technology investment, which includes investment in enterprise systems software, than will manufacturing organizations. If those low levels of return on investment are associated with a tendency to customize enterprise systems, then it would not be unreasonable to infer that customization may be associated with lower productivity gains from enterprise systems investment and may at least partially cause the information technology paradox.

The analysis was based on the emphasis placed by the information technology executives polled on customization rights, in the context of enterprise systems contracts previously signed by them. It was assumed that the emphasis would reflect future behavior, which is arguably a fairly reasonable assumption (otherwise the related contract clauses would not have been there in the first place). Figure 9.3 shows the results of the data analysis in connection with emphasis on customization rights, that is, rights allowing the acquiring organization to revise, or change, the enterprise system that they purchased. More specifically, Figure 9.3 shows the averages obtained from the data analysis in connection with the emphasis on customization rights displayed by information technology executives in service and manufacturing sector organizations.

Another facet of the analysis was the emphasis placed by the information technology executives polled on portability rights in enterprise systems contracts previously signed by them. Portability rights are defined as rights allowing the acquiring organization to port the enterprise system to different hardware platforms that the acquiring organization has adopted or may adopt in the future. It was assumed that the emphasis on portability rights would show a trend opposite to the trend regarding the emphasis on customization rights, because interest in portability suggests interest in using the system "as is" for a long time—enterprise systems platforms (e.g., hardware, operating systems) do not usually change very often, owing to the costs involved. Figure 9.4 shows the averages obtained from the data analysis in connection with the emphasis on portability rights displayed by information technology executives in service and manufacturing sector organizations.

Based on Figures 9.3 and 9.4, one can reasonably argue that service sector organizations generally display a preference toward customizing software, which is supported by evidence indicating that information technology executives of service sector organizations perceive enterprise systems customization rights as approximately 10 percent more important than information technology executives of manufacturing sector organizations. One can also conclude, based on Figures 9.3 and 9.4, that manufacturing sector organizations generally display a preference

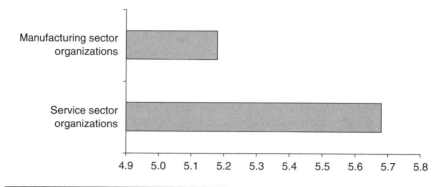

Figure 9.3   Emphasis on Customization Rights

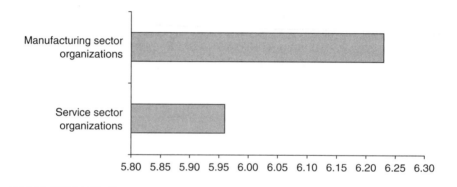

Figure 9.4   Emphasis on Portability Rights

toward acquiring portable software, which is also supported by evidence indicating that the difference in importance of enterprise portability rights is approximately 5 percent, with information technology executives in the manufacturing sector perceiving those rights as more important.

These results generally support the information technology productivity paradox notion and also suggest a new explanation for it. The new explanation is that service sector organizations tend to adopt a more revisionist, or change-oriented, approach to software acquisition, which in turn contributes in part to making them reap lower productivity gains from software spending than their counterparts in the manufacturing sector. One could argue that customization of large, complex, and expensive software products such as enterprise systems may not be a good idea. This claim may be seen as more or less counterintuitive, depending on which software vendors' views are considered. Those vendors that rely heavily on post-sale software maintenance services for much of their revenues, which comprise many enterprise systems vendors today, may find the claim counterintuitive. Those vendors that rely heavily on license-based revenues and that provide post-sale software maintenance as a bonus to their customers may find the claim perfectly reasonable.

In-House Development

As mentioned before in this chapter, the in-house development alternative to business process implementation generally entails "creating" a technology solution in-house, that is, inside the organization that houses the business process being implemented. For example, let us consider a large pharmaceutical company that has recently redesigned its new drug development processes. The company then implements the new business processes through the development of a secure Web-based document routing and control system, which essentially routes and controls the flow of the several documents involved in the development of drugs among the several departments and areas involved (e.g., lab testing area, statistical analysis department). For the sake of discussion, let us assume that the document routing and control system was developed using a development suite commercialized by Oracle, which the pharmaceutical company acquired specifically for the project in question.

In this example, the pharmaceutical company purchased (and likely customized) a commercial package, namely the Oracle development suite. Nevertheless, the example is one of in-house development, because the Oracle development suite was not used to automate the new drug development process per se. Rather, the suite served as a basis on which a new technology solution was created. That new technology solution was the secure Web-based document routing and control system.

There are many software development suites available on the market. The following are only a few examples: Oracle JDeveloper 10g (by Oracle Corporation); Microsoft Access and Microsoft Visual Studio .NET (both by Microsoft Corporation); Sun Java Studio (by Sun Microsystems); and WebSphere Studio (by IBM Corporation). Quite often, in-house development of a software solution to partially or fully automate a redesigned business process is conducted based on a software development suite such as those just mentioned. Nevertheless, the acquisition of a software development suite does not characterize a business process implementation project as being of the commercial package customization type.

Today, in-house development is a much less frequently employed business process implementation solution than business process outsourcing and commercial package customization. There are many reasons for this, one of which is cost. Because of the many risks and complexities associated with in-house development, the likelihood is very high that its total cost will be as much as twice (if not more than) that of an equivalent business process outsourcing or commercial package customization solution (if one such solution is commercially available, of course). However, not-very-seasoned information technology managers and professionals often fall into the trap of believing that in-house development is the cheapest choice for the implementation of a new business process.

The main reason for the above is the inability to recognize all of the different types of direct and indirect costs associated with in-house development, an inability that more often than not is displayed by inexperienced information technology managers and professionals. For example, it is often assumed that information technology support staff can be reallocated from nondevelopment activities (e.g., help desk support, networking infrastructure troubleshooting) to in-house development activities at no or minimum extra cost. Another mistake is to assume that inexperienced developers (e.g., student interns) can develop software in-house that is of quality comparable to that of commercial software packages. Yet another mistake is to assume no overhead costs as associated with in-house development (e.g., copying, telephone, secretarial support). Finally, a big and very common mistake is to ignore maintenance costs, that is, costs associated with maintaining, operating, and fixing the software system developed in-house (after it is developed and installed for use). Maintenance costs are believed to amount to as much as 80 percent of the total costs associated with many in-house system development projects.

More than a few of these costs are absent from commercial package customization or business process outsourcing projects. Moreover, the costs associated with commercial package customization or business process outsourcing are usually more predictable, which facilitates multiyear budgeting. This improves the relationship between the chief information and financial officers' offices, which is very important since in most organizations, the chief financial officer's office is constantly asked to approve all sorts of information technology expenditures.

In a sense, in-house development can be seen as an extreme form of commercial package customization. And, given the discussion in the previous section in connection with customization, one could conclude that in-house development should be avoided at all costs. However, in some cases, in-house development is the most appropriate alternative, if not unavoidable. These situations are illustrated in Figure 9.5.

Figure 9.5 lists three main situations that call for in-house development. One of those situations is that involving very specialized business processes, such as the process involved in the management multimedia resources (e.g., VCRs, projectors) used by instructors in educational organizations. In this type of situation, it is possible that there will be no commercial packages or business process outsourcing solutions available for purchase, or that the available solutions will be adaptations of technology solutions designed to support different (but similar) types of business processes. One thing to bear in mind regarding commercial package and business process outsourcing solutions is that those solutions are usually offered by companies that want to make a profit, either by designing solutions that can be used

---

When to do in-house development?

- When the business process is very specialized
  - Management of multimedia components used for class enrichment
- When the business process is very simple (local/narrow processes)
  - Control of multimedia carts routinely used in three conference rooms
- When the business process is very strategic
  - Counterterrorism intelligence gathering and sharing process managed by the CIA

Figure 9.5   Situations in Which In-House Development Is a Good Choice

by a large number of customers (a General Motors–like approach, to use a car design analogy) or by designing specialized solutions for a small number of customers and charging a premium for them (a Porsche-like approach).

Another situation illustrated in Figure 9.5 that calls for in-house development is that involving very simple business processes, such as managing and controlling the use of multimedia carts (i.e., portable carts with multimedia equipment such as VCRs and projectors) used in three conference rooms. This is a simple business process that essentially entails allocating multimedia carts and having them delivered to different conference rooms upon request and making sure that they are returned to the multimedia room where they are kept and maintained. This type of business process can easily be enabled by in-house development based on relatively inexpensive office technologies, such as a spreadsheet with macros developed to support basic functions such as the identification of scheduling conflicts. Given its simplicity, the best alternative here is in-house development.

Finally, a third situation illustrated in Figure 9.5 that calls for in-house development is that involving very strategic business processes, such as the process of intelligence gathering and sharing managed by the U.S. Central Intelligence Agency (CIA). The reason why in-house development may be the best alternative here is that the organization retains full control over the business process and the technology used to implement it. Another example would be a business process that involves a novel algorithm, which the organization may want to keep in secrecy until a patent is obtained. For example, Amazon.com has developed and patented proprietary algorithms for customization of electronic commerce Web sites based on a customers' buying history. In that case, Amazon.com benefited from resorting to an in-house development strategy, even though Amazon.com is primarily an online retailer, not a software developer.

Summary and Concluding Remarks

This chapter began by providing an answer to the question of how one goes from a relatively abstract business process representation, such as a communication flow diagram, to a clear pre-implementation understanding of how technologies will be used to enable a new business process. This chapter's answer to that question was what is referred to here as a rich pictorial representation of the new business process, which is based on a flexible graphical tool inspired by a similar concept proposed many years ago by Peter Checkland as part of his soft systems methodology. Rich pictorial representations help a business process redesign team move relatively smoothly from an abstract representation of a business process to a reasonably clear view of how the business process will be implemented in practice with the use of information technologies.

While rich pictorial representations provide a clearer view of how technology can be used to implement a new business process than do more abstract representations, such as communication flow diagrams, the clearer technological lenses that they provide are primarily used to set the stage for important decisions as to what strategy will be used in that implementation.

As far as business process implementation strategies, the main focus of this chapter has been on three main strategies: business process outsourcing, commercial package customization, and in-house development. Business process outsourcing essentially entails farming out the execution of the business process to an outside organization. Commercial package customization involves buying a packaged technology solution to implement the new business process and using it with some modifications aimed to accommodate the business process. In-house development essentially consists of creating a technology solution in-house, that is, inside the organization that houses the business process being implemented.

After being involved in several business process redesign projects involving technology-based implementation decisions, one starts noticing some patterns in terms of the practical elements of the situations faced and the strategies that are most recommended under the circumstances. Table 9.1 summarizes some realistic practical situations and recommended strategies. For the sake of simplicity, it is assumed in Table 9.1 that the recommended strategies can be implemented—for example, that the necessary business process outsourcing options, or commercial packages, are available in the market.

In Table 9.1, the term *process quality metrics* refers to measurement instruments or approaches that are related to how certain business process attributes are

Table 9.1   Practical Situations and Recommended Implementation Strategies

Practical Situation	Recommended Strategy
Very standardized and regulated process; many reliable process quality metrics available	Business process outsourcing
Very standardized and regulated process; no reliable process quality metrics available	Commercial package customization
Very specialized and nonstandardized process created to address a new business opportunity	In-house development
Complex support area process unrelated to the main mission of the organization	Business process outsourcing
Complex core process directly related to the main mission of the organization	Commercial package customization
Very simple process addressing a local need of a small department or unit	In-house development
Very strategic and general process using and generating nonsensitive information	Business process outsourcing
Very strategic and general process using and generating sensitive information	Commercial package customization
Very strategic and unique process using and generating sensitive information	In-house development

perceived by the customers of the business process. For example, let us consider a question used for measurement of the perceived usefulness of the computer applications support provided through a help desk process. Let us assume that the question is measured on a scale from 1 (not satisfied) to 7 (extremely satisfied). A variable that summarizes the answers to the question, by the calculation of the average answer, for instance, is an example of a quality metric associated with a business process carried out by the help desk department of an organization.

Another term used in Table 9.1 that could be clarified is *unrelated to the main mission of the organization.* Let us consider a car rental company, for the sake of illustration. The broad business process associated with renting cars to customers is closely related to the main mission of the organization. The business process associated with maintaining the engines of the cars in the rental company's fleet in good working order is a support process that is arguably unrelated to the main mission of the organization—which is primarily to rent cars, not to fix them.

The recommendations in Table 9.1 should, of course, be implemented with caution and common sense. For example, the commercial package customization strategy is recommended in a practical situation involving a very strategic and general busing process using and generating sensitive information. In this case, it would probably be a good idea to find out whether the organization that developed or commercialized the software package has access to the sensitive information stored by the system for each customer. If it has, then it might be advisable to find another vendor, request a change in the commercial package's configuration to protect sensitive information, or obtain a written assurance from the vendor that the sensitive information will be handled in a confidential manner. Such written assurances are essentially contract clauses and thus should be accompanied by penalty clauses to be invoked in cases of noncompliance.

Review Questions

1. Rich pictorial representations are:
   (a) Less abstract, in terms of making it clear how technology is used to implement a business process, than communication flow representations.
   (b) Too abstract to provide an effective view of how the business process will be automated.
   (c) More abstract, in terms of making it clear how technology is used to implement a business process, than communication flow representations.
   (d) The most abstract type of representation available, in terms of making it clear how technology is used to implement a business process.

2. It is incorrect to say that rich pictorial representations:
   (a) Are lightly standardized, not using very well-defined symbols.
   (b) Have been proposed as part of the work conducted by Peter Checkland in the 1980s.

(c) Are heavily standardized, using very well-defined symbols.

(d) Are inspired in a type of representation of the same name, proposed as part of the soft systems methodology.

3. Business process outsourcing essentially entails:

(a) Centralizing the execution of one or more business processes inside the organization.

(b) Farming out the execution of one or more business processes to an outside organization.

(c) Creating an infrastructure for the execution of one or more support processes inside the organization.

(d) Signing a franchising contract to outsource the execution of one or more support processes to a national defense–related organization.

4. Which of the following alternatives is incorrect?

(a) Commercial package customization is one of the most widely used alternatives for the implementation of business processes, together with business process outsourcing.

(b) For standardized business processes that are very similar across a large number of organizations, commercial package customization is usually a good solution.

(c) Commercial package customization entails purchasing a commercial software package "off the shelf" to automate a business process.

(d) Commercial package customization entails buying cardboard boxes and customizing them for sale to selected customers.

5. Which of the following alternatives in connection with in-house development is correct?

(a) Costs associated with maintaining, operating, and fixing software systems are usually not part of in-house development project implementations.

(b) In-house development is a much more frequently employed business process implementation solution than commercial package customization, particularly in companies that do not develop technology themselves (e.g., hospitals and car manufacturers).

(c) In-house development can be seen as an extreme form of commercial package customization.

(d) In restaurant chains, in-house development is a much more frequently employed business process implementation solution than commercial package customization.

Discussion Questions

1. Develop a detailed scenario involving a knowledge-intensive business process in a service sector organization (e.g., a university, a consulting services firm). The business process in question should incorporate at least three information

repositories and five interactions involving information exchanges. Develop a communication flow and related rich pictorial representation of the business process in question.

2. Based on a Web-based review, identify business process outsourcing and commercial package customization solutions to implement the business process developed in response to Discussion Question 1. Develop a table comparing the solutions along a number of dimensions that you believe are important from a decision-making perspective (e.g., cost). Decide which is the best alternative between the two, and explain why.

3. Develop a detailed description of an in-house development solution to implement the business process you developed in response to Discussion Question 1. The description should incorporate estimated implementation costs along several dimensions (e.g., labor, hardware, software, training). Compare this solution with the business process outsourcing and commercial package customization solutions you identified in response to Discussion Question 2. Decide which is the best alternative of the three, and explain why.

CHAPTER 10

Redesigning Little Italy Restaurants

For quite some time now, case studies have been successfully used to illustrate the application of ideas, methods, and techniques in real-world contexts. The Harvard Business School is widely recognized as a leader in the use of case studies to teach business concepts and ideas to management students. In this chapter, a case study is used to describe in some detail a practical business application of the ideas, methods, and techniques discussed in previous chapters. This is done here following the Harvard method, which usually involves an in-depth analysis of business context and a conceptual illustration that is not overly simplified. The goal is to show more or less how a real business process redesign project would be carried out, using the general redesign approach proposed in this book.

The case study involves the redesign of the order fulfillment process of an Italian restaurant chain, referred to here as Little Italy Restaurants. It is based on several actual business process redesign projects, including one key project that incorporated many of the elements of this case study; the actual project in question involved the redesign of a restaurant chain that was in many aspects similar to Little Italy Restaurants. The case has also been used in several university classes, at both undergraduate and graduate levels, which helped in its refinement over the years and hopefully in making it more pedagogically appealing.

Little Italy Restaurants: Background Information

Many of the popular restaurant chains where we eat today started with one single restaurant whose food, service, or both had a particular appeal to its clientele. Little Italy Restaurants was no exception. It grew from one single restaurant located in a high-growth city in southern Brazil, which then had about 700,000 people. In only about 10 years, the restaurant chain had grown from 1 restaurant to 30 restaurants, all located in and around the same city. All 30 restaurants initially had their own independent kitchens, where the dishes and their ingredients were all prepared from scratch. The city's population had grown to approximately 1.7 million people in 10 years, a compound annual growth rate of more than 14 percent, which helped support the restaurant chain's expansion.

Some of the elements that separated the Little Italy Restaurants chain from the competition were the atmosphere and service in its restaurants. Unlike other pasta restaurants, whose atmosphere attempted to replicate a part of Italy (even though pasta was actually invented in China), Little Italy Restaurants adopted an innovative approach to creating a unique dining atmosphere. The restaurant chain tried to appeal to its local customers by decorating its restaurants to extol the accomplishments of local sports and media celebrities, as well as to highlight certain events of importance to the city. Waiters and waitresses were trained so as to add to and strengthen that atmosphere, often wearing clothes related to a city event–related theme. Examples of city events inspiring themes included a local soccer championship, a major arts exhibition being held in the downtown area of the city (which was also a regional cultural center), an ecological campaign being promoted by the city and state governments, and the inauguration of a new animal habitat at the local zoo.

Notwithstanding the atmosphere and service, perhaps the most unique aspect that set Little Italy Restaurants apart from the competition was the quality of its dishes, all prepared with ingredients produced in-house. Among those ingredients, the key ones were the pastas (e.g., spaghetti, linguine, penne) and the sauces (e.g., meatball, Bolognese, marinara). The pastas developed in Little Italy Restaurants' kitchens had a distinctive flavor because they were prepared with semolina imported from Italy, and their al dente cooking enhanced that flavor.

As the Little Italy Restaurants chain grew, it became increasingly difficult and costly to have full kitchens in each of its restaurants. A key difficulty was that dish items, such as a particular type of pasta and sauce, had to be prepared in exactly the same way in each restaurant so that their taste would be uniformly the same across different restaurants of the same chain—something that was very hard to accomplish.

Another problem was the amount of space that the full kitchens occupied in each restaurant. This is a key problem with any restaurant that has a lot of demand, and it is also a source of revenue losses. For example, let us consider a restaurant where the kitchen occupies about half of the restaurant's space. This means that the restaurant has roughly half of the sitting capacity that it would have if it had no kitchen, and a loss in sitting capacity can be translated into a loss of revenues if the demand for food is higher than the supply in the restaurant. If the restaurant has yearly revenues of $1 million, which is a conservative estimate of revenues for a small restaurant, a 50 percent loss in revenues would translate to an actual loss of $500,000 in sales every year! With a gross profit margin of 10 percent, that would translate into an absolute cash flow loss of $50,000 per year. Multiplied by 30, the number of restaurants in the Little Italy Restaurants chain, that would yield a cash flow loss of $1.5 million per year.

The above was not the actual cash flow loss that the Little Italy Restaurants chain was incurring every year due to several reasons. For example, the full kitchens in its restaurants varied in size and did not usually take up half of the sitting space in the restaurants. Also, one cannot assume that the kitchens could be simply eliminated from the restaurants, because even with the centralization of food item preparation elsewhere, at least some kitchen space would be necessary to put food items together and prepare them in a simplified way (e.g., heat them up, add spice to them according to order, "dress" the dishes) prior to serving the dishes to the customers. Nevertheless, even if we consider that Little Italy Restaurants was losing a third of the aforementioned estimate, that would be half a million a year, which is by no means a negligible cash flow loss amount for a small business enterprise.

A possible solution, mentioned above, was the centralization of dish item preparation in a central kitchen. That was exactly what the owner of the Little Italy Restaurants' chain decided to do to increase sitting space in each of the restaurants of the chain and ensure that the dish items would taste the same across different restaurants. A new industrial kitchen was built, using mostly new and modern cooking equipment. The full kitchens in each restaurant were reduced in size to about one third of their former space, which led to an average increase in sitting capacity in the restaurants of about 30 percent. The estimated increase in annual revenues as a result of those changes was about $9 million. Figure 10.1 shows the new chain configuration in a schematic way.

A restaurant chain that grows as fast as the Little Italy Restaurants chain did could not be categorized as anything other than a very successful organization. However, growth and change usually lead to problems as well. Key problems facing the Little Italy Restaurants chain were related to the interaction between the restaurants in the chain and the central kitchen. Those problems are discussed in the next section.

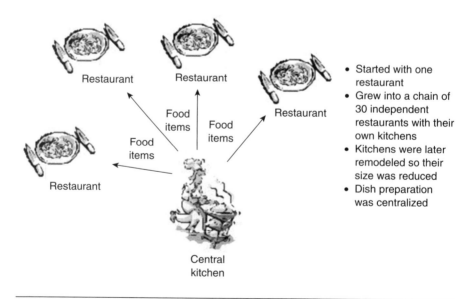

Figure 10.1   Little Italy Restaurants' Organizational Structure

Little Italy Restaurants' Key Problems

While centralizing food item production in a central kitchen was a smart move, it was also a significant change in the way the Little Italy Restaurants chain operated. Change of that magnitude usually leads to problems, which, in the Little Italy Restaurant chain's case, were mostly related to the interaction between each of the 30 restaurants and the central kitchen, in what we will refer to here as the "order fulfillment process." This process could be seen as involving two key entities, namely the restaurant placing a food items order and the central kitchen, which would fulfill the order—that is, produce the component food items and deliver them to the restaurant that placed the order.

In theory, the central kitchen would receive orders for food items (e.g., pasta and sauce items) from the restaurants, produce those food items, and then ship them to the restaurants on time so that the restaurants could then use those food items to prepare dishes for their customers in their small kitchens. The reality was that, at the end of the first year of the centralization of food item preparation in the central kitchen, several things were going terribly wrong, and the restaurant chain was starting to lose customers as a result.

In approximately 40 percent of the deliveries made by the central kitchen, food items arrived late in the restaurants. For example, a restaurant located near a highway would request a number of food items in preparation for a visit by a large group of tourists whose tour bus would be stopping at the restaurant for lunch on a Wednesday. The food items would arrive on Friday, which would leave the customers and the restaurant manager infuriated; some of the unused food items would have to be shipped back to the central kitchen, due to the limited storage capacity in the restaurant.

Additionally, in approximately 20 percent of the deliveries, the food items went to the wrong restaurants. Moreover, about 60 percent of the food orders from the restaurants to the central kitchen were only partially fulfilled. For example, an order for 20 gallons of carbonara sauce would be placed, but only 15 gallons would arrive.

All of the aforementioned problems led to reactions by the restaurant managers, which ranged from repeated complaints to preventive measures, such as ordering more than what was needed and providing "just in case" deadlines (e.g., ordering food items for a Wednesday, when the items were actually needed on a Friday). The combination of the problems and reactions led to a rather chaotic and wasteful situation. The central kitchen was seemingly ill equipped to deal with the volume of orders being placed.

After many attempts at addressing the Little Italy Restaurant chain's quandary by the owner of the chain, several of which involved the kitchen and restaurant managers, an external consulting team was hired. An initial analysis suggested that the problems were due to what seemed to be primarily communication difficulties associated with the order fulfillment process. That is, apparently there was nothing wrong with the food items production process or with the restaurants themselves.

What really needed to be fixed was the communication interface between the restaurants and the central kitchen, which involved several steps of information

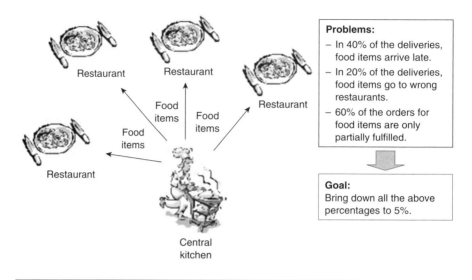

Figure 10.2   Little Italy Restaurants' Problems and Business Process Redesign Goal

exchange and storage. Based on an overall assessment of the restaurant industry, the consulting team felt that what was needed was a systematic business process redesign effort. The consulting team also felt that a reasonable goal for the business process redesign effort would be to bring down the percentages associated with the problems discussed above to about 5 percent (see Figure 10.2).

Although there were benchmarks available, which the external consulting team used to propose the goal above, the goal was also based on a detailed analysis of the order fulfillment process. That analysis included the development of a communication flow representation of the business process, as well as detailed textual descriptions of the different activities involved in the process. Key elements of that analysis are summarized below.

The Order Fulfillment Process

The business process whereby the central kitchen fulfills orders from each of the 30 restaurants starts with a request by the restaurant's manager of food items that are soon expected to be out of stock. Requests are usually made over the phone, all with very high-priority stipulations and expectations, and answered by an overworked and rather stressed central kitchen's manager (see Figure 10.3). From the central kitchen's manager perspective, each restaurant's manager usually acts as though his or her restaurant is the most important of the chain.

As mentioned before, the central kitchen's manager receives each restaurant's request typically over the phone or, in some cases, by fax. Restaurant managers

Figure 10.3   The Restaurant Request Stage of the Order Fulfillment Process

prefer the telephone as a food items order–placing medium because it gives them a sense of commitment on the part of the central kitchen's manager; that is, they generally want to hear the central kitchen's manager say that the restaurant orders will be fulfilled, right on the spot.

The above happened frequently, even though most orders ended up not being fulfilled as promised, and most restaurant managers knew that the orders would not be fulfilled as promised. That tended to irritate the restaurant managers even more, because their reactive attempts to ensure order delivery seemed to be leading nowhere. It was not clear to them that it was not the central kitchen manager's intentional low prioritization of their orders that was causing the problem.

Now, let us go back to the description of the order fulfillment process. Upon receipt of a food items request by a restaurant manager, the central kitchen's manager fills out a form that is sent to his assistant manager, who places the form in an in-box. This form specifies the food items requested and the restaurant whose manager made the request.

When processing a food items request, the assistant manager of the central kitchen always checks the request with each restaurant's manager over the phone. There are two reasons for this. First, the assistant manager always wants to make sure that the list of food items is correct, since mistakes are commonly made in the phone communication of a food items request. Second, given that the central kitchen's staff is generally overworked and behind schedule in the production and delivery of food items orders, the central kitchen's assistant manager wants to find out when the items can be delivered at the latest.

Once the assistant manager of the central kitchen is done checking the request, he then forwards the form with the appropriate corrections and usually with a handwritten priority code (e.g., urgent, 1-day delivery) to the central kitchen's chef, who places the request form near the top right corner of his desk. As soon as the central kitchen's chef has some time—he is always busy coordinating the production of food items—he schedules food items production by pinning up the request forms on a notice board. The request forms are pinned up in a way that suggests their planned order of production.

In the meantime, the central kitchen's chef coordinates the work of his kitchen staff, as well as controlling his own stock of ingredients. The chef interacts with his staff by instructing them to carry out simple tasks such as filling up a large pan with water, cleaning a batch of shrimps, or adding onion to a mix. When the food items associated with a request are ready, they are first packed, then labeled, and finally left on a delivery pallet by the chef's team. The labels on the packets describe the contents of the packets and the address of the restaurants to which they have to be delivered. The request form is then returned to the assistant manager with a note indicating that the order is ready for delivery.

Upon receipt of the request form, with a note indicating that the order is ready for delivery, the assistant manager then signs the request form returned by the chef, fills a control book with information about the completed order (including size, food items, and date), and sends the signed request form to the central kitchen's delivery team. The delivery team makes no delivery until they receive the signed request form from the central kitchen's assistant manager.

After receiving a signed request form from the assistant manager, the central kitchen's delivery team checks with the chef as to whether there are other orders coming out soon, before making a delivery. They do so to reduce the mileage they cover whenever they have to make deliveries to restaurants that are near each other, which happens frequently. That is, if one delivery to a restaurant is ready, and another delivery to a nearby restaurant will be ready in an hour, it makes sense to wait until the second is ready and make both deliveries in one single trip. After checking with the chef for upcoming deliveries, the delivery team then plans its itinerary and makes the pending delivery or deliveries (see Figure 10.4).

Some details are worth noting regarding the communication flow representation of the order fulfillment process shown in Figure 10.4. First, the representation does not incorporate any knowledge repository or knowledge flow. One could argue that knowledge repositories and/or flows should have been included in the representation, which is a fair contention given our discussion in previous chapters on knowledge use and representation in business processes. Nevertheless, in the real project that served as the basis for this application example, it seemed to the business process redesign team that there were no knowledge-related elements worth representing in the process, at least from a business process redesign perspective. As can be seen from the description above, the business process is not very knowledge intensive, and most of its activities are rather simple and manual in nature.

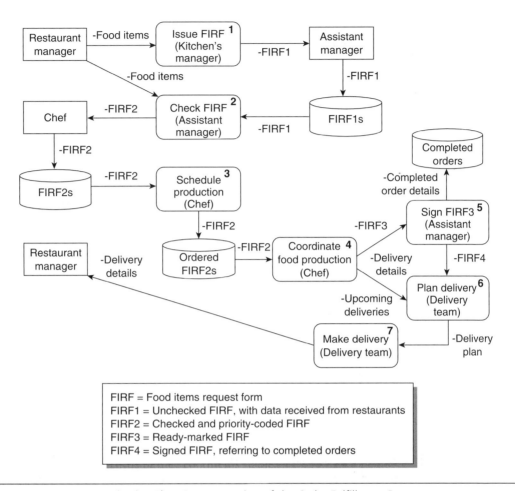

Figure 10.4   Communication Flow Representation of the Order Fulfillment Process

A second point worth noting in connection with Figure 10.4 is that its representation is one of several possible communication flow representations of the order fulfillment process. If all of those possible representations were to be generated and compared, the conclusion would probably be that they were very similar to each other and that their differences would be generally irrelevant from the point of view of the application of the business process redesign techniques previously discussed in this book. Nevertheless, there might have been small differences, such as different locations in the representation of different symbols, or different terms used (e.g., "FoIRFm" could have been used instead of "FIRF").

A final point that merits discussion regarding the business process representation in Figure 10.4 is that, like any communication flow representation of a business process, it does not indicate the flow of materials, such as the actual food items being delivered by the central kitchen's delivery team to a restaurant. This is why the element that flows between the activity titled "make delivery" (carried out by the central kitchen's delivery team) and the restaurant manager is a piece of information—namely, the delivery details. Those delivery details are transferred from the central kitchen to the restaurant manager through the label on the order delivery packet. As discussed earlier in this book, it would be incorrect to represent a material flow (e.g., food items) as part of a communication flow representation of a business process.

Redesigning the Order Fulfillment Process

Previously in this book, several techniques for the redesign of business processes have been discussed, including the following: encouraging asynchronous communication of information, reducing information duplication in static repositories, eliminating unnecessary information flow, reducing contact points in a process, minimizing knowledge transfer in operational processes, and maximizing knowledge transfer in organizational learning processes.

In this section, the power of the previously discussed techniques is demonstrated by the application of only the first three techniques just mentioned to the redesign of the order fulfillment process at Little Italy Restaurants. That is, the techniques used are as follows: encouraging asynchronous communication of information, reducing information duplication in static repositories, and eliminating unnecessary information flow. As will be shortly seen, even though only three techniques are employed, the outcomes in terms of business process simplification are quite dramatic.

Encouraging Asynchronous Communication of Information

This technique is implemented in the context of the order fulfillment process at Little Italy Restaurants by eliminating the synchronous food items request interaction between each restaurant manager and the kitchen's manager (see Figure 10.5). Restaurant managers are now allowed to enter information about needed food items directly into a "food items requests" information repository.

As previously discussed in this chapter, the order fulfillment process starts with a request by a restaurant's manager of food items that are soon expected to be out of stock, a request that is usually made over the phone. Since the request is made over the phone, the representation of the corresponding information exchange interaction indicates that the interaction is synchronous. This means that the two individuals involved in the communication interaction, namely the restaurant manager and the central kitchen's manager, have to interact at the same time. This also means that there is no information repository acting as intermediary between those two individuals.

It is not important at this point to establish exactly how the redesigned communication interaction will take place—for example, whether it will take place using the Internet or a private wide area network. What is important at the redesign stage is to establish that the new communication interaction will be asynchronous, which

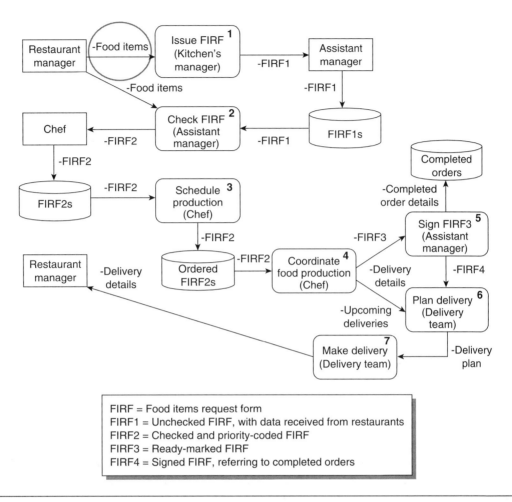

Figure 10.5   Encouraging Asynchronous Communication of Information

implies that an information repository will be used. It is usually a good idea to name the new information repository. In the example discussed here, the new information repository is tentatively called "food items requests" (this will be shown later, in the communication flow representation of the redesign business process).

Reducing Information Duplication in Static Repositories

This business process redesign technique is implemented in the example discussed here through the elimination of the "completed orders" information repository (see Figure 10.6), by making "food items requests" a static information repository.

As previously discussed in this chapter, before the assistant manager sends the signed request form to the central kitchen's delivery team, which indicates that the

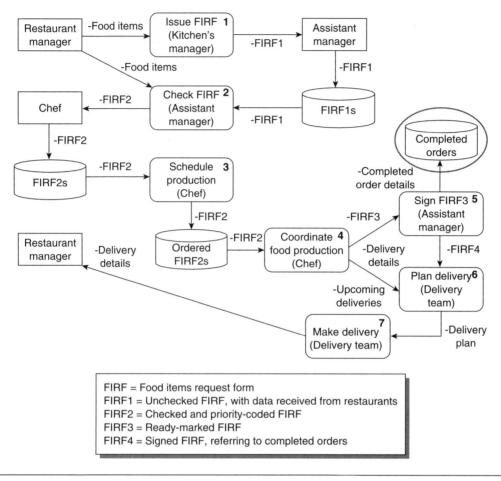

Figure 10.6   Reducing Information Duplication in Static Repositories

delivery team has the "green light" to make a delivery, he first creates an entry in a control book with information about the completed order (including size, food items, and date). The delivery team makes no delivery until they receive the signed request form from the central kitchen's assistant manager. The control book is represented in Figure 10.6 by the "completed orders" information repository.

Eliminating Unnecessary Information Flow

This business process redesign technique can be implemented through the elimination of duplicated information flows caused by what is referred to here as "polygonation" of information. This type of polygonation occurs when a piece of information (e.g., the information set contained in a form), which is meant to flow between a source (e.g., a staff assistant) and a destination (e.g., the staff assistant's manager), first passes through an intermediary (e.g., the assistant manager), who

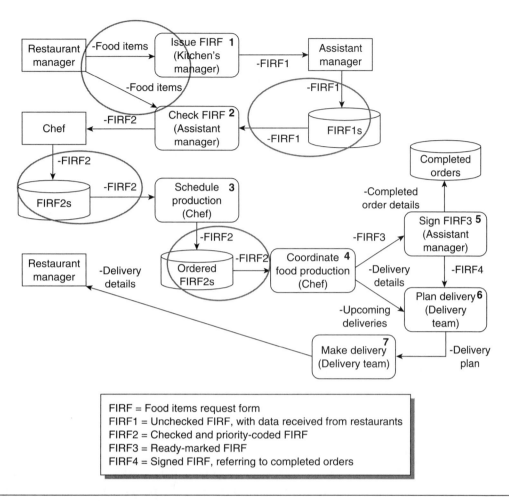

Figure 10.7   Eliminating Unnecessary Information Flow

does nothing with the piece of information. That is, unnecessary information polygonation takes place when a piece of information goes through organization functions that add no value to that piece of information. For example, the piece of information "food items," provided by a restaurant manager, needs to reach the assistant manager. But it first goes to the central kitchen's manager, which is an unnecessary step in the business process—a polygonation of the piece of information represented by "food items" in the diagram in Figure 10.7. Information polygonation is often associated with a sense by those involved in the business process that there are too many unnecessary information handoffs in the process.

The business process redesign technique of eliminating unnecessary information flow can also be implemented by the elimination of information flow instances between organizational functions and themselves, where usually those organization functions first receive information in a synchronous way and then store that information for later use by themselves. Two examples are the central kitchen's assistant

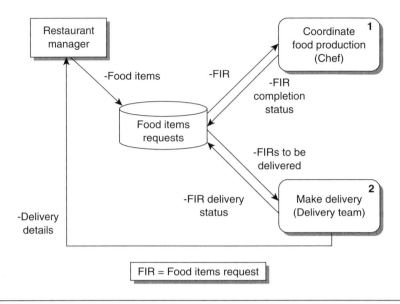

Figure 10.8 Redesigned Order Fulfillment Process

manager's storing unchecked FIRFs (or FIRF1s) for later use, the central kitchen's chef storing FIRF2s for later use, and the chef storing ordered FIRF2s for later use.

The above discussion illustrates the application of the three business process redesign techniques previously called in this book encouraging asynchronous communication of information, reducing information duplication in static repositories, and eliminating unnecessary information flow. Those three techniques are only a subset of the business process redesign techniques discussed in previous chapters. Nevertheless, their application to the order fulfillment process led to what could be reasonably seen as a dramatic simplification of the business process. The communication flow representation of the redesigned order fulfillment process is shown in Figure 10.8.

In the redesigned business process shown in Figure 10.8, each restaurant manager now enters information about the food items being requested directly into a food items requests information repository. That information is now directly accessed by the central kitchen's chef, who coordinates the food production by his team of cooks. Once the food items associated with a request are ready, they are first packed, then labeled, and finally left on a delivery pallet by the chef's team. That team now updates the status of the food items request to "complete" in the food items requests information repository, which signals to the delivery team that the food items order can be delivered to the restaurant that requested it. Upon its return from a delivery trip, the delivery team updates the status of the food items request to "delivered" and enters the details of the delivery into the food items requests information repository, which is now a static repository.

The communication flow representation shown in Figure 10.8 leaves out some details that need to be spelled out so that the business process is properly implemented. For example, how is the production of food items orders scheduled after they are received? Previously, the chef scheduled food items production by pinning up the request forms on a notice board. Now, since there is no human intervention indicated, one has to assume that those orders are produced in the sequence in which they are received. In the real case that served as the basis for the example discussed in this chapter, that was essentially what happened after the business process was redesigned. That was possible because the new redesigned order fulfillment process was much more efficient than the previous one, which significantly reduced the need to prioritize orders.

It is not clear from Figure 10.8 how the scheduling of the deliveries is carried out in the redesigned business process. Previously, the central kitchen's delivery team checked with the chef as to whether there were other orders coming out soon, before making a delivery, so as to reduce the mileage they covered whenever they had to make deliveries to restaurants that were near each other. Since that happened frequently, one has to assume that something analogous happened in the redesigned order fulfillment process. In the real case that served as the basis for the example discussed in this chapter, the scheduling of deliveries in the redesign process was automated based on a simple algorithm that grouped together deliveries to restaurants that were geographically close to each other. This can easily be done based on the numeric coordinates of each restaurant on a bi-dimensional plane covering the whole geographical area where the restaurants were distributed.

As previously discussed in this book, communication flow diagrams are relatively abstract business process representations, which are not very good for providing a clear pre-implementation understanding of how technologies will be used to enable a new business process. Rich pictorial representations of the new business process are a solution to this problem. Figure 10.9 provides such a representation of the redesigned order fulfillment process.

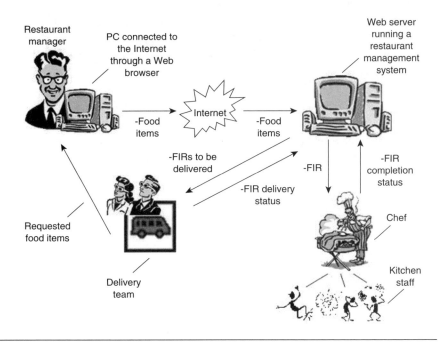

Figure 10.9   Rich Pictorial Representation of the Redesigned Order Fulfillment Process

Notice that the rich pictorial representation shown in Figure 10.9 makes explicit how information technology will be used to implement the redesigned business process, in a way that complements the communication flow representation of the redesigned process. However, the rich pictorial representation of the redesigned process does not go into much detail; otherwise, it might have been impossible to have the complete representation in one single diagram. For example, the names of the computer systems used are largely omitted, and so are the specifications of the hardware used. Nevertheless, some of the elements in Figure 10.9 add substantial insights into the generic types of technologies and technological infrastructures that will be used to implement the new business process (e.g., Web servers and Web browsers interacting through the Internet infrastructure).

Summary and Concluding Remarks

There is no doubt that the business process redesign project described in this chapter led to major simplifications in the order fulfillment process. But what about the bottom-line gains for Little Italy Restaurants? Were there any? If yes, were they significant enough to justify the project? To answer those questions, we have to refer back to the real case that served as the basis for the example discussed in this chapter and make some assumptions based on the pedagogical adaptations made to the case here to best illustrate the applications of the three business process redesign techniques employed.

All assumptions made, it is safe to say that the large simplification in the business process through the redesign project led to significant gains in both quality and productivity. The productivity gains, as far as the business process is concerned, can be estimated at around roughly 75 percent, including labor savings—notice that the redesigned order fulfillment process no longer shows the central kitchen's manager and assistant manager, which were organizational functions that were present in the pre-redesign version of the business process. The reason why the central kitchen's manager function is no longer shown is that the role of that function was significantly reduced in the process. But the central kitchen's manager still played a high-level supervisory role in the redesigned process (which is not shown in the redesigned process), rather than getting involved in the nitty-gritty of the process as he was doing before. The assistant manager's role, however, was completely eliminated. Did he lose his job? This question will be addressed shortly below.

The business process redesign project also led to major improvements in quality. Recall that the business process redesign project was motivated by a few serious problems being faced by Little Italy Restaurants. In 40 percent of the deliveries made by the central kitchen, food items arrived late in the restaurants. Additionally, in 20 percent of the deliveries, the food items went to the wrong restaurants. Moreover, 60 percent of the food orders from the restaurants to the central kitchen were only partially fulfilled. The problems often led to a key outcome, namely the restaurants' routinely running out of food items, which restricted their customers' choices. That, in turn, was leading to lower customer satisfaction levels (i.e., a loss in perceived service quality).

All of the aforementioned percentages were brought down to the initial goal of 5 percent, in some cases falling below that. For example, the percentage of food orders that were only partially fulfilled was reduced to close to zero percent. Those percentage reductions were primarily due to the improvement in the communication-related activities involving the central kitchen and the restaurants, whose associated problems created bottlenecks that often prevented orders from moving forward through the business process as they should have—that is, the bottlenecks decreased business process throughput.

Let us now address the issue of what happened with the assistant manager of the central kitchen. After all, given his involvement in the order fulfillment process, the business process redesign project could not have been successfully completed without his help. If he had been fired at the end of the project, he would probably have felt somewhat like a turkey who had been asked to help with Thanksgiving preparations.

Since Little Italy Restaurants had an established brand, one of the best ways for it to continue expanding its chain of restaurants (a strategic goal of the owner of the Little Italy Restaurants chain) was to employ an expansion approach that is often referred to in marketing and sales circles as "franchising." Franchising essentially entails selling one's brand and business processes expertise to independent business operators, who in turn pay a franchising fee to the franchise owner. Many fast-food restaurant chains operate in this manner (e.g., McDonald's, KFC, Taco Bell, Burger King).

However, to expand its operations through franchises, Little Italy Restaurants had to establish a franchise division. To lead that division, they needed someone with solid knowledge of the key business processes that made Little Italy Restaurants' operation so successful. That is where the former assistant manager of the central kitchen comes into the picture. He was eventually hired to lead Little Italy Restaurants' franchise division. Not only was he promoted, but he also received a sizable raise in salary to take over that new challenging position.

It is important to follow this happy ending with a caveat. Business process redesign projects usually lead to happy endings in organizations that conduct business process redesign in "times of plenty," that is, when revenues are going up rather than down. Unfortunately, most business process redesign projects take place against the backdrop created by cash flow losses, decreases in revenues, and other serious bottom-line organizational problems. In those cases, it is almost impossible to avoid layoffs, since in most organizations, the largest fixed cost component is that of labor.

Review Questions

1. The need to redesign the order fulfillment process at the Little Italy Restaurants chain resulted from:
   (a) Major losses in revenues by half of the restaurants that made up the chain in the previous 10 years.
   (b) Several changes aimed at, among other things, increasing the variety of past dishes offered to customers in half of the restaurants that made up the chain.

(c) A change aimed at, among other things, increasing the seating capacity in each of the restaurants that made up the chain.

(d) A major change aimed at allowing each of the restaurants that made up the chain to offer customized past dishes that met specific local tastes.

2. It is not correct to say that the order fulfillment process was selected for redesign because:

(a) It was seen as an optimal business process.

(b) It was seen as a suboptimal business process.

(c) It was perceived as a problematic business process.

(d) In approximately 40 percent of the deliveries made by the central kitchen, food items arrived late in the restaurants—a problem that was seen as caused by the design of that business process.

3. How is the business process redesign technique "encouraging asynchronous communication of information" used in the context of the order fulfillment process at Little Italy Restaurants?

(a) Through the elimination of the asynchronous food items delivery interaction between each restaurant manager and the kitchen's manager, right at the beginning of the order fulfillment process.

(b) Through the elimination of the second half of the order fulfillment process, whereby food items are delivered to the central kitchen's chef.

(c) Through the reduction in the number of restaurants that made up the Little Italy Restaurants chain, and the outsourcing of the order fulfillment process to an insurance company specializing in property insurance.

(d) Through the elimination of the synchronous food items request interaction between each restaurant manager and the kitchen's manager, right at the beginning of the order fulfillment process.

4. Which of the following examples is not a good illustration of the business process redesign technique "reducing information duplication in static repositories"?

(a) The "completed orders" information repository is eliminated, by making "food items requests" a static information repository.

(b) Before the assistant manager sends the signed request form to the central kitchen's delivery team, which indicates that the delivery team has the "green light" to make a delivery, he first creates an entry in a control book with information about the completed order.

(c) Upon its return from a delivery trip, the delivery team updates the status of the food items request to "delivered" and enters the details of the delivery into the "food items requests" information repository, which is now a static repository.

(d) The assistant manager no longer needs to create an entry in a control book with information about a completed order, because all of that information is already stored in the static information repository called "food items requests."

5. An instance of the general phenomenon referred to in this chapter as "polygonation" of information can be defined as:
   (a) A situation where a tangible item (e.g., a car part), which is meant to flow between a source and a destination, first passes through an intermediary, who does not add any value to the item.
   (b) A situation where the information set contained in a form, which is meant to flow between a source (e.g., a staff assistant) and a destination (e.g., the staff assistant's manager), first passes through an intermediary (e.g., the assistant manager), who does nothing with the form (other than keeping it for a few hours).
   (c) A situation where a piece of knowledge (e.g., the knowledge related to a cancer discovery), which is meant to flow between a researcher and an organization, first passes through a law enforcement officer, who prevents the knowledge from moving forward.
   (d) A situation where a piece of information, which is meant to flow between a source and a destination, first passes through an intermediary, who does not modify the piece of information in any way.

Discussion Questions

1. Develop a detailed scenario involving a car part design process (i.e., a business process through which car parts such as brakes and windshields are designed) in an automaker that will later outsource the manufacturing of the car parts to outside suppliers. Please bear in mind that successful car parts design usually involves not only engineers, but also other parties, such as salespeople, car parts suppliers, and customers. The business process in question should incorporate at least three information repositories and five interactions involving information exchanges. Develop a communication flow representation of the business process in question.

2. Apply each of the business process redesign techniques discussed in this chapter to the scenario you developed in Discussion Question 1. Explain how the changes modified the business process in question (i.e., the car part design process). Generate a communication flow representation of the redesigned business process.

3. Develop a rich pictorial representation of the business process redesigned through Discussion Question 2. The rich pictorial representation should be accompanied by a detailed textual description of how information technology will be used to implement the redesigned business process.

PART V

Advanced Technology Issues

Part V Case:
Denver International
Airport's Baggage Handling System

The Denver International Airport (DIA) was designed to be the most modern and majestic airport in the United States. Its design was approved in 1989. It occupies a total area of 53 square miles, making it twice the size of Manhattan. More than 100 million cubic yards of earth had to be moved to make way for its construction. The initial plans assumed that DIA would be opened to the public in 1993, supporting the operation of more than 20 major airlines. It was designed with five runways, allowing three simultaneous landings in most weather conditions. Its total estimated building cost was $1.7 billion (although it ended up costing about $2.5 billion more than that).

An airport of such dimensions and grandeur was perceived as also needing a jumbo-sized and supermodern baggage handling system. The system's price tag was initially estimated at $193 million. Its development and installation was contracted with BAE Automated Systems, a leading designer, integrator, and operator of baggage handling systems based in Carrollton, Texas (it was later acquired by G&T Conveyor Co., a Florida-based company).

DIA's baggage handling system was designed to run on a large number of networked computers. Some accounts place that number at around 50, while others claim that more than 300 computers were used. The networked computers controlled thousands of remote-controlled carts (called "telecarts") operating on a 21-mile track system. Laser scanners would read barcodes off baggage tags. Photocells would track the movement and location of the remote-controlled carts, which would enable the system to reroute them as needed (e.g., in case a departing flight changed gates at the last minute).

In early 1994, BAE Automated Systems and the City of Denver were gearing up for the first test of the baggage handling system, which was supposed to move 7,000 bags. The test was a fiasco of major proportions. So many problems were discovered with the system that the test had to be halted. Reporters were able to see and document some of the results of the problems, which included piles of clothes and personal items lying under the remote-controlled carts and around the tracks.

Apparently some software bugs led to serious problems in the system's operation, even before it was fully online. Those software bugs were at the source of the problems identified in the first public test and subsequent tests. Remote-controlled carts were often misrouted and crashed. Baggage items were often lost or damaged. These problems delayed DIA's opening. Since the airport operators had fixed costs to pay (e.g., personnel salaries), the loss of revenue led to a daily hemorrhaging of funds in amounts upward of $1 million.

The City of Denver decided then to abandon the baggage handling system project and install an alternative standard system. This met with strong opposition from United Airlines, which had earlier contracted with BAE Automated Systems to develop a similar but smaller-scale baggage handling system exclusively for its own use. The development of that smaller system had been stopped due to DIA's decision to build the larger system to automate baggage handling for the entire airport.

United Airlines was no stranger to air travel–related technologies and had played key roles in pioneering technology-related projects in this past. Notably, it had been one of the pioneers (together with American Airlines) in the development and use of travel reservation systems. Its APOLLO travel reservation system, in operation since the late 1960s and early 1970s, contributed to its becoming one of the leading airlines in the United States and around the world.

United Airlines' previous success with its APOLLO travel reservation system probably bolstered its confidence in being a potential key player in the implementation of airport technologies. Since it was one of the largest carriers operating out of Denver, in 1994 United Airlines decided to take the lead in the fixing and further development of the new baggage handling system at DIA.

When DIA opened in 1995, 2 years after originally planned, several additional millions of dollars had been spent to fix the problems with the baggage system. But many problems remained. While the system had originally been planned for use by all airlines operating out of DIA, for the most part only one airline used it—United Airlines.

In mid-2005, after more than a decade of trying to make its baggage handling system work, United Airlines announced that it would abandon it and return to its tried-and-tested manual baggage handling process. By then, the baggage handling system had cost DIA and United Airlines about $230 million. Since that system never fully worked as expected, a conventional baggage handling system was purchased at an additional cost of $70 million.

Bruce Webster, a consultant that advises companies with troubled technology projects, suggests that one main lesson had been learned from DIA's baggage handling system fiasco: ". . . the best way to build a large, complex system is to evolve it from a small system that works. No one bothered to get a small system up and running in the first place—they went for the big bang."

Sources

Knill, B. (2004). New inspiration from the old Denver airport disaster. *Material Handling Management, 59*(1).

Montealegre, R., & Keil, M. (2000). De-escalating information technology projects: Lessons from the Denver International Airport. *MIS Quarterly, 24*(3).

Weiss, T. R. (2005, June 13). United to scrap baggage system at Denver airport. *Computerworld.*

Yamanouchi, K. (2005, February 22). Computer glitch leads to delays for United Airlines flights leaving Denver. *Knight Ridder Tribune Business News.*

CHAPTER 11

Database Design Concepts and Issues

As we have seen in previous chapters of this book, business process redesign does not always lead to in-house systems development as the chosen alternative to implement new business processes. In fact, in the majority of cases, business process outsourcing and commercial package customization are the chosen alternatives, with in-house development trailing far behind.

In spite of the above, a good knowledge of fundamental database design concepts and issues is always useful, regardless of the redesigned business process implementation alternative chosen. In business process outsourcing, for example, decisions regarding the use of certain database structures and file formats by one outsourcing services provider may lead to cost savings when the database is integrated with a different database used by another provider. In certain commercial package customization-based implementations of new business processes, some amount of effort in connection with database design may also be needed if the level of customization required goes beyond a certain threshold—with related decisions driven by extant database structures and configurations employed by an organization.

In the case of in-house software development, which may not happen all the time but constitutes a critical success factor when it does happen, a working knowledge of key database design concepts and issues is usually a *sine qua non* condition for success. The reason is that the vast majority of in-house software development projects, especially those aimed at enabling new business process designs, start with key decisions regarding the design of one or more databases. Key concepts and related techniques that come into play in those types of projects are the following: sequential and structure files, entity-relationship diagramming, and normalization. Those concepts and techniques are covered in this chapter, together with the more recent data warehousing and mining, which are being increasingly used in organizations to support all kinds of decision-making processes.

Sequential and Structured Files

Structured files are fundamentally different from what are often referred to as sequential files (or "flat" files). In the former, data are organized into units that are usually called "records." The latter (i.e., sequential files) store data without much organization, with the storage unit being usually a byte (or an alphanumeric character). One of the key disadvantages of sequential files is that the data stored in them usually has to be retrieved sequentially. That is, if a particular piece of data that is of interest to a user is in the middle of the file, all of the data up to that point need to be retrieved before that piece of data can be found—see Figure 11.1.

Sometimes sequential files are referred to as "ASCII files" because, quite often, the bytes that they store are encoded according to a standard known as ASCII (American Standard Code for Information Interchange). The ASCII standard was previously discussed in this book. It was developed by the American National Standards Institute and is one of the most widely used standards for byte-to-character conversion (and vice versa) in the computing world.

In spite of their disadvantages when compared with structured files, sequential files are extensively used in companies, particularly to store backup data. It is generally easier to compress unstructured than structure files, and backup data is usually stored in a compressed way. Moreover, the types of media normally used by data backups are sequential by nature, in the sense that they allow for sequential data retrieval only (e.g., magnetic tapes). These are among the main reasons why unstructured files are used for data backups.

The record-based organization of data into structured files makes those files look like tables with rows and columns. For this reason, structured files are often called tables in textbooks and other professional publications dealing with database issues. Figure 11.2, for example, shows part of the content stored in a structured file called "Orders." The "Orders" structured file, or table, stores information about the details of orders placed by customers. The "Orders" table shown in Figure 11.2 is adapted from the Northwind Traders database example provided by Microsoft with its Access database management system.

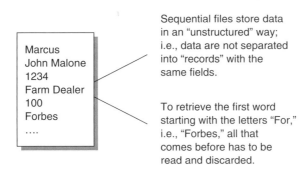

Marcus
John Malone
1234
Farm Dealer
100
Forbes
....

Sequential files store data in an "unstructured" way; i.e., data are not separated into "records" with the same fields.

To retrieve the first word starting with the letters "For," i.e., "Forbes," all that comes before has to be read and discarded.

Figure 11.1   Sequential File

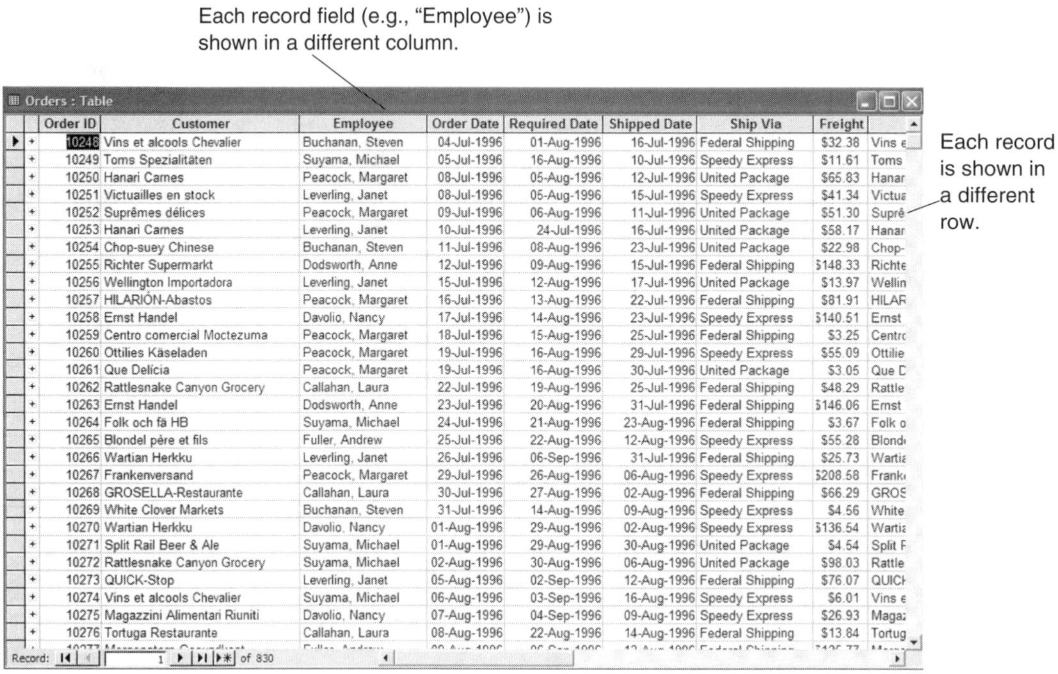

Each record field (e.g., "Employee") is
shown in a different column.

Each record
is shown in
a different
row.

Figure 11.2 Structured File

In a structured file, or table, each row corresponds to a record in the table. Each record, in turn, is made up of several fields. One of the key advantages of organizing data into tables is that the data stored in an individual record can be easily accessed through a search in only one of the fields of the record (e.g., "Order ID," in Figure 11.2). A search procedure is particularly efficient when the following conditions are met: (a) the search field is a numeric field, (b) the search field contains a unique value for each record, and (c) the records are ordered according to the search field.

Databases and Entity-Relationship Diagrams

A database is essentially a set of tables (or structured files) that are related to each other in a particular way and that store related data. Figure 11.3 shows one of the most widely used representations of databases, an entity-relationship diagram, where several tables that make up a database are shown. Each table is represented as an entity that encapsulates several fields. Entity-relationship diagrams are discussed in more detail later in this chapter.

A one-to-many relationship between two tables is normally established by means of a particular field, often referred to as the "key" field. That type of relationship is usually represented through a line containing the symbols 1 and ∞ at each end, respectively. One example of a key field used to establish a relationship between two tables, shown in Figure 11.3, is "ProductID." That field enables the one-to-many relationship between the tables "Products" and "Order Details."

Different tables (e.g., "Suppliers," "Orders") make up a database.

Tables that are part of the same database are usually related to each other, usually through one-to-many relationships. These are represented through lines containing the symbols "1" and "∞" at each end, respectively.

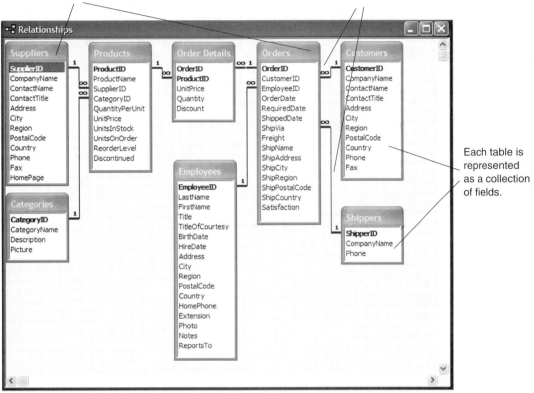

Each table is represented as a collection of fields.

Figure 11.3 An Entity-Relationship Representation of a Database

A one-to-many relationship between two tables essentially means that for each record in the table at the "one" end of the relationship, many records may exist in the table at the "many" end of the relationship. The expectation that one record in one table may be linked to many records in another table is defined by the "one" and "many" symbols near each table that makes up the relationship (in Figure 11.3, the symbols used are 1 and ∞, respectively). The underlying values to which the symbols refer (i.e., "one" or "many") are also referred to as the *cardinalities* associated with each table that makes up the relationship. Generally speaking, the cardinalities in a one-to-many relationship are either "one" or "many."

In Figure 11.3, we can see that the tables "Customers" and "Orders" have a one-to-many relationship, where "one" customer is related to "many" orders. This means that the same customer may appear many times in the "Orders" table, which reflects the notion that one customer may place many orders.

As will be seen later in this chapter, the establishment of one-to-many relationships between tables is useful in reducing duplication of data across different tables. Without those relationships, the data would have to be stored in larger tables with redundant data. Again, let us use the relationship between the "Customers" and "Orders" tables. If those two tables were to be merged into one table, whenever customer data were to be entered into this larger table, the data for each of its fields (e.g., "ContactName") would also have to be entered. This would lead to duplicate entries for each of the fields in the original "Customers" table. This type of duplication is generally undesirable in databases that support day-to-day operations of an organization.

Normalization of Databases

The process whereby duplication of data in databases is reduced to a minimum is called normalization. Through this process, a database is usually transformed from a non-normalized configuration to one of several "normal forms." The most common normal forms discussed in the literature on database design are the first, second, and third normal forms. The transformation of a database from a non-normalized configuration to one of the normal forms is usually done by splitting tables of the database, with the goal of eliminating redundancies.

The whole idea behind normalization is elimination of data redundancies, which played a key role in reducing the size of databases in the 1970s and 1980s. Given today's relatively cheap data storage solutions and abundant storage capacity in organizations, one may question whether it makes sense to go through the somewhat painful process of normalizing databases. The truth is that normalization reduces not only the size of databases, but also repetition in the process of data entry, which is one of the main reasons why normalization is very important, even with today's low cost of storage and abundant capacity.

There are a few situations, however, in which the use of normalized databases is problematic, and de-normalization is often necessary. One of these situations, which will be discussed in more detail later in this chapter, is when one wants to "mine" a database. Generally speaking, data mining is the process of discovering relationships between different fields of a database. For that to happen in an efficient way, a normalized database is first de-normalized, leading to a large table containing all of the fields of the previously normalized database. This large table is often referred to as a "data warehouse" or a "data mart."

First Normal Form

To go from a non-normalized database configuration to a database in first normal form, one splits one or more tables to remove repeating fields. Usually, each non-normalized table that makes up the database is split into two tables. The resulting tables contain one common field, normally a primary key field in one of the tables, which is used to create a one-to-many relationship between the tables. That common field is still repeated in one of the tables. The other table has no repeating fields.

The above is illustrated in Figure 11.4, where a one-table non-normalized database (i.e., a non-normalized database with only one table in it) is shown at the top part of the figure. That database stores information about food items orders placed

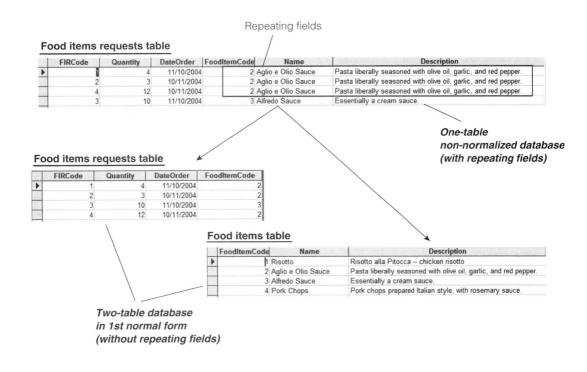

Figure 11.4   Getting a Database in the First Normal Form

by a restaurant to a central kitchen and contains six fields: "FIRCode" (the code of the food item request), "Quantity" (the quantity of food items being requested), "DateOrder" (the date the request or order was placed), "FoodItemCode" (the code identifying the food item requested), "Name" (the name of the food item requested), and "Description" (the description of the food item requested).

At the bottom of Figure 11.4, we see a two-table database in first normal form. The resulting tables are the "Food items requests" and "Food items" tables. The common field of the two resulting tables is now "FoodItemCode," which allows for the creation of a one-to-many relationship between the two tables, where the "Food items" table is at the "one" end of the relationship. Note that there are no repeating fields in the "Food items" table, and that the repetition of data in the "Food items requests" table is limited to a single field, namely the "FoodItemCode" field.

Second Normal Form

Getting a database into the second normal form requires that the database be in the first normal form. A database in the second normal form is defined as a database in which certain dependencies between non-key fields and key fields do not exist. So, to set the stage for the discussion of the second normal form, let us first start with a brief discussion of what a key field is.

A key (or "primary key") of a table is a set of fields (usually one) that uniquely identify each record of the table. When the key for a table is made up of one single field, then that key is called an "atomic" key. When the key for a table is made up of two or more fields, it is called a "compound" key.

Usually, when a particular code is created to uniquely identify each of the records of a table, the code in question ends up becoming an atomic key, for example, "FIRCode" (or food items request code) in Figure 11.5. Alternatively, the database designer may opt for defining a set of fields as the key for a table, instead of creating a code, with the set of fields uniquely defining (as a group) each record of the table. That set of fields becomes then a compound key—see the bottom part of Figure 11.5.

The compound key of the table shown at the bottom of Figure 11.5 is made up of four fields, namely "FoodItemCode" (the code of a food item being ordered), "RestaurantCode" (the code of the restaurant ordering the food item), "Quantity" (the quantity of the food item being ordered), and "DateOrder" (the date on which the order is being placed). Defining a compound key in such a way implies that each row of the table will be uniquely identified by a combination of these four fields. Or, in other words, it is assumed that no food items order will have the same food item code, restaurant code, quantity, and date.

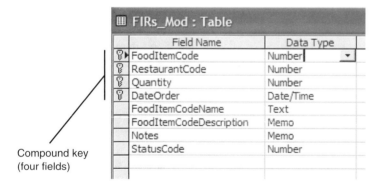

Figure 11.5   Atomic and Compound Keys

When a non-key field in a table depends on only part of a compound key (e.g., one of the fields of the compound key), then the table is said to have a partial dependency in it. For example, in the table shown at the bottom of Figure 11.5, the fields "FoodItemCodeName" (the name of a food item) and "FoodItemCodeDescription" (the description of the food item) depend only on one of the fields of the compound key, namely the field "FoodItemCode." The other two fields of the table, namely "Notes" (notes about the order) and "StatusCode" (the code that defines the status of the order—e.g., being produced, delivered), refer to the order as a whole. As such, they depend on the entire compound key and thus do not characterize a partial dependency.

For a database to be in second normal form, all of its tables must be in first normal form and also free of partial dependencies. The elimination of partial dependencies is achieved by splitting tables that contain partial dependencies into sets of tables (e.g., usually with two "children" tables, but sometimes more) that do not contain partial dependencies. When a table contains partial dependencies, the process of splitting it usually involves moving the non-key fields that depend on part of a compound key to a separate table (see Figure 11.6).

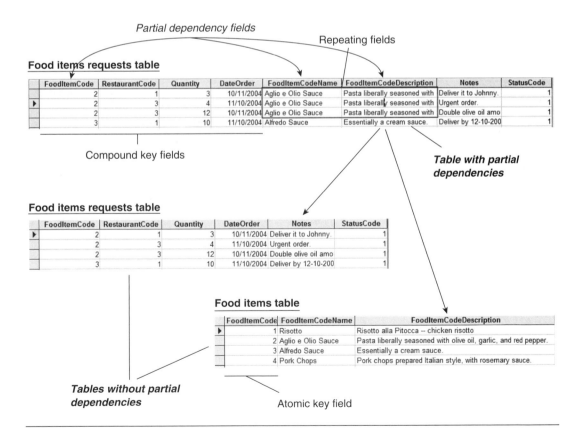

Figure 11.6   Eliminating Partial Dependencies

As can be seen from Figure 11.6, partial dependencies lead to data redundancy, which is normally reflected in the presence of repeating fields (top part of Figure 11.6). Once the table with partial dependencies is split into tables (two, in the case in question) without partial dependencies, the repeating fields are eliminated. In the example provided in Figure 11.6, the key of one of the tables is an atomic key (i.e., single-field key), which is precisely the field in the original compound key associated with the partial dependency.

Third Normal Form

When a non-key field in a table depends on another non-key field (or fields), then the table is said to have one or more transitive dependencies in it. For example, in the table shown at the top of Figure 11.7, the field "Name" (the name of a food item) depends on a non-key field, namely the field "FoodItemCode." Given that, the relationship between "Name" and "FoodItemCode" is a transitive dependency relationship.

For a database to be in third normal form, all of its tables must be in second normal form and also free of transitive dependencies. Analogous to previous normalization steps, the process of eliminating transitive dependencies involves splitting tables that contain transitive dependencies into sets of two or more tables that

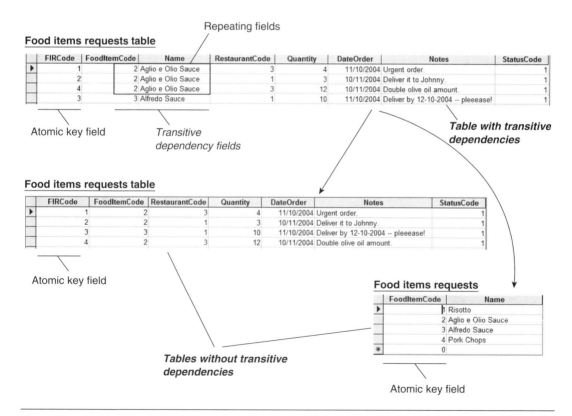

Figure 11.7   Eliminating Transitive Dependencies

do not contain any transitive dependency. When a table contains transitive dependencies, the process of splitting it usually involves moving the non-key fields that characterize each transitive dependency to a separate table. As illustrated by Figure 11.7, in the new table created, one of the previous non-key fields will become a key field.

Similar to what happens in previous normalization steps, the elimination of transitive dependencies also leads to the elimination of data redundancy, which is normally reflected in the presence of repeating fields (see top part of Figure 11.7). Once the table with transitive dependencies is split into two or more tables, each free of transitive dependencies, the repeating fields are usually removed as well.

Data Warehousing and Mining

Let us assume that a supermarket manager needs to know which products are usually purchased together, in the same supermarket visit, so that the shelving arrangement of those products is done appropriately. One way in which this can be accomplished is by analyzing purchasing data stored in the computer system that controls the supermarket's cash registers. Those analyses require two main steps, usually known as data warehousing and data mining.

The data on supermarket purchases are most likely stored in one or more normalized databases. As we have seen earlier in this chapter, database normalization is generally advisable for data repositories that are used on a daily basis to keep track and coordinate an organization's operations. However, normalized databases are not particularly good when they serve as the basis for data analysis, particularly the computation-intensive types of data analyses required for data mining. For that, non-normalized tables are generally better. The process of building non-normalized tables for data mining, based on normalized databases, is normally referred to as data warehousing.

The data warehousing process also involves a variety of "data cleaning and expansion" steps, such as correcting data that were entered wrong, entering missing data, reconciling data stored in different formats (e.g., numeric and alphanumeric data), and generating additional data based on calculations applied to existing fields (e.g., totaling a set of fields, or subtracting two fields, to obtain a composite measure). The final outcome of the data warehousing process is the "data warehouse," which is normally a large table stored in a particular database file format (e.g., Access, Oracle, Sybase). Small data warehouses storing data about a particular area (e.g., a department of a large organization) and used for localized analyses are often called "data marts."

Data mining is essentially a process in which relationships between fields are discovered based on the analysis of a data warehouse. Generally speaking, only numeric data can be used in data mining. Moreover, only those fields that can be meaningfully analyzed with a particular goal in mind are useful for data mining. The goal may be to answer a particular question, such as which among a set of factors involved in a particular service delivery is the strongest determinant of customer satisfaction with the service.

Let us take, for example, the orders table whose structure is shown in Figure 11.8, which stores data about orders placed against a trading company called Northwind

Orders : Table		
Field Name	Data Type	
OrderID	AutoNumber	Unique order number.
CustomerID	Text	Same entry as in Customers table.
EmployeeID	Number	Same entry as in Employees table.
OrderDate	Date/Time	
RequiredDate	Date/Time	
ShippedDate	Date/Time	
ShipVia	Number	Same as Shipper ID in Shippers table.
Freight	Currency	
ShipName	Text	Name of person or company to receive the shipment.
ShipAddress	Text	Street address only -- no post-office box allowed.
ShipCity	Text	
ShipRegion	Text	State or province.
ShipPostalCode	Text	
ShipCountry	Text	
Satisfaction	Number	Customer satisfaction with order.

Figure 11.8   Orders Table

Traders (adapted from a database example provided by Microsoft with its Access database management system). Let us also assume that our goal is to find out which of the following three is the strongest determinant of customer satisfaction with an order delivery: (a) the shipping delay, calculated as the difference between the shipping and order dates; (b) the extent to which the required date was met, calculated as the difference between the required and shipping dates; and (c) the cost of the freight. The customer satisfaction score goes from 1 to 7 and is stored in the field "Satisfaction" (shown at the bottom of Figure 11.8).

Figure 11.9 shows a small data warehouse generated based on the orders table. Given its size in terms of number of fields, and the fact that it stores data only that refers to a specific area of the Northwind Traders organization, the data warehouse shown in Figure 11.9 could also be called a data mart. The fields "ShippingDelay" and "MetRequired" are calculated based on other fields. "ShippingDelay" has been calculated as the difference, in number of days, between the shipping and order dates ("ShippedDate" and "OrderDate," respectively). "MetRequired" has been calculated as the difference, in number of days, between the required and shipping dates ("RequiredDate" and "ShippedDate," respectively).

Once the data warehouse is ready, the next steps involve (a) establishing a data mining goal, (b) selecting a data mining technique to achieve the goal, and (c) selecting a software tool that implements the data mining technique. Establishing a data mining goal can be achieved by building a diagram that represents the key question that needs to be answered through the data mining process.

As discussed earlier, the goal here is to find out which of the following three factors is the strongest determinant of customer satisfaction with an order delivery: the shipping delay, the extent to which the required date was met, or the cost of the freight. This goal is represented in the diagram shown in Figure 11.10, where three arrows point to "Satisfaction," each coming from one of three variables representing the three factors just mentioned, that is, "ShippingDelay," "MetRequired," and "Freight." What we want is essentially to find out the strengths of the links represented by the arrows, which are signaled by the question marks above each of the arrows.

Fields with values calculated
based on other fields

	A	B	C	D	E	F	G
1	OrderDate	RequiredDate	ShippedDate	ShippingDelay	MetRequired	Freight	Satisfaction
2	4-Jul-96	1-Aug-96	16-Jul-96	12.00	16.00	$32.38	3
3	5-Jul-96	16-Aug-96	10-Jul-96	5.00	37.00	$11.61	6
4	8-Jul-96	5-Aug-96	12-Jul-96	4.00	24.00	$65.83	5
5	8-Jul-96	5-Aug-96	15-Jul-96	7.00	21.00	$41.34	2
6	9-Jul-96	6-Aug-96	11-Jul-96	2.00	26.00	$51.30	6
7	10-Jul-96	24-Jul-96	16-Jul-96	6.00	8.00	$58.17	5
8	11-Jul-96	8-Aug-96	23-Jul-96	12.00	16.00	$22.98	4
9	12-Jul-96	9-Aug-96	15-Jul-96	3.00	25.00	$148.33	2
10	15-Jul-96	12-Aug-96	17-Jul-96	2.00	26.00	$13.97	6
11	16-Jul-96	13-Aug-96	22-Jul-96	6.00	22.00	$81.91	5
12	17-Jul-96	14-Aug-96	23-Jul-96	6.00	22.00	$140.51	3
13	18-Jul-96	15-Aug-96	25-Jul-96	7.00	21.00	$3.25	7
14	19-Jul-96	16-Aug-96	29-Jul-96	10.00	18.00	$55.09	6
15	19-Jul-96	16-Aug-96	30-Jul-96	11.00	17.00	$3.05	7
16	22-Jul-96	19-Aug-96	25-Jul-96	3.00	25.00	$48.29	1
17	23-Jul-96	20-Aug-96	31-Jul-96	8.00	20.00	$146.06	2
18	24-Jul-96	21-Aug-96	23-Aug-96	30.00	-2.00	$3.67	7
19	25-Jul-96	22-Aug-96	12-Aug-96	18.00	10.00	$55.28	6
20	26-Jul-96	6-Sep-96	31-Jul-96	5.00	37.00	$25.73	4
21	29-Jul-96	26-Aug-96	6-Aug-96	8.00	20.00	$208.58	1
22	30-Jul-96	27-Aug-96	2-Aug-96	3.00	25.00	$66.29	5
23	31-Jul-96	14-Aug-96	9-Aug-96	9.00	5.00	$4.56	7
24	1-Aug-96	29-Aug-96	2-Aug-96	1.00	27.00	$136.54	3
25	1-Aug-96	29-Aug-96	30-Aug-96	29.00	-1.00	$4.54	7
26	2-Aug-96	30-Aug-96	6-Aug-96	4.00	24.00	$98.03	4
27	5-Aug-96	2-Sep-96	12-Aug-96	7.00	21.00	$76.07	5
28	6-Aug-96	3-Sep-96	16-Aug-96	10.00	18.00	$6.01	7
29	7-Aug-96	4-Sep-96	9-Aug-96	2.00	26.00	$26.93	4
30	8-Aug-96	22-Aug-96	14-Aug-96	6.00	8.00	$13.84	6
31	9-Aug-96	6-Sep-96	13-Aug-96	4.00	24.00	$125.77	3

⏮ ◀ ▶ ⏭ \ **DataWarehouse** /

Figure 11.9   Data Warehouse Containing Orders Data

The next step, namely selecting a data mining technique to achieve the goal, is taken through the selection of a technique called multiple regression, which is implemented through a software tool called SPSS—this takes care of the following step as well, namely the step of selecting a software tool that implements the data mining technique. The multiple regression technique allows for the calculation of coefficients associated with each of the arrows shown in Figure 11.10.

The higher the coefficient, the stronger is the influence of the factor in question (e.g., "ShippingDelay") on the variable to which all the arrows point (i.e., "Satisfaction," also known as the dependent variable). The coefficients calculated through multiple regression usually vary from −1 to +1. A coefficient of +1 indicates a very strong positive relationship between the factor in question and the dependent variable; a coefficient of −1 indicates a very strong negative relationship. If the coefficient is close to zero, the relationship between the factor in question and the dependent variable is very weak (or nonexistent, if the coefficient equals zero).

In multiple regression, each coefficient is usually accompanied by another coefficient known as "sigma," which is associated with the confidence level on the first coefficient (i.e., the one that ranges from −1 to +1, often called "standardized

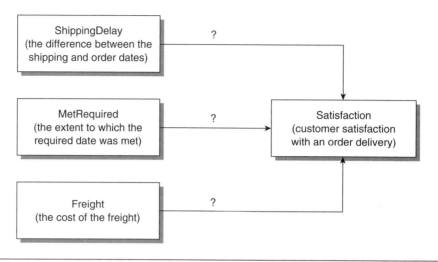

Figure 11.10 Diagram Representing the Data Mining Goal

beta" or simply "beta"). The lower the sigma, the better the confidence on the respective beta obtained through the data mining analysis. A low sigma essentially means a low degree of likelihood that a high beta value (i.e., a value that deviates significantly from zero) is due to measurement errors or other uncontrolled factors. Often, a minimum threshold of 5 percent (i.e., 0.05) is set for the sigma so that the value of beta can be considered significant. That is, for values of sigma above 0.05, the respective betas are considered insignificant.

Figure 11.11 illustrates the data mining process. At the top-left corner, we see part of the screen snapshot of the multiple regression data mining function of SPSS being used. The independent variable is set as "Satisfaction" (abbreviated to fit the variable name size limit imposed by SPSS). The aforementioned factors are referred to in SPSS as independent variables. In the middle-right part of Figure 11.11 is a screen snapshot of part of the output generated by SPSS, with the betas (called standardized beta coefficients) and the sigmas (confidence levels) circled.

At the bottom-left part of Figure 11.11, we see the final interpretation of the data mining results, vis-à-vis the original data mining goal. That final interpretation is that (a) the extent to which the required date was met, or "MetRequired," has an insignificant effect on the customer satisfaction with an order delivery; (b) the difference between shipping and order dates, or "ShippingDelay," has a weak effect on satisfaction; and (c) the freight cost has a strong negative effect on customer satisfaction, meaning that lower freight costs are associated with high levels of satisfaction. The effect of "Freight" on "Satisfaction" is almost 6 times stronger than the effect of "ShippingDelay."

Data mining results can be used as a basis for a variety of business-related decisions, including decisions in connection with business process redesign. For instance, the results summarized above suggest that if we were to redesign the order delivery process at Northwind Traders, it would be advisable to target activities that could minimize the cost of freight. The reason is that, according to the data mining

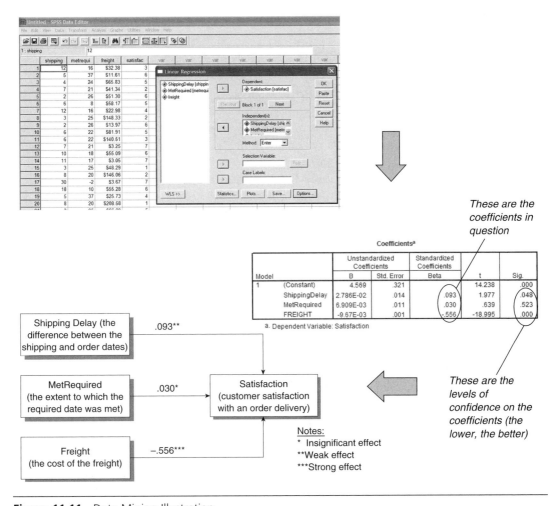

Figure 11.11   Data Mining Illustration

analysis summarized above, customers are 6 times more concerned about freight costs than shipping delays.

Summary and Concluding Remarks

The key difference between sequential and structured files is that the latter are organized in terms of sets of fields, whereas the former are essentially "flat" and made up of sequences of bytes with no higher-level unit of organization. This difference underlies a fundamental notion of database design, which is that databases are collections of structured files (better known as tables) that incorporate relationships with each other. The set of fields that make up the basic structure of a table is known as a record, and populated tables are in fact collections of records (the rows of the table).

More often than not, novice database designers think of one single, large table as an appropriate data repository for an organization, especially when the organization is relatively small. But, even in small organizations or business processes within those organizations, storing all of the relevant data in one single table is likely to lead to data redundancy. That, in turn, can lead to such a level of repetition in terms of data entry and maintenance (e.g., updates) as to significantly add to the labor costs associated with storing and using data to support even one single business process. Moreover, data redundancy can lead to higher storage costs, as more storage space is needed—an issue that is not of as much concern as increased labor costs, owing to the relatively low cost of storage media today.

Normalization is the process through which data redundancies are eliminated from a database. Normalizing a table or database usually involves breaking single tables into pairs of "children" tables, where the children tables do not have the same level of data repetition across different records. Most database designers employ a three-stage normalization method, through which they transform a non-normalized database into a database in first normal form, then second normal form, and then third normal form. Other normal forms exist beyond the third, but those are not traditionally employed in most practical situations.

The final concepts and techniques addressed in this chapter are those in connection with data warehousing and mining. Data mining is normally better accomplished on non-normalized databases, where all of the different tables that make up a database in third normal form are essentially joined together into a large table. This large table is called a data warehouse, or, in some cases, a data mart (this term means, roughly speaking, a mini data warehouse). The main goal of data mining is to unveil relationship among the fields that make up a database, which can be used as a basis for business decision making in a variety of scenarios. One scenario that is discussed in this chapter is that in which data mining is used to identify the most important factor in connection with customer satisfaction with an order delivery process, which is then presented as the main factor that should be targeted in an effort to redesign the order delivery process with the goal of improving its perceived quality.

Review Questions

1. In "flat," or unstructured, files, data are:
   (a) Organized into structured units, which are usually called records.
   (b) Stored without much organization, with the storage unit being usually a byte or an alphanumeric character.
   (c) Organized into unstructured units, which are usually called flattened records.
   (d) Organized into rows and columns, where different columns refer to different fields of a table, and where different rows refer to different records of a table.

2. Which of the following statements is incorrect?
   (a) In structured files, data are organized into units that are usually called records.

(b) One of the key disadvantages of sequential files is that the data stored in them usually has to be retried sequentially.

(c) A search procedure is only considered efficient when the field being searched is an alphanumeric field, rather than a numeric field.

(d) The ASCII standard was developed by the American National Standards Institute and is one of the most widely used standards for byte-to-character conversion in computers.

3. Which of the statements below does not refer to a goal of the database normalization process?

(a) To prepare a database for data mining.

(b) To reduce to a minimum the duplication of data in a database.

(c) To eliminate data redundancies in a database.

(d) To minimize repetition in the data entry process in connection with a database.

4. The main goal behind putting a database in second normal form is:

(a) To split each table of the database into two other tables.

(b) To remove repeating fields.

(c) To eliminate transitive dependencies.

(d) To eliminate partial dependencies.

5. Which of the following statements is incorrect?

(a) Database normalization is generally advisable for data repositories that are used on a daily basis to keep track and coordinate an organization's operations.

(b) Normalized databases are not particularly good when they serve as the basis for data analysis, particularly the computation-intensive types of data analyses required for data mining.

(c) Small data warehouses storing data about a particular area (e.g., a department of a large organization) are sometimes called data marts.

(d) Database normalization is generally advisable for data repositories that are used on a daily basis for large and complex data mining projects.

Discussion Questions

1. Develop a detailed scenario involving a service sector organization (e.g., a university, a restaurant, a consulting services firm) in need of storing data about its clients and the delivery of a key service to those clients. Create the structure of one large table that will store all of the data needed for that purpose. Implement that table using a standard database management suite (e.g., Microsoft Access), and populate it with data. A minimum of 20 records must be created.

2. Describe each of the steps involved in normalizing the one-table database created in Discussion Question 1, going up to the third normal form. For each of the steps, generate an entity-relationship diagram of the database. Implement the

resulting database in third normal form using a standard database management suite (e.g., Microsoft Access).

3. Develop a detailed scenario in which the normalized database generated in Discussion Question 2 is used as the basis for a data mining project. Create a corresponding data warehouse (or data mart), and execute the data mining project using a standard data mining package (e.g., SPSS, SAS, PLS Graph). Provide a detailed discussion of the results of the data mining project.

CHAPTER 12

Object-Oriented Design Concepts and Issues

The software development approach generally known as object-oriented programming has found widespread acceptance among professional programmers, especially those who develop large and complex computer programs on a regular basis. This adoption success led to the development of object-oriented systems analysis and design ideas and methods, whose general goal has been to facilitate the move from business process modeling to automation employing object-oriented programming languages and techniques.

This chapter introduces the notion of a software object as an abstraction that allows computer programmers to "encapsulate," and thus protect from improper access, both data and data manipulation code. A brief discussion of object-oriented programming is then provided, followed by a discussion of object-oriented analysis and design. Two forms of object-oriented design are subsequently discussed. The first involves the creation of software object classes, whereas the second involves the use of previously created software object classes. It is argued that the latter form is the most widely used form in in-house systems development projects aimed at automating newly designed business processes, particularly those employing a Web-based development paradigm.

What Is a Software Object?

A software object is an abstract entity used in computer programming to represent a set of related pieces of data and a set of programming functions that operate on those data pieces. One distinctive characteristic of object-oriented programming, which distinguishes it from the more traditional structured programming, is that the data and the programming functions that operate on those data are encapsulated into the same software object.

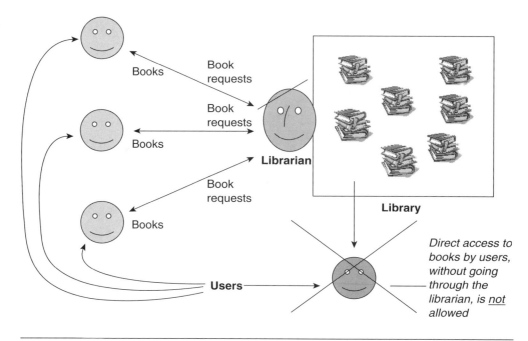

Figure 12.1 A Library Analogy

This encapsulation notion and its apparent usefulness are notoriously difficult to understand, which is one of the major roadblocks to the understanding of object-oriented design. The notion can be clarified by our drawing an analogy between a fictitious library and a software object. This library, like most libraries, stores data in the form of books (see Figure 12.1). Can book users go into the library and take the books themselves? The answer is "no," because if that was allowed, most likely some of the users would return their books, after they used them, to the wrong places. This would gradually make books more and more difficult to find in the library, as more and more users misplaced their returned books. So, how could users have access to books? The answer is simple: The users would place their book requests with a librarian, who would be responsible for keeping the library organized.

A software object is somewhat like the library in the example above. In the same way as the library, it stores data, which other program modules may need to use. Those program modules could be seen as analogous to the book users in the example. They need access to the data stored in the software object, but they can mess up those data, if given direct access to them. The librarian is analogous to the program functions that are part of the software object. In the same way that the librarian is the only one with direct access to the books stored in the library, a software object's functions (often called "methods," in object-oriented design jargon) are the only program functions with direct access to the data stored in a software object.

Object-Oriented Programming

Many believe that the first object-oriented programming language was Smaltalk, developed in the 1970s by a group of researchers at Xerox. Over the years, object-oriented programming has become very successful and is now the standard software development approach in large programming projects. Among the most widely used object-oriented programming languages are C++ and Java. C++ was created and refined over the years by AT&T Labs researcher and Texas A&M University Professor Bjarne Stroustrup. Java was developed by a group of researchers at Sun Microsystems.

As mentioned above, one of the key differences between object-oriented and traditional, or structured, programming is that in the former, the program modules of a software object are designed to operate on the software object's variables only. This basic premise behind object-oriented programming can be explained through an example. If a computer programmer were to create a software object associated with a real object, such as a life insurance policy holder (an object that is, in fact, a person), that software object would have some variables that would store information about policy holders, such as their age, general health, and whether they are smokers or not.

The program modules associated with the life insurance policy holder object (as previously mentioned, these are also called methods, in object-oriented programming lingo) would operate on the policy holder object variables only and would be part of the same software object definition. In traditional, or structured, programming, program modules would be defined separately from the policy holder variables and would be allowed to operate on those variables as well as any other variables in the computer program (see Figure 12.2). This independence between variables and program modules, which differentiates structured programming from object-oriented programming, makes structured programming code much more difficult to debug (or maintain) than object-oriented programming code.

This advantage in connection with debugging is particularly true for large programs with thousands of lines of code. In fact, the advantages of object-oriented programming become increasingly noticeable as the size of a computer program increases. For small programs (e.g., programs with a few lines of code), it often seems like object-oriented programming is unnecessarily cumbersome. Indeed, that is generally true.

On the other hand, very large computer programs, with thousands of lines of code, are very difficult to manage if they are built with structured programming techniques. The reason behind this is that when different program modules have direct access to the same variables, it is often difficult to figure out which program module is improperly manipulating the variables in the case of a programming error. And, as most programmers know, it is almost impossible to generate a large computer program that is completely error-free in "one sitting." More often than not, a large computer program must be debugged many times before it works properly.

Structured programming code

Object-oriented programming code

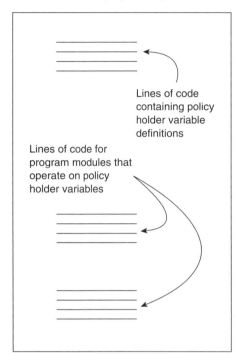

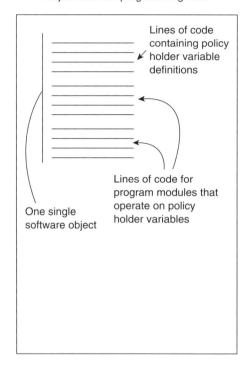

Lines of code
containing policy
holder variable
definitions

Lines of code for
program modules that
operate on policy
holder variables

One single
software object

Lines of code
containing policy
holder variable
definitions

Lines of code for
program modules that
operate on policy
holder variables

Figure 12.2 Structured Versus Object-Oriented Programming

Object-Oriented Analysis and Design

Apparently due to the success of object-oriented programming, the 1990s saw the emergence of object-oriented analysis and design as a widely touted approach for business process analysis, as well as an important stage preceding computers systems design and specification. Among leading early proponents of this approach were Grady Booch, James Rumbaugh, and Ivar Jacobson, as well as others such as Coad, Yourdon, and Firesmith. Object-oriented analysis and design seems to have emerged as an answer to the following question: How can we devise an approach that would allow us to move more quickly from analysis and design to coding using object-oriented programming techniques than the software development life cycle?

As with the software development life cycle, different flavors of object-oriented analysis and design methodologies soon emerged. An important component of those methodologies, which helped to differentiate them from each other, was the standard notation that each of them proposed for modeling business processes and real-world objects. These standard notations have been incorporated into several diagram types. After a while, a new set of standard notations for object-oriented analysis and design was developed with the goal of unifying three existing methodologies—Grady Booch's methodology, aimed at describing groups of related software objects and their associations; James Rumbaugh's methodology, called Object-Modeling Technique; and Ivar Jacobson's methodology, centered on a notion that was referred to as the "use-case."

This new set of standard notations became known as unified modeling language, or UML. Twelve types of diagrams made up the unified modeling language. Those diagrams are divided into three main categories, namely structural diagrams, behavior diagrams, and model management diagrams. Structural diagrams are used to represent the structure and static relationship of software objects—for example, which data and operation modules are shared by which software objects. Behavior diagrams are used to represent the operation of a computer system in terms of its objects, including the dynamic relationship among software objects—that is, how the software objects interact with each other when the computer system is being executed. Model management diagrams are used to represent the organization of computer system modules around software objects.

Object-oriented analysis and design has apparently been presented as an approach that allows computer systems developers to move swiftly from analysis and design to coding using object-oriented programming techniques. And it seems that object-oriented analysis and design has been reasonably triumphant in connection with that arguably narrow goal. However, unlike its object-oriented programming cousin, object-oriented analysis and design has been only modestly successful from a more general perspective. One of the key indications of that is that object-oriented analysis and design is still not used by the vast majority of systems analysts, who more often than not employ some variation of the software development life cycle.

T. Chuang and S. Yadav coauthored an article published in the journal *Database for Advances in Information Systems* in which they provide an explanation for the above state of affairs. In the article, titled "A Decision-Driven Approach to Object-Oriented Analysis," the authors argue that traditional object-oriented analysis and design approaches have not been very successful because they provide an impoverished view of how information exchanges take place in business processes. Chuang and Yadav expand their discussion by proposing their own approach to object-oriented analysis and design, which is based on an information exchange perspective.

The arguments put forth in this book are in general agreement with Chuang and Yadav's conclusions. However, this may appear to be contradictory with the conclusion that we reached a few paragraphs ago, that is, that object-oriented analysis and design has apparently been a successful answer to the call for an approach that would allow us to move more quickly from analysis and design to coding using object-oriented programming techniques. And we cannot forget that object-oriented programming has found wide acceptance among those who make a living developing computer code. Given this, doesn't the other conclusion, that object-oriented analysis and design has been somewhat unsuccessful, sound a bit paradoxical? Arguably it does, and an explanation is certainly warranted.

An important point made throughout this book is that we need more information exchange–oriented approaches to systems analysis and design. In fact, this is one of the key points made in this book, which sets the stage for another key contribution of this book, namely a set of methodological solutions to the lack of information exchange orientation of extant systems analysis and design approaches.

Nevertheless, one of the big reasons (and perhaps the main reason) why object-oriented analysis and design has not been as successful as originally expected is that it addresses somewhat poorly the need to redesign business processes *before* we even start thinking about how to automate them. If a business process is badly designed—for example, a form in a business process has to be signed by 10 people when only 2 would be enough—automating it will not solve the problem. The business process will have to be changed first, by doing away with the related formal procedure requiring 10 signatures.

In some cases, the inefficient activities of a nonoptimal business process will be carried out faster with computer automation, but the marginal gain in productivity will not be enough to offset the extra costs associated with automation. That is, computer automation per se rarely leads to business process productivity gains (as suggested by some of the quantitative evidence presented earlier in this book). This is, one could argue, one of the main problems with current systems analysis and design approaches, whether they are based on the object-oriented paradigm or the software development life cycle model.

Creating Classes of Software Objects

Object-oriented design, in its purest form, involves the design and implementation of software object classes. Software object classes are implemented through object-oriented programs, which are written in object-oriented computer programming languages such as C++ and Java. Software object classes are then "instantiated," which means that they are initialized and used in a computer program.

Structured programming, in contrast, does not involve the design and implementation of software object classes or their instantiation into software objects. As mentioned before in this chapter, in structured programming variables are accessed directly throughout a computer program. That is, those variables are not protected through their encapsulation into a software object. Figure 12.3 shows a piece of computer programming code written in the C language, which is not object-oriented.

The program shown in Figure 12.3 is complete—the code itself is shown on the top-left part of the figure. It allows a user to provide 10 numbers to the program, which then calculates the sum, product, and average of those 10 numbers. The output of the program, as seen on a computer screen, is shown on the bottom-right part of the figure. The program lines starting with "//" are comment lines, which means that they are ignored by the computer running the program. In fact, all code followed by "//" is computer programming commentary and is ignored by the computer. The goal of that commentary is to make a computer program easy to understand by other computer programmers.

The variables are defined at the beginning of the program shown in Figure 12.3. For example, the "float n;" statement defines the variable "n," which will be used to store a number. The variable type "float" refers to a rational number. The "int c = 0;" statement defines the variable "c," which will be used as a number entry "counter"—so that the program stops running after 10 numbers are entered. The variable type "int" refers to an integer number. The "int c = 0;" statement, in addition to defining the variable "c," also initializes that variable with the value zero.

Program written in the C programming language

```
// Calculates the sum, product and average of 10 numbers

#include <iostream.h>

float n; // input: number
float s = 0, p = 1, a; // outputs: sum, product and average
int c = 0; // Flag: counter

void main () {

while (c++<10) {
cout<< "Enter number: "; cin>>n;
 s+=n;
 p*=n;
} // end while
a = s/10;

cout<<"Sum="<<s<<endl;
cout<<"Product="<<p<<endl;
cout<<"Average="<<a<<endl;
}//end main
```

Program variables are defined at the beginning of the program and directly accessible throughout the program.

This part of the program code allows users to enter values and calculates the sum, product, and average of those values (which are stored in the previously defined variables "s," "p," and "a").

The "cout" statements are responsible for the program outputs, which appear on the computer screen.

```
Enter number: 12
Enter number: 2.3
Enter number: 4.5
Enter number: 1.2
Enter number: 3.4
Enter number: 5
Enter number: 6
Enter number: 7
Enter number: 1.2
Sum = 45.6
Product = 383092
Average = 4.56
```

Figure 12.3   Structured Programming Example

As can be seen from Figure 12.3, the program statements below the "void main ()" statement access the variables, defined at the beginning of the program, directly. For example, the statement "s += n;" adds the value stored in "n" to whatever is in the variable "s" (e.g., if "s" is 10, and "n" is 5, then "s" will become 15). This direct manipulation of variables within a computer program is what differentiates structured from object-oriented programming.

The C++ programming language is the object-oriented version of the C language. Figure 12.4 shows three pieces of code on the top-left, top-right, and bottom-left parts of the figure. Those pieces of object-oriented programming code illustrate a software object class definition, implementation, and use, respectively. They together form a complete program that performs a rather simple task, namely the task of incrementing and decrementing (i.e., adding 1 to and subtracting 1 from) the value stored by a software object called a "counter." The computer screen output of the program is shown on the bottom-right part of Figure 12.4.

C++ program code: Class definition

```
#include <iostream.h> // cin & cout definitions

//*********************************
//Definition of the class counter
//*********************************

class counter {
public:
        counter();
        void increment();
        void decrement();
        int access_value();
private:
        int value;
};
```

C++ program code: Class implementation

```
//************************************************
//Implementation of the class counter
//************************************************

counter::counter() {
    value = 0;
} // end counter (constructor member function)

void counter::increment() {
    value++;
}

void counter::decrement() {
    value--;
}

int counter::access_value() {
    return value;
}
```

C++ program code: Class use

```
//************************************************
//Use of the class counter in a program
//************************************************

void main() {
    counter c;

    cout <<"Initial value of counter:"<<c.access_value();

    c.increment();
    cout<< endl;
    cout<<"Value of counter after one increment:" << c.access_value();

    c.decrement(); c.decrement();
    cout<< endl;
    cout<<"Value of counter after two decrements:" << c.access_value();
}
```

Program output (screen)

Initial value of counter: 0
Value of counter after one increment: 1
Value of counter after two decrements: −1

Figure 12.4 Object-Oriented Programming Example

A software class definition usually involves listing the variables stored by a particular software object, as well as the functions that operate on those variables. Those functions are referred to as the "methods" (or "member functions") of the software object. As can be seen from the top-left part of the Figure 12.4, the software object class "counter" contains one variable, called "value" and defined as being of the type "integer." Also, the software object class "counter" is defined as having four methods—"counter," "increment," "decrement," and "access_value." These methods perform operations on the variable "value."

On the top-right part of Figure 12.4, we can see the implementation of the software object class "counter," which essentially is the coding of the methods that make up the class. The first method shown, indicated as "counter::counter()" simply initializes the variable "value" with the value zero. This method is referred to as the "constructor" method of the class. A constructor method usually has the same name as the software object class and is executed immediately upon the instantiation of the class.

The methods "increment" and "decrement," indicated as "counter::increment()" and "counter::decrement()," simply add 1 and subtract 1 from the variable "value," respectively. Finally, the method "access_value," indicated as "counter::access_ value()," returns the value of the variable "value." This latter method is necessary, since software object encapsulation prevents outside code from having access to the variable "value," which is hidden inside the software object.

At the bottom-left part of Figure 12.4, we see the use of the software object class "counter." The first step in using the "counter" class is to instantiate it, which is done through the statement "counter c;." This statement effectively creates a software object "c" with the same structure as defined in the class "counter," where the variable "value" is started with the value zero by the constructor method.

Once a software object class is instantiated into a software object (e.g., the software object "c," in Figure 12.4), its methods are normally used within a computer program through calls that include the name of the software object, a "dot," the name of the method, and any parameters used by the method (usually included within parentheses). For example, the method "increment" is used through the call "c.increment()."

Using Previously Created Classes of Software Objects

One of the advantages of developing classes of software objects is that their reusability potential is very high. Unlike pieces of programming code that have to be edited (sometimes extensively) when they are moved from one program to another, software object classes can be easily reused in different computer programs. This can be accomplished even when the classes are created in a programming language different from the one in which they are being used, as long as a standard for interaction with different objects is available. One such standard is CORBA, which stands for Common Object Request Broker Architecture.

Web-based programming is becoming one of the most popular alternatives for new business process implementation using the in-house development approach (as opposed to business process outsourcing or commercial package customization). There are many software development tools and computer languages available for Web-based programming. One of them is JavaScript, developed by Netscape Corporation—see code in Figure 12.5.

JavaScript is a programming language that is interpreted by many Web browsers. The Web-based programming example illustrated through Figure 12.5 employs JavaScript to access two methods of the software object class "window," which allow users to manipulate characteristics of a Web browser window—that is, the window of the Web browser that is interpreting the JavaScript programming code. Those methods are "resizeTo" and "moveTo," which resize the Web browser window and move it to a particular position on the computer screen, respectively. The computer screen output of the JavaScript code, after it is executed, is shown at the bottom-right part of Figure 12.5.

This example illustrates one of the most common forms of what many refer to as object-oriented programming, used to develop Web-based applications in-house to enable new business process designs. However, as can be seen from Figure 12.5, no software object class is created. Therefore, object-oriented programming is not,

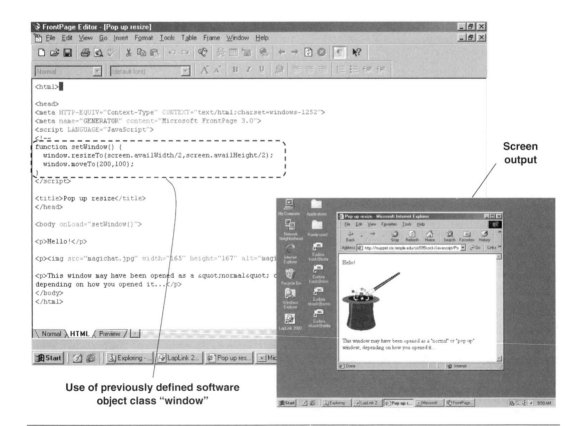

Figure 12.5   Using Previously Created Objects in Web-Based Programming

in its strictest sense, really taking place. Nevertheless, this form of "object-oriented programming" can be used as a basis to develop complete database-based commercial applications, not only small and simple programs like the one whose code is shown in Figure 12.5. This will be illustrated later in this book, through the development of a relatively complete prototype Web-based system.

The use of previously created software object classes illustrated in Figure 12.5, which we could call a "weak" form of object-oriented programming, is probably the most common form of object-oriented programming used to implement the in-house development alternative to automating redesigned business processes. And, for someone to successfully use this weak form of object-oriented programming, it arguably makes relatively little difference whether that person employs an object-oriented approach to systems analysis and design, instead of the more traditional software development life cycle.

Summary and Concluding Remarks

Software objects are widely used in business applications. Their widespread use is a reflection of the success of the object-oriented programming paradigm, which has been very popular among developers of large and complex business programs—for example, those that implement software development environments, operating systems, and large commercial applications. Many believe that the first object-oriented programming language was Smalltalk, developed in the 1970s by a group of researchers at Xerox.

In a business application context, a software object can be defined as a software representation of a business entity, such as a customer, a product, or a customer order. One distinctive characteristic of object-oriented design is that software objects encapsulate both (a) data, in the form of object-specific variables, and (b) the object-specific functions that access and manipulate those data. Those functions are often referred to as "methods," in the terminology employed by object-oriented programmers.

The encapsulation of data and methods in software objects essentially means that data that are part of one software object cannot be directly accessed by programming code outside the software or by methods from other software objects. In large programs, this makes it much easier for programmers to debug, reuse, and extend object-oriented code than is possible in traditional structured programming. In the latter (i.e., structured programming), data and functions are not encapsulated. Therefore, in large programs, invariably several functions will access the same data, which may lead to what some software developers would call "strange" program behavior (e.g., a screen freeze, keyboard lockups, and other unexpected events). Since many functions access the same data, large chunks of programming code generated using structured programming techniques tend to have more bugs than equivalent code generated using object-oriented techniques. Structured code tends to be harder to debug as well.

The success of object-oriented programming has led to the development of new approaches to systems analysis and design that were different from the software development life cycle and that better aligned the underlying notions of object-oriented programming. The basic motivation behind the development of those approaches was the perception that traditional software development life cycle techniques were not entirely appropriate for use by software developers who wanted to move quickly from analysis and design to coding using object-oriented programming techniques.

The above led to the emergence of object-oriented analysis and design in the 1990s. It seems that object-oriented analysis and design has been reasonably triumphant in connection with its goal of allowing software developers to move relatively quickly from analysis and design to object-oriented coding. However, unlike its object-oriented programming cousin, object-oriented analysis and design has been only modestly successful from a more general perspective. It is still not used by the vast majority of systems analysts, who more often than not employ some variation of the software development life cycle.

There are many possible reasons why object-oriented systems analysis and design has not been as successful as originally expected. For example, it is possible that adoption of object-oriented systems analysis and design is not currently more widespread because there are still many systems analysts who have been trained in traditional systems analysis and design techniques. That is, those systems analysts may not be using object-oriented techniques and methods simply due to a resistance-to-change phenomenon.

Based on the discussion presented in previous chapters of this book, it seems plausible that one of the main reasons why object-oriented analysis has not been as successful as originally predicted is that it addresses in a rather limited way the urgent need to redesign business processes *before* any decisions are made regarding how those processes will be automated. Object-oriented systems analysis and design assumes to a certain extent that automation will take place through the creation and use of software objects. But most business process automation efforts today rely on either business process outsourcing or commercial package customization. And, in the relatively small number of instances where automation is done through in-house development, previously created software object classes are reused and no new objects are actually created.

Review Questions

1. A software object is:
   (a) An abstract entity used in computer programming to represent a set of related pieces of data and a set of programming functions that operate on those data pieces.
   (b) A real and tangible entity used in computer programming to represent a set of related table fields and a set of programming functions that operate on those fields.
   (c) An abstract entity used in object-oriented programming, which was developed by Bjarne Stroustrup in response to what is known as the "Java revolution"—spearheaded by a group of programmers working for the Starbucks Corporation.

(d) An abstract entity used in object-oriented programming to represent a set of related pieces of data and a set of programming functions, where the functions operate on data pieces that are outside the software object.

2. Which of the statements below is incorrect?
   (a) Many believe that the first object-oriented programming language was Smaltalk, developed in the 1970s by a group of researchers at Xerox.
   (b) One of the key differences between object-oriented and traditional, or structured, programming is that in the former, the program modules of a software object are designed to operate on the software object's variables only.
   (c) Over the years, object-oriented programming has become only moderately successful, never matching the popularity of object-oriented analysis and design.
   (d) In the context of large and complex computer programs, structured programming code is generally more difficult to "debug" (or maintain) than object-oriented programming code.

3. Object-oriented analysis and design:
   (a) Has achieved, from its inception, much more success than the waterfall model.
   (b) Has traditionally been used by programmers to encapsulate operations and data.
   (c) Has replaced structured programming.
   (d) Has been unified through UML.

4. It is incorrect to say that a software class definition involves:
   (a) Creating an instance of the software class to be used in a program.
   (b) Listing the variables stored by a particular software object.
   (c) Writing a list of the functions that operate on a software object's variables.
   (d) Creating a list of the methods that make up a software object.

5. One of the advantages of developing classes of software objects is that:
   (a) Their methods can never be accessed directly by outside variables.
   (b) They can be reused relatively easily in different computer programs.
   (c) They can be instantiated in the real world, which makes them much easier to use in manufacturing activities, particularly as parts of car engines.
   (d) They can be directly used to classify different structured computer programs in what many see as "natural" program categories.

Discussion Questions

1. As mentioned earlier in this chapter, one of the key differences between object-oriented and traditional, or structured, programming is that in the former, the program modules of a software object are designed to operate on the software object's variables only. Based on this simple idea, develop a software development

scenario related to the automation of a manufacturing process. The scenario should illustrate the advantages of this difference in favor of the object-oriented programming approach and should be as realistic as possible.

2. Conduct Web-based research on the history of object-oriented programming. Based on that research, develop a timeline showing the main developments in the history of object-oriented programming, along with dates and key individuals involved.

3. Develop two detailed mutually exclusive business scenarios involving either a service or a manufacturing organization. One scenario should illustrate the advantages of using an object-oriented analysis and design approach, whereas the other scenario should illustrate the advantages of using a non–object-oriented analysis and design approach. Each scenario should illustrate the advantages of one approach over the other, and both scenarios should be as realistic as possible.

CHAPTER 13

Business Process Automation With ASP

Should systems analysts know how to program? This is an issue that is often debated in systems analysis and design circles, as well as in university programs where systems analysis and design courses are taught. On one side of the debate are those who believe that systems analysis and design courses should be more technical and emphasize programming. The rationale presented by this constituency is often that systems analysts should sometimes "eat their own dog food," so to speak, by placing themselves in the shoes of the programmers who will have to implement the technology solutions they design. On the other side of the debate are those who believe that systems analysis and design courses should be entirely conceptual, since (a) it is not the job of a systems analyst to implement the system he or she designs and (b) computer programming is usually covered in other courses.

It may be advisable to take the middle ground on the aforementioned debate. In other words, one may reasonably take the stand that systems analysts should "eat their own dog food" but not spend too much time with computer programming in a systems analysis and design course. After all, most technology-based implementations of new business processes employ one of two business process implementation strategies: business process outsourcing or commercial package customization. Neither strategy's focus is on computer programming, as has been discussed in previous chapters. Nevertheless, a third business process implementation strategy, in-house development, does involve computer programming and other technological issues.

To implement this "middle ground" perspective, one of the best approaches in the context of a systems analysis and design course seems to be that of conducting a prototype implementation of a designed technology solution to implement a business process. To have the prototype implementation completed within the time frame of a semester-long course, the choice of prototype development environment should arguably rest with a relatively "high-level" environment, that is, one in which several components of the prototype system (e.g., elements of the user interface, such as buttons and forms) would be already available for use with minimal programming.

Another criterion to be used in the selection of a prototype development environment is that it is widely used commercially, for two reasons. One is that the environment would be relatively easy to set up for student use in computer laboratories and other similar facilities. The other reason is that, by employing a development environment that is widely used commercially, the students will be acquiring useful technological skills.

The choice of development environment to which this chapter refers revolves primarily around what is generally known as active server pages (ASP). ASP-based prototype development can be implemented through a relatively "high-level" environment, which is usually made up of several software development products produced and commercialized by Microsoft Corporation, including Access (a database development environment), FrontPage (a Web page and applications development environment), and Internet Information Services (Web server software). Also, from a commercial perspective, ASP-based development is one of the most widely used development approaches.

The Redesigned Process at Little Italy Restaurants

The rich pictorial representation shown in Figure 13.1 is of the redesigned order fulfillment process of the Italian restaurants chain called Little Italy Restaurants,

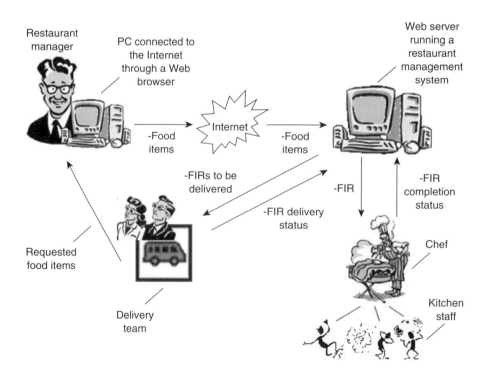

Figure 13.1   Rich Pictorial Representation of the Redesigned Order Fulfillment Process

whose case was discussed in some detail earlier in this book. The implementation of the redesigned business process assumes the use of Internet technologies, particularly those based on a client-server infrastructure made up of standard Web browsers (on the client side—the restaurant manager) and a Web server (on the server side—the central kitchen).

Figure 13.1 suggests that the order fulfillment process at Little Italy Restaurants starts with a request for food items being issued by a restaurant manager. That is done through a Web browser. The food items request then becomes available to a team based in a central kitchen. The team produces the food items requested and packs them for delivery. The delivery team, which is also based in the central kitchen, then delivers the food items requested to the restaurant that issued the request over the Web.

The Little Italy Restaurants Web System must have some key components to enable the order fulfillment process. It must provide the means by which food items requests data are entered, modified, and deleted, using a standard Web browser. An underlying database is needed to store those data. Moreover, a variety of Web-based reports must be made available to central kitchen employees, to properly fulfill food items requests, as well as to restaurant managers, to keep track of the status of their food item requests.

What Are Active Server Pages?

Just about every Web-based transaction involves two key elements: a Web browser and a Web server. The Web browser usually runs on a user's computer, which accesses the Web through one of the many services available (e.g., AOL's dial-up service or a broadband Internet service provided by a cable company). The Web server usually runs on an organization's computer, usually a bigger one than that used by the user, which makes itself available to Web browser users through a static Internet protocol (IP) address (e.g., 207.171.166.102) and/or a universal resource locator (URL) (e.g., www.amazon.com). More often than not, both IP address and URL can be used to access a Web server (or cluster of servers associated with the same IP address and URL). For example, at the time of this writing, Amazon.com's main Web site was accessible through a Web browser by entering either of the following on its search field (at the top part of the browser) and pressing the enter key: "http://207.171.166.102," or "http://www.amazon.com."

ASP pages are Web pages that contain code that is processed by a user's Web browser, as well as some code that is processed by a Web server. The code processed at the Web browser is usually written in HTML, a language used to compose most Web pages that hold static content. The code processed by the Web server is habitually referred to as "script" code. The most common script code generation (or scripting) languages used to create Web-based programs are JavaScript and VBScript. JavaScript bears some similarities to the popular programming language called Java, developed by Sun Microsystems. Analogously, VBScript bears similarities to the programming language underlying Visual Basic, a programming environment developed by Microsoft, and supporting the use of a version of the programming language BASIC (one of the early programming languages, aimed at novice programmers).

ASP is one of several software technologies that use content generated by HTML pages on a Web browser as inputs and that produce as output content that can be shown as part of HTML pages by the same Web browser. For example, a user may enter a search term such as "Texas A&M" through a Web browser form, which will then send it to an ASP page. The ASP page will then conduct a search for that term on a database of Web sites and compile all of the URLs of all of the Web sites that contain the term "Texas A&M," which it (i.e., the ASP page) will send back to the Web browser. The Web browser will then show those URLs as part of an HTML page.

ASP pages usually have the extension ".asp" and are stored and run on Web servers running Microsoft's Internet Information Services (also known as IIS). The ASP software technology is seen by many as a much-awaited replacement for common gateway interface (CGI)–enabled applications. The CGI standard enables Web pages to pass on data to compiled computer programs written in a variety of programming languages (e.g., C, C++, Visual Basic) and receive data from those programs, which are then shown on an HTML page. ASP code is generally seen as easier to write and more efficient (in terms of processing time and use of computer resources) than the code underlying CGI-enabled applications.

The Little Italy Restaurants Web System

In the following sections, we will discuss a simple prototype called the Little Italy Restaurants Web System. The goal of that discussion is to cover a minimum set of software techniques using ASP and other related software technologies. It is hoped that, based on that minimum set of techniques, readers will be able to develop fully functional and operational Web-based systems—with functionality that goes well beyond that of the prototype discussed in this chapter.

The Little Italy Restaurants Web System is made up of several components, which allow users to enter, modify, and delete data stored in an underlying database. The database stores information about food items (i.e., components of past dishes), restaurants, food items requests (i.e., a quantity of food items requested by a given restaurant), and status options associated with food items requests (e.g., ordered, delivered). The Little Italy Restaurants Web System also allows users to obtain Web-based reports of the information stored in the database. Figure 13.2 shows the main menu Web page with links for the different components of the Little Italy Restaurants Web System.

The set of components illustrated by the Web links in Figure 13.2 is a simplified one; a commercial system would probably have more components. Also, some of those components could be combined (e.g., data entry with update and deletion). The reason why they are presented in that way is to allow for a relatively simplified discussion of the basic ASP functionality needed to develop much more complex Web-based systems.

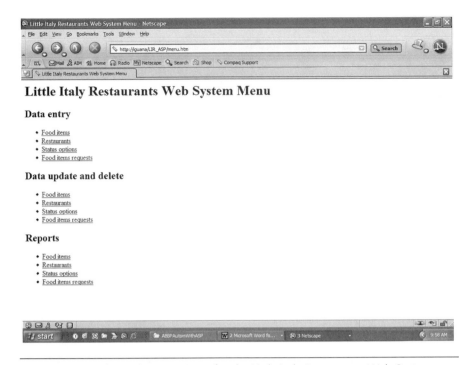

Figure 13.2   The Main Menu Page for the Little Italy Restaurants Web System

Creating the Database for the System

ASP-enabled Web systems that operate on data are usually made up of "front-end" Web pages with data manipulation code (e.g., HTML forms, VBScript) and "back-end" databases that are used to store the data that the Web pages operate on. Those databases can be developed with many different database management systems, such as Microsoft Access, Oracle, IBM's DB2, and Microsoft SQL Server. More often than not, each database management system employs a different database format. For example, Oracle's database format is different from that used by Access, which in part makes Oracle databases more efficient than Access databases in situations where the number of records stored in the database, or the number of simultaneous "queries" on the database, is large.

In our discussion here, we will use Microsoft Access, since Access is one of the most widely available database management systems around. Access comes as a standard component of the Microsoft Office suite, together with Word, Excel, and FrontPage—also widely popular tools for word processing, spreadsheet calculations, and Web page design, respectively. Incidentally, a commercial and fully functional version of the prototype Little Italy Restaurants Web System presented here could also use Access and perform quite well. Both the number of records stored and simultaneous accesses (from, e.g., geographically distributed restaurant managers) are likely to be well below the thresholds that would make Access less efficient as a database than Oracle or SQL Server, for example.

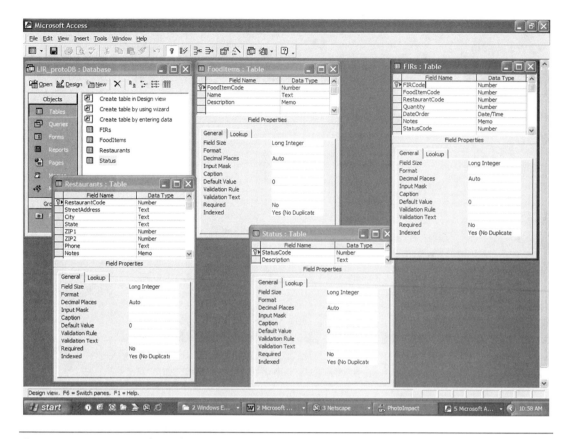

Figure 13.3   Creating the Little Italy Restaurants Web System Database

Let us assume that at the design stage, it was decided that the Little Italy Restaurants Web System database would contain four main tables and that those tables would store information about food items, restaurants, status options for food items requests, and the food items requests themselves. We would then have to create that database and the related tables using Access. This is done by defining the fields of each of the tables in the database, using Access table design feature (see Figure 13.3).

Figure 13.3 shows each of the four tables (or files) that make up the Little Italy Restaurants Web System database. The four tables are named "FoodItems" (which stores data about food items), "Restaurants" (which stores data about each of the restaurants in the Italian restaurant chain), "Status" (which stores data about status options for each food item request), and "FIRs" (which stores data about food items requests). Each table contains several fields, which store data in records associated with each table. For example, the fields of the "FoodItems" table will all store data for each record entered into the table, and each record will refer to a different food item (e.g., risotto, Alfredo sauce).

Following database design conventions, the first field of each table is defined as the primary key field for the table (shown with a key icon on the left). A primary key field is a unique field of each table and cannot be repeated in two or more different records. For example, if "FoodItemCode" stores information about a unique code for each food item (e.g., 1 for risotto, 3 for Alfredo sauce), then two food items cannot have the same code (1 for risotto and 1 also for Alfredo sauce). As can be seen in Figure 13.3, the primary key fields are "FoodItemCode," "StatusCode," "RestaurantCode," and "FIRCode."

The table structure of the Little Italy Restaurants Web System contains separate tables for data in connection with, say, food items and food items requests. Could only one table store all of the data? The answer is "yes," but that would cause some problems in terms of duplication in the database, duplicated data entry in Web forms, and other related issues. For example, a restaurant manager should not have to enter all of a food item's information (e.g., name, how it is prepared) every single time she enters a food items request. She should be allowed to enter only a summarized piece of data in connection with the food item in question, for example, the food item's code, together with the other details of the food items request (e.g., quantity). The food item's code would be related to a particular food item (and related information) stored in a separate table, the food items table. This way, a food item's description would have to be entered only once, even if 10 food items requests were entered every day, all containing a reference to the same food item.

Using ODBC to Create a Data Source Name

Once a database has been created, we must create a data source name (DSN) by which the database will be referred to in our ASP pages. This is accomplished through a standard for database connectivity called Open Database Connectivity (ODBC), which is implemented in Microsoft Windows through a program labeled ODBC Data Source Administrator. This program is usually available through the "Control Panel" in Windows, sometimes under "Administrative Tools." It should be run on the Web server computer that will host the ASP code associated with the Little Italy Restaurants Web System.

Once ODBC Data Source Administrator is up and running, several tab options will appear across the top of the window (see Figure 13.4). The "System DSN" tab should be selected for the creation of a DSN to be used by ASP code running on the Web server. This will ensure that the database will be accessible from the Web site ASP code, regardless of who is browsing the Web site. Since the Little Italy Restaurants Web System database has been created as an Access database, a "Microsoft Access Driver" should be selected.

Once a particular driver has been chosen, the next step involves naming the DSN and selecting the actual database file that will store the data manipulated through the DSN connection. In Figure 13.5, the chosen name for the DSN is "LIRACC," which will be referenced in the ASP code that will make up the Little Italy Restaurants Web System. The database file selected to be associated with that DSN is "LIR_protoDB.mdb," which Figure 13.5 suggests is in the "c:/Temp" folder of the Web server.

As can be seen in Figure 13.5, the option "Select Database" was used. That option was activated by clicking on the "Select" button under the "Database" area of the "ODBC Microsoft Access Setup" window. Just below that, there is an area named

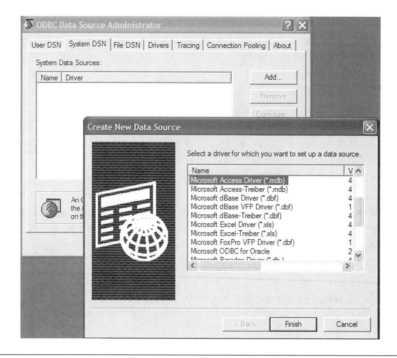

Figure 13.4 Choosing a DSN Driver for the Access Database

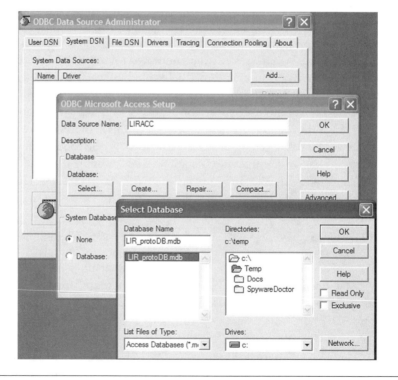

Figure 13.5 Naming a DSN and Selecting a Related Access Database

"System Database," which should not be used unless the Access database is being used as a shared database—that is, a database used by a workgroup. Shared Access databases require username and password entries to be set up for them so that they can be used on a Web site.

Database Manipulation With SQL

SQL stands for structured query language. It is a standard programming language used for the manipulation of most relational databases (as well as some object-oriented databases). SQL's broad standard status is reflected in its being registered with both the American National Standards Institute (ANSI) and the International Organization for Standardization (often referred to as ISO), a worldwide federation of national standards bodies from more than 100 countries.

There are four main SQL standard statements, widely seen as the "most important" elements of the SQL syntax. These four standard statements are often referred to as SELECT, INSERT, UPDATE, and DELETE. Combined, these four standard statements allow for just about any database operation—from data entry to modification and deletion. Their generic syntax is shown below, where clauses within brackets "[]" are optional and those separated by a vertical line "|" can be used alternatively.

```
SELECT select_list [INTO new_table] FROM table_name(s)
[WHERE search_condition(s)]
[ORDER BY sort_criteria]

INSERT INTO table_name (column_list)
VALUES (values_list) | select_statement

UPDATE table_name SET column_name=expression, . . .
[WHERE search_condition(s)]

DELETE FROM table_name
[WHERE search_condition(s)]
```

A SELECT statement, when used alone, will often be aimed at generating a selection of records, which will then be used in some way. SELECT statements are used for the creation of temporary tables, which in turn can be combinations of other tables or simply replicas of the original tables used for intermediate operations. For example, the SQL statement below is used to select all records from the table "Status" and copy them into a temporary table called "Temp." Often, SQL statements end with a semicolon.

```
SELECT * INTO Temp FROM Status;
```

An INSERT statement is used to enter data into a table, which in turn is part of a database (i.e., a database is a collection of tables). INSERT statements essentially create new records in the specified table. For example, the SQL statement below is used to create a new record in the table "FoodItems," where the value "3" is assigned to the field "FoodItemCode," the text "Risotto" is assigned to the field "Name," and the text "Good" is assigned to the field "Description."

```
INSERT INTO FoodItems (FoodItemCode, Name, Description)
SELECT '3' AS FoodItemCode, 'Risotto' AS Name, 'Good' AS Description;
```

An UPDATE statement will be used to modify the data that currently exists in a table. For example, the SQL statement below updates the fields "StatusCode" and "Description" in the table "Status," making the first equal "3" and the second equal "Delivered." This update refers to the record in which "StatusCode" equals "3" (the search condition).

```
UPDATE Status SET StatusCode = '3', Description = 'Delivered'
WHERE StatusCode = '3';
```

Finally, a DELETE statement will be used to remove a particular record from a table. For example, the SQL statement below will delete one record from the table Status. The record delete will be the one where the field "StatusCode" equals "3" (the search condition).

```
DELETE FROM Status
WHERE StatusCode = '3';
```

As can be seen from these examples, the four SQL statements (i.e., SELECT, INSERT, UPDATE, and DELETE), allow for a wide range of database manipulation operations. Earlier, it was mentioned that SQL is used for the manipulation of data in relational databases. In fact, relational databases are often defined as databases that can be manipulated through SQL, either directly or indirectly (e.g., through data manipulation functions that interpret SQL statements). That characteristic is often used to differentiate relational databases from object-oriented databases.

Creating Web-Based Data Entry Forms

The two main components of any computer system that operates on a database are normally referred to as "forms" and "reports," whether the system is Web based or not. Forms enable data entry, modification, and deletion. Reports have one main function: showing what is on the database in a convenient format (e.g., a list of records in a table, ordered by the primary key of the table).

One of the most popular techniques for building Web-based forms is the use of an HTML element called "form." That HTML element is used to allow a user to enter data into a set of variables using a Web browser. Once the data is entered in the form of values assigned to a set of variables, those values are then transferred to a Web page containing ASP code, where the values will be used as inputs for database operations.

The piece of code below shows how the HTML element "form" is used to allow for values to be entered for the variables "FoodItemCode," "Name," and "Description." Those values correspond to the fields of the table "FoodItems," but they are not actually those fields—they are in fact intermediate variables that hold values corresponding to those fields. Once those values are entered, they are sent to the Web page "DataEntryFoodItemsProc.asp," which contains the ASP code that will process the data input entered through the variables "FoodItemCode," "Name," and "Description."

```
<form method="POST" action="DataEntryFoodItemsProc.asp">
  <p>Food item code: <input type="text" name="FoodItemCode"
  size="10"> </p>
  <p>Name: <input type="text" name="Name" size="50"></p>
  <p>Description: <textarea rows="10" name="Description" cols="50">
  </textarea></p>
  <p><input type="submit" value="Submit" name="SubmitButton">
      <input type="reset" value="Reset" name="ResetButton"></p>
</form>
```

In this piece of code, the first and last lines, starting with "<form method . . ." and ending with "</form>," mark the beginning and end of the Web-based form. Figure 13.6 shows how the form looks on a Web browser. The lines starting with "<p>" and ending with "</p>" indicate separate paragraphs. Each new paragraph starts with a label to be shown on the browser screen for each variable (e.g., "Food item code" is shown as a label for "FoodItemCode"), and is followed by a piece of code.

Most of the lines of code that generate the Web browser output shown in Figure 13.6 contain the "<input . . ." statement. The following HTML elements usually follow the word "input": the type of variable (e.g., type="text"); the name of the variable (e.g., name="Name"); and, in some cases, the size of the variable (e.g., size="50"). The "<textarea . . . /textarea> statement specifies a text box with

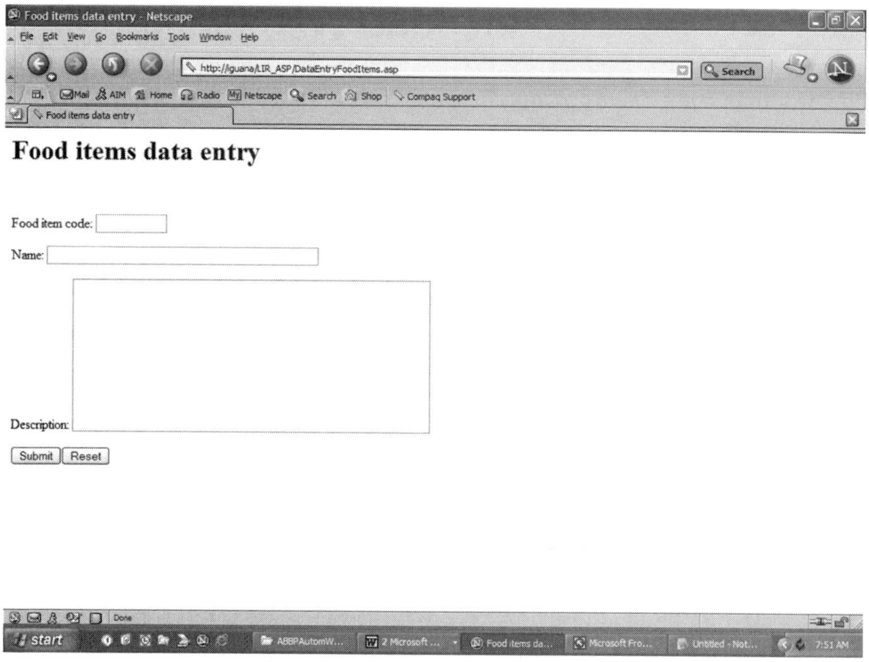

Figure 13.6 Web-Based Form for Data Entry

several lines and its dimensions. The input types "submit" and "reset" refer to form buttons.

The HTML code associated with a Web-based form can be entered directly, through a text editor, for example, or indirectly, by means of a Web page design tool. One such tool is FrontPage, which is a standard component of the Microsoft Office suite. FrontPage provides a relatively user-friendly interface for Web-based form design, including a menu bar from which all of the main form components can be selected and inserted into a Web page (see Figure 13.7).

Now let us go back to the piece of code (shown a few paragraphs earlier) illustrating how the HTML element "form" is used to allow for values to be entered for the variables "FoodItemCode," "Name," and "Description." For that piece of code to work as part of a Web page, it has to be inserted within the necessary HTML code "wrapping," which will then form a complete Web page that can be processed through a Web browser. Below is the HTML code for such a complete Web page, stored in the file "DataEntryFoodItems.asp," which includes the previously shown piece of code illustrating the use of the HTML element "form."

```
<html>
<body>
<h1>Food items data entry</h1>
<form method="POST" action="DataEntryFoodItemsProc.asp">
```

```
<p>Food item code: <input type="text" name=vFoodItemCode"
size=v10"> </p>
<p>Name: <input type="text" name="Name" size="50"></p>
<p>Description: <textarea rows="10" name="Description" cols="50">
</textarea></p>
<p><input type="submit" value"="Submit" name="SubmitButton">
    <input type="reset" value="Reset" name="ResetButton"></p>
</form>
</body>
</html>
```

The complete Web page code above contains a few additional elements that provide a "wrapping" around the code illustrating the use of the HTML element "form." Among those elements are the "<html>" and "</html>" statements, on the first and last lines, which indicate that the code between them is HTML code. Also among those elements are the "<body>" and "</body>" statements, which indicate the beginning and end of the Web page's main body. Both "<html> . . . </html>"

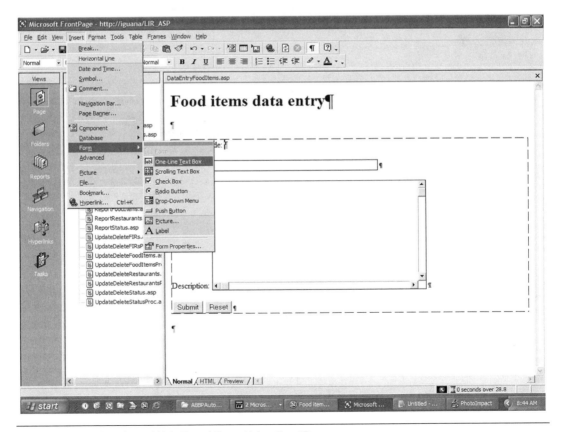

Figure 13.7   Creating a Web-Based Form Using FrontPage

and "<body> . . . </body>" elements could be removed from the code above without any effect on the functioning of the Web page. Finally, the "<h1>Food items data entry</h1>" statement indicates the heading of the Web page, which is shown at the top of the page whenever it is viewed with a Web browser.

Inserting New Records Through Web-Based Forms

It should be noted that the complete Web page code discussed in the previous section contains only HTML elements, no ASP code per se. The page whose file name is "DataEntryFoodItemsProc.asp," referred to at the top of the "form" HTML element, is the page that will incorporate the ASP code used to process the content of the variables "FoodItemCode," "Name," and "Description." That ASP code is shown below. It is possible to have the ASP code that will process the Web-based form inputs in the page that contains the "form" HTML element, but many ASP developers consider this to be bad programming practice.

```
<%
If (Request("ResetButton") = "Reset") Then
Response.Redirect "DataEntryFoodItems.asp"
End If
%>
<%
Set LIRDbObj = Server.CreateObject("ADODB.Connection")
LIRDbObj.Open "DSN=LIRACC;UID=;PWD=;"
strSQLStatement = "INSERT INTO FoodItems " _
& "(FoodItemCode, Name, Description) " _
& "SELECT '" & Request("FoodItemCode") & "' AS FoodItemCode, '" _
& Request("Name") & "' AS Name, '" _
& Request("Description") & "' AS Description;"
LIRDbObj.Execute(strSQLStatement)
%>
<%
LIRDbObj.Close
SET LIRDbObj = Nothing
%>
```

ASP code can be inserted in the middle of HTML code (e.g., between "<body> . . . </body>" statements) as long as it is enclosed within "<% . . . %>." The "<%" and "%>" terms indicate that whatever code is between them should be processed by the Web server. Code that is not enclosed within "<% . . . %>" is processed by the Web browser (e.g., HTML code). The ASP code above can be split into three main parts, each enclosed within "<% ... %>." The first part starts with "If (Request ... ," the second starts with "Set LIRDbObj ... ," and the third starts with "LIRDbObj.Close."

The ASP code part that starts with "If (Request ..." compares the content of the variable "ResetButton," received from "form" HTML element contained in the file "DataEntryFoodItems.asp," with "Reset." This is the value that would have been assigned to the "ResetButton" if the person filling out the Web-based form had clicked on the "Reset" button. If the content of the variable "ResetButton" equals "Reset," then the user is directed back to the original page that contained the form, and any values previously entered in the form fields are cleared. This content clearing feature is the reason why the type of that button (i.e., "ResetButton") was set to "reset," instead of "submit," like most form buttons.

If the content of the variable "ResetButton" is different from "Reset," then the person filling out the Web-based form clicked on the "Submit" button, and the system proceeds to the second part of the ASP code—the one starting with "Set LIRDbObj. ..." This second part of ASP code begins by creating an instance of an object of the type "ADODB.Connection" called "LIRDbObj." Objects of the type "ADODB.Connection" can be linked to databases, which in turn can be manipulated through SQL statements. Through the "LIRDbObj.Open" command, the object "LIRDbObj" is linked to the Access database associated with the DSN labeled "LIRACC," previously created by the ODBC Data Source Administrator (discussed earlier in this chapter). The line starting with "strSQLStatement = ..." and the four following lines simply assign to the variable "strSQLStatement" the text string corresponding to the SQL statement that will insert a new record into the FoodItems table. That SQL statement is then executed through the "LIRDbObj.Execute" command in the following line.

The aforementioned SQL statement is essentially the one shown below, where the "_" and "&" symbols have been removed. The "_" and "&" symbols serve to connect separate ASP code lines and line segments, respectively, making sure that those lines and line segments are processed by the Web server as though they were part of the same (long) line, containing the "strSQLStatement" text content specification. The "Request" commands return the values previously entered for the associated variables (indicated within parentheses, after the term "Request") in the Web-based form contained in the file "DataEntryFoodItems.asp."

```
INSERT INTO FoodItems (FoodItemCode, Name, Description)
SELECT 'Request("FoodItemCode")' AS FoodItemCode,
'Request("Name")' AS Name,
'Request("Description")' AS Description;
```

The ASP code part that starts with "LIRDbObj.Close" performs two functions. First, it closes the database connection opened through the "LIRDbObj.Open" command. Then it "clears" the "LIRDbObj" object for future use, if necessary (this means that the object can be used for other database connections). Clearing objects that had been previously instantiated (or created) is a widely used practice in object-oriented programming.

Updating or Deleting Records Through Web-Based Forms

Earlier in this chapter, we discussed a piece of code showing how the HTML element "form" was used to allow for values to be entered for the variables "FoodItemCode," "Name," and "Description." Those variables were part of the table "FoodItems" of the Access database stored in the file "LIR_protoDB.mdb," for which an ODBC connection had been created.

The piece of code below performs a similar function, that is, a data entry function. The data entered through the Web page can be passed on to a separate Web page with ASP code. The ASP code will then perform operations on the ODBC-connected database. A different aspect of the piece of code below is that it implements two new buttons, labeled "Delete" and "Update," which in turn activate different pieces of ASP code in the Web page referred to at the top of the "<form . . ." statement, namely "UpdateDeleteFoodItemsProc.asp."

```
<form method="POST" action="UpdateDeleteFoodItemsProc.asp">
<p>Food item code: <input type="text" name="FoodItemCode"
size="10"></p>
<p>(Values below only needed if updating data)</p>
<p>Name: <input type="text" name="Name" size="50"></p>
<p>Description: <textarea rows="10"
name="Description"cols="50"></textarea></p>
<p><input type="submit" value="Delete" name="DeleteButton">
<input type="submit" value="Update" name="UpdateButton">
<input type="reset" value="Reset" name="ResetButton"></p>
</form>
```

As with the form-related code shown previously in this chapter, in the piece of code above, the first and last lines, starting with "<form method . . ." and ending with "</form>," mark the beginning and end of the Web-based form. Figure 13.8 shows how the form looks on a Web browser.

Below is the ASP code that processes the data entered through the Web-based form shown in Figure 13.8. The ASP code shown below is part of the Web page contained in the file named "UpdateDeleteFoodItemsProc.asp," which is referred to at the top of the "<form . . ." statement associated with the Web-based form that receives the input to be processed through the ASP code on the next page.

Figure 13.8   Web-Based Form for Updating or Deleting Records

```asp
<%
If (Request("ResetButton") = "Reset") Then
Response.Redirect "UpdateDeleteFoodItems.asp"
End If
%>
<%
Set LIRDbObj = Server.CreateObject("ADODB.Connection")
LIRDbObj.Open "DSN=LIRACC;UID=;PWD=;"
%>
<%
If (Request("DeleteButton") = "Delete") Then
strSQLStatement = "DELETE FROM FoodItems " _
& "WHERE FoodItemCode = " & Request("FoodItemCode") & ";"
Else
strSQLStatement = "UPDATE FoodItems " _
& "SET FoodItemCode = " & Request("FoodItemCode") & "," _
& " Name = '" & Request("Name") & "'," _
& " Description = '" & Request("Description") & "'" _
& "WHERE FoodItemCode = " & Request("FoodItemCode") & ";"
End If
LIRDbObj.Execute(strSQLStatement)
%>
<%
```

```
LIRDbObj.Close
SET LIRDbObj = Nothing
%>
```

This ASP code contains virtually the same elements as the ASP code discussed earlier in this chapter for the insertion of new records. The key difference is that different SQL statements are executed depending on whether the variable "DeleteButton" equals "Delete" or not. If it does, that means the person filling out the Web-based form clicked on the "Delete" button, with the goal of having a record deleted. This triggers the execution of the SQL statement starting with "DELETE FROM FoodItems. . . ." Otherwise, the SQL statement starting with "UPDATE FoodItems . . ." is executed, and the respective record in the FoodItems table is updated.

Creating Web-Based Reports

Human beings are not very good at memorizing the type of data that is normally stored in computer databases; this is, in fact, one of the main reasons why computer databases are so popular. Once a few records are entered into a table, it becomes difficult to remember their details. So, someone would need a way of viewing those records before he or she could decide which records should be deleted or updated and, in the latter case, what fields should be modified and how. This is one of the functions of Web-based reports in situations where database manipulation is conducted through the Web.

The ASP code below, stored in the file named "ReportFoodItems.asp," shows the content of the following fields of the "FoodItems" table, side by side and in a tabular format: "FoodItemCode," "Name," and "Description." It mixes up HTML and ASP code. The main HTML element used is the "<TABLE . . . /TABLE>" element.

```
<%
SET LIRDbObj = Server.CreateObject("ADODB.Connection")
LIRDbObj.Open "DSN=LIRACC;UID=;PWD=;"
SET oRs = LIRDbObj.Execute("SELECT * FROM FoodItems;")
%>
<TABLE BORDER=3>
<% WHILE NOT oRs.EOF %>
<TR>
<TD> <%=oRs.Fields("FoodItemCode").Value %> </TD>
<TD> <%=oRs.Fields("Name").Value %> </TD>
<TD> <%=oRs.Fields("Description").Value %> </TD>
```

```
<TR>
<% oRs.MoveNext %>
<% WEND %>
</TABLE>
<%
LIRDbObj.Close
SET LIRDbObj = Nothing
%>
```

This piece of code has three main segments. The first and third segments are the ASP code parts contained within "<% . . . %>" at the beginning and end of the piece of code. They are similar to the code segments found in the same locations seen in previous sections and perform similar functions. Let us discuss the third (and last) code segment first, because it is the simplest. It is the code segment that starts with "LIRDbObj.Close." It simply closes the database connection opened through the "LIRDbObj.Open" command and "clears" the "LIRDbObj" object for future use, if necessary.

The first code segment, starting with "Set LIRDbObj . . ." creates an instance of an object of the type "ADODB.Connection" called "LIRDbObj." Then, through the "LIRDbObj.Open" command, the object "LIRDbObj" is linked to the Access database associated with the DSN labeled "LIRACC." The following command (shown separately below) stores in the text variable "oRs" the output generated by the SQL statement "SELECT * FROM FoodItems," which is essentially a long text string containing all of the records in the "FoodItems" table.

```
SET oRs = LIRDbObj.Execute("SELECT * FROM FoodItems;")
```

The second code segment is the one shown within "<TABLE . . . /TABLE>." It contains a specification of the size of the table border (i.e., "BORDER=3") and, immediately below that, a "WHILE . . . WEND" programming loop. The loop runs continuously until the end of file is reached—this is the meaning of the "WHILE NOT oRs.EOF" statement at the beginning of the loop. Within the loop, "<TR>" indicates a new table row, and "<TD> . . . </TD>" indicates a table column within a given row. Within each "<TD> . . . </TD>" area, the contents of each field of the table "FoodItems" are shown. For example, the following statement returns the content of the "FoodItemCode" field in the "FoodItems" table: "=oRs.Fields("FoodItemCode"). Value." Figure 13.9 shows how the report looks on a Web browser, as a pop-up window.

A few additional code elements, beyond the code discussed above, play a role in generating the output shown in Figure 13.9. The pop-up window listing the food items is launched after the link "Food Items," under "Reports," is clicked on the Little Italy Restaurants Web System Menu page (in the background). That pop-up

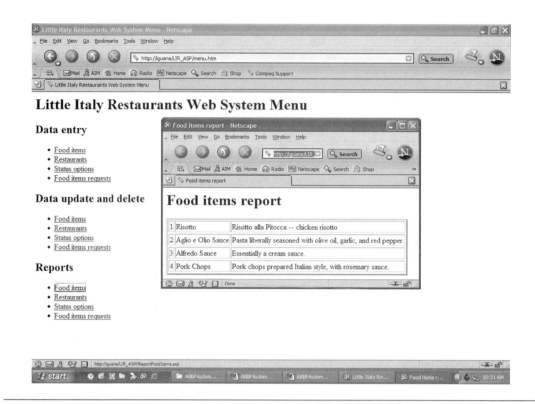

Figure 13.9 Web-Based Report Example

window also contains a heading, titled "Food items report"; the actual HTML code for that heading is "<h1>Food items report</h1>."

Only the most important pieces of code associated with the Little Italy Restaurants Web System have been discussed in this chapter. Those pieces of HTML and ASP code incorporate most of the functionality needed to build a similar Web system or expand the current system to incorporate additional functions and features. A complete set of screen snapshots for the Little Italy Restaurants Web System, as well as the complete code associated with each screen snapshot, are shown later in this book, in Appendix A.

Summary and Concluding Remarks

A commercial Web-based system would probably have more components than the ones discussed in this chapter and would probably combine data entry with data update and deletion. Moreover, a commercial Web-based system would probably have different menu pages for different types of users (e.g., restaurant manager, central kitchen manager, chef's team member) and a user authentication module that would log users into the system based on passwords and route them to the appropriate menus.

Since our goal here is to illustrate basic ASP functionality, the extended functionality and commercial system elements mentioned above are not part of the system discussed in this chapter. Nevertheless, the basic ASP functionality discussed here is enough to implement a substantially enhanced set of application features as part of the system, including the ones mentioned. For example, take the functionality used to allow data entry, changes, and deletions on a food items file. That same functionality can be used to do the same with a "users" file containing user types, passwords, and specific rules on what Web pages in the system those users can and cannot access.

Review Questions

1. Active server pages (ASP) are:
   (a) Web pages that contain code that is processed by a user's Web browser, as well as some code that is processed by the Web browser running on the Web server.
   (b) Web pages that contain variables that are only accessed by a user's Web browser, as well as at least 10 variables that are accessed only by a Web server.
   (c) Web pages that contain code that is processed by a user's Web browser, as well as some code that is processed by a Web server.
   (d) Web pages that contain Java code that is processed by a user's Web browser, as well as code that is processed by a Web server, the latter primarily being always written in the JavaScript programming language.

2. Which of the following statements is incorrect?
   (a) Once a database has been created, one must create an IP address and a universal resource locator (URL) by which the database will be referred to in our ASP pages.
   (b) ODBC stands for Open Database Connectivity.
   (c) A data source name (DSN) refers to a database, which can be manipulated by ASP pages through that DSN.
   (d) The creation of a "System DSN" on a Web server used to implement a Web site ensures that the associated database is accessible from the Web site's ASP code, regardless of who is browsing the Web site.

3. SQL, which stands for structured query language, is:
   (a) A standard programming language that is never used for the manipulation of object-oriented databases.
   (b) A standard programming language used for the manipulation of most relational databases.
   (c) Made up of four main standard statements, which are often referred to as TABLE, FIELD, UPDATE, and DELETE.
   (d) Used primarily to compress databases so that their normalized versions can be used in shop floor simulations.

4. Web-based data entry forms are not:
   (a) Used for data entry, modification, and deletion.
   (b) Often developed using the HTML element called "form."
   (c) Used to transfer values to Web pages containing ASP code, where the values are used as inputs for database operations.
   (d) Used for displaying business data on a computer screen using one of many reporting formats.

5. In Web-based programming using HTML and ASP:
   (a) The HTML code associated with a Web-based form can be entered directly, through a text editor, for example, or indirectly, by means of a Web page design tool.
   (b) The HTML code associated with a Web-based form can never be written with a text editor, always requiring a reasonably sophisticated Web page design tool.
   (c) HTML code cannot be mixed with ASP code in the same Web page.
   (d) The HTML code associated with a Web-based report can be entered directly (e.g., through a text editor), but that associated with a Web-based form cannot.

Discussion Questions

1. Develop a detailed business scenario involving a knowledge-intensive business process in a service sector organization (e.g., a university, a consulting services firm). Develop a normalized database to store data about the customers of the organization.

2. Create a Web-based system for customer relationship management using ASP. The Web-based system should contain forms for data entry and reports and should allow one to store data about customers and their transactions.

3. Conduct Web-based research on at least five major software programming tools and/or languages that compete with ASP. Create a table summarizing the main advantages and disadvantages of the programming tools selected, using ASP as the benchmark for comparison.

CHAPTER 14

Conclusion

B usiness process redesign can be conducted in a somewhat radical and one-shot manner, as well as in a way that is more aligned with incremental and continuous change. The former usually leads to clearly noticeable changes in a business process and is better aligned with the notion of business process reengineering, which has been discussed earlier in this book. The latter often leads to changes in a business process that are not very noticeable and is well aligned with the notion of total quality management, pioneered by Deming and also discussed earlier in this book.

This book's main emphasis is on one-shot forms of business process redesign, whereby a business process is redesigned in such a way that the changes in it are clearly noticeable after their implementation with the help of information technologies. Nevertheless, this chapter argues that incremental and continuous improvement is also very important. More specifically, it is argued here that some incremental fine-tuning, in the form of continuous business process redesign, should be conducted immediately after a radical business process redesign project. Sometimes that fine-tuning is necessary even before the new business process is ready for final implementation with information technology, which means that, ideally, the fine-tuning should be conducted in a pilot implementation of the business process.

It is also argued in this chapter that business process redesign must take into consideration the view of the customer, that is, the customer (or customers) of the business process that is being targeted for redesign. That customer may be inside or outside the organization that houses the business process. This is expanded in this chapter into a broader argument, which is that the impact on quality indicators (e.g., customer satisfaction) of the changes in the business process should be carefully evaluated before the changes are implemented.

Finally, this chapter emphasizes the notion (briefly touched upon in previous chapters) that business process redesign changes must be accompanied by benefits to those organization members who will directly help to implement those changes, not only the managers—who usually reap the leadership-related benefits from a successful business redesign project whose bottom-line impact affects the organization in a positive way. More specifically, the impact of redesign changes on business process team members (i.e., employees) should be assessed, and rewards (social and financial) should be created for those from whom extra time, effort, and dedication will be required to make the new business process work.

Radical Versus Incremental Business Process Change

The dichotomy between radical and incremental business process change is somewhat artificial and was created to a large extent by the proponents of the business process reengineering movement, discussed earlier in this book. Some of the proponents of that movement wanted to differentiate their management ideas from those associated with the total quality management movement, which was widely influential within the business community up until the early 1990s. The idea that reengineering is radical and therefore "better" than total quality management might well have been, to a large extent, a marketing ploy by some of the forerunners of the business process reengineering movement.

If this ploy existed, it was not very successful, since soon it became clear that radical and incremental forms of business process redesign often had to be used in a combined way, which incidentally is one of the main points of this chapter. That is, radical business process change is not necessarily better than incremental change. The former usually implies a larger amount of change taking place faster, whereas the latter implies a smaller amount of change taking place slower. Each may be advisable, depending on the circumstances of the organization that houses the business process and the economic environment that surrounds the organization.

For example, many car parts' manufacturers seek ISO 9001 certification. ISO 9001 is a standard developed by the International Organization of Standardization that is widely used by manufacturing organizations to show that they adopt good business process practices, from product design to manufacturing, and that they possess the capabilities to continuously improve their business processes. More often than not, organizations have to document their business processes in detail to show that they meet ISO 9001 requirements, as well as develop business process quality measurement schemes and approaches to address quality-related problems (e.g., defective parts).

However, it is not usually necessary to show that business processes undergo major changes to obtain ISO 9001 certification. In fact, the general orientation proposed by the ISO 9001 standard, as well as other similar quality standards, is better aligned with the notion of changing business processes incrementally over time, with the primary objective of achieving gradual and cumulative improvements in the quality of the products generated through the business processes.

Deming's total quality management ideas underlie the development of ISO 9001 and other quality-related certification standards, and those ideas are particularly well aligned with the Japanese economic recovery after World War II. Japan slowly improved the quality of its products, particularly in the electronics and automotive industries, by incrementally and systematically perfecting business processes over a period of more than 30 years—from the early 1950s to the 1980s. In doing so, the Japanese economic recovery became one of the best examples of what incremental business process redesign can do for organizations in the long run, since in those 30 years Japanese organizations went from being seen as third-class copiers to playing a surprisingly dominant role in the electronics and automotive industries.

While obtaining ISO 9001 certification may seem like quite an undertaking, and in fact it is, the amount of business process change required for a car part manufacturing organization to show that its car parts manufacturing process meets ISO 9001 requirements is arguably significantly smaller than the amount of business process change involved in, say, completely automating the car parts manufacturing process using robotics-based technologies—assuming that the process did not use those types of technologies before. Robotics-based automation of this type of magnitude is most likely to require major business process changes so that work practices are aligned with the technologies that are going to be used—it is very likely that layoffs will occur as well. This is illustrated in Figure 14.1, which lists examples of business process change classified according to amount of change and speed with which the change takes place.

The type of business process change depicted in the top-right corner of the table shown in Figure 14.1 is what is often referred to as radical change. Not only is the amount of change substantial, but also the time frame in which that change takes place is relatively short. Radical business process redesign projects involve situations where drastic change happens rather suddenly. The bottom-left corner depicts a situation that would likely be considered one of incremental change. There, the amount of change is arguably small and is taking place over a relatively long period of time.

Generally speaking, radical change is riskier and harder to implement than is change of a more incremental nature. Moreover, most of the empirical research literature on business process redesign suggests that radical change projects tend to fail more often than incremental change projects. Nevertheless, radical change is often absolutely necessary, particularly when the alternative is even more drastic (e.g., bankruptcy). For example, many information technology organizations had

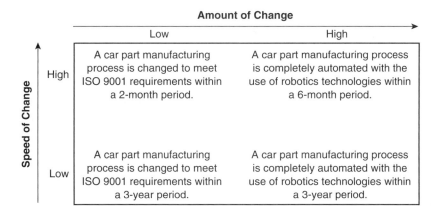

Figure 14.1   Examples of Business Process Change

to undergo major changes in the aftermath of the "technology bubble burst" that took place in the years that followed the year 2000 (this event was discussed earlier in this book). As a result, radical business process change became commonplace in those years, in spite of the poor reputation that radical forms of business process redesign, such as business process reengineering, acquired in the 1990s. As previously discussed in this book, that poor reputation came as a result of the publication of a large number of cases describing business process reengineering projects that failed to achieve their goals—those goals being major productivity and quality improvement in connection with the business processes targeted for redesign.

The Importance of Combining Radical and Incremental Change

Regardless of how change is important to organizations, the people who make up those organizations are generally opposed to change, especially when they do not understand the reason for change or when the change requires them to do more work than they were doing before. This holds true for change that comes in the form of business process redesign projects, as well as other types of initiatives (not all change is related to business process redesign).

Speaking in psychological terms, the truth of the matter is that, in the short run, change is uncomfortable to most people. It more often than not requires people to learn new skills, adapt their behavior to new work practices, and walk away from benefits that are associated with their hard-won specialized knowledge. In other words, change causes disruption, which is why very few people embrace it.

What would happen if (or when) brain interfaces were created that enabled university students to acquire all of the knowledge involved in a university program (e.g., a marketing major program) by simply plugging a chip into a brain interface and running a learning program for about 1 hour (sort of like in the first of the *The Matrix* movies)? A 1-hour process of knowledge assimilation through the brain interface would replace the longer 4-year learning process. Incidentally, that longer 4-year learning process is the general process around which most universities with undergraduate programs are structured today.

One could safely bet that this situation would lead to strong opposition from university professors, who would argue against it from all sorts of angles—ethical issues, learning quality problems, the loss of the social component of the learning process, and so on. But isn't it possible that the aforementioned situation would change the way university professors do their work for the better? It is hard to tell, since it is not usually obvious how change can be advantageous to those affected by it in the long run, especially when the impact seems at first to be negative, which clouds people's minds a bit.

One thing is certain, though. A reduction in knowledge acquisition time from 4 years to 1 hour would be too attractive to be rejected by the universities' main clients, the students (and most of their parents, particularly if a corresponding reduction in tuition followed). It would not be too daring to predict that, if the technology and related processes were available, change toward that direction would be inevitable. And conflict would be inevitable as well, as those who saw themselves as being negatively affected by the change would get organized and put up a strong opposition.

As a general rule, it is reasonable to assume that the degree of change involved in a business process redesign project is positively correlated with the degree of opposition that the project is likely to face. And, when opposition is strong, small mistakes and problems may easily be amplified and used as a basis to call for a boycott of the business process redesign project. In fact, one of the key reasons why radical business process change projects fail is because the new redesigned business processes end up having several problems. Those new business processes may be much better than the old ones that they replaced. Nevertheless, those who strongly oppose change will certainly explore the problems as much as possible and, at the same time, turn a blind eye on the benefits associated with the new business processes.

The reality seems to be that, when radical business process redesign takes place, the final result is likely to be a "diamond in the rough." The new business process may allow the organization housing the process to save a substantial amount of money, but the process may also incorporate a few problems that will lead to complaints from its customers. Interestingly, the empirical literature on business process redesign suggests that most of the problems left in a redesign process are quality related; that is, they have something to do with how satisfied the customers are with the products generated by the business process. This is one of the main reasons why customers should be involved in the business process redesigned project—a point that will be discussed in more detail later in this chapter. This is also one of the main reasons why it is important to have periods of incremental business process change following bursts in which radical change occurs. This is illustrated in Figure 14.2.

Several connected dotted lines are shown in Figure 14.2, where each dotted line represents a business process redesign project. The vertical axis represents the degree of change of each project, and the horizontal axis represents the time

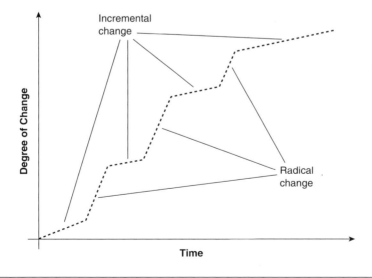

Figure 14.2   Sequencing Radical and Incremental Change

duration of each project. The lines with a relatively smooth upward inclination represent projects associated with incremental change. The steep lines refer to business process redesign projects associated with radical change. In Figure 14.2, radical and incremental projects are alternated, with the incremental projects (except the first) being follow-up efforts to the more radical ones that precede them. That is, the incremental business process change projects are essentially refinements on radical projects that happened before, with both projects addressing the same business process (or processes).

Given what was discussed above regarding radical and incremental business process change, it should be clear that Figure 14.2 depicts what is generally believed to be an appropriate way of conducting business process redesign in an organization. Starting with an incremental business process change project is perfectly okay; what is not okay is to implement radical change and not follow it up with incremental change, where the incremental change is aimed at refining the radical change that preceded it. Let us look at an example to further illustrate the general idea depicted in Figure 14.2.

Let us consider the dish item preparation process of a fast-food restaurant chain specializing in low-carbohydrate dishes—the term *dish* is meant here to refer to something like a salad, a sandwich, or a wrap. The chain is made up of 30 restaurants, all with their own full kitchens, and all operating in the same metropolitan area. An example of a dish item would be a particular type of salad, say, a Caesar salad. Since each restaurant has its own kitchen, the dish preparation process is decentralized and carried out in each kitchen separately, producing dishes of somewhat similar taste and quality.

The owner of the chain hired some consultants to conduct a business study for her. The main outcome of the study is that the described restaurant chain configuration is bad for business, because the full kitchens take up space that could be used to accommodate tables and thus seat additional customers. The study suggested that, since the restaurants were always full of customers, reducing the size of the kitchens in half could increase the restaurant chain sales by 20 percent, bringing its annual sales up from $10 million to $12 million.

Given the above, the restaurant owner then led a business process redesign project whose outcome was a radically new restaurant chain structure. All dish item preparation is now centralized in one central industrial kitchen, allowing each of the kitchens to be reduced in size by about half. This leads to a significant change in the way dishes are prepared for customers, with the now smaller restaurant kitchens being used primarily for combination of dish items previously prepared in the central industrial kitchen. This is an example of what most would call a radical business process redesign project.

However, the new configuration led to a number of small problems, one of which was related to the processing of food items requests, which are issued regularly by the managers of the restaurants to the central industrial kitchen. Due to a set of inefficient communication procedures, about 10 percent of food items requests routinely were arriving late at the restaurants. To address that problem, as well as a few other related problems, a set of small-scope business process redesign projects was conducted. The problems left by the radical business process redesign project were then eliminated. The changes associated with the small-scope business process redesign projects are examples of incremental business process changes, which are necessary, following the radical changes that previously led to the reduction of the size of the kitchens.

By looking at the aforementioned example, it should not be difficult for the reader to understand why many radical business process redesign projects fail as a result of not being followed by incremental redesign projects. The main goal of the latter type of business process redesign project is, of course, to "polish" the "diamond in the rough" that was produced in the former, more radical type of redesign project.

Bringing the Customer's Voice Into the Redesign

One of the most basic mistakes made in business process redesign projects is that of not making the customer's voice heard enough during the project. In other words, many business process redesign projects are conducted entirely based on the views of those who execute and manage the business processes targeted for redesign. Those projects almost entirely ignore the views of those who consume the products generated by the business process.

Let us take, for example, the case of an engineering company that specializes in the development of budgets for large civil construction projects overseen by public organizations. For example, if the state of Texas were considering building a new university, its representatives would then go to this engineering company and ask them for an independent budget for the building of the university (we are referring primarily to the physical plant here, not university program curricula or the administrative structure of the university).

The engineering company used to employ a civil engineering project budgeting computer program, which was developed in-house, to produce their project budgets. However, they were not happy with the computer program, because it made use of an antiquated coding system for construction materials, which required a great deal of manual entry and addition of construction material information each time a project budget was generated. Examples of construction materials are concrete, insulating materials, masonry materials, metals, plastics, and wood.

Given these problems, the engineering company decided to adopt a new computer program, developed by a software development firm that specializes in civil engineering software applications. The new computer program used a more modern coding system for construction materials.

Before adopting the new computer program and changing the business process associated with developing project budgets, the engineering company briefly consulted with its customers, mostly branches of the Texas State Government, to make sure that they were okay with the changes. That brief consultation uncovered no problems, and the engineering company went ahead with the business process and computer program changes.

Later, the engineering company found out that civil construction coordination teams of several branches of the Texas state government had adopted the construction material coding system of the old budget generation computer program—the one previously used by the engineering company. That led to strong opposition against the adoption of the new computer program, which the engineering company decided to keep, since it had also redesigned its budget generation process around it. As a result, the Texas state government decided to hire a competitor. The loss of its main customer eventually led the engineering company to go bankrupt.

This example illustrates an important issue regarding bringing the customer's voice into business process redesign decisions, which is that there must be a high degree of communication and a high level of collaboration between the organization that houses the business process being redesigned and the customers of the business process. The involvement of the customers should be deeper than simply filling out a questionnaire or having someone assigned to act as a liaison between the business process team and them (i.e., the customers).

However, if questionnaires are used, they should be administered to all of the customers of the business process, and they should be comprehensive enough to allow for the gathering of multiple perspectives about the consequences of the changes and their impact on business process quality and productivity. The problem with comprehensive questionnaires is that they are also long and tedious, which leads many customers to not want to fill them out. Some business process redesign teams resort to interviews to avoid this problem, since giving interviews is not usually perceived to be as boring as completing questionnaires. The trouble with interviews is that they require much more time and effort to conduct and compile, from the part of the business process redesign team members, than do questionnaires.

Ideally, the customers of the business process should be as engaged as the other business process redesign team members from the outset of the business process redesign effort. The more customer representatives participate, the better. Some recent research has suggested that engaging customers in business process redesign projects electronically (e.g., via e-mail or Web-based conferencing) can be useful in bringing as many customer representatives' perspectives as necessary in a business process redesign effort, without tying so much of their time as to make them unwilling to get involved.

Rewarding Those Who Will Make the New Process Work

Similar to nearly all changes that affect the work practices of teams of individuals, business process redesign usually creates an imbalance between those who will benefit from the new business process design and those who will have to do extra work because of that new design. Jonathan Grudin once pointed out, in a seminal article titled "Groupware and Social Dynamics: Eight Challenges for Developers," that the same is true for groupware systems. These are systems that support the work of groups of individuals engaged in collaborative tasks; such systems are also known by other terms, like *group support systems* or *electronic collaboration systems*.

Grudin provided the example of the adoption of an electronic calendaring system, which illustrates in a simple but clear way the work imbalance that often follows change and that is analogous to the imbalance associated with business process redesign–related change. An electronic calendaring system allows personal calendars to be shared on a computer network—for example, a local area network, or the Internet, which is a wide area network. Their use is relatively simple. Since all users are expected to keep their personal calendars up to date, a manager who wants to set up a meeting can simply find a time in which a group of individuals is available by inspecting their individual calendars and then scheduling the meeting. The electronic calendaring system will then update all personal calendars with details about the new meeting.

In the above example, the adoption of the electronic calendaring system obviously leads to advantages for the meeting convener, the manager. But it imposes an extra cost on the other users, who have to keep their individual calendars up to date with their schedules. This imbalance between those who benefit from the electronic calendaring system and those who have to do extra work to make the system work properly has been presented by Grudin as one of the main reasons why electronic calendaring systems are not as widely used in organizations as other types of electronic collaboration systems, such as the simple yet ubiquitous e-mail.

What is the solution to this problem? One could argue that throwing money at those who will do the additional work is the solution. But the reality is that sometimes money is not enough of an attraction to bring the employees in question on board, and sometimes there is not enough money to go around, especially in situations where business process redesign is itself being carried out to reduce or eliminate certain types of costs. For example, the organization where the business process is housed may be facing financial difficulties due to a sudden reduction in sales.

So, as with many organizational issues that involve people, the solution is a bit more complex than throwing money at the problem. The first step in addressing the imbalance between those who will have to do additional work and those who do not is to clearly identify those in the former category. Those individuals will not always be fully aware of the additional demands on them after the implementation of the new business process. Therefore, the next step is to approach those individuals, explain the situation to them, and essentially ask them how they feel about it and what the organization could do for them in return. In many cases, their own preferences will not be directly associated with a promotion or pay raise.

For example, those individuals on which additional demands will result from the implementation of the new business process may want the organization to do one or more of the following: sponsor their participation in external activities that involve formal training (e.g., information technology certification courses) or informal knowledge and skill acquisition (e.g., professional conferences), provide some sort of formal mentorship for them with the potential for future promotion, give them a greater level of time flexibility in connection with their work (e.g., the ability to telecommute on certain weekdays), or create some form of symbolic social recognition for their extra good work (e.g., an award given out at a formal ceremony).

In a nutshell, the imbalance in work demands after the implementation of a new business process cannot be ignored, but addressing that imbalance requires common sense and consultation with those who will be negatively affected by the new work demands. As employees are consulted, it may become clear that nonfinancial rewards are higher on their list of preferences than financial rewards, such as pay raises and grants of company ownership shares (e.g., stock grants and options).

Summary and Concluding Remarks

Radical business process change involves implementing drastic change in work practices within a short period of time. Incremental change involves implementing small changes in work practices over a long period of time. Radical business process change is riskier and harder to implement than is change of a more incremental nature, which partially explains why radical change projects tend to fail more often than incremental change projects. Nevertheless, radical change is often absolutely necessary, particularly when the alternative is even more drastic, such as in a situation involving an organization that is facing imminent bankruptcy.

When radical business process redesign takes place, the final result is likely to be a "diamond in the rough" in the form of a new and yet-to-be-polished business process. The new, redesigned business process may allow the organization housing it to save a substantial amount of money. However, the redesigned business process may also add new problems of its own, leading to unexpected consequences, such as complaints from the process' customers and the creation of indirect costs in other areas. This is among the main reasons why it is important to have periods of incremental business process change following the often inevitable bursts of radical change.

An issue that needs to be addressed after any type of business process redesign, but that is quite common when the change is of a more radical nature, is the imbalance in work demands on different individuals after the implementation of a new business process. Addressing that imbalance requires common sense and consultation with those who will be negatively affected by the new work demands. As employees are consulted, it may become clear that nonfinancial rewards are seen as more important than financial rewards such as pay raises or stock grants. Some examples of nonfinancial rewards are sponsorship for participation in information technology certification courses or professional conferences, mentorship opportunities, and the ability to telecommute on certain weekdays.

Review Questions

1. Why was the dichotomy between radical and incremental business process redesign emphasized in the early 1990s?
   (a) So that total quality management could be presented as a desirable replacement for business process reengineering.
   (b) So that Deming's approach to business process change could be presented as more effective than Hammer's approach to business process change.
   (c) So that business process reengineering could be clearly differentiated from total quality management.

(d) So that business process reengineering could be equated to total quality management.

2. Which of the examples below is not one of radical business process change?
   (a) A university completely changes its organizational structure in one semester so that student registration for courses is no longer needed— that is, all courses adopt a walk-in policy.
   (b) A university professor improves her information technology teaching process by revising its course over a 2-year period.
   (c) A traditional consulting company completely revamps its hourly fee– based consulting services within a 1-year period, subsequently allowing clients unlimited access to its consultants for a fixed fee.
   (d) A Chinese restaurant chain drastically restructures its dish item (e.g., Hunan pork, soft noodles) preparation process during a 2-month busi- ness process redesign period, primarily by centralizing the production of those Chinese dish items.

3. The degree of change involved in a business process redesign project is usually correlated with:
   (a) The inverse of the degree of incremental change necessary after the project is completed.
   (b) The degree of opposition that the project is likely to face.
   (c) The degree of support likely to be received from a labor union.
   (d) The degree of support likely to be received from those employees who will have to do extra work to implement the new business process.

4. Which of the statements below is incorrect?
   (a) One of the most basic mistakes made in business process redesign projects is that of making the customer's voice loud enough during the project.
   (b) Many business process redesign projects are conducted entirely based on the views of those who execute and manage the business process targeted for redesign.
   (c) Many business process redesign projects largely ignore the views of those who consume the products generated by the business process.
   (d) The involvement of the business process customers in business process redesign projects should be deeper than simply filling out a questionnaire.

5. Business process redesign projects often lead to:
   (a) A more balanced set of work demands on different individuals after the implementation of a new business process.
   (b) Absolutely no change in the business process targeted for redesign.
   (c) The organizations that engage in those projects going bankrupt in less than 1 year.
   (d) An imbalance in work demands on different individuals after the implementation of a new business process.

Discussion Questions

1. Develop a detailed scenario involving a set of alternated business process redesign projects where an incremental project follows a radical project, which is then followed by another incremental project, and so on. The business process should be part of a food production type of organization (e.g., an organization that manufactures canned food). The scenario should start with a radical business process redesign project and should end with an incremental project.

2. Develop a detailed scenario involving a core production process of a service sector organization whose main product is packaged in the form of data (e.g., a news services organization, a packaged software retailer, a software developer). The scenario should illustrate a situation in which initially the customer's voice was not brought into the redesign project—something that was later corrected (this should also be part of the scenario).

3. Develop a detailed scenario involving an online customer service process provided by a service sector organization (e.g., an online stockbroker, an Internet-based networking equipment store). The scenario should illustrate a situation in which the business process was radically redesigned and no attention was paid to the imbalance between those who benefited from the new business process design and those who had to do extra work because of that new design. The scenario should illustrate the negative consequences that the imbalance oversight led to in the context of the project.

Appendix A

Complete ASP Code Examples

Below are the full active server pages (ASP) code examples for the Little Italy Restaurants Web System, which has been discussed earlier in this book together with an introductory discussion of ASP as a basis for the implementation of redesigned business processes. The code is preceded by screen snapshots illustrating the features implemented through it. Necessary HTML elements (e.g., <form> ... </form>) routinely used with ASP code are also included.

Little Italy Restaurants Web System Menu

Data entry

- Food items
- Restaurants
- Status options
- Food items requests

Data update and delete

- Food items
- Restaurants
- Status options
- Food items requests

Reports

- Food items
- Restaurants
- Status options
- Food items requests

Main Menu

The code presented below, following the screen snapshots, is meant to be fully functional. That is, it is meant to provide all of the elements needed to implement the features and functionality shown on the screen snapshots. Since actual file names are referenced throughout the code, the code contained in each separate file is shown here under the file name used in the actual prototype Web system (e.g., Menu.htm, DataEntryFoodItems.asp, and DataEntryFoodItemsProc.asp). The code shown in this appendix has been generated using FrontPage.

Menu.htm

```html
<html>

<head>
<meta http-equiv="Content-Type" content="text/html; charset=windows-1252">
<meta http-equiv="Content-Language" content="en-us">
<title>Little Italy Restaurants Web System Menu</title>
<meta name="GENERATOR" content="Microsoft FrontPage 4.0">
<meta name="ProgId" content="FrontPage.Editor.Document">
</head>

<body>
<h1>Little Italy Restaurants Web System Menu</h1>
<h2>Data entry</h2>
<ul>
  <li><a href="DataEntryFoodItems.asp">Food items</a></li>
  <li><a href="DataEntryRestaurants.asp">Restaurants</a></li>
  <li><a href="DataEntryStatus.asp">Status options</a></li>
  <li><a href="DataEntryFIRs.asp">Food items requests</a></li>
</ul>
<h2>Data update and delete</h2>
<ul>
  <li><a href="UpdateDeleteFoodItems.asp">Food items</a></li>
  <li><a href="UpdateDeleteRestaurants.asp">Restaurants</a></li>
  <li><a href="UpdateDeleteStatus.asp">Status options</a></li>
  <li><a href="UpdateDeleteFIRs.asp">Food items requests</a></li>
</ul>
<h2>Reports</h2>
<ul>
  <li><a href="ReportFoodItems.asp" target="_blank">Food items</a></li>
  <li><a href="ReportRestaurants.asp" target="_blank">Restaurants</a></li>
  <li><a href="ReportStatus.asp" target="_blank">Status options</a></li>
```

```
  <li><a href="ReportFIRs.asp" target="_blank">Food items requests</a></li>
</ul>
</body>

</html>
```

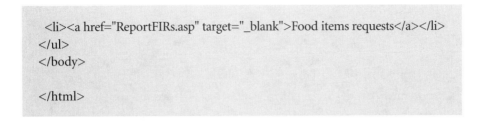

Food Items Data Entry

DataEntryFoodItems.asp

```
<html>

<head>
<meta http-equiv="Content-Language" content="en-us">
<meta http-equiv="Content-Type" content="text/html; charset=windows-
1252">
<meta name="GENERATOR" content="Microsoft FrontPage 4.0">
<meta name="ProgId" content="FrontPage.Editor.Document">
<title>Food items data entry</title>
</head>
```

```
<body>

<h1>Food items data entry</h1>
<p> </p>
<form method="POST" action="DataEntryFoodItemsProc.asp">
  <p>Food item code: <input type="text" name="FoodItemCode" size="10">
(<a href="ReportFoodItems.asp" target="_blank">See
  current food items report</a>)</p>
  <p>Name: <input type="text" name="Name" size="50"></p>
  <p>Description: <textarea rows="10" name="Description"
cols="50"></textarea></p>
  <p><input type="submit" value="Submit" name="SubmitButton"><input
type="reset" value="Reset" name="ResetButton"></p>
</form>
<p> </p>

</body>

</html>
```

DataEntryFoodItemsProc.asp

```
<%@ LANGUAGE="VBSCRIPT" %>
<html>

<head>
<meta http-equiv="Content-Language" content="en-us">
<meta http-equiv="Content-Type" content="text/html;
charset=windows-1252">
<meta name="GENERATOR" content="Microsoft
FrontPage 4.0">
<meta name="ProgId"
content="FrontPage.Editor.Document">
<title>Food items data entry processing page</title>
</head>

<body>

<%
If (Request("ResetButton") = "Reset") Then
  Response.Redirect "DataEntryFoodItems.asp"
End If
%>
```

```
<%
Set LIRDbObj = Server.CreateObject("ADODB.Connection")
LIRDbObj.Open "DSN=LIRACC;UID=;PWD=;"
strSQLStatement = "INSERT INTO FoodItems " _
        & "(FoodItemCode, Name, Description) " _
        & "SELECT '" & Request("FoodItemCode") & "' AS FoodItemCode, '" _
        &           Request("Name") & "' AS Name, '" _
        &           Request("Description") & "' AS Description;"
LIRDbObj.Execute(strSQLStatement)
%>

<%
LIRDbObj.Close
SET LIRDbObj = Nothing
%>

<h1>Food items data entered successfully!</h1>
<p><a href="DataEntryFoodItems.asp">Return to food items data entry
page.</a></p>

</body>
</html>
```

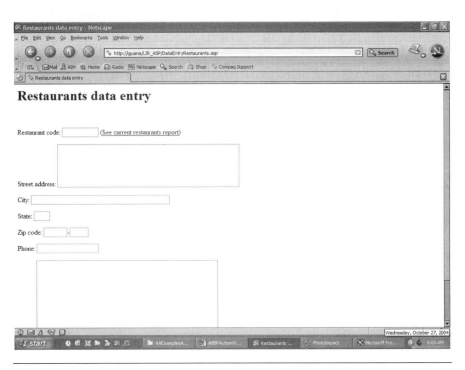

Restaurants Data Entry

DataEntryRestaurants.asp

```
<html>

<head>
<meta http-equiv="Content-Language" content="en-us">
<meta http-equiv="Content-Type" content="text/html; charset=windows-
1252">
<meta name="GENERATOR" content="Microsoft FrontPage 4.0">
<meta name="ProgId" content="FrontPage.Editor.Document">
<title>Restaurants data entry</title>
</head>

<body>

<h1>Restaurants data entry</h1>
<p> </p>
<form method="POST" action="DataEntryRestaurantsProc.asp">
  <p>Restaurant code: <input type="text" name="RestaurantCode"
size="10"> (<a href="ReportRestaurants.asp" target="_blank">See
  current restaurants report</a>)</p>
  <p>Street address: <textarea rows="5" name="StreetAddress"
cols="50"></textarea></p>
  <p>City: <input type="text" name="City" size="50"></p>
  <p>State: <input type="text" name="State" size="2"></p>
  <p>Zip code: <input type="text" name="ZIP1" size="5">-<input
type="text" name="ZIP2" size="3"></p>
  <p>Phone: <input type="text" name="Phone" size="20"></p>
  <p>Notes: <textarea rows="10" name="Notes" cols="50"></textarea></p>
  <p><input type="submit" value="Submit" name="SubmitButton"><input
type="reset" value="Reset" name="ResetButton"></p>
</form>
<p> </p>

</body>

</html>
```

DataEntryRestaurantsProc.asp

```
<%@ LANGUAGE="VBSCRIPT" %>
<html>

<head>
<meta http-equiv="Content-Language" content="en-us">
```

```
<meta http-equiv="Content-Type" content="text/html; charset=windows-
1252">
<meta name="GENERATOR" content="Microsoft FrontPage 4.0">
<meta name="ProgId" content="FrontPage.Editor.Document">
<title>Restaurants data entry processing page</title>
</head>

<body>

<%
If (Request("ResetButton") = "Reset") Then
  Response.Redirect "DataEntryRestaurants.asp"
End If
%>


<%
Set LIRDbObj = Server.CreateObject("ADODB.Connection")
LIRDbObj.Open "DSN=LIRACC;UID=;PWD=;"
strSQLStatement = "INSERT INTO Restaurants " _
      & "(RestaurantCode, StreetAddress, City, State, ZIP1, ZIP2, Phone,
Notes) " _
      & "SELECT '" & Request("RestaurantCode") & "' AS RestaurantCode, '" _
      &          Request("StreetAddress") & "' AS StreetAddress, '" _
      &          Request("City") & "' AS City, '" _
      &          Request("State") & "' AS State, '" _
      &          Request("ZIP1") & "' AS ZIP1, '" _
      &          Request("ZIP2") & "' AS ZIP2, '" _
      &          Request("Phone") & "' AS Phone, '" _
      &          Request("Notes") & "' AS Notes;"
LIRDbObj.Execute(strSQLStatement)
%>


<%
LIRDbObj.Close
SET LIRDbObj = Nothing
%>


<h1>Restaurants data entered successfully!</h1>
<p><a href="DataEntryRestaurants.asp">Return to restaurants data entry
page.</a></p>

</body>
</html>
```

Status Options Data Entry

DataEntryStatus.asp

```
<html>

<head>
<meta http-equiv="Content-Language" content="en-us">
<meta http-equiv="Content-Type" content="text/html; charset=windows-
1252">
<meta name="GENERATOR" content="Microsoft FrontPage 4.0">
<meta name="ProgId" content="FrontPage.Editor.Document">
<title>Status options data entry</title>
</head>

<body>

<h1>Status options data entry</h1>
<p> </p>
<form method="POST" action="DataEntryStatusProc.asp">
  <p>Status code: <input type="text" name="StatusCode" size="10">
(<a href="ReportStatus.asp" target="_blank">See
  current status options report</a>)</p>
```

```
  <p>Status description: <textarea rows="5" name="Description"
cols="50"></textarea></p>
  <p><input type="submit" value="Submit" name="SubmitButton"><input
type="reset" value="Reset" name="ResetButton"></p>
</form>
<p> </p>

</body>

</html>
```

DataEntryStatusProc.asp

```
<%@ LANGUAGE="VBSCRIPT" %>
<html>

<head>
<meta http-equiv="Content-Language" content="en-us">
<meta http-equiv="Content-Type" content="text/html; charset=windows-
1252">
<meta name="GENERATOR" content="Microsoft FrontPage 4.0">
<meta name="ProgId" content="FrontPage.Editor.Document">
<title>Status options data entry processing page</title>
</head>

<body>

<%
If (Request("ResetButton") = "Reset") Then
  Response.Redirect "DataEntryStatus.asp"
End If
%>


<%
Set LIRDbObj = Server.CreateObject("ADODB.Connection")
LIRDbObj.Open "DSN=LIRACC;UID=;PWD=;"
strSQLStatement = "INSERT INTO Status " _
        & "(StatusCode, Description) " _
        & "SELECT '" & Request("StatusCode") & "' AS StatusCode, '" _
        &          Request("Description") & "' AS Description;"
LIRDbObj.Execute(strSQLStatement)
%>
```

```
<%
LIRDbObj.Close
SET LIRDbObj = Nothing
%>

<h1>Status options data entered successfully!</h1>
<p><a href="DataEntryStatus.asp">Return to status options data entry
page.</a></p>

</body>
</html>
```

DataEntryFIRs.asp

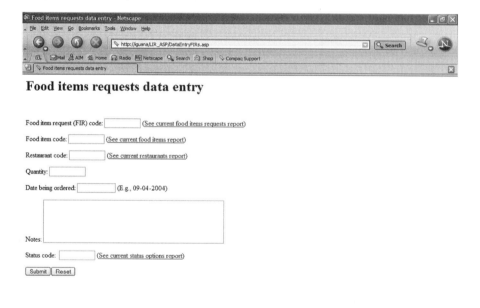

Food Items Requests Data Entry

```
<html>
```

```
<head>
<meta http-equiv="Content-Language" content="en-us">
<meta http-equiv="Content-Type" content="text/html; charset=windows-
1252">
<meta name="GENERATOR" content="Microsoft FrontPage 4.0">
```

```
<meta name="ProgId" content="FrontPage.Editor.Document">
<title>Food items requests data entry</title>
</head>

<body>

<h1>Food items requests data entry</h1>
<p> </p>
<form method="POST" action="DataEntryFIRsProc.asp">
  <p>Food item request (FIR) code: <input type="text" name="FIRCode"
size="10">
 (<a href="ReportFIRs.asp" target="_blank">See current food items requests
 report</a>)</p>
  <p>Food item code: <input type="text" name="FoodItemCode" size="10">
(<a href="ReportFoodItems.asp" target="_blank">See
 current food items report</a>)</p>
    <p>Restaurant code: <input type="text" name="RestaurantCode"
size="10"> (<a href="ReportRestaurants.asp" target="_blank">See
 current restaurants report</a>)</p>
  <p>Quantity: <input type="text" name="Quantity" size="10"></p>
  <p>Date being ordered: <input type="text" name="DateOrder" size="11">
(e.g., 09-04-2004)</p>
  <p>Notes: <textarea rows="5" name="Notes" cols="50"></textarea></p>
  <p>Status code:  <input type="text" name="StatusCode" size="10">
(<a href="ReportStatus.asp" target="_blank">See
 current status options report</a>)</p>
  <p><input type="submit" value="Submit" name="SubmitButton"><input
type="reset" value="Reset" name="ResetButton"></p>
</form>
<p> </p>

</body>

</html>
```

DataEntryFIRsProc.asp

```
<head>
<meta http-equiv="Content-Language" content="en-us">
<meta http-equiv="Content-Type" content="text/html; charset=windows-
1252">
```

```
<meta name="GENERATOR" content="Microsoft FrontPage 4.0">
<meta name="ProgId" content="FrontPage.Editor.Document">
<title>Food items requests data entry processing page</title>
</head>


<body>


<%
If (Request("ResetButton") = "Reset") Then
  Response.Redirect "DataEntryFIRs.asp"
End If
%>


<%
Set LIRDbObj = Server.CreateObject("ADODB.Connection")
LIRDbObj.Open "DSN=LIRACC;UID=;PWD=;"
strSQLStatement = "INSERT INTO FIRs " _
        & "(FIRCode, FoodItemCode, RestaurantCode, Quantity,
DateOrder, Notes, StatusCode) " _
        & "SELECT '" & Request("FIRCode") & "' AS FIRCode, '" _
        &         Request("FoodItemCode") & "' AS FoodItemCode, '" _
        &         Request("RestaurantCode") & "' AS RestaurantCode, '" _
        &         Request("Quantity") & "' AS Quantity, '" _
        &         Request("DateOrder") & "' AS DateOrder, '" _
        &         Request("Notes") & "' AS Notes, '" _
        &         Request("StatusCode") & "' AS StatusCode;"
LIRDbObj.Execute(strSQLStatement)
%>


<%
LIRDbObj.Close
SET LIRDbObj = Nothing
%>


<h1>Restaurants data entered successfully!</h1>
<p><a href="DataEntryFIRs.asp">Return to food items requests data entry
data entry page.</a></p>


</body>
</html>
```

Food Items Data Update or Delete

UpdateDeleteFoodItems.asp

```
<html>

<head>
<meta http-equiv="Content-Language" content="en-us">
<meta http-equiv="Content-Type" content="text/html; charset=windows-
1252">
<meta name="GENERATOR" content="Microsoft FrontPage 4.0">
<meta name="ProgId" content="FrontPage.Editor.Document">
<title>Food items data update or delete</title>
</head>

<body>

<h1>Food items data update or delete</h1>
<p> </p>
<form method="POST" action="UpdateDeleteFoodItemsProc.asp">
 <p>Food item code: <input type="text" name="FoodItemCode" size="10">
(<a href="ReportFoodItems.asp" target="_blank">See
 current food items report</a>)</p>
 <p>(Values below only needed if updating data)</p>
 <p>Name: <input type="text" name="Name" size="50"></p>
```

```html
  <p>Description: <textarea rows="10" name="Description"
cols="50"></textarea></p>
  <p><input type="submit" value="Delete" name="DeleteButton">
    <input type="submit" value="Update" name="UpdateButton">
    <input type="reset" value="Reset" name="ResetButton"></p>
</form>
<p> </p>

</body>

</html>
```

UpdateDeleteFoodItemsProc.asp

```asp
<%@ LANGUAGE="VBSCRIPT" %>
<html>          .

<head>
<meta http-equiv="Content-Language" content="en-us">
<meta  http-equiv="Content-Type"  content="text/html;  charset=windows-
1252">
<meta name="GENERATOR" content="Microsoft FrontPage 4.0">
<meta name="ProgId" content="FrontPage.Editor.Document">
<title>Food items update or delete processing page</title>
</head>

<body>

<%
If (Request("ResetButton") = "Reset") Then
  Response.Redirect "UpdateDeleteFoodItems.asp"
End If
%>

<%
Set LIRDbObj = Server.CreateObject("ADODB.Connection")
LIRDbObj.Open "DSN=LIRACC;UID=;PWD=;"
%>

<%
If (Request("DeleteButton") = "Delete") Then
  strSQLStatement = "DELETE FROM FoodItems " _
          & "WHERE FoodItemCode = " & Request("FoodItemCode") & ";"
Else
```

```
    strSQLStatement = "UPDATE FoodItems " _
            & "SET FoodItemCode = " & Request("FoodItemCode") & "," _
            &    " Name = '" & Request("Name") & "'," _
            &    " Description = '" & Request("Description") & "'" _
            & "WHERE FoodItemCode = " & Request("FoodItemCode") & ";"
End If

LIRDbObj.Execute(strSQLStatement)
%>


<%
LIRDbObj.Close
SET LIRDbObj = Nothing
%>
```

```html
<h1>Food items data updated or deleted successfully!</h1>
<p><a href="UpdateDeleteFoodItems.asp">Return to food items update or
delete page.</a></p>


</body>
</html>
```

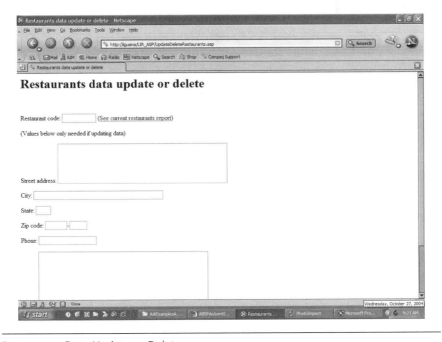

Restaurants Data Update or Delete

UpdateDeleteRestaurants.asp

```
<html>

<head>
<meta http-equiv="Content-Language" content="en-us">
<meta http-equiv="Content-Type" content="text/html; charset=windows-1252">
<meta name="GENERATOR" content="Microsoft FrontPage 4.0">
<meta name="ProgId" content="FrontPage.Editor.Document">
<title>Restaurants data update or delete</title>
</head>

<body>

<h1>Restaurants data update or delete</h1>
<p> </p>
<form method="POST" action="UpdateDeleteRestaurantsProc.asp">
  <p>Restaurant code: <input type="text" name="RestaurantCode"
size="10"> (<a href="ReportRestaurants.asp" target="_blank">See
  current restaurants report</a>)</p>
  <p>(Values below only needed if updating data)</p>
  <p>Street address: <textarea rows="5" name="StreetAddress"
cols="50"></textarea></p>
  <p>City: <input type="text" name="City" size="50"></p>
  <p>State: <input type="text" name="State" size="2"></p>
  <p>Zip code: <input type="text" name="ZIP1" size="5">-<input
type="text" name="ZIP2" size="3"></p>
  <p>Phone: <input type="text" name="Phone" size="20"></p>
  <p>Notes: <textarea rows="10" name="Notes" cols="50"></textarea></p>
  <p><input type="submit" value="Delete" name="DeleteButton">
    <input type="submit" value="Update" name="UpdateButton">
    <input type="reset" value="Reset" name="ResetButton"></p>
</form>
<p> </p>

</body>

</html>
```

UpdateDeleteRestaurantsProc.asp

```
<%@ LANGUAGE="VBSCRIPT" %>
<html>

<head>
<meta http-equiv="Content-Language" content="en-us">
```

```
<meta http-equiv="Content-Type" content="text/html; charset=windows-
1252">
<meta name="GENERATOR" content="Microsoft FrontPage 4.0">
<meta name="ProgId" content="FrontPage.Editor.Document">
<title>Restaurants data update or delete processing page</title>
</head>

<body>

<%
If (Request("ResetButton") = "Reset") Then
 Response.Redirect "UpdateDeleteRestaurants.asp"
End If
%>


<%
Set LIRDbObj = Server.CreateObject("ADODB.Connection")
LIRDbObj.Open "DSN=LIRACC;UID=;PWD=;"
%>


<%
If (Request("DeleteButton") = "Delete") Then
 strSQLStatement = "DELETE FROM Restaurants " _
         & "WHERE RestaurantCode = " & Request("RestaurantCode")
& ";"
Else
 strSQLStatement = "UPDATE Restaurants " _
         & "SET RestaurantCode = " & Request("RestaurantCode") & "," _
         &   " StreetAddress = '" & Request("StreetAddress") & "'," _
         &   " City = '" & Request("City") & "'," _
         &   " State = '" & Request("State") & "'," _
         &   " ZIP1 = '" & Request("ZIP1") & "'," _
         &   " ZIP2 = '" & Request("ZIP2") & "'," _
         &   " Phone = '" & Request("Phone") & "'," _
         &   " Notes = '" & Request("Notes") & "' " _
         & "WHERE RestaurantCode = " & Request("RestaurantCode")
& ";"
End If

LIRDbObj.Execute(strSQLStatement)
%>


<%
LIRDbObj.Close
```

```
SET LIRDbObj = Nothing
%>

<h1>Restaurants data updated or deleted successfully!</h1>
<p><a href="UpdateDeleteRestaurants.asp">Return to restaurants data
update or delete page.</a></p>

</body>
</html>
```

Status Options Data Update or Delete

UpdateDeleteStatus.asp

```
<html>

<head>
<meta http-equiv="Content-Language" content="en-us">
<meta http-equiv="Content-Type" content="text/html;
charset=windows-1252">
<meta name="GENERATOR" content="Microsoft
```

```
FrontPage 4.0">
<meta name="ProgId" content="FrontPage.Editor.Document">
<title>Status options data update or delete</title>
</head>

<body>

<h1>Status options data update or delete</h1>
<p> </p>
<form method="POST" action="UpdateDeleteStatusProc.asp">
  <p>Status code: <input type="text" name="StatusCode" size="10"> (<a
href="ReportStatus.asp" target="_blank">See
  current status options report</a>)</p>
  <p>(Values below only needed if updating data)</p>
  <p>Status description: <textarea rows="5" name="Description"
cols="50"></textarea></p>
  <p><input type="submit" value="Delete" name="DeleteButton">
    <input type="submit" value="Update" name="UpdateButton">
    <input type="reset" value="Reset" name="ResetButton"></p>
</form>
<p> </p>

</body>

</html>
```

UpdateDeleteStatusProc.asp

```
<%@ LANGUAGE="VBSCRIPT" %>
<html>

<head>
<meta http-equiv="Content-Language" content="en-us">
<meta http-equiv="Content-Type" content="text/html; charset=windows-
1252">
<meta name="GENERATOR" content="Microsoft FrontPage 4.0">
<meta name="ProgId" content="FrontPage.Editor.Document">
<title>Status options data update or delete processing page</title>
</head>

<body>

<%
```

```
If (Request("ResetButton") = "Reset") Then
  Response.Redirect "UpdateDeleteStatus.asp"
End If
%>


<%
Set LIRDbObj = Server.CreateObject("ADODB.Connection")
LIRDbObj.Open "DSN=LIRACC;UID=;PWD=;"
%>


<%
If (Request("DeleteButton") = "Delete") Then
  strSQLStatement = "DELETE FROM Status " _
        & "WHERE StatusCode = " & Request("StatusCode") & ";"
Else
  strSQLStatement = "UPDATE Status " _
        & "SET StatusCode = " & Request("StatusCode") & "," _
        & " Description = '" & Request("Description") & "' " _
        & "WHERE StatusCode = " & Request("StatusCode") & ";"
End If

LIRDbObj.Execute(strSQLStatement)
%>


<%
LIRDbObj.Close
SET LIRDbObj = Nothing
%>

<h1>Status options data updated or deleted successfully!</h1>
<p><a href="UpdateDeleteStatus.asp">Return to status options data update
or delete page.</a></p>

</body>
</html>
```

UpdateDeleteFIRs.asp

```
<html>

<head>
<meta http-equiv="Content-Language" content="en-us">
<meta http-equiv="Content-Type" content="text/html; charset=
  windows-1252">
```

Food Items Requests Data Update or Delete

```
<meta name="GENERATOR" content="Microsoft FrontPage 4.0">
<meta name="ProgId" content="FrontPage.Editor.Document">
<title>Food items requests data update or delete</title>
</head>

<body>

<h1>Food items requests data update or delete</h1>
<p> </p>
<form method="POST" action="UpdateDeleteFIRsProc.asp">
  <p>Food item request (FIR) code: <input type="text" name="FIRCode"
size="10"> (<a href="ReportFIRs.asp" target="_blank">See
  current food items requests report</a>)</p>
  <p>(Values below only needed if updating data)</p>
  <p>Food item code: <input type="text" name="FoodItemCode" size="10">
(<a href="ReportFoodItems.asp" target="_blank">See
  current food items report</a>)</p>
  <p>Restaurant code: <input type="text" name="RestaurantCode"
size="10"> (<a href="ReportRestaurants.asp" target="_blank">See
  current restaurants report</a>)</p>
  <p>Quantity: <input type="text" name="Quantity" size="10"></p>
  <p>Date being ordered: <input type="text" name="DateOrder" size="11">
  (e.g., 09-04-2004)</p>
```

```
 <p>Notes: <textarea rows="5" name="Notes" cols="50"></textarea></p>
 <p>Status code:  <input type="text" name="StatusCode" size="10">
(<a href="ReportStatus.asp" target="_blank">See
 current status options report</a>)</p>
 <p><input type="submit" value="Delete" name="DeleteButton"> <input
type="submit" value="Update" name="UpdateButton">
 <input type="reset" value="Reset" name="ResetButton"></p>
</form>
<p> </p>

</body>

</html>
```

UpdateDeleteFIRsProc.asp

```
<%@ LANGUAGE="VBSCRIPT" %>
<html>

<head>
<meta http-equiv="Content-Language" content="en-us">
<meta http-equiv="Content-Type" content="text/html; charset=windows-
1252">
<meta name="GENERATOR" content="Microsoft FrontPage 4.0">
<meta name="ProgId" content="FrontPage.Editor.Document">
<title>Food items requests data update or delete processing page</title>
</head>

<body>

<%
If (Request("ResetButton") = "Reset") Then
  Response.Redirect "UpdateDeleteFIRs.asp"
End If
%>

<%
Set LIRDbObj = Server.CreateObject("ADODB.Connection")
LIRDbObj.Open "DSN=LIRACC;UID=;PWD=;"
%>
<%
If (Request("DeleteButton") = "Delete") Then
  strSQLStatement = "DELETE FROM FIRs " _
          & "WHERE FIRCode = " & Request("FIRCode") & ";"
```

```
Else
  strSQLStatement = "UPDATE FIRs " _
          & "SET FIRCode = " & Request("FIRCode") & "," _
          &   " FoodItemCode = " & Request("FoodItemCode") & "," _
          &   " RestaurantCode = " & Request("RestaurantCode") & "," _
          &   " Quantity = " & Request("Quantity") & "," _
          &   " DateOrder = '" & Request("DateOrder") & "'," _
          &   " Notes = '" & Request("Notes") & "'," _
          &   " StatusCode = " & Request("StatusCode") & "," _
          & "WHERE FIRCode = " & Request("FIRCode") & ";"
End If

LIRDbObj.Execute(strSQLStatement)
%>

<%
LIRDbObj.Close
SET LIRDbObj = Nothing
%>

<h1>Restaurants data updated or deleted successfully!</h1>
<p><a href="UpdateDeleteFIRs.asp">Return to food items requests data
update or delete page.</a></p>

</body>

</html>
```

Food items report

1	Risotto	Risotto alla Pitocca -- chicken risotto
2	Aglio e Olio Sauce	Pasta liberally seasoned with olive oil, garlic, and red pepper.
3	Alfredo Sauce	Essentially a cream sauce.
4	Pork Chops	Pork chops prepared Italian style, with rosemary sauce.

Food Items Report

ReportFoodItems.asp

```
<%@ LANGUAGE="VBSCRIPT" %>
<html>

<head>
<meta http-equiv="Content-Language" content="en-us">
<meta http-equiv="Content-Type" content="text/html; charset=windows-
1252">
<meta name="GENERATOR" content="Microsoft FrontPage 4.0">
<meta name="ProgId" content="FrontPage.Editor.Document">
<title>Food items report</title>
</head>

<body>

<h1>Food items report</h1>

<%
SET LIRDbObj = Server.CreateObject("ADODB.Connection")
LIRDbObj.Open ""DSN=LIRACC;UID=;PWD=;""
SET oRs = LIRDbObj.Execute(""SELECT * FROM FoodItems;"")
%>

<TABLE BORDER=3>
<% WHILE NOT oRs.EOF %>
<TR>
<TD> <%=oRs.Fields(""FoodItemCode"").Value %> </TD>
<TD> <%=oRs.Fields(""Name"").Value %> </TD>
<TD> <%=oRs.Fields(""Description"").Value %> </TD>
<TR>
<% oRs.MoveNext %>
<% WEND %>

</TABLE>

<%
LIRDbObj.Close
SET LIRDbObj = Nothing
%>

</body>
</html>
```

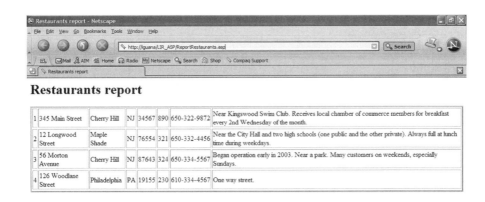

Restaurants Report

ReportRestaurants.asp

```
<%@ LANGUAGE="VBSCRIPT" %>
<html>
<head>
<head>
<meta http-equiv="Content-Language" content="en-us">
<meta http-equiv="Content-Type" content="text/html;
charset=windows-1252">
<meta name="GENERATOR" content="Microsoft
FrontPage 4.0">
<meta name="ProgId"
content="FrontPage.Editor.Document">
<title>Restaurants report</title>
</head>

<body>
```

```
<h1>Restaurants report</h1>

<%
SET LIRDbObj = Server.CreateObject("ADODB.Connection")
LIRDbObj.Open "DSN=LIRACC;UID=;PWD=;"
SET oRs = LIRDbObj.Execute("SELECT * FROM Restaurants;")
%>

<TABLE BORDER=3>
<% WHILE NOT oRs.EOF %>
<TR>
<TD> <%=oRs.Fields("RestaurantCode").Value %> </TD>
<TD> <%=oRs.Fields("StreetAddress").Value %> </TD>
<TD> <%=oRs.Fields("City").Value %> </TD>
<TD> <%=oRs.Fields("State").Value %> </TD>
<TD> <%=oRs.Fields("ZIP1").Value %> </TD>
<TD> <%=oRs.Fields("ZIP2").Value %> </TD>
<TD> <%=oRs.Fields("Phone").Value %> </TD>
<TD> <%=oRs.Fields("Notes").Value %> </TD>
<TR>
<% oRs.MoveNext %>
<% WEND %>

</TABLE>

<%
LIRDbObj.Close
SET LIRDbObj = Nothing
%>

</body>
</html>
```

Status Options Report

ReportStatus.asp

```
<%@ LANGUAGE="VBSCRIPT" %>
<html>

<head>
<meta http-equiv="Content-Language" content="en-us">
<meta http-equiv="Content-Type" content="text/html; charset=windows-
1252">
<meta name="GENERATOR" content="Microsoft FrontPage 4.0">
<meta name="ProgId" content="FrontPage.Editor.Document">
<title>Status options report</title>
</head>

<body>

<h1>Status options report</h1>

<%
SET LIRDbObj = Server.CreateObject("ADODB.Connection")
LIRDbObj.Open "DSN=LIRACC;UID=;PWD=;"
```

```
SET oRs = LIRDbObj.Execute("SELECT * FROM Status;")
%>

<TABLE BORDER=3>
<% WHILE NOT oRs.EOF %>
<TR>
<TD> <%=oRs.Fields("StatusCode").Value %> </TD>
<TD> <%=oRs.Fields("Description").Value %> </TD>
<TR>
<% oRs.MoveNext %>
<% WEND %>

</TABLE>


<%
LIRDbObj.Close
SET LIRDbObj = Nothing
%>

</body>
</html>
```

Food items requests report

1	2	3	4	11/10/2004	Urgent order.	1
2	2	1	3	10/11/2004	Deliver it to Johnny.	1
3	3	1	10	11/10/2004	Deliver by 12-10-2004 -- pleeease!	1
4	2	3	12	10/11/2004	Double olive oil amount.	1

Food Items Requests Report

ReportFIRs.asp

```
<%@ LANGUAGE="VBSCRIPT" %>
<html>

<head>
<meta http-equiv="Content-Language" content="en-us">
<meta http-equiv="Content-Type" content="text/html; charset=
windows-1252">
<meta name="GENERATOR" content="Microsoft FrontPage 4.0">
<meta name="ProgId" content="FrontPage.Editor.Document">
<title>Food items requests report</title>
</head>

<body>

<h1>Food items requests report</h1>

<%
SET LIRDbObj = Server.CreateObject("ADODB.Connection")
LIRDbObj.Open "DSN=LIRACC;UID=;PWD=;"
SET oRs = LIRDbObj.Execute("SELECT * FROM FIRs;")
%>

<TABLE BORDER=3>
<% WHILE NOT oRs.EOF %>
<TR>
<TD> <%=oRs.Fields("FIRCode").Value %> </TD>
<TD> <%=oRs.Fields("FoodItemCode").Value %> </TD>
<TD> <%=oRs.Fields("RestaurantCode").Value %> </TD>
<TD> <%=oRs.Fields("Quantity").Value %> </TD>
<TD> <%=oRs.Fields("DateOrder").Value %> </TD>
<TD> <%=oRs.Fields("Notes").Value %> </TD>
<TD> <%=oRs.Fields("StatusCode").Value %> </TD>
<TR>
<% oRs.MoveNext %>
<% WEND %>

</TABLE>

<%
LIRDbObj.Close
SET LIRDbObj = Nothing
%>

</body>
</html>
```

Appendix B

Chapter 1:
Introduction

1. b.
2. a.
3. c.
4. d.
5. d.

Chapter 2:
Data, Information, and
Knowledge Flow in Business Processes

1. c.
2. a.
3. d.
4. c.
5. d.
6. a.
7. d.
8. c.
9. b.
10. b.
11. c.
12. a.

13. c.
14. b.
15. b.

Chapter 3:
Return on Investment in Technology

1. d.
2. b.
3. a.
4. d.
5. a.
6. b.
7. a.
8. c.
9. d.
10. d.

Chapter 4:
The Past, Present, and Future
of Business Process Redesign

1. a.
2. c.
3. b.
4. d.
5. a.
6. c.
7. a.
8. b.
9. c.
10. d.

Chapter 5:
Business Process Modeling Approaches and Diagrams

1. b.
2. c.
3. a.
4. d.
5. b.

6. c.

7. a.

8. d.

9. b.

10. c.

Chapter 6:
Selecting a Target for Successful
Business Process Redesign

1. d.

2. c.

3. a.

4. b.

5. a.

Chapter 7:
Representing Information and
Knowledge in Business Processes

1. b.

2. a.

3. d.

4. c.

5. a.

Chapter 8:
Redesigning Business Processes

1. c.

2. d.

3. a.

4. c.

5. a.

6. d.

7. b.

8. a.

9. d.

10. b.

Chapter 9:
Using IT to Enable New Process Designs

1. a.
2. c.
3. b.
4. d.
5. c.

Chapter 10:
Redesigning Little Italy Restaurants

1. c.
2. a.
3. d.
4. b.
5. d.

Chapter 11:
Database Design Concepts and Issues

1. b.
2. c.
3. a.
4. d.
5. d.

Chapter 12:
Object-Oriented Design Concepts and Issues

1. a.
2. c.
3. d.
4. a.
5. b.

Chapter 13:
Business Process Automation With ASP

1. c.
2. a.

3. b.
4. d.
5. a.

Chapter 14: Conclusion

1. c.
2. b.
3. b.
4. a.
5. d.

Bibliography

Alge, B. J., Wiethoff, C., & Klein, H. J. (2003). When does the medium matter? Knowledge-building experiences and opportunities in decision-making teams. *Organizational Behavior and Human Decision Processes, 91*(1), 26–37.

Alonzo, M., & Aiken, M. (2004). Flaming in electronic communication. *Decision Support Systems, 36*(3), 205–214.

Archer, R., & Bowker, P. (1995). BPR consulting: An evaluation of the methods employed. *Business Process Re-Engineering & Management, 1*(2), 28–46.

Argyris, C. (1964). *Integrating the individual and the organization.* New York: John Wiley & Sons.

Argyris, C. (1977). Double loop learning organizations. *Harvard Business Review, 55*(5), 115–125.

Argyris, C. (1992). *On organizational learning.* Cambridge, MA: Blackwell.

Arnold, K. L. (1994). *The manager's guide to ISO 9000.* New York: The Free Press.

Atkins, R. (2003). Computer contracts: Capturing requirements and apportioning responsibilities. *International Review of Law, Computers and Technology, 17*(2), 219–231.

Bao, J., Zhang, W., & Lee, P. (2003). Decentralized fault-tolerant control system design for unstable processes. *Chemical Engineering Science, 58*(22), 5045–5054.

Bartlett, F. (1932). *Remembering: A study in experimental and social psychology.* Cambridge, UK: Cambridge University Press.

Bartlett, F. (1958). *Thinking: An experimental and social study.* New York: Basic Books.

Bashein, B. J., & Markus, M. L. (1994). Preconditions for BPR success. *Information Systems Management, 11*(2), 7–13.

Bell, R. K. (1994). Case study: Dow Corning. In E. White & L. Fischer (Eds.), *The workflow paradigm* (pp. 267–285). Alameda, CA: Future Strategies.

Belmonte, R. W., & Murray, R. J. (1993). Getting ready for strategic change: Surviving business process redesign. *Information Systems Management, 10*(3), 23–29.

Berryman, K., & Seaberg, J. (2004). The outlook for enterprise software. *McKinsey Quarterly, 1*(1), 66–68.

Biggs, M. (2000). Enabling a successful e-business strategy requires a detailed business process map. *InfoWorld, 22*(10), 64.

Boaz, N. T., & Almquist, A. J. (1997). *Biological anthropology: A synthetic approach to human evolution.* Upper Saddle River, NJ: Prentice Hall.

Boland, R. J., Jr., & Tenkasi, R. V. (1995). Perspective making and perspective taking in communities of knowing. *Organization Science, 6*(4), 350–372.

Booch, G. (1991). *Object-oriented design with application.* Redwood City, CA: Benjamin-Cummings.

Booch, G., Jacobson, I., & Rumbaugh, J. (1998). *The unified modeling language user guide.* New York: Addison-Wesley.

Boroson, W. (1997). *Keys to investing in mutual funds.* Hauppauge, NY: Barron's Educational Series.

Boyce, M. E. (1996). Organizational story and storytelling: A critical review. *Journal of Organizational Change Management, 9*(5), 5–26.

Brynjolfsson, E. (1993). The productivity paradox of information technology. *Communications of the ACM, 36*(12), 66–77.

Brynjolfsson, E., & Hitt, L. M. (1998). Beyond the productivity paradox. *Communications of the ACM, 41*(8), 49–55.

Brynjolfsson, E., & Yang, S. (1997). The intangible benefits and costs of investments: Evidence from financial markets. In K. Kumar & J. I. DeGross (Eds.), *Proceedings of the 18th International Conference on Information Systems* (pp. 147–166). New York: The Association for Computing Machinery.

Burke, G., & Peppard, J. (1995). Business process re-engineering: Research directions. In G. Burke & J. Peppard (Eds.), *Examining business process re-engineering* (pp. 25–37). London: Kogan Page.

Burke, G., & Peppard, J. (Eds.). (1995). *Examining business process re-engineering.* London: Kogan Page.

Buss, D. M. (1995). *The evolution of desire: Strategies of human mating.* New York: Basic Books.

Buzacott, J. A. (1996). Commonalities in reengineered business processes: Models and issues. *Management Science, 42*(5), 768–782.

Callatay, A. M. (1986). *Natural and artificial intelligence.* Amsterdam: North-Holland.

Camerer, C. F., & Johnson, E. J. (1991). The process-performance paradox in expert judgment: How can experts know so much and predict so badly? In K. A. Ericsson & J. Smith (Eds.), *Toward a general theory of expertise: Prospects and limits* (pp. 195–217). Cambridge, UK: Cambridge University Press.

Carlzon, J. (1989). *Moments of truth.* New York: HarperCollins.

Caron, J. R., Jarvenpaa, S. L., & Stoddard, D. B. (1994). Business reengineering at CIGNA Corporation: Experiences and lessons learned from the first five years. *MIS Quarterly, 18*(3), 233–250.

Carr, N. G. (2003). IT? Does it matter? *Network Magazine, 18*(7), 6–10.

Carr, N. G. (2003). IT doesn't matter. *Harvard Business Review, 81*(5), 41–50.

Casey, D. (1993). *Managing learning in organizations.* Buckingham, UK: Open University Press.

Champy, J. (1995). *Reengineering management.* New York: Harper Business.

Checkland, P. (1981). *Systems thinking, systems practice.* New York: John Wiley & Sons.

Checkland, P., & Scholes, J. (1990). *Soft systems methodology in action.* New York: John Wiley & Sons.

Chen, C., & Tai, W. (2003). An information push-delivery system design for personal information service on the Internet. *Information Processing & Management, 39*(6), 873–888.

Chen, P. (1976). The entity-relationship model: Towards a unified view of data. *ACM Transactions on Database Systems, 1*(1), 9–36.

Chervany, N., & Dickson, G. (1974). An experimental evaluation of information overload in a production environment. *Management Science, 20*(10), 1335–1344.

Childe, S. J., Maull, R. S., & Benett, J. (1994). Frameworks for understanding business process re-engineering. *International Journal of Operations & Productions Management, 14*(12), 22–34.

Choi, T. Y. (1995). Conceptualizing continuous improvement: Implications for organizational change. *Omega, 23*(6), 607–624.

Choi, T. Y., & Liker, J. K. (1995). Bringing Japanese continuous improvement approaches to U.S. manufacturing: The roles of process orientation and communications. *Decision Sciences, 26*(5), 589–620.

Chuang, T., & Yadav, S. B. (2000). A decision-driven approach to object-oriented analysis. *Database for Advances in Information Systems, 31*(2), 13–34.

Clutterbuck, D., & Crainer, S. (1990). *Makers of management.* London: Macmillan.

Coad, P., & Yourdon, E. (1991). *Object oriented analysis* (2nd ed.). Englewood Cliffs, NJ: Yourdon Press.

Cohen, H. B. (1994). Results: The forgotten element of quality programs, *SAM Advanced Management Journal, 59*(3), 24–31.

Connoly, T. M., & Begg, C. E. (2002). *Database systems: A practical approach to design, implementation, and management.* New York: Addison-Wesley.

Cooprider, J. G., & Victor, K. M. (1993). The construction of shared knowledge to IS group performance. In J. I. Degross, R. P. Bostrom, & D. Robey (Eds.), *Proceedings of the 14th International Conference on Information Systems* (pp. 285–297). New York: The Association for Computing Machinery.

Couger, J. D. (1973). Evolution of business system analysis techniques. *Computing Surveys, 5*(3), 167–198.

Craig, T. (1996). The Japanese beer wars: Initiating and responding to hypercompetition in new product development. *Organization Science, 7*(3), 302–321.

Crosby, P. B. (1980). *Quality is free: The art of making quality certain.* New York: Mentor.

Crosby, P. B. (1984). *Quality without tears: The art of hassle-free management.* New York: McGraw-Hill.

Daft, R. L., & Lengel, R. H. (1986). Organizational information requirements, media richness and structural design. *Management Science, 32*(5), 554–571.

Damanpour, F. (1988). Innovation type, radicalness, and the adoption process. *Communications Research, 15,* 545–567.

Damaševičius, R., & Štuikys, V. (2004). Application of the object-oriented principles for hardware and embedded system design. *The VLSI Journal, 38*(2), 309–339.

Danesh, A. (2005). *IT-enabled process redesign: Using communication flow optimization theory in an information intensive environment.* Doctoral dissertation, Temple University, Philadelphia.

Darwin, C. (1859). *On the origin of species by means of natural selection.* Cambridge, MA: Harvard University Press. (Facsimile of 1st ed., reprinted in 1966)

Darwin, C. (1871). *The descent of man and selection in relation to sex.* London: Murray.

Davenport, T., & Prusak, L. (2000). *Working knowledge.* Cambridge, MA: Harvard Business School Press.

Davenport, T. H. (1993). Need radical innovation and continuous improvement? Integrate process re-engineering and total quality management. *Planning Review, 21*(3), 6–12.

Davenport, T. H. (1993). *Process innovation.* Boston: Harvard Business Press.

Davenport, T. H., & Beck, J. C. (2001). *The attention economy: Understanding the new currency of business.* Cambridge, MA: Harvard Business School Publishing.

Davenport, T. H., & Beers, M. C. (1995). Managing information about processes. *Journal of Management Information Systems, 12*(1), 57–80.

Davenport, T. H., Harris, J. G., & Cantrell, S. (2004). Enterprise systems and ongoing process change. *Business Process Management Journal, 10*(1), 16–27.

Davenport, T. H., & Short, J. E. (1990). The new industrial engineering: Information technology and business process redesign. *Sloan Management Review, 31*(4), 11–27.

Davenport, T. H., & Stoddard, D. B. (1994). Reengineering: Business change of mythic proportions? *MIS Quarterly, 18*(2), 121–127.

Davidow, W. H., & Malone, M. S. (1992). *The virtual corporation.* New York: HarperCollins.

Davidson, W. H. (1993). Beyond re-engineering: The three phases of business transformation. *IBM Systems Journal, 32*(1), 17–26.

Dawkins, R. (1986). *The blind watchmaker.* New York: W. W. Norton.

Dawkins, R. (1990). *The selfish gene.* Oxford, UK: Oxford University Press.

De Bono, E. (1994). *Water logic.* London: Penguin Books.

Dehning, B., Dow, K. E., & Stratopoulos, T. (2003). The info-tech "productivity paradox" dissected and tested. *Management Accounting Quarterly, 5*(1), 31–40.

DeMarco, T. (1979). *Structured analysis and system specification.* Englewood Cliffs, NJ: Prentice-Hall.

Deming, W. E. (1986). *Out of the crisis.* Cambridge: Center for Advanced Engineering Study, Massachusetts Institute of Technology.

Dennett, D. C. (1991). *Consciousness explained.* Boston: Little, Brown.

Dennett, D. C. (1995). *Darwin's dangerous idea: Evolution and the meaning of life.* New York: Simon & Schuster.

Dennis, A. R., & Wixom, B. H. (2000). *Systems analysis and design: An applied approach.* New York: John Wiley & Sons.

DeRosa, D. M., Hantula, D. A., Kock, N., & D'Arcy, J. P. (2004). Communication, trust, and leadership in virtual teams: A media naturalness perspective. *Human Resources Management Journal, 34*(2), 219–232.

Devaraj, S., & Kohli, R. (2002). *The IT payoff: Measuring the business value of information technology investments.* Upper Saddle River, NJ: Prentice Hall PTR.

Dos Santos, B. L., & Peffers, K. (1995). Rewards to investors in innovative information technology applications: First movers and early followers in ATMs. *Organization Science, 6*(3), 241–259.

Dozier, R. W., Jr. (1992). *Codes of evolution.* New York: Crown.

Drucker, P. F. (1989). *The new realities.* New York: Harper & Row.

Drucker, P. F. (1993). Professional's productivity. *Across the Board, 30*(9), 50.

Drucker, P. F. (1994). The theory of business. *Harvard Business Review, 72*(5), 95–104.

Drucker, P. F. (1995). The information executives truly need. *Harvard Business Review, 73*(1), 54–62.

Dunbar, R. I. M. (1993). Coevolution of neocortical size, group size and language in humans. *Behavioral and Brain Sciences, 16*(4), 681–735.

Duncan, J. (1989). *Great ideas in management.* San Francisco: Jossey-Bass.

Earl, M. J. (1994). The new and the old of business process redesign. *Journal of Strategic Information Systems, 3*(1), 5–22.

Earl, M. J., Sampler, J. L., & Short, J. E. (1995). Strategies for business process reengineering: Evidence from field studies. *Journal of Management Information Systems, 12*(1), 31–56.

Ebbinghaus, H. (1913). *Memory: A contribution to experimental psychology.* New York: Teachers College, Columbia University. (Originally published 1885)

Ehin, C. (1995). The quest for empowering organizations: Some lessons from our foraging past. *Organization Science, 6*(6), 666–671.

Ericsson, K. A., & Smith, J. (Eds.). (1991). *Toward a general theory of expertise.* Cambridge, UK: Cambridge University Press.

Eysenck, M. W., & Keane, M. T. (1990). *Cognitive psychology.* East Sussex, UK: Lawrence Erlbaum Associates.

Feldman, J. (1986). On the difficulty of learning from experience. In H. P. Sims, Jr., & D. A. Gioia (Eds.), *The thinking organization* (pp. 263–292). San Francisco: Jossey-Bass.

Foster, D. (1975). *The intelligent universe*. London: Abelard.

Fowler, D. N., & Nissen, M. E. (2001). Innovating the federal acquisition process through intelligent agents. *Acquisition Review Quarterly, 8*(3), 151–166.

French, W. L., & Bell, C. H., Jr. (1990). *Organization development*. Englewood Cliffs, NJ: Prentice Hall.

Galbraith, J. K. (1973). *Designing complex organizations*. Reading, MA: Addison-Wesley.

Galbraith, J. K. (1977). *Organizational design*. Reading, MA: Addison-Wesley.

Galbraith, J. K. (1990). *A short history of financial euphoria*. New York: Penguin Books.

Gallivan, M. J., Hofman, J. D., & Orlikowski, W. J. (1994). Implementing radical change: Gradual versus rapid pace. In J. I. DeGross, S. L. Huff, & M. C. Munro (Eds.), *Proceedings of the 15th International Conference on Information Systems* (pp. 325–340). New York: The Association for Computing Machinery.

Gardner, H. (1985). *The mind's new science*. New York: Basic Books.

Garratt, R. (1994). *The learning organization*. London: HarperCollins.

George, C. S., Jr. (1972). *The history of management thought*. Englewood Cliffs, NJ: Prentice-Hall.

Ghertman, M., & Allen, M. (1984). *An introduction to the multinationals*. London: Macmillan.

Gibson, M. L., & Hughes, C. T. (1994). *Systems analysis and design: A comprehensive methodology with CASE*. Danvers, MA: Boyd & Fraser.

Gillespie, G. (2004). Data mining: Solving care, cost capers. *Health Data Management, 12*(11), 52–57.

Gioia, D. A., & Sims, H. P., Jr. (1986). Social cognition in organizations. In H. P. Sims, Jr., & D. A. Gioia (Eds.), *The thinking organization* (pp. 1–48). San Francisco: Jossey-Bass.

Glazer, R., Steckel, J. H., & Winer, R. S. (1992). Locally rational decision making: The distracting effect of information on managerial performance. *Management Science, 38*(2), 212–227.

Gleick, J. (1993). *Chaos: Making a new science*. London: Abacus.

Goldratt, E. (1990). *Theory of constraints*. New York: North River Press.

Goldratt, E. (1991). *The haystack syndrome: Sifting information out of the data ocean*. New York: North River Press.

Goldratt, E., & Cox, J. (1986). *The goal: A process of ongoing improvement*. New York: North River Press.

Goldratt, E. M., & Fox, R. E. (1986). *The race*. New York: North River Press.

Gouillart, F. J. (1994). Spend a day in the life of your customers. *Harvard Business Review, 72*(1), 116–125.

Graham, I. (1992). *TQM in service industries: A practitioner's manual*. New York: Technical Communications.

Grant, G. G. (2003). Strategic alignment and enterprise systems implementation: The case of Metalco. *Journal of Information Technology, 18*(3), 159–176.

Greenspan, A. (1999). The interaction of education and economic change. *The Region, 13*(1), 6–11.

Grote, G. (2004). Uncertainty management at the core of system design. *Annual Reviews in Control, 28*(2), 267–274.

Grudin, J. (1994). Groupware and social dynamics: Eight challenges for developers. *Communications of the ACM, 37*(1), 93–105.

Guha, S., Kettinger, W. J., & Teng, J. T. (1993). Business process reengineering, building a comprehensive methodology. *Information Systems Management, 10*(3), 13–22.

Hackett, G. P. (1990). Investment in technology: The service sector sinkhole? *Sloan Management Review, 31*(2), 97–103.

Hall, G., Rosenthal, J., & Wade, J. (1993, November/December). How to make reengineering really work. *Harvard Business Review, 71*(6), 119–131.

Hamel, G. (2001). Take it higher. *Fortune, 143*(3), 169–170.

Hammer, M. (1990). Reengineering work: Don't automate, obliterate. *Harvard Business Review, 68*(4), 104–114.

Hammer, M. (2000). Reengineering redux. *CIO Magazine, 13*(10), 143–156.

Hammer, M., & Champy, J. (1993). *Reengineering the corporation.* New York: Harper Business.

Hammer, M., & Stanton, S. A. (1995). *The reengineering revolution.* New York: HarperCollins.

Harrington, J. H. (1991). *Business process improvement.* New York: McGraw-Hill.

Harrington, J. H., Esseling, E. K. C., & Van Nimwegen, H. (1998). *Business process improvement workbook: Documentation, analysis, design, and management of business process improvement.* New York: McGraw-Hill.

Harrison, A. (1995). Business processes: Their nature and properties. In G. Burke & J. Peppard (Eds.), *Examining business process re-engineering* (pp. 60–69). London: Kogan Page.

Hasan, B. (2002). End users and developers in systems analysis and design. *Journal of Information Systems Education, 13*(1), 3–6.

Hay, E. J. (1988). *The just-in-time breakthrough.* Chichester, UK: John Wiley & Sons.

Heap, J. (1992). *Productivity management.* New York: Cassell.

Hendricks, K. B., & Singhal, V. R. (1996). Quality awards and the market value of the firm: An empirical investigation. *Management Science, 42*(3), 415–436.

Hendricks, K. B., & Singhal, V. R. (1997). Does implementing an effective TQM program actually improve operating performance? Empirical evidence from firms that have won quality awards. *Management Science, 43*(9), 1258–1274.

Hernandez, A. (1993). *Just-in-time quality.* Englewood Cliffs, NJ: Prentice-Hall.

Hewitt, F., & Yeon, K. H. (1996). BPR perceptions, practices and expectations: A UK study. *Business Change & Re-engineering, 3*(3), 47–55.

Hirschheim, R. A. (1985). *Office automation: A social and organizational perspective.* New York: John Wiley & Sons.

Hitt, L. M., & Brynjolfsson, E. (1996). Productivity, business profitability, and consumer surplus: Three different measures of information technology value. *MIS Quarterly, 20*(2), 121–142.

Hofstede, G. (1980). *Culture's consequences: International differences in work-related values.* Beverly Hills, CA: Sage.

Hofstede, G. (2001). *Culture's consequences: Comparing values, behaviors, institutions, and organizations across nations.* Thousand Oaks, CA: Sage.

Holyoak, K. J. (1991). Symbolic connectionism: Toward third-generation theories of expertise. In K. A. Ericsson & J. Smith (Eds.), *Toward a general theory of expertise* (pp. 301–335). Cambridge, UK: Cambridge University Press.

Hormazi, A. M., & Giles, S. (2004). Data mining: A competitive weapon for banking and retail industries. *Information Systems Management, 21*(2), 62–72.

Hsieh, N. (2004). An integrated data mining and behavioral scoring model for analyzing bank customers. *Expert Systems With Applications, 27*(4), 623–633.

Hutchins, D. (1985). *Quality circles handbook.* London: Pitman.

Im, K. S., Dow, K. E., & Grover, V. A. (2001). A reexamination of IT investment and the market value of the firm: An event study methodology. *Information Systems Research, 12*(1), 103–118.

Ishikawa, K. (1986). *Guide to quality control.* Tokyo: Asian Productivity Organisation.

Jacobson, I. (1992). *Object-oriented software engineering.* Reading, MA: Addison-Wesley.

Jacobson, I., Ericsson, M., & Jacobson, A. (1995). *The object advantage.* New York: Addison-Wesley.

Jaques, E. (1990). In praise of hierarchy. *Harvard Business Review, 69*(1), 127–133.

Jerva, M. (2001). BPR and systems analysis and design: Making the case for integration. *Topics in Health Information Management, 21*(4), 30–38.

Jerva, M. (2001). Systems analysis and design methodologies: Practicalities and use in today's information systems development efforts. *Topics in Health Information Management, 21*(4), 13–21.

Juran, J. (1989). *Juran on leadership for quality.* New York: The Free Press.

Karahanna, E., & Evaristo, J. R. (2001). *Innovation adoption and mental workload: An empirical investigation* (Research Rep.). Athens: Terry College of Business, University of Georgia.

Katzenbach, J. R., & Smith, D. K. (1993). *The wisdom of teams: Creating the high-performance organization.* Boston: Harvard Business School Press.

Katzenstein, G., & Lerch, F. J. (2000). Beneath the surface of organizational processes: A social representation framework for business process redesign. *ACM Transactions on Information Systems, 18*(4), 383–422.

Kavanagh, J. (2004, January 27). Use your contracts as checklists for managing risk on IT projects. *Computer Weekly,* p. 42.

Keen, P. G. W. (1999). *Competing in Chapter 2 of Internet business.* Delft, The Netherlands: Eburon.

Keil, M., Tan, B. C. Y., Wei, K., Saarinen, T., Tuunainen, V., & Wassenaar, A. (2000). A cross-cultural study on escalation of commitment behavior in software projects. *MIS Quarterly, 24*(2), 299–325.

Ketchum, L. D., & Trist, E. (1992). *All teams are not created equal.* Newbury Park, CA: Sage.

Kettinger, W. J. (1995). Global measures of information service quality: A cross-national study. *Decision Sciences, 26*(5), 569–588.

Kettinger, W. J., & Grover, V. (1995). Toward a theory of business change management. *Journal of Management Information Systems, 12*(1), 9–30.

Kock, N. (1995). *Process reengineering, PROI: A practical methodology* [in Portuguese]. São Paulo, Brazil: Editora Vozes.

Kock, N. (1997). Myths in organisational action research: Reflections on a study of computer-supported process redesign groups. *Organizations & Society, 4*(9), 65–91.

Kock, N. (1998). Government transformation and structural rigidity: Redesigning a service acquisition process. *Acquisition Review Quarterly, 5*(1), 1–18.

Kock, N. (1999). *Process improvement and organizational learning: The role of collaboration technologies.* Hershey, PA: Idea Group.

Kock, N. (2000). Benefits for virtual organizations from distributed groups. *Communications of the ACM, 43*(11), 107–113.

Kock, N. (2000). Information overload: A process-centered view. *Knowledge and Process Management, 7*(4), 256–264.

Kock, N. (2001). Asynchronous and distributed process improvement: The role of collaborative technologies. *Information Systems Journal, 11*(2), 87–110.

Kock, N. (2001). Changing the focus of business process redesign from activity flows to information flows: A defense acquisition application. *Acquisition Review Quarterly, 8*(2), 93–110.

Kock, N. (2001). Compensatory adaptation to a lean medium: An action research investigation of electronic communication in process improvement groups. *IEEE Transactions on Professional Communication, 44*(4), 267–285.

Kock, N. (2002). Managing with Web-based IT in mind. *Communications of the ACM, 45*(5), 102–106.

Kock, N. (2003). Communication-focused business process redesign: Assessing a communication flow optimization model through an action research study at a defense contractor. *IEEE Transactions on Professional Communication, 46*(1), 35–54.

Kock, N. (2004). The three threats of action research: A discussion of methodological antidotes in the context of an information systems study. *Decision Support Systems, 37*(2), 265–286.

Kock, N. (2005). What is e-collaboration? *International Journal of e-Collaboration, 1*(1), i–vii.

Kock, N., Auspitz, C., & King, B. (2000). Using the Web to enable industry-university collaboration: An action research study of a course partnership. *Informing Science* [Special issue on Organizational Learning], *3*(3), 157–167.

Kock, N., & Davison, R. (2003). Can lean media support knowledge sharing? Investigating a hidden advantage of process improvement. *IEEE Transactions on Engineering Management, 50*(2), 151–163.

Kock, N., Davison, R., Ocker, R., & Wazlawick, R. (2001). E-collaboration: A look at past research and future challenges. *Journal of Systems and Information Technology, 5*(1), 1–9.

Kock, N., Davison, R., Ocker, R., & Wazlawick, R. (Eds.). (2001). *E-collaboration* [Special issue of the *Journal of Systems and Information Technology*]. Joondalup, Australia: Edith Cowan University, Department of Information Systems.

Kock, N., & Lau, F. (2001). Information systems action research: Serving two demanding masters. *Information Technology & People, 14*(1), 6–12.

Kock, N., & McQueen, R. J. (1996). Is re-engineering possible in the public sector? A Brazilian case study. *Business Change and Re-engineering, 3*(3), 3–12.

Kock, N., & McQueen, R. J. (1996). Product flow, breadth and complexity of business processes: An empirical study of fifteen business processes in three organizations. *Business Process Re-engineering & Management, 2*(2), 8–22.

Kock, N., McQueen, R. J., & Baker, M. (1996). Learning and process improvement in knowledge organizations: A critical analysis of four contemporary myths. *The Learning Organization, 3*(1), 31–41.

Kock, N., McQueen, R. J., & Corner, J. L. (1997). The nature of data, information and knowledge exchanges in business processes: Implications for process improvement and organizational learning. *The Learning Organization, 4*(2), 70–80.

Kock, N., McQueen, R. J., & Scott, J. L. (1997). Can action research be made more rigorous in a positivist sense? The contribution of an iterative approach. *Journal of Systems and Information Technology, 1*(1), 1–24.

Kock, N., & Murphy, F. (2001). *Redesigning acquisition processes: A new methodology based on the flow of knowledge and information.* Fort Belvoir, VA: Defense Acquisition University Press.

Kock, N., Tomelin, C. A., & Asper-y-Valdes, G. J. (1999). *PMQP: Total quality management in practice* [in Portuguese]. Rio de Janeiro, Brazil: IBPI Press.

Kodratoff, Y. (1988). *Introduction to machine learning.* London: Pitman.

Kofman, F., & Senge, P. M. (1993). The heart of learning organizations. *Organization Dynamics, 22*(2), 5–23.

Kogut, B., & Zander, U. (1992). Knowledge of the firm, combinative capabilities, and the replication of technology. *Organization Science, 3*(3), 383–397.

Kohli, R., & Gupta, J. N. D. (2002). Effectiveness of systems analysis and design education: An exploratory study. *Journal of Organizational and End User Computing, 14*(3), 16–32.

Kryt, J. (1997). Information conundrum: Semantics . . . with a payoff! *Informatica*, *21*(2), 305–319.

Kurke, L. B., & Aldrich, H. E. (1983). Mintzberg was right! A replication and extension of the nature of managerial work. *Management Science*, *29*(8), 975–984.

Laudon, K. C., & Laudon, J. P. (1996). *Management information systems: Organization and technology*. Upper Saddle River, NJ: Prentice Hall.

Leidner, D. E., & Elam, J. J. (1995). The impact of executive information systems on organizational design, intelligence, and decision making. *Organization Science*, *6*(6), 645–664.

Linke, P., & Kokossis, A. (2004). Advanced process systems design technology for pollution prevention and waste treatment. *Advances in Environmental Research*, *8*(2), 229–245.

Lord, R. G., & Foti, R. J. (1986). Schema theories, information processing and organizational behaviour. In H. P. Sims, Jr., & D. A. Gioia (Eds.), *The thinking organization* (pp. 20–48). San Francisco: Jossey-Bass.

Lu, W. F., & Deng, Y. (2004). A system modelling methodology for materials and engineering systems design integration. *Materials & Design*, *25*(6), 459–469.

Lubit, R. (2001). Tacit knowledge and knowledge management: The keys to sustainable competitive advantage. *Organizational Dynamics*, *29*(3), 164–178.

Luger, G. F., & Stubblefield, W. A. (1989). *Artificial intelligence and the design of expert systems*. Redwood City, CA: Benjamin-Cummings.

Mann, F. C., Indik, B. P., & Vroom, V. H. (1963). *The productivity of work groups*. Ann Arbor: Institute for Social Research, University of Michigan.

Martin, J. (1991). *Rapid application development*. New York: Macmillan.

Maslow, A. H. (1954). *Motivation and personality*. New York: Harper & Row.

Maull, R. S., Weaver, A. M., Childe, S. J., Smart, P. A., & Bennett, J. (1995). Current issues in business process re-engineering. *International Journal of Operations and Production Management*, *15*(11), 37–52.

Mayo, E. (1945). *The social problems of an industrial civilization*. New York: Macmillan.

Mayr, E., & Provine, W. B. (1998). *The evolutionary synthesis: Perspectives on the unification of biology*. Cambridge, MA: Harvard University Press.

McGill, M. E., & Slocum, J. W., Jr. (1993). Unlearning the organization. *Organization Dynamics*, *22*(2), 67–79.

McGrath, J. E. (1984). *Groups: Interaction and performance*. Englewood Cliffs, NJ: Prentice-Hall.

McLeod, R. (1996). Comparing undergraduate courses in systems analysis and design. *Communications of the ACM*, *39*(5), 113–122.

Middleton, P. (1999). Implementing business policy through information technology: A test of the structured systems analysis and design method. *International Journal of Management*, *16*(4), 557–567.

Miller, G. A. (1956). The magical number seven, plus or minus two: Some limits on our capacity for processing information. *The Psychological Review*, *63*, 81–97.

Mills, H. D., Linger, R. C., & Hevner, A. R. (1986). *Principles of information systems analysis and design*. Orlando, FL: Harcourt Brace Jovanovich.

Miner, A. S., & Mezias, S. J. (1996). Ugly duckling no more: Pasts and futures of organizational learning research. *Organization Science*, *7*(1), 88–99.

Mintzberg, H. (1975, July/August). The manager's job: Folklore and fact. *Harvard Business Review*, *53*(4), 49–61.

Misic, M. M., & Russo, N. L. (1999). An assessment of systems analysis and design courses. *The Journal of Systems and Software*, *45*(3), 197–203.

Misic, M. M., & Russo, N. L. (2000). Reading between the lines: An examination of systems analysis and design texts. *Journal of Systems and Software*, *50*(1), 65–73.

Misterek, S. D., Dooley, K. J., & Anderson, J. C. (1992). Productivity as a performance measure. *International Journal of Operations & Production Management, 12*(1), 29–45.

Mittra, S. S. (1983). Information system analysis and design. *Journal of Systems Management, 34*(4), 30–35.

Morik, K. (Ed.). (1989). *Knowledge representation and organization in machine learning.* Berlin, Germany: Springer-Verlag.

Naisbitt, J. (1994). *Global paradox.* London: Nicholas Brealey.

Napier, R. W., & Gershenfeld, M. K. (1993). *Groups: Theory and experience.* Boston: Houghton Mifflin.

Natter, M., Mild, A., Feurstein, M., Dorffner, G., & Taudes, A. (2001). The effect of incentive schemes and organizational arrangements on the new product development process. *Management Science, 47*(8), 1029–1045.

Necco, C. R., Gordon, C. L., & Tsai, N. W. (1987). Systems analysis and design current practices. *MIS Quarterly, 11*(4), 461–478.

Neo, B. S. (1988). Factors facilitating the use of information technology for competitive advantage: An exploratory study. *Information & Management, 15*(4), 191–201.

Nissen, M. E. (1998). Redesigning reengineering through measurement-driven inference. *MIS Quarterly, 22*(4), 509–534.

Nissen, M. E. (2001). *Toward a program of research on knowledge flow in the very-large enterprise* (Research Rep. No. NPS-GSBPP-01-003). Monterey, CA: Naval Postgraduate School.

Ohmae, K. (1982). *The mind of the strategist: The art of Japanese business.* New York: McGraw-Hill.

Olson, D. L., & Courtney, J. F., Jr. (1992). *Decision support models and expert systems.* New York: Macmillan.

Osborne, D., & Gaebler, T. (1992). *Reinventing government.* Reading, MA: Addison-Wesley.

Parente, R., Kock, N., & Sonsini, J. (2004). An analysis of the implementation and impact of speech recognition technology in the health care sector. *Perspectives in Health Information Management, 1*(A.5), 1–23.

Peters, T. J., & Waterman, R. H., Jr. (1982). *In search of excellence.* New York: Harper & Row.

Piaget, J. (1971). *Biology and knowledge.* Chicago: University of Chicago Press.

Pimentel, K., & Teixeira, K. (1993). *Virtual reality.* New York: McGraw-Hill.

Plotnick, N. (2000). *The IT professional's guide to managing systems, vendors and end users.* Berkeley, CA: McGraw-Hill.

Porter, M. E. (1980). *Competitive strategy: Techniques for analyzing industries and competitors.* New York: The Free Press.

Porter, M. E. (1985). *Competitive advantage.* New York: The Free Press.

Porter, M. E. (1991). From competitive advantage to corporate strategy. In C. A. Montgomery & M. E. Porter (Eds.), *Strategy: Seeking and securing competitive advantage* (pp. 225–255). Boston: Harvard Business School Press.

Porter, M. E. (1991). How competitive forces shape strategy. In C. A. Montgomery & M. E. Porter (Eds.), *Strategy: Seeking and securing competitive advantage* (pp. 11–25). Boston: Harvard Business School Press.

Porter, M. E., Takeuchi, H., & Sakakibara, M. (2000). *Can Japan compete?* Cambridge, MA: Basic Books.

Postrel, S. (2002). Islands of shared knowledge: Specialization and mutual understanding in problem-solving teams. *Organization Science, 13*(3), 303–320.

Power, M. D. (1995). Back to the future: A commentary on the quest for empowering organizations. *Organization Science, 6*(6), 671–676.

Pressman, R. (1987). *Software engineering: A practitioner's approach.* New York: McGraw-Hill.

Quinn, R. E. (1988). *Beyond rational management.* San Francisco: Jossey-Bass.

Rai, A., Patnayakuni, R., & Patnayakuni, N. (1997, July). Technology investment and business performance. *Communications of the ACM, 40*(7), 89–97.

Ramsey, D. K. (1987). *The corporate warriors.* Boston: Houghton Mifflin.

Redding, J. C., & Catalanello, R. F. (1994). *Strategic readiness: The making of the learning organization.* San Francisco: Jossey-Bass.

Reijers, H. A., Limam, S., & Van der Aalst, W. M. P. (2003). Product-based workflow design. *Journal of Management Information Systems, 20*(1), 229–263.

Restle, F. (1974). Critique of pure memory. In R. L. Solso (Ed.), *Theories in cognitive psychology: The Loyola Symposium* (pp. 203–217). Potomac, MD: Lawrence Erlbaum Associates.

Roach, S. (1991). Services under siege: The restructuring imperative. *Harvard Business Review, 69*(5), 82–92.

Roach, S. (1994, September 19). Lessons of the productivity paradox. *Computerworld,* p. 55.

Romme, A. G. L. (1996). A note on the hierarchy-team debate. *Strategic Management Journal, 17*(5), 411–417.

Ross, J. W., & Beath, C. M. (2002). New approaches to IT investment. *Sloan Management Review, 43*(2), 51–60.

Roth, I., & Bruce, V. (1995). *Perception and representation.* Buckingham, UK: Open University Press.

Roth, W. (1993). *The evolution of management theory.* Orefield, PA: Roth & Associates.

Rumbaugh, J., Blaha, M., Premerlani, W., Eddyy, F., & Lorensen, W. (1991). *Object-oriented modeling and design.* Englewood Cliffs, NJ: Prentice-Hall.

Rumbaugh, J., Jacobson, I., & Booch, G. (1998). *The unified modeling language reference manual.* New York: Addison-Wesley.

Russel, S., & Norvig, P. (1995). *Artificial intelligence: A modern approach.* Upper Saddle River, NJ: Prentice Hall.

Sawyer, S., & Guinan, P. J. (1998). Software development: Processes and performance. *IBM Systems Journal, 37*(4), 552–569.

Schein, E. H. (1993, Winter). How can organizations learn faster? The challenge of entering the green room. *Sloan Management Review, 34*(2), 85–92.

Semler, R. (1989, September/October). Managing without managers. *Harvard Business Review, 67*(5), 76–84.

Semler, R. (1993). *Maverick.* London: Arrow.

Senge, P. M. (1990). *The fifth discipline.* New York: Doubleday.

Senge, P. M., Roberts, C., Ross, R. B., Smith, B. J., & Kleiner, A. (1994). *The fifth discipline fieldbook.* London: Nicholas Brealey.

Shang, S., & Seddon, P. B. (2002). Assessing and managing the benefits of enterprise systems: The business manager's perspective. *Information Systems Journal, 12*(4), 271–300.

Shaw, M. (1981). *Group dynamics: The psychology of small group behavior.* New York: McGraw-Hill.

Sheridan, T. B. (Ed.). (2002). *Human and automation: System design and research issues.* New York: John Wiley & Sons.

Simon, H. A., & Chase, W. G. (1973). Skill in chess. *American Scientist, 61*(4), 394–403.

Sims, H. P., Jr., & Lorenzi, P. (1992). *The new leadership paradigm: Social learning and cognition in organizations.* Newbury Park, CA: Sage.

Smith, A. (1910). *The wealth of nations* (Vol. 1). London: J. M. Dent & Sons. (Originally published 1776)

Smith, A. (1910). *The wealth of nations* (Vol. 2). London: J. M. Dent & Sons. (Originally published 1776)

Soles, S. (1994). Work reengineering and workflows: Comparative methods. In E. White & L. Fischer (Eds.), *The workflow paradigm* (pp. 70–104). Alameda, CA: Future Strategies.

Solso, R. L. (Ed.). (1974). *Theories in cognitive psychology: The Loyola Symposium.* Potomac, MD: Lawrence Erlbaum Associates.

Spector, B., & Beer, M. (1994). Beyond TQM programmes. *Journal of Organizational Change Management, 7*(2), 63–70.

Sprague, R. H., Jr. (1995). Electronic document management: Challenges and opportunities for information systems managers. *MIS Quarterly, 19*(1), 29–49.

Stacey, R. D. (1995). The science of complexity: An alternative perspective for strategic change processes. *Strategic Management Journal, 16,* 477–495.

Stoddard, D. B., & Jarvenpaa, S. L. (1995). Business process redesign: Tactics for managing radical change. *Journal of Management Information Systems, 12*(1), 81–107.

Strassmann, P. (1997). *The squandered computer.* New Canaan, CT: The Information Economics Press.

Strassmann, P. A. (1996). *The value of computers, information and knowledge* (Working Paper). New Canaan, CT: Strassmann.

Takeishi, A. (2002). Knowledge partitioning in the interfirm division of labor: The case of automotive product development. *Organization Science, 13*(3), 321–338.

Tapscott, D., & Caston, A. (1993). *Paradigm shift.* New York: McGraw-Hill.

Taylor, F. W. (1885). *A piece rate system.* New York: McGraw-Hill.

Taylor, F. W. (1911). *The principles of scientific management.* New York: W. W. Norton.

Teichman, J., & Evans, K. C. (1995). *Philosophy: A beginner's guide.* Oxford, UK: Blackwell.

Thelen, S., Mottner, S., & Berman, B. (2004). Data mining: On the trail to marketing gold. *Business Horizons, 47*(6), 25–32.

Toffler, A. (1970). *Future shock.* New York: Bantam Books.

Toffler, A. (1985). *The adaptive corporation.* Hampshire, UK: Gower.

Toffler, A. (1991). *Powershift.* New York: Bantam Books.

Venkatraman, N. (1994). IT-enabled business transformation: From automation to business scope redefinition. *Sloan Management Review, 35*(2), 73–87.

Voehl, F., Jackson, P., & Ashton, D. (1994). *ISO 9000: An implementation guide for small and mid-sized businesses.* Delray Beach, FL: St. Lucie Press.

Walsh, J. P. (1995). Managerial and organizational cognition: Notes from a trip down memory lane. *Organization Science, 6*(3), 280–321.

Walton, M. (1989). *The Deming management method.* London: Mercury.

Walton, M. (1991). *Deming management at work.* London: Mercury.

Ward, J. A. (1994). Continuous process improvement. *Information Systems Management, 11*(2), 74–76.

Waring, S. P. (1991). *Taylorism transformed.* Chapel Hill: University of North Carolina Press.

Wastell, D. G., White, P., & Kawalek, P. (1994). A methodology for business process redesign: Experiences and issues. *Journal of Strategic Information Systems, 3*(1), 23–40.

Weick, K. E., & Bougon, M. G. (1986). Organizations as cognitive maps: Charting ways to success and failure. In H. P. Sims, Jr., & D. A. Gioia (Eds.), *The thinking organization* (pp. 102–135). San Francisco: Jossey-Bass.

White, L., & Taket, A. (1994). The death of the expert. *Journal of the Operational Research Society, 45*(7), 733–748.

Williams, I. (1994). Competing for quality: Competition in the supply of central government services. In R. Lovell (Ed.), *Managing change in the new public sector* (pp. 216–227). Harlow, Essex, UK: Longman.

Willmott, H. (1995). Will the turkeys vote for Christmas? The re-engineering of human resources. In G. Burke & J. Peppard (Eds.), *Examining business process re-engineering* (pp. 306–315). London: Kogan Page.

Windsor, J. C. (1986). Are automated tools changing systems analysis and design? *Journal of Systems Management, 37*(11), 28–33.

Winograd, T., & Flores, F. (1986). *Understanding computers and cognition.* Norwood, NJ: Ablex.

Wirfs-Brock, R. J., & Johnson, R. E. (1990). Surveying current research in object-oriented design. *Communications of the ACM, 33*(9), 104–124.

Woofford, J. C. (1994). Getting inside the leader's head: A cognitive processes approach to leadership. *SAM Advanced Management Journal, 59*(3), 4–9.

Wren, D. A. (1979). *The evolution of management thought.* New York: John Wiley & Sons.

Zack, M. (1999). Managing codified knowledge. *Sloan Management Review, 40*(4), 45–58.

Zander, A. (1971). *Motives and goals in groups.* New York: Academic Press.

Zeleny, M. (1982). *Multiple criteria decision making.* New York: McGraw-Hill.

Index

Abbott Laboratories, 26
Abstract concepts, 80
Access (program), 166, 230, 233–234, 236–237
Accuracy of information, 21–22
Active server pages (ASP), 229–249
   business process automation, 231–232
   creating database, 233–235
   creating Web-based data entry forms,
      239–242
   creating Web-based reports, 246–248
   database manipulation with SQL, 237–238
   inserting new records through
      Web-based forms, 242–244
   Little Italy Restaurants Web System,
      231, 232–248
   updating or deleting records through
      Web-based forms, 244–246
   using ODBC to create data source name,
      235–237
Active server pages code examples, 263–291
   food items data entry, 265–267
   food items data update or delete, 275–277
   food items report, 285–286
   food items requests data entry, 272–274
   food items requests data update or delete,
      282–285
   food items requests report, 290–291
   menu, 263–265
   restaurants data entry, 267–269
   restaurants data update or delete, 277–280
   restaurants report, 287–288
   status options data entry, 270–272
   status options data update or delete,
      280–282
   status options report, 289–290
Activities, exploding into diagram, 101
Activity flow-oriented approaches, 82–85
   auto parts ordering and production process,
      69, 70
   emphasis on, 65, 67–68
   predictive car maintenance example, 84
   symbols, 83
   usefulness of, 71–74

"ADODB.Connection" objects, 243, 247
Adopters, technology, 50–51
Advancedness of information, 21–22
Amazon.com, 171, 231
American Airlines, 42, 51, 196
American Customer Drying, 71–74
American National Standards Institute (ANSI),
      199, 237
American Standard Code for Information
      Interchange (ASCII):
   code, 20, 199
   files, 199
Analysis step (software development life cycle
      model), 6
ANSI. *See* American National Standards
      Institute
APOLLO travel reservation system, 196
Argyris, Chris, 33
ASCII. *See* American Standard Code for
      Information Interchange
ASP. *See* Active server pages
Assembly language, 2
Assertions, 20
Asynchronous communication,
      136–139, 184–185
ATMs. *See* Automatic teller machines
Atomic keys, 204, 205, 206
Auditing for fraud, 159
Auto insurance company
      example, 143
Automated Case System (FBI), 13–14
Automatic teller machines (ATMs), 50
Automobile manufacturing, 32–33,
      42, 43, 140–141
     See also Manufacturing sector
Automobile parts, 68–69, 70,
      157–159, 252–253

Backup, data, 141
BAE Automated Systems, 195–197
Bankruptcy, 164
Banks, 50
Bartlett, Frederick, 24

Beginner's All-Purpose Symbolic Instruction
Code (BASIC), 2, 231–232
Behavior diagrams, 92–93, 219
Belarus, outsourcing of programming to,
153–155
Betas, in multiple regression, 209–210
"Beyond the Productivity Paradox"
(Brynjolfsson & Hitt), 48–49
Bigchalk.com, 71–74
Bits, 1, 20
Booch, Grady, 92, 218
Boolean data searches, 14
Bottlenecks, 145–146
Brynjolfsson, Erik, 48–49
Bugs, software, 2–3, 4, 53, 154, 217
Business process diagrams, 97–101, 130–133
Business processes:
    operational, 127, 147–148
    representing knowledge flow in, 124–126,
        127–128
    rigidity of, 118–119
    simple, 170, 171
    specialized, 170–171
    strategic, 96, 170, 171
    support, 127, 147
    types of, 126–127
Business process implementation strategies,
157, 161–171
    commercial package customization,
        9, 157, 165–168, 198
    in-house development, 157, 161,
        162, 169–171, 198
    See also Business process outsourcing
Business Process Improvement (Harrington),
68, 82
Business Process Improvement Workbook
(Harrington & colleagues), 68, 69
Business process outsourcing:
    advantages of, 162–163
    as business process implementation strategy,
        157, 161, 162–165
    database design knowledge and, 198
    of help desk support, 9, 161, 164
    potential problems with, 164
    of programming to Belarus, 153–155
Business process redesign, 136–150
    current approaches to systems analysis and
        design and, 9
    Department of Defense, 59–61
    eliminating unnecessary information flow,
        142–145
    encouraging asynchronous communication,
        136–139
    importance of, 10
    involving customers in, 257–258
    as knowledge sharing catalyst, 149
    maximizing knowledge transfer in
        organizational learning
        processes, 148–149

    methods, 62–74
    minimizing knowledge transfer in
        operational processes, 147–148
    optimal duration of projects, 102–103
    reducing contact points, 145–147
    reducing information duplication in static
        repositories, 139–142
    software development life cycle
        model and, 6–7
    See also Little Italy Restaurants (case study)
Business process redesign target selection,
110–120
    business process rigidity, 118–119
    cost-benefit analysis, 112–115
    employee resistance, 117
    management support, 115–117
    problem identification, 111–112
    stakeholder resistance, 118
Business process reengineering, 65–67
    difficulties with, 110, 116, 254
    overview, 49
    radical business process change
        and, 251, 252
    versions, 115–116
Bytes, 20

C, 2, 8, 220, 221
C++, 8, 217, 221, 222
Calendaring systems, electronic, 259
Cardinalities, 201
Carlzon, Jan, 146
Carr, Nicholas, 50
CASE. *See* Computer-aided software
engineering
Case studies:
    Denver International Airport, 195–197
    Department of Defense, 59–61
    FBI's Virtual Case File, 13–15
    IBM Global Financing, 107–109
    Investars, Inc., 153–155
    See also Little Italy Restaurants (case study)
Case study method, 176
Causal knowledge, 23, 28
Center for Research on Information Technology
and Organizations (CRITO), 51–52
CGI. *See* Common gateway interface
Champy, James, 65, 66, 116
Change:
    combining radical and incremental change,
        255–257
    opposition to, 254–255
    radical versus incremental, 251, 252–254
Charting tools, commercial, 160
Chartist, 98
Checkland, Peter, 95, 156
Chess players, 32
Children tables, 205
Chuang, T., 67, 219
CIA. *See* U.S. Central Intelligence Agency

Civil construction projects, 119
COBRA. *See* Common Object Request Broker Architecture
Coca-Cola, 21
Coding, testing, and implementation step (software development life cycle model), 6
Coefficients, in multiple regression, 209–210
Cognitive chunking, 131
Cognitive maps, 24
Comment lines, 220
Commercial package customization, 9, 157, 165–168, 198
Common gateway interface (CGI), 232
Common Object Request Broker Architecture (COBRA), 223
Communication:
    asynchronous, 136–139, 184–185
    synchronous, 136–138
Communication flow-oriented approach, 88–92
    auto parts examples, 69, 70, 157–159
    Computer Sciences Corporation, 60
    knowledge flow represented in, 124–126, 127–128
    Little Italy Restaurants, 182–184, 188–189
    predictive car maintenance example, 90–91
    symbols, 89–90
    usefulness of, 71–74
Communication flows, importance of, 67, 68
Completeness of information, 21–22
Compound keys, 204–205
Computer-aided software engineering (CASE), 3, 7, 88, 97–98
Computer languages, 2, 8
    See also specific languages
Computer literacy course redesign example, 111–112
Computer science, as new discipline, 1–3
Computer Sciences Corporation (CSC), 59–61
Concepts, abstract, 80
Confidence levels, in multiple regression, 209–210, 211
Connectors, in PowerPoint, 100, 101
Consciousness Explained (Dennett), 23
Contact points, reducing, 145–147
Context diagrams, 95
Contractual issues, in business process outsourcing, 164
Control activities, 142–143
Core competencies, 163
Correlational knowledge, 23, 26, 28
Cost-benefit analysis, 112–115
Costs:
    business process outsourcing, 162–163, 170
    in-house development, 169–170
    maintenance, 3, 5, 170
    production, 43
Couger, J. Daniel, 3

CRITO. *See* Center for Research on Information Technology and Organizations
CSC. *See* Computer Sciences Corporation
Customers, 45, 257–258
Customization of commercial packages, 9, 157, 165–168, 198

Data:
    backup of, 141
    defined, 19–20
    exchange of, 30–31
    redundancies in, 202
    relationship to information and knowledge, 16–19, 27–29
    synchronization of, 141–142
Database design concepts and issues, 198–212
    databases and entity-relationship diagrams, 200–202
    data warehousing and mining, 202, 207–211
    first normal form, 202–203
    importance of, 198
    normalization of databases, 202
    second normal form, 203–206
    sequential and structured files, 199–200
    third normal form, 206–207
Database management systems, 233
Databases:
    analysis of, 6, 7
    creating, 233–235
    defined, 200
    design and specification step, 6, 7
    and entity-relationship diagrams, 200–202
    manipulating with SQL, 237–238
    normalization of, 202
    relational versus object-oriented, 238
Data entry forms, Web-based:
    creating, 239–242
    food items, 265–267
    food items requests, 272–274
    restaurants, 267–269
    status options, 270–272
Data flow diagrams, 86–88, 95
Data marts, 207
Data mining, 202, 207, 208–211
Data source name (DSN), 235–237
Data update or delete examples:
    food items, 275–277
    food items requests, 282–285
    restaurants, 277–280
    status options, 280–282
Data warehousing, 207–208, 209
Davenport, Thomas, 65, 116
"Decision-Driven Approach to Object-Oriented Analysis, A" (Chuang & Yadav), 219
Deduction, knowledge building through, 25
Delete, data, examples. *See* Data update or delete examples
"DeleteButton" code, 245–246
DELETE statements (SQL), 237, 238

DeMarco, Tom, 2–3
Deming, William E., 45, 64, 251, 252
Dennett, Daniel, 23
De-normalization, 202
Denver International Airport, 195–197
Dependencies:
    partial, 205–206
    transitive, 206–207
Dependent variables, in multiple regression, 209
Design step (software development life cycle
    model), 6, 7
Diagrams:
    behavior, 92–93, 219
    breaking into smaller diagrams, 130–133
    business process, 97–101, 130–133
    context, 95
    data flow, 86–88, 95
    entity-relationship, 200, 201
    exploding into, 101
    holistic system, 96
    Level 0, 95
    Level 1, 131, 132
    Level 2, 131, 132
    model management, 93, 219
    structural, 92, 219
    tool types, 97–98
    unified modeling language, 219
    use-case, 93–94
    using PowerPoint, 98–101
Disk mirroring, 141
Documentation, 3–4
DoD. *See* U.S. Department of Defense
Dos Santos, Brian, 50
Drucker, Peter, 17, 66, 67
Drug development process, 119
DSN. *See* Data source name
Dumping, 47
Dynamic information repositories, 139

Early technology adopters, 50–51
Ebbinghaus, H., 24
E-Collaboration Research Center, 68–69, 71–74
Elance Online, 154
Electronic calendaring systems, 259
Electronic collaboration systems, 258–259
E-mail, 128, 129, 137–138
Employee orientation, 148
Employee resistance, 117
Employee rewards, 258–260
Encapsulation, 215–216
Engineering company example, 257–258
Enterprise resource planning (ERP) systems,
    10, 165, 166–168
Entity-relationship diagrams, 200, 201
ERP. *See* Enterprise resource planning (ERP)
    systems
"Evolution of Business System Analysis
    Techniques" (Couger), 3
Excel (program), 166, 233
External customers, 45

Federal Bureau of Investigation (FBI), 13–15
Fields:
    key, 200, 204–205
    non-key, 205, 206–207
    primary key, 234–235
Files:
    sequential, 199
    structured, 199–200
First-generation computer languages, 2
First normal form, 202–203
Flat files, 199
Flowcharts, functional, 83–84
Focus groups, 46
Forms:
    as database component, 239
    design of, 31
    as HTML element, 239–242
Forms, Web-based:
    creating data entry forms, 239–242
    inserting new records through, 242–244
    updating or deleting records through,
        244–246
    See also Data entry forms, Web-based
FORTRAN, 2
43-minute rule, in steel plants, 23
Franchising, 191
Fraud, auditing for, 159
FrontPage, 230, 233, 240, 241
Functional flowcharts, 83–84
Functional heterogeneity, 119

Gantt charts, 7
Gouillart, F., 46
Governance committees, 117
Group knowledge, 31–32
"Groupware and Social Dynamics" (Grudin),
    258–259
Groupware systems, 258–259
Grudin, Jonathan, 258–259

Hackett, Gregory, 47
Hammer, Michael, 49, 65, 116
Harrington, J. H., 68, 69, 82
Harvard Business School, 176
Hawthorne effect, 64
Health services organization example, 162–163
Help desk support:
    business process redesign example, 116
    outsourcing of, 9, 161, 164
    productivity and quality of, 44–45
    Temple University, 71–74
Heterogeneity, functional, 119
"High-level" environment, 229–230
Hitt, Lorin, 48–49
Holiday Boutique, 71–74
Holistic systems approaches, 95–97
Hopper Specialty, 28–29
HTML, 231–232, 239–242, 246–247, 248
Humanist movement, 63–64
Hypercommunication, 30, 34–36

IBM:
  Global Financing, 107–109
  gross profit margins, 163
  Semi-Automatic Business Research
      Environment, 42
If-then statements, 24
Induction, knowledge building
      through, 25
Industry-university gap, 8–9
Information:
  accuracy of, 21–22
  advancedness of, 21–22
  asynchronous communication of,
      136–139, 184–185
  completeness of, 21–22
  defined, 20
  duplication of, 139–142, 185–186
  exchange of, 30–31
  legally sensitive, 138
  monetary value of, 21–22
  personal, 138
  polygonation of, 186–188
  relationship to data and knowledge,
      16–19, 27–29
  synchronous communication of,
      136–138
Information buffers, 143, 144, 145
Information filters, 143–144, 145
Information flow, 66–67, 142–145, 186–188
  See also Communication flow-oriented
      approach
Information repositories:
  dynamic, 139
  static, 139–142, 185–186
Information technology productivity paradox,
      41, 47–49, 166–168
In-house development, 157, 161,
      162, 169–171, 198
INSERT statements (SQL), 237, 238
Instantiation, 220, 223
Internal customers, 45
International Organization for Standardization
      (ISO), 237, 252–253
Internet, 10
Internet Explorer, 47
Internet protocol (IP) address, 231
Interviews, customer, 258
Investars, Inc., 153–155
"Investment in Technology" (Hackett), 47
IP address. *See* Internet protocol (IP) address
ISO. *See* International Organization for
      Standardization
"IT Doesn't Matter" (Carr), 50

Jacobson, Ivar, 92, 218, 219
Japan, economic recovery after World War II,
      252–253
Java, 217, 231
JavaScript, 224, 231
Juran, Joseph, 64

Key fields, 200, 204–205
Keys:
  atomic, 204, 205, 206
  compound, 204–205
  primary, 204
Knowledge:
  causal, 23, 28
  communication of, 128–130
  correlational, 23, 26, 28
  defined, 22–24
  group, 31–32
  monetary value of, 24–27
  organizational, 27
  of programming, by systems
      analysts, 229
  relationship to data and information,
      16–19, 27–29
  team, 31–32
Knowledge flow representation, 124–126,
      127–128
Knowledge fragmentation, 31–33, 34–36
Knowledge transfer, 33–34, 147–149

Labor unions, 117
Late technology adopters, 50
Lean diagramming tools, 97–98
Learning organizations movement, 33
      See also Organizational learning processes
Legal issues, in business process
      outsourcing, 164
Legally sensitive information, 138
Legal regulation, 118–119
Level 0 diagrams, 95
Level 1 diagrams, 131, 132
Level 2 diagrams, 131, 132
Library analogy, 216
Likert-type scale, multi-point, 45
"LIRDbObj" objects, 243–244, 247
Little Italy Restaurants (case study), 176–191,
      230–231, 232–248, 263–291
  background information, 176–178
  communication flow representation,
      182–184, 188–189
  creating database, 233–235
  creating Web-based data entry forms,
      239–242
  creating Web-based reports, 246–248
  database manipulation with SQL,
      237–238
  eliminating unnecessary information flow,
      186–188
  encouraging asynchronous communication,
      184–185
  food items data entry, 265–267
  food items data update or delete, 275–277
  food items report, 285–286
  food items requests data entry, 272–274
  food items requests data update or delete,
      282–285
  food items requests report, 290–291

inserting new records through
Web-based forms, 242–244
key problems, 179–180
menu, 263–265
order fulfillment process, 180–184
redesigned process, 188–190, 230–231
redesigning order fulfillment process,
184–190
redesign results, 190–191
reducing information duplication, 185–186
restaurants data entry, 267–269
restaurants data update or delete, 277–280
restaurants report, 287–288
rich pictorial representation, 189–190,
230–231
status options data entry, 270–272
status options data update or delete,
280–282
status options report, 289–290
updating or deleting records through
Web-based forms, 244–246
using Open Database Connectivity to create
data source name, 235–237
Loan covenants, 108
Lockheed Martin, 60–61

Machine language, 2
Macros, 166
Magical number 7 rule, 130–131
Mainframes, 1
Maintenance costs, 3, 5, 170
Management support, 115–117
Managers, middle, 143–144
Manufacturing sector, 47–48, 51–52, 167–168
See also Automobile manufacturing
Mayo, Elton, 63–64
Media naturalness, 128–130
Meta-process, 149
Methods (software object functions),
216, 217, 223
Microsoft Corporation:
business process outsourcing,
164–165
dumping, 47
gross profit margins, 163
legally sensitive information, 138
software development products,
230, 232
stakeholder concerns, 118
Microsoft Office suite, 160, 166, 233, 240
Microsoft Windows, 235
Middle managers, 143–144
Millennium bug problem, 53, 154
Miller, George, 130
Mnemonic codes, 2
Model management diagrams, 93, 219
Mueller, Robert, III, 14
Multiple regression, 209–210, 211
Multi-point Likert-type scale, 45

NCR, 28–29
Netologic, Inc. *See* Investars, Inc.
Netscape, 47
Netscape Communications, 47, 138
Neural networks, 18
New Mexico, statute of limitations in, 28–29
Non-key fields, 205, 206–207
Normal form:
first, 202–203
second, 203–206
third, 206–207
Normalization of databases, 202

Object-oriented analysis and design,
7–8, 92–94, 218–220
See also Software object classes; Software
objects
Object-oriented databases, 238
Object-oriented programming, 8, 217–218
Objects. *See* Software objects
ODBC. *See* Open Database Connectivity
ODBC Data Source Administrator, 235
One-to-many relationship, between
tables, 200–202
Open Database Connectivity (ODBC), 235–237
Operational business processes, 127, 147–148
See also Business processes
Operational duplication, 141
Operation and maintenance step (software
development life cycle model), 6
Oracle, 169, 233
Organizational knowledge, 27
Organizational learning processes,
127, 148–149
See also Business processes
Orientation for new employees, 148
Out of the Crisis (Deming), 45
Outsourcing. *See* Business process outsourcing

Partial dependencies, 205–206
Pascal, 2, 7
Payroll management, 163
PDAs. *See* Personal digital assistants
Peffers, Ken, 50
Pepsi, 21
Personal digital assistants (PDAs), 141
Personal information, 138
Phone conversations, 136–137, 138
Planning, importance of, 3–4
Polygonation of information, 186–188
Portability rights, 167–168
PowerPoint, 98–101, 160
Predictive car maintenance example,
81–82, 96–97, 124–126
Pressman, Roger, 4
Primary key fields, 234–235
Primary keys, 204
Problem identification, 111–112
Process quality metrics, 172–173

Production capacity, 42–43
Production cost, 43
Production rules, 24
Productivity:
    gains in 1990s, 51–52
    Little Italy Restaurants case study, 190
    measuring, 42–43
    profits and, 46–47
    quality and, 44–45
    role of, 49–51
Profits, 46–47
Programming:
    knowledge of, 229
    object-oriented, 8, 217–218
    structured, 217–218, 220, 221
    Web-based, 224
Programming languages, 2, 8
    See also specific languages
Program modules, 217, 218
Prototype development environment,
    229–230

Quality:
    Little Italy Restaurants case study, 190–191
    measuring, 45–46
    process quality metrics, 172–173
    productivity and, 44–45
    service quality metrics, 164
Questionnaires, customer, 258

Rai, Arun, 50
RAID-1. *See* Redundant array
    of independent disks
Records:
    inserting through Web-based forms,
        242–244
    in structured files, 199, 200
    updating or deleting through
        Web-based forms, 244–246
Redundant array of independent disks
    (RAID-1), 141
Relational databases, 238
Remote synchronization, 141, 142
Reports, as database component, 239
Reports, Web-based:
    creating, 246–248
    food items, 285–286
    food items requests, 290–291
    restaurants, 287–288
    status options, 289–290
Repositories:
    dynamic, 139
    static, 139–142, 185–186
Requirements definition step (software
    development life cycle model), 6
"ResetButton" code, 242, 243
Restaurants, 146–147, 256–257
    See also Little Italy Restaurants
        (case study)

"Rewards to Investors in Innovative Information
    Technology Applications" (Dos Santos
    & Peffers), 50
Rich pictorial representations,
    159–160, 189–190, 230–231
Roach, Steven, 47
Robotics technologies, 253
Rumbaugh, James, 92, 218–219

SABRE. *See* Semi-Automatic Business Research
    Environment
SAIC. *See* Science Applications International
    Corporation
SAP/R3, 166
Schemas, 24
Science Applications International Corporation
    (SAIC), 13–14
Scientific management, 63, 66, 74
Script code, 231–232
Second-generation computer languages, 2
Second normal form, 203–206
SELECT statements (SQL), 237–238
Semi-Automatic Business Research
    Environment (SABRE), 42, 51
Senge, Peter, 33
Sentinel Project (FBI), 14
Sequential files, 199
Service quality metrics, 164
Service sector, 47–48, 51–52, 167–168
Sigmas, in multiple regression, 209–210, 211
Simon, Herbert A., 32
Simple business processes, 170, 171
Smaltalk, 217
Soft systems methodology, 156
Software asset management, 9, 164–165
Software crisis, 4–5
Software development life cycle model, 5–7
Software development suites, 169
Software engineering, 2–3
Software licensing savings, 162–163
Software object classes:
    creating, 220–223
    defining, 222, 223
    implementing, 222, 223
    using, 222, 223
    using previously created, 223–225
Software objects, 92, 215–216, 243–244
Solow, Robert, 42
Specialized business processes, 170–171
Specification stage, 3–4, 6, 7
"Spend a Day in the Life of Your Customers"
    (Gouillart), 46
SPSS, 209, 210, 211
SQL. *See* Structured query language
Stakeholder resistance, 118
Standardized betas, in multiple regression,
    209–210
Static information repositories,
    139–142, 185–186

Steel plants, 23
Strassmann, Paul, 26
Strategic business processes, 96, 170, 171
Structural diagrams, 92, 219
Structured English, 7
Structured files, 199–200
Structured programming, 217–218, 220, 221
Structured query language (SQL), 237–238
Supply-chain processes, 127, 147–148
    See also Business processes
Support business processes, 127, 147
    See also Business processes
Symbols:
    active server pages, 243
    activity flow representation, 83
    communication flow representation, 89–90
    data flow diagram, 86–87
    use-case diagram, 93
Synchronization:
    data, 141–142
    remote, 141, 142
Synchronous communication, 136–138
Systems analysis and design, origins of, 3–5
Systems analysts, knowledge of
    programming, 229

Tables, 200–202, 205
Tasks and communication, 30
Taylor, Frederick, 3, 63, 66, 74
Team knowledge, 31–32
Technology bubble, 52–53, 154, 253–254
"Technology Investment and Business
    Performance" (Rai), 50
Technology productivity paradox,
    41, 47–49, 166–168
Telephone conversations, 136–137, 138
Temple University, 68–69, 71–74
Texas A&M International University, MIS and
    Decision Sciences Department, 166–167
Texas state government, 257–258
Third-generation computer languages, 2
Third normal form, 206–207
Total quality management,
    64–65, 251, 252
Transitive dependencies, 206–207
TurboTax, 129

Unified modeling language (UML),
    92–93, 95, 219
Unions, labor, 117
United Airlines, 196
United Parcel Service, 51

Universal resource locator (URL), 231
University of California at Irvine, 51–52
University of Connecticut Huskies basketball
    team, 127–128
UPDATE statements (SQL), 237, 238
URL. *See* Universal resource locator
U.S. Central Intelligence Agency (CIA), 170, 171
U.S. Department of Defense (DoD):
    business process redesign approach, 68
    knowledge flow representation, 125
    software procurement from Computer
        Sciences Corporation, 59–61
Use-case diagrams, 93–94

Value of Computers, Information and Knowledge,
    The (Strassmann), 26
Variables:
    dependent, 209
    structured versus object-oriented
        programming, 217, 218, 220–221
VBA. *See* Visual Basic for Applications
VBScript, 231–232
Video clips, 129
Virtual Case File system (FBI), 13–15
Visio, 98, 101
Visual Basic for Applications (VBA), 166

Warehouse Manager, 28–29
Warehousing:
    business process redesign
        example, 113–115
    of data, 207–208, 209
"War of the Ghosts, The," 24
Waterfall model, 5–7
Web-based forms. *See* Data entry forms,
    Web-based; Forms, Web-based
Web-based programming, 224
Web-based reports. *See* Reports, Web-based
Web browsers, 231
Web Java programmers, salaries of, 27
Web servers, 231
Webster, Bruce, 196–197
Word (program), 166, 233
Work demands, and new business
    process, 258–260
Workflow-oriented approaches. *See* Activity
    flow-oriented approaches

Xerox, 217

Yadav, S., 67, 219
Year 2000 problem, 53, 154

About the Author

Ned Kock (Nereu Florencio Kock, Jr.) is Associate Professor and Chairperson of the Department of MIS and Decision Science at Texas A&M International University. He holds degrees in electronics engineering (B.E.E.), computer science (M.Sc.), and management information systems (Ph.D.). Ned has authored several books, and published in a number of journals, including *Communications of the ACM*; *Decision Support Systems*; *IEEE Transactions on*: *Education, Engineering Management*, and *Professional Communication*; *Information & Management*; *Information Systems Journal*; *Information Technology & People*; *Journal of Organizational Computing and Electronic Commerce*; *Journal of Systems and Information Technology*; *MIS Quarterly*; and *Organization Science*. He is the Editor-in-Chief of the *International Journal of e-Collaboration*, Associate Editor of the *Journal of Systems and Information Technology*, and Associate Editor for Information Systems of the journal *IEEE Transactions on Professional Communication*. His research interests include action research, ethical and legal issues in technology research and management, e-collaboration, and business process improvement.